D0687983

LUXURY

JOHN SEKORA

Luxury

THE CONCEPT IN
WESTERN THOUGHT,
EDEN TO
SMOLLETT

THE JOHNS HOPKINS UNIVERSITY PRESS
BALTIMORE AND LONDON

This book has been brought to publication with the
generous assistance of the Andrew W. Mellon Foundation.

Manufactured in the United States of America

The Johns Hopkins University Press, Baltimore, Maryland 21218
The Johns Hopkins Press Ltd., London

Library of Congress Catalog Card Number 77-4545
ISBN 0-8018-1972-5

Library of Congress Cataloging in Publication data
will be found on the last printed page of this book.

FOR BILL,
AND FOREVER RUTH

CONTENTS

PART TWO: SMOLLETT AND LUXURY

PART THREE: THE ATTACK UPON LUXURY AND THE FORMS OF *HUMPHRY CLINKER*

CONCLUSION

PREFACE

Running through eighteenth-century English writing—considered broadly enough to embrace Ned Ward as well as Edward Gibbon—is a typology of values and characters that, much simplified, would include the following: young – mature, urban – country, feminine – masculine, innovative – traditional, unnatural – natural, uncontrolled – serene, immoderate – temperate, irrational – wise, dull – witty, unruly – obedient, corrupt – virtuous, subjects – rulers, the mob – men of substance, "they" – "we." It was in the attempt to discover the roots of such polarities, usually described as simple conventions, that this book began. The search led as a matter of course to earlier literature and, because the typology is as much moral as literary, to philosophers, theologians, and eventually lawmakers. To give short circuit to a long journey, all paths led to the ancient concept of luxury. One of the most inclusive theories of human relationships employed in antiquity, the concept of luxury explained much about the polar relationships employed in the later period. But the initial task I had set myself proved not as restricted as I had assumed. For I could discover no adequate published scholarship to draw upon: neither on the influence and transmission of the concept from antiquity, its effect upon eighteenth-century controversy, its place in the thinking of any valued writer, nor its significance to any major literary work.

At that point the study lost its original focus upon literary convention and took on its present concentration upon luxury, with special reference to the eighteenth century. For it became clear that that century was a turning point in men's thinking about luxury; in 1700 the edifice of laws and attitudes surrounding the concept seems wholly intact; yet by 1800 it is rubble. Hence this period of English history and literature offered not one but several opportunities, principally for three concrete and interrelated kinds of illustration: an account of the polemics surrounding the classical conception of luxury during its twilight and sunset; an analysis of an important author who absorbed himself within the classical tradition; and a description of how the concept shaped one highly regarded literary work. The goal may be conceived as a series of concentric and concentrating circles.

The study is equally historical and literary. I present the complex of relationships subsumed under the concept of luxury in historical terms: the way it evolved, accumulating power and influence over time. That history is given point and precision when it is brought to bear upon a writer who was immersed in the intellectual currents of his own day and who is still respected in ours. Standing alone, the historical discussion of luxury would be incomplete and perhaps inconclusive. Standing alone, the literary study would be vacuous, perhaps incomprehensible. Standing together, they encompass one of the oldest and most potent traditions of Western literary and intellectual life. As examples of the literary influence of the idea of luxury during its final years of potency, as many as two dozen significant writers are available. The novelist Tobias Smollett proved especially appropriate, for he is probably the last major English writer to accept wholly the classical conception, and his career spans the last outburst of controversy and its later moderation. And as culmination *Humphry Clinker* is similarly apt: it is Smollett's last work as well as his best, the finest novel of the 1770s, and the last major English literary work to be informed by the older sense of luxury.

From the decision to treat Smollett at length, three possibilities ensued. One was to treat the whole range of his historical, journalistic, and miscellaneous writings as well as his better-known fiction. The second was to treat only one novel but to treat it fully, not as a cultural anthropologist collecting artifacts, but as a literary critic searching for value and meaning. To add *Ferdinand Count Fathom* or *Launcelot Greaves* (or *Tom Jones*) would mean either expanding the study greatly or reducing the value of individual works to the level of mere examples. This gave rise to a third possibility: to note as fully as might be pertinent previous evaluations of Smollett's work generally and his achievement in *Humphry Clinker* in particular. If my reading of the novel is to have merit, that is, it should be able to stand with the judgments of those critics from whom I have learned so much. I do not intend a specialist's study, chiefly for those already interested in Smollett; yet such a study is included. Like most readers I admire scholarly books that are lean and swiftly to the point; contemplating the pages that follow, I console myself with the hope that I have written such a book—indeed, several of them.

If the concept of luxury is as momentous as I believe it to be, it follows that my own contribution to its understanding can be no more than partial, tentative, and suggestive. Only an encyclopedic work by many scholars in many fields could do it full justice. Rather than the encyclopedia, I offer a series of related essays. The Introduction compares classical and modern conceptions of luxury, reviews scholarship on the idea (practically all of which is founded on the modern sense), and questions the place Smollett is usually assigned in literary history. Chapter 1 traces the attack upon luxury from the Hebrews to about 1700 and notes the sumptuary laws drawn to enforce the attack. Chapters 2 and 3 treat in more detail the fierce disputes that arose between 1700 and the mid-1760's, after which the concept was often given a 180-degree turn of meaning. Chapters 4, 5, and 6 concentrate upon the role of luxury in the novelist's many-sided works of the 1750s and 1760s. The first of these, on the historical writings, presents his account of the origin, rise, and consequences of luxury in English life. The concrete day-to-day progress of the vice as he viewed it during the most critical period of his career—indeed his maturity—is described in chapters 5 and 6; these seek also to identify as particularly as possible the contemporary persons and behavior he considered luxurious. Chapters 7 through 9 suggest some of the implications of the attack regarded as a literary mode, using as exempla the political nature, the characterization, and the narrative structure of *Humphry Clinker*. The Conclusion attempts a final synthesis and reinterpretation of the concept and of Smollett's achievement. Throughout I have resisted several strong temptations. Presenting an anthology of the chief discussions of luxury, with commentary, would establish more vividly than I can in these pages the strength and continuity of the concept; but the result would be barely readable and would detract from a larger purpose—to indicate the ways the concept was put to practical use. Another temptation was to give a full account of sumptuary and related legislation as it regulated conduct beyond spending; though one is certainly needed, I could not provide it here. And while I have not tried to respond to all the studies that see luxury as merely the obverse of primitivism, I do notice the most prominent. It is sufficient at the outset to say that an approach by way of primitivism cannot account for the social, political, or theological implications of luxury, or for the repeated attacks upon the alleged luxury of women, slaves, and paupers.

Much that is of interest in the history of luxury, moveover, lies before and after the three millennia treated here. The origin of the concept is obscure. There are indications that even before the Hebrews it was a deduction from religious dogma, a luxurious act being construed as human enjoyment of that intended as sacrifice to the gods: for example, gold, birds, animals, children, and virgins. There are other indications that the crime of luxury was associated with justifications for slavery. What is clear—as well as commonplace—is that the main Western philosophical systems posited perfect (i.e., absolute) forms of degradation as well as models of perfect virtue and freedom. To describe the decline into depravity of an individual or group, they created various theories of entropy, the concept of luxury being among the most prominent. Such theories sought to comprehend the origins of depravity, its nature, psychology, stages of development, and inevitable consequences. Their attractions remain visible in our language today as in our odd phrase "falling in love." To mark the decline and fall of a person or nation, we enjoy a vocabulary rich in nuance and technical distinction. But to describe the kinds and stages of success and fulfillment, we make do with a stock of bloodless yet incessantly used platitudes. In the ancient world the concept of luxury withstood all sorts of historical change: poverty as well as prosperity, republican as well as imperial governments, benighted as well as advancing civilizations. It was largely unaffected by Chrisitanity and came to the end of its classical phase in Europe only when certain economic and political circumstances undermined its original assumptions. But those assumptions did not themselves wither away, for many were transplanted to that new birth of freedom, America, where the ideas and often the exact language of the classical attack upon luxury were used to defend the most brutal form of slavery the world has known.

For the study that follows, 1776 is of cardinal significance as the year of Adam Smith's *Wealth of Nations* and the affirmation of American independence from European corruption. Yet it was also the year Congress struck from the Declaration of Independence Jefferson's charge that George III had carried on "cruel war against human nature" by capturing and enslaving many of his fellowmen. For the American slave no less than the Athenian slave, freedom was considered a luxury, something for which he had neither need nor right. The assumption held fast beyond the legal demise of slavery, to the extent that, in an address to the National Education Association in 1910, a southern superintendent of schools knew he would find sympathy for his region's policy of keeping black schools isolated and poor:

> Public peace and the safety of the state demand that the less developed race be subordinated to the more developed, under conditions as they exist in the South today. The Caste of Kin is the practice of the theory that blood is thicker than water. . . . If these widely different races cannot blend their blood—and instinct and science say nay—the only real foundation for democracy, equality actual or potential, does not exist and cannot be created. . . . Southerners understand the apparent cruelty imputed to the God of Israel who is represented as commanding the extermination of non-assimilable peoples. But the more refined killing of today in the South is not the taking of a negro's life but the impassive and relentless murder of a people's hopes. But better this than worse that might be.

To bring the record nearer to the present, one could cite three stories reported by the *New York Times* within one month during 1976. A white woman who heads a group in Boston opposed to school bussing explained that, "Black parents aren't really interested in desegregated schools. They care about more essential things like jobs." A male legislator from Florida said he was leading the opposition to the Equal Rights Amendment in his state because "Women already have more rights than they can handle." And a district court judge in Illinois ruled that, while uncovering graves of persons of European descent was "criminal desecration," the same act regarding native American graves was "legitimate archeology." All these attitudes and incidents represent atavisms of the ancient distinction between necessity and luxury and the ancient choice of who should draw the distinction.

Notwithstanding the good counsel I have received from many generous scholars, specialists in several fields may, at the minimum, question my decisions of emphasis and selection. I cannot yet resolve to my own satisfaction important issues raised by Smollett's work; it is far less likely that I can say anything conclusive about Sallust or Bolingbroke. For another instance, I have sorted out the phases of eighteenth-century discussion of luxury according to domestic controversy; a specialist in diplomatic affairs could well perceive international influences I have missed. And it is true that English writers on painting and gardening occasionally speak of luxury in a favorable sense I have not attempted to treat here. The few sentences I offer concerning the Romans or major English authors are simply illustrative and do not attempt to gauge their richness. While Smollett does receive the bulk of attention, that attention is again selective. I treat his social and political attitudes insofar as they are included within his conception of luxury, leaving largely un-touched such otherwise important areas as his Scottish background.

It may be enough to say that, although I have not been able to resolve them, I am aware of the problems of dealing with a copious heterogene-ity of material and with large, philosophically charged questions of historical change and description. Since any study that includes political controversy must cross lines closely guarded by the followers and doubters of Namier, the joining of certain controversies has been unavoidable. Without wishing to enter either list, I can plead that in general I follow Smollett's habitual uses of the terms *Whig* and *Tory*. I accept Namier's contention that well before midcentury England had for practical purposes (and in contemporary terms) a one-party govern-ment, and also Plumb's thesis that Walpole followed Cromwell in find-ing means to reconcile the interests of land and money. By 1756 Smollett apparently accepted as fact—not as enthusiastically, but as certainly, as a Pitt or a Beckford—that England was set on an unalter-able commercial course. The battles he wished to lead were over hard political divisions and questions that yet remained: What kind of men would regulate national commerce and garner most of its profits? What products would be traded and with whom? Would commerce be made servant and guardian of the traditional English order of things? Or would it be permitted to undermine that order? Although he lagged behind many of his contemporaries in understanding political economy, he grasped more acutely than most the politics of status and privilege. He certainly knew what he meant when he dismissed an opponent as "a mere Whig" (and so did the opponent), and the divisions he posed were, indisputably, historical phenomena. They are not retrospective con-structs or categories but are divisions embodied in living people at a discernible time over interests perceived as vital. This is one point among many made most recently by John Brewer in *Party Ideology and Popular Politics at the Accession of George III* (Cambridge, 1976).

A final stylistic point. Like most authors before him, Smollett uses the word *luxury* variously for the intellectual concept, the moral vice, and some concrete thing. In context such usage is seldom confusing, and to avoid distracting repetitions of "the concept of luxury" or "the vice of luxury" I have normally followed his practice. All citations from *Humphry Clinker* are drawn from the edition by Lewis M. Knapp in the Oxford English Novels series (London, 1966). In the last portion of the study, devoted to the novel, I revert to Smollett's way of dating the fictional letters—month first, then day—which Knapp and other editors have retained.

Any book like this depends upon the research and generous advice of many scholars. Although I would claim for it a moiety of originality, it would have been quite impossible but for the work of many eminent scholars, particularly M. I. Finley, David Brion Davis, P. A. Brunt, and Sarah Pomeroy on the ancient world; J. G. A. Pocock, Isaac Kramnick, Caroline Robbins, and George Rudé on eighteenth-century England; and Lewis M. Knapp, Paul-Gabriel Boucé, Byron Gassman, and Robert Donald Spector on Smollett. Having ventured into many fields, I am especially indebted and equally aware of the risks of having tried so much, and I will not excuse my errors by pressing them upon those who have helped me. Yet the errors I have made would have been far greater had not portions of the manuscript been read by Louis A. Landa, Lawrence Lipking, Henry Knight Miller, Ian R. Christie, Duncan Isles, Ronald Paulson, Jean H. Hagstrum, and J. G. A. Pocock. I mourn the circumstance that three gracious men who saw early drafts—Jack W. Jessee, Geoffrey Tillotson, and Lewis M. Knapp—will not see the final version. For their patience in enduring many hours of talk on the subject and their persistence in clarifying many of its problems, I am grateful to my friends Steven Bates, Anne Hargrove, June Frazer, Paul-Gabriel Boucé, William Park, and Anthony Wadden. I owe thanks to the National Endowment for the Humanities for a fellowship that allowed me to complete the manuscript. William P. Sisler of the Johns Hopkins University Press, an editor's editor and an author's friend, put it all together.

Whatever value this study may ultimately possess owes most to those teachers who offered a model as admirable as it was demanding. Toward Josephine A. Pearce, Warren F. Dwyer, G. E. Bentley, Louis A. Landa, and Henry Knight Miller, I feel a sense of obligation this volume cannot exhaust; yet I am happy for the chance to express it publicly. And only that teacher I know best, Ruth my wife, can realize how much this was written with and for her.

LUXURY

Introduction

WHY LUXURY? WHY SMOLLETT?
SOME PRELIMINARY
OBSERVATIONS

This is the study of a relationship—one compassing a major intellectual tradition, its twilight in England, a writer who during that twilight became its spokesman, and the masterpiece he created. For us, luxury is less a concept than a mere term, far less a single coherent social theory than the merest part of many theories.[1] Although the term has retained a mite of its ancient power, its conceptual significance has been absorbed by modern political philosophies, principally the varying "isms" that condition life in the contemporary world. The devaluation from transcendental principle to quibbling word was so slow as to be imperceptible to all but the most sensitive. Even in retrospect it is obscured by related but more palpable and dramatic changes: the Enlightenment, the French and American Revolutions, the founding of the British Empire, the Industrial Revolution, the growth of cities and of the bourgeoisie. As an intimate part of all of these, the changes in meaning of the concept of luxury represent nothing less than the movement from the classical world to the modern. For the concept of luxury

1

is one of the oldest, most important, and most pervasive negative principles for organizing society Western history has known. As an intellectual construct it is similar to the Great Chain of Being and other such figures for metaphysical relationships; on a "lower" level it is akin to such ideas as the divine right of kings, law and order, and manifest destiny in European and American history. In its more abstract senses, the concept was used to explain God's plan for mankind and thus the movement of human destiny. Rendered concrete through politics and the law, it evolved into a potent element of the whole range of secular institutions, expressing man's plan for man and thus the desired movement of everyday social affairs.

As over centuries the concept of luxury grew more influential, it also became increasingly complex and controversial. Tension, conflict, and controversy were inevitable as eminent men used the concept to identify those things within their societies they most distrusted. By the eighteenth century in England such controversy was climactically fierce, for the traditional concept was thought to be endangered, losing by degrees the religious and political sanction it had possessed since antiquity. To many prominent Englishmen it was most precious when most threatened. After centuries as a tacit, axiomatic supposition, it was now occasionally challenged, reinterpreted, and, stranger still, even ignored. The debate that ensued was pivotal in intellectual history, yielding a general sense of luxury radically different at the end of the century from what it had been at the beginning. A short list of the major figures who took part would include Mandeville, Addison, Steele, Defoe, Pope, Swift, Bolingbroke, Fielding, Chesterfield, Hume, Johnson, Pitt father and son, Walpole father and son, Goldsmith, Gibbon, Ferguson, Steuart, Wesley, and Adam Smith.

By midcentury a central position in the controversy had been assumed by Tobias Smollett (1721-71), whose distinction it is to have been one of the last, most adamant, and most forceful proponents of the classical view. In the early 1750s, while writing his first major history, Smollett became absorbed in social and political issues of national import and thereafter did as much as any single writer to keep the dangers of luxury ever before the public eye. To this task he brought distinct advantages. After 1754, when Fielding died and Richardson published his last work, Smollett was often praised as the most talented novelist in England. He was at the same time one of the nation's foremost political journalists, serving as defender of Leicester House, then Bute and George III, and directing two major reviews. He also came to be regarded as the most influential historian after Hume, and he was easily the most prolific, producing three dozen volumes within a decade. The specific vehicles of his involvement were the seventy volumes of nonfiction he wrote or edited between 1756 and 1771: The *Critical Review* (1756-), the *British Magazine* (1760-), the *Briton* (1762-63), *The Complete History of England* (1757-58), *The Continuation of the Complete History* (1760-65), *The Modern Part of the Universal History* (1759-65), the *Travels through France and Italy* (1766), *The History and Adventures of an Atom* (1769), and *The Present State of All Nations* (1768-69).[2] Several hundred times in these volumes he resorted to the concept of luxury to explain what he considered seriously wrong in England and the world.

In his last years, after more than a decade of intense activity, Smollett left England, ill and disillusioned with the state of national politics, to concentrate a large portion of his remaining energies upon the novel by which he is known best today, *The Expedition of Humphry Clinker.* Published just three months before his death in September 1771, this final book can be seen in retrospect as equally masterpiece and testament, his preeminent creation as well as his summing up of the lessons of history, experience, and natural law. He utilized the concept of luxury variously and repeatedly within the larger patterns of meaning, structure, and characterization. For him it was the hinge linking the two aspects of the novel, which is at once a harsh indictment of the newer England he repudiated and a nostalgic memoir of the Old England he honored. For us it demonstrates again that a work of art exists within a tradition, the artist perfecting and completing the work of his predecessors. For us too it may provide a further definition of *masterpiece*: a work that not only grows out of a tradition but actually contains it.

Whether this argument is valid and substantial is something that must emerge over subsequent chapters. Yet, put this baldly, it cuts across various assumptions current in social, literary, and intellectual history. It certainly raises a series of legitimate objections, which in summary form might run as follows. "We already know everything of consequence about the canard of luxury, during Smollett's lifetime as well as before. Moralists of the eighteenth century were naturally concerned with increasing signs of extravagance and self-indulgence within their society. And, in any case, what is valuable in Smollett has little to do with luxury or any other concept. In no genre is his work notable for its ideas, and *Humphry Clinker* owes its vitality not to any intellectual content but to its easy flow of comic characters and situations. Even if he sometimes did refer to luxury in the novel, there would be little point to a book-length gloss of a single idea in a single work by so unintellectual a writer."

Each of these judgments must be considered before we proceed, for each represents a serious objection to the entire process of revaluation attempted here. I have abbreviated the objections and limited them to the most pertinent; yet I have not tried by caricature to reduce their force. There is no satisfaction in besting straw men, and all can be pursued in the notes to their original sources. The basic question concerns the state of our knowledge of the concept of luxury. Even within the relatively new and always difficult study of the history of ideas, luxury presents an unusual problem in meaning, since it is not susceptible to ready definition. Context is important, and during three thousand years this has shifted many times and in many ways. Ideas concerning, say, death or marriage or monarchy are more easily sorted, for they possess a definite subject. Luxury, however, embraces a network of fluctuating social, philosophic, and theological presuppositions. For eighteenth-century Englishmen, certainly, it was not so much an idea to be analyzed as an idea to be lived by—or at least lived with. In Michel Foucault's valuable phrase, it is a system of discourse: both the mental discourse that guides thought and the social discourse that governs behavior.

Most perplexing for modern students is the additional complication that luxury represents a *lost* system of discourse, the loss disguised by a superficial resemblance between the classical and the modern usage of the term. On the lower level of modern usage, our ordinary language is of course something of a churchyard of ancient philosophies, and present-day references to luxury are to the original as a gravemarker is to an ebullient human life. On the higher level of doctrine, although the vocabulary and social vehemence are often the same, there is as little similarity between a classical opponent of luxury like Augustine and a modern one like Marx as between patristic theology and messianic socialism. We seem to recognize fully that Aquinas and Darwin mean quite different things by the phrase "natural law," but we have yet to draw such distinctions regarding luxury. Perhaps the most informative analogues lie in that specialized branch of the history of ideas, the history of architecture. A temple erected during the reign of Marcus Aurelius has recently been reconstructed to house concerts of popular music. The harmony of a Roman temple was as much cultural as physical; its mass, power, and plastic body were expressions of political philosophy as much as of aesthetic theory. To a modern Roman the rehabilitated shell might argue a renewal of history or a sign of its continuity; but its altered interior speaks volumes of profound change. For another example, a contemporary visitor to the Kremlin could well view Uspenski cathedral as an instance of permanent, unyielding grandeur, for its outward form has been carefully preserved since the fifteenth century. Yet its function and inner spirit have undergone vast upheavals between the czars who built it and the soviets who use it.

Ideas associated with a particular kind of social, religious, political, or economic organization can be finely analyzed long after the organization itself has lapsed or changed. The situation is quite different with ideas like luxury, which appear to absorb and comprehend many varieties of historical change. Like temple and cathedral, luxury has endured.

To indicate briefly that durability over time and fashion, one might examine the opinions of two Englishmen very different from Tobias Smollett. Roger Ascham devotes a large part of the opening Book of *The Scholemaster* (1570) to an exposure of Italian luxury and its imported effect upon educated English youth. When young men become luxurious or "Italianate," there begins a chain of events that ends in certain national degeneracy. First, individual youths dress absurdly and grow vain, lustful, and idolatrous. Contentious factions then develop within families and cities, and the public virtues of respect, honesty, and learning are forever lost. For Ascham luxury is "that sweet and perilous poison of all youth" that has directly caused the chaotic state of private and public life in sixteenth-century Italy. He concludes with the warning that vigilance against luxury must never waver, for the vice is not "open, fond and common," but always "subtle, cunning, new, and divers."[3] Writing two centuries later, Henry Fielding redirects Ascham's warning as he seems to repeat it. Fielding's *Enquiry into the Cause of the late Increase of Robbers* (1751) is a semiofficial report upon a specific situation at midcentury, and he feels obligated to review English history to account for that situation. He finds that the "vast Torrent of Luxury which of late Years hath poured itself into this Nation" has altered and disrupted all levels of society, but he is most alarmed that it has "almost totally changed the Manners, Customs, and Habits of the People, more especially of the lower Sort." A *political* evil, luxury has inspired in the poor a desire for things they may not and cannot have, hence what Fielding considers their wickedness, profligacy, idleness, and dishonesty. Like Ascham, he ends with a call for public vigilance, but of the kind made permanent by stringent laws.[4]

Brief, out of context, and randomly chosen from thousands of possible examples, these two instances cannot reveal much about the nature or history of luxury. Yet they can demonstrate something of its protean quality. The one concurs with the other that luxury is as potent an enemy as England faces. But Ascham's anxiety for the morals of wealthy, educated young Englishmen, while an important facet of the Renaissance conception of luxury, is not wholly congruent with the common eighteenth-century alarm over the luxury of the illiterate poor. Moreover, both Ascham and Fielding are concerned with states of interior wholesomeness, whether of persons or nations, and this characteristic alone is sufficient to distinguish the classical or pre-nineteenth-century concept of luxury from its modern version, with its emphasis on externals like extravagant spending and the waste of natural resources. The distinction between classical and modern conceptions will be taken up later in this chapter.

Notwithstanding the tens of thousands of references to luxury in Western literature, there is as yet, so far as I can discover, no thorough investigation of the concept. Before the eighteenth century, European readers had little need to question its meaning and significance, for they were living in the midst of a vital tradition, one that asserted itself every time a classical text or author was cited. Scholars and other readers since the eighteenth century have in the main assumed that the meaning of luxury was self-evident and self-contained, that it referred to the kind of ostentatious indulgence every right-minded person would oppose.[5] Studies of the eighteenth century generally, of other writers concerned with luxury, and of Smollett have shared this assumption.[6] I have tried to forego the particularity of previous definitions of luxury —definitions that are often more rigorous than the material will allow and that fall victim to misplaced concreteness—attempting instead to discover the assumptions all have in common. Luxury has been always despised and always loved, Voltaire ventured in the *Philosophical Dictionary*. The issue is compounded, consequently, as much by paradox and ambiguity as by controversy; the history of luxury is as much one of various attempts to *enforce* a single meaning over all others as of inevitably evolving meanings. It also encloses the full range of human expression, from the "higher" peaks of philosophical speculation to the "lower" depths of disorganized sentiment and ineffable passion. The power to unite men of differing goals and values—at least tenuously and perhaps below the level of consciousness—remains one of the most fascinating features of the idea.

If a revaluation of luxury is possible, then a redress of judgment regarding Smollett will follow. For several reasons, his prominence and importance in the intellectual life of the middle decades of the eighteenth century have never been fully recognized. The very topicality of much of his writing provides part of the explanation and at least indicates why there is no brilliantly caustic portrait by Macauley to rebut. But the main reason is seemingly temperamental, for Smollett was a perpetual outsider, standing against or aloof from the influential literary coteries of his day. He would find no welcome among the Whig circle of patrons, writers, and booksellers; Horace Walpole saw to that. He was too busy, too irascible, too pugnacious to compete for honors within The Club, and therefore remained beyond the preservative power of Boswell's pen. What time he did have for social diversion seems to have been spent with his *own* circle of family and close associates. And this group, with the partial exceptions of John Moore and Alexander Carlyle, did not leave informative letters or memoirs. Smollett's own letters are relatively few, usually short, and generally utilitarian. They do not provide what we would most wish, "his own life in his own words." Indeed he appears to have been too much the proud Scotsman either (like Johnson) to feel altogether comfortable anywhere in London or (like Pope) to use personal letters to broadcast his fame.

The contention that Smollett's work is unintellectual is relatively recent, predicated on a superficial reading of his fiction and an almost total neglect of his nonfiction. In a brief essay in *Reason and Romanticism* (1926), Herbert Read argued that Smollett's mind "is innocent of ideas, and indeed of abstractions of any sort."[7] With the revival of interest in Smollett's fiction in succeeding decades, this presumption guided interpretations of the whole canon and of particular novels, Smollett becoming the pure storyteller among the great eighteenth-century novelists. Writing of *Peregrine Pickle,* James L. Clifford summarizes the most learned version of this view: "Although the writing is largely free from abstract ideas, this does not mean that Smollett's work lacks serious purpose. He merely refuses to philosophize, to brood, or to waste time in useless introspection. He is a story-teller, who is also an observer and satirist, with a world of folly to expose. But the demands of the narrative always have first claim."[8] Nor could critics like Alan D. McKillop discern any "philosophizing" in his final work. "The world of *Clinker* is still Smollett's world, a jungle in which amazing fauna are to be found, a region of endless absurdities, but there is no longer so much talk about fierce indignation [as in earlier novels]. There is a general parallel with Sterne here: while the great world may rage without, the obliquities of these originals are harmless, and manifest themselves in a well-grounded order of things. . . . Smollett's humorous characters never require long study."[9]

One kind of response to the misgivings of a magisterial man of letters like Read—and those who agree with him—is to bring to court the opinion of another. W. H. Auden has written:

> we cannot fully understand Pope and any other writers of his period without knowing something about the general climate of thought and opinion by which they were surrounded. It was one of the few historical periods in which one could with accuracy speak of an educated élite who, whether as writers or as readers, shared the same artistic tastes and general ideas about Nature, Man, and Society—a period, therefore, when "originality" and "alienation" were not regarded as the hallmarks of genius.[10]

Another response is to note that Read's notion of an idea was not Smollett's, nor that of numerous other eighteenth-century figures justly respected as thinkers. To a progressive critic like Read, *idea* connotes novelty, originality, innovation, bold speculation, a leap beyond the margins of conventional thought. But to Locke, Dryden, Swift, Pope, Johnson, Goldsmith, Reynolds, and Smollett, to cite but a few, intellectual apprehension was something quite different.[11] To call upon Johnson, it was a revelation of "the general truths of nature," "just and universal truths," "general and transcendental truths, which will always be the same." In the *Life of Cowley* appear the distinction of three levels of wit, the disparagement of novel insights as merely "metaphysical," and the famous summary, "Great thoughts are always general, and consist in positions not limited by exceptions, and in descriptions not descending to minuteness."[12] Whatever his other differences and disagreements with these contemporaries, Smollett shared their view of truth and the goals of meaningful thought. To him possession of an idea was a process of ever-growing, ever-deepening apprehension of a truth known from time immemorial. To hold an idea meant to make it one's own, to feel it, to use it, to renew its strength, to apprehend its manifestations, to become sensitive to its immediate implications; and to exercise the imagination meant to give an idea force, vitality, and immediacy. Like the old priest in Graham Greene who twice daily for fifty years polished the gilt crucifix he had received at ordination, Smollett furbished his conception of luxury with many volumes of what he considered closely argued prose.

A secondary objection, related to Read's, is that Smollett rarely appears self-consciously concerned with abstractions of any sort. It is perhaps this very habit of mind, common to active writers, that has obscured Smollett's stature as a thinker. To a contemplative philosopher like Hume, luxury could be an object of detached curiosity, a fascinating study in the clashes and combinations of various attitudes. But to Smollett it was of necessity something else—a tool for use, an automatic, reflexive instrument to simplify and clarify his work. Once accepted, the classical approach to luxury took on for him the strength of doctrine. It was to him what the Pauline epistles were to Wesley—not a pale relic of a remote culture, but a vivid, immediate presence of timeless certainty. It is hence not surprising that at no point in the seventy volumes he wrote after 1756, with their hundreds of references to luxury, did he define his use of the concept or reduce it to its essentials. He had no more use for such a definition than Wesley had for a definition of the Incarnation. Rather his habit is to associate it with other concepts and events or to illustrate it through its social consequences. It existed not to be defined, but to be displayed, vivified, personified, worked with, written from. It began with people, described people, and returned to people. Finding the concept equally fertile and crucial, he turned time and again to luxury to guide his thinking and his writing, for the truth could easily bear incessant repetition. To John Locke the process of association would have been a familiar one, for "once set going" predominant ideas "continue in the same steps they have been used to, which by often treading, are worn into a smooth path, and the motion in it becomes easy, and as it were natural."

In such a "motion," moreover, the novelist was neither lax nor confused; he was reflecting the common habit of his time. The enveloping context and vocabulary of the controversy over luxury had been established perhaps as long as three millennia before he was born and were not to be revised substantially until after the publication of *The Wealth of Nations,* five years after his death. To this context and vocabulary the vast majority of Smollett's countrymen who wrote on the subject gave their assent, regarding the idea not as hackneyed or indeterminate, but as resonant with the implications of experience and the lessons of history. To most literate Englishmen of his lifetime, the continual reminders of the fall of Rome appear to have been like the annual feasts of the Jewish and Christian calendars, regular commemorations of the most important event in European history. Such reminders enabled eighteenth-century Englishmen to develop what was to them a sharp sense of history and thereafter to carry that sense with them day after day, generation after generation. As many Europeans would today say "Never again!" to the atrocities of Nazi Germany, just so did many Englishmen then respond to the luxuries of ancient Rome.

This legacy of dread had manifold consequences for eighteenth-century English thought. Since nearly all moralists assumed that luxury was one of the most dire forms of human vice, the only dispute possible was over its manifestations. In a century of accelerated change, these manifestations were to be found virtually everywhere. Politicians saw luxury rampant within the church, and clergymen found it infesting Westminster. While military men blamed the merchants, the merchants blamed the literati. Save for one conspicuous break, the controversy would have been flawlessly circular. Almost all writers on luxury blamed The People. As that amorphorous body found its spokesmen and then its own voice, the controversy over luxury reached probably its highest peak in European history. Although it may be impossible ultimately to assess the influence of an idea, particularly such a protean one, it is arguable that luxury was the single most significant social and political idea of eighteenth-century England. It became a popular cliché flowing easily from the pens of aspiring writers on religion, society, political economy, and politics. Yet it is also at the center of many works of the first order: from *Leviathan* to *The Wealth of Nations*, from *The Fable of the Bees* to *The Decline and Fall of the Roman Empire*, from *Tom Jones* to *The Man of Feeling*, from the *Spectator* to the *Annual Register*, and from Pope's *Epistles* to *The Deserted Village*. In his review of Jenyns's *Free Inquiry*, Johnson ventures the audacious, divining in the Platonic doctrine of plenitude a profound philosophical contradiction. With somewhat more temerity, critics occasionally called attention to the theoretical and practical inconsistencies present in the conventional concept of luxury.

Discussing the idea of the Great Chain during the eighteenth century, Lovejoy argued that questions of rank and power could be tacitly absorbed into the higher unity of theological metaphysics. Many Englishmen were simultaneously aware that questions of political and legal privilege, the concentration of wealth and property, the state of education and the arts, and many related issues could be absorbed openly into the allegedly higher unity of luxury. Although the position of literature in this process has been little noticed by literary historians, an economic historian, Jacob Viner, has essayed a general description. Regarding satirists from the Restoration to about 1760, Viner writes: "Satire was . . . an upper-class preserve in the main, with the satirists in the free or paid service of their social superiors. . . . I have not succeeded in finding a clear-cut *English* instance in which a satirist, on an economic issue, was attacking a social group clearly higher than the one he belonged to or had been hired to serve."[13] He argues further that during this period satire "had its darts pointed horizontally or downwards in the social scale, but not upwards." Smollett was not a satirist in the strict sense, and his last novel did not appear until 1771; yet his work otherwise falls within such a pattern. Later chapters indeed will seek to suggest his affinity with the earlier generation of Tory satirists. Viner recommends additional study of the interrelations of literature and society. Knowledge of the manner in which the concept of luxury influenced a major novelist goes far, I believe, to explain what he calls "institutional *status quo* conservatism." If language does in fact greatly influence perception, then the conservative perceptions of many eighteenth-century Englishmen were influenced by an intellectual tradition whose taproots lay deep in the soil of antiquity.[14]

Viner's researches help to anticipate the objections of literary scholars who, while granting the importance of luxury to the history of ideas, would question its pertinence to literary history. In the concluding portion of this study I argue that the attack upon luxury represents a literary mode as distinct and as ancient as the idea itself. If Smollett had never written a line, there would be value in a wholly literary investigation of luxury, on a scale I can only indicate here. For even beyond the question of narrative mode, condemnations of luxury possess a quality rare outside Gothic fiction and eschatological homilies—an eloquence of horror. Heuristic figures and flourishes abound, and the imagination is compelled to number the abominations of desolation. Frequently there is the further fascination of an author or fictional speaker extending himself to befoul that which he most ardently and most secretly covets, as in the rhetorical glory of lascivious clerics in Webster and Diderot.

The final pair of objections involve the nature of Smollett's achievement in *Humphry Clinker*. The one holds that his two decades of journalistic labor were an unfortunate distraction from his mature work as a novelist, rather than a contribution to it.[15] The other regards the novel as too much a comic tour de force to depend upon a "serious" or controversial context.[16] Both assume a series of disjunctions within his career and can be treated together. Regarding a major writer of voluminous output, literary historians usually are able to perceive that, when taken together, his different creations form a single, consistent oeuvre, one portion of which illuminates all others. But this overarching assessment has not been carried out for Smollett. Because of the obscurity of eighteenth-century controversy and his role in it, and because he did not publish an important novel between 1751 and 1771, it has generally been assumed that he had entered an arid period, writing much but accomplishing little. Contemporary readers, however, apparently had little difficulty recognizing the consistency and continuity his work possesses. They came to *Humphry Clinker* fully aware of his numerous nonfictional works of the 1750s and 1760s and of the positions he assumed during these last decades of his life. Of these decades, Herbert Read aptly notes that they were "years of the most unremitting literary labour, and to omit to reckon them in any estimate of Smollett is as though we were to ignore in Milton's case the twenty years that elapsed between *Lycidas* and *Paradise Lost*."[17] But Smollett's contemporaries, of course, could not omit these years in their evaluation of the writer. While they may have known him as "the author of *Roderick Random*," as the title pages of all the novels proclaimed him, they did not know him exclusively, or even primarily, as a novelist. For his fiction is but a small fraction of his total work, and at no time in his career was he a full-time novelist. Rather, they knew him as the contentious editor of the *Critical Review* and the *Briton,* the writer equally praised and damned for his histories of Europe and England, the jaundiced observer of the *Travels,* and the acidulous creator of the *Atom.* For them, as potentially for us, his authority derived from his immersion in the intellectual currents of his age: as a leading controversialist and defender of the king's causes, a man of medicine, a historian of his country, and the guiding spirit of some of the most considerable periodicals of the day. Indeed the Italian physician who visited him during his last days was informed that Smollett was a writer of "political and historical studies."

Whether hostile or favorable, contemporary estimates of Smollett's nonfiction remark upon two qualities: the ease of his narratives (i.e., his ability to shape large masses of material into a meaningful whole) and the force of his ideas. He was himself proud of the breadth of his reading and his interests and professed that he formed his opinions from "the best thoughts of our age and those of the past." It is part of his power that he genuinely believed he could absorb all of what was known to the English world of ideas. Since much of what was known was summarized by the traditional concept of luxury, Smollett could write rapidly and economically—expressing a constant theme with many variations. Like any comprehensive social concept, luxury gave him the habit and the ability to think in terms of *types* of people, *classes* of events, and *patterns* of behavior. In the histories he revealed the theme through people, events, and behavior of the past; in the periodicals, through those of the present. The habit and the ability combined to make him the eighteenth-century Aristarch of luxury. And in this respect he does far more than merely echo his time; to use Roy Fuller's phrase, he is its very ticking.

By revealing the way eighteenth-century Englishmen read *Humphry Clinker,* the contemporary reception of his last novel serves to affirm the respect Smollett's ideas received. First, the descriptive and expository portions of the novel were commonly distinguished and discussed apart from the narrative. I have located thirty-two notices published within three months of the appearance of the novel, and of these twenty-seven were devoted almost exclusively to the facts and opinions Smollett had included. Virtually all of the twenty extracts that were printed were of this kind of material and were given such titles as "The Present State of Bath," "The Present State of London," "Description of Harrigate," "A Description of Edinburgh," "Some Observations on Glasgow and Lachlomond," and "Considerations on the Union by . . . Dr. Smollett."[18] Second, these portions of the novel were seen, in the words of a reviewer for the *Universal Magazine,* as a "conduit-pipe, through which our author conveys his own real sentiments of men and things." "The work is by no means a novel or romance," the *Gentleman's Magazine* announced, "nor is it indeed principally a narration of events, but rather a miscellany containing dissertations on various subjects, exhibitions of characters, and descriptions of places." The *London Magazine* in its turn called it "a cyclopedia of opinion." The presence of two misanthropic characters notwithstanding, no reviewer doubted that the serious opinions expressed were the author's own.[19] Third, although placed in an imaginative setting, the descriptive and expository passages were granted as much authority as Smollett's earlier writings in current affairs, history, and travel, seemingly because they were read as extensions and continuations of those works. As the editors of contemporary periodicals realized and as Louis Martz has reminded us, *Humphry Clinker* was frequently accepted as a fictional rendering of *The Present State of England and Scotland.* John Moore, one of the novelist's editors and closest friends, gave one kind of support to this view when he wrote, in a memoir to the 1798 edition of the works, that Smollett "hardly attempted any story" in his last novel, but used the plot as "a mere vehicle for characters and remarks on life and manners." Horace Walpole provided another in his *Memoirs of the Reign of King George the Third,* calling the book "a party novel, written by the profligate hireling Smollett, to vindicate the Scots and cry down juries." (*Profligate,* it should be noted, was one of Smollett's own favorite terms of abuse.) Thackeray, one of the most sympathetic readers the novelist has had, put the situation with admirable brevity: Smollett, he said, "did not invent much."

Thus those readers most familiar with Smollett's previous work were neither surprised nor disappointed to find in *Humphry Clinker* a miscellany of fiction and opinion, and no critic, friendly or harsh, had difficulty finding amid the several points of view represented in the novel those most characteristic of the author. Such unanimity argues not critical naivité, but the reverse. With the examples of Pope and Swift, Fielding and Hogarth before them, eighteenth-century readers expected a blend of general and particular satire and realized that profound moral themes could be expressed as well through humor as through wrath. In the *Treatise of Human Knowledge* (1739), Hume accepted the challenge to define "what is commonly, and in a popular sense, called reason." This he decided is "nothing but a general and a calm passion which takes a comprehensive and distant view of its object." And what is commonly termed "strength of mind" is actually but "the prevalence of calm passions over the violent." In a similar fashion the essential distinction between, say, Smollett's essays in the *Critical Review* on the one hand and *Humphry Clinker* on the other is not that the novelist had grown less political, or had altered his social views, or had become a better writer. Rather it is that he had gained sufficient time and favorable circumstances to write another kind of book. We indeed know that during the early 1760s, while he was writing for the *Critical,* he was also gathering material that would later be incorporated into *Humphry Clinker.* Moreover, we find in the *Critical,* the *Briton,* and the *Present State of All Nations* anticipations of specific portions of the novel.

When Smollett gave over the exigencies of periodical journalism for travel and rest, he did not relinquish his combat with luxury. He selected new weapons.

To distinguish sharply between "the appealing humor" of *Humphry Clinker* and its "mere essay material," as many critics have done, is to create a false dichotomy, certainly one Smollett would not have permitted. For at heart the issue is one of elementary literary craftsmanship. Nearly all the humor as well as the "essay matter" is conveyed by two characters, Bramble and Jery. Smollett must convince us, as he did his original readers, that the uncle and nephew are worthy, responsible reporters of events; otherwise their humor would be as reflexive and their characters as absurd as those of Tabby and Dr. L——n (Linden). It is in fact a measure of his success that *Humphry Clinker* can be at once (as Thackeray wrote) "the most laughable story that has ever been written since the goodly art of novel-writing began" and one of the most despairing. Smollett had learned well the art of limits and balances, and the world he created in his final novel is rich and full because of the lesson.

It was as familiar a paradox to eighteenth-century critics as to those of the twentieth that fiction is often truer than philosophy. If Smollett's social and political ideas are accepted as essential elements in his creation of *Humphry Clinker,* they may still be interpreted in different ways. From a formalist point of view, they call attention not so much to themselves as to the characters and situations they animate. Fiction does not shackle its readers to a dogma from which we must later free ourselves. Rather it repeats, reorders, and reveals anew the values we already possess. A fine novel disengages us from ourselves by placing us in the midst of an assembly of fascinating characters. Ideas here must be not true, but ample, compelling, vivifying. A great novel gives not ideas to affirm, but a fullness of experience to appreciate. Against this view, a contemporary structuralist would say that most fiction, most of the time, offers an author's promise of deliberate commentary upon the phenomenal world; that Smollett—no less than Dickens, Balzac, Zola, and Richard Wright—is urging the truth of his ideas upon us. [20] To come to *Humphry Clinker* by way of his political and historical writing is, I think, to offer a way to resolve such theoretical questions. As Hardy late in his life turned in disappointment from fiction, so Smollett turned to it. Over the social reality he described in his nonfiction there was little dispute. It was there: simple, solid, and palpable. And many of his readers were repelled. But when he recreated that reality in *Humphry Clinker* they were delighted. In this last work he is among the *masters,* in Pound's sense of the term, authors who, "apart from their own inventions, are able to assimilate and co-ordinate a large number of preceding inventions . . . they either start with a core of their own and accumulate adjuncts, or they digest a vast mass of subject-matter, apply a number of known modes of expression, and succeed in pervading the whole with some special quality or some special character of their own, and bring the whole to a state of homogeneous fullness."[21]

It is no detraction, but plain fact, to observe that large portions of human existence were closed to Smollett. There was much in English life that he either missed or dismissed. Yet what he saw, he saw clearly. He was for many years preoccupied with the social, political, and literary relations of his time, and regarding these he was able to penetrate the immediate surface of mid–eighteenth-century events to a depth perhaps only a Swift could appreciate. Like Burke and Paine in their zeal a generation later, he believed he had been given special sight into the fundamental workings of human history. Gifted with such sight, he was able to create, in *Humphry Clinker* and elsewhere, a vital order of vision—what he would have called knowledge of the nature of things—that he could himself draw upon while also sharing with others. It is with questions about the nature of such an order that this study is ultimately concerned: what it sought from the Western intellectual tradition, how it accommodated change in human relationships, where it demanded continuity and where reversal and return.

Such questions encompass the whole of Smollett's later career but have special application to his last novel. In it he invested the routine, ordinary bustle of Bath, London, Edinburgh, and other places with a transcendental significance it surely did not of itself possess. Why, one may ask, did he weave into such rich and original cloth the features of a commonplace nemesis, luxury? Why is one of Smollett's voices, Bramble, so appalled by what another, Mr. S——, finds quite engaging? Why, on its surface, is *Humphry Clinker* savage, witty, silly, and tender by turns? If Walpole was just in calling it "a party novel," why has it been enjoyed by readers of all shades of political opinion across Europe and America (as editions and translations reveal it to have been)? If the early English novel as a genre offers a view of the world that is "subjective, individualistic, private," why does *Humphry Clinker* return to the objective, social, and public orientation of the classical world? If Sterne had converted English critics after 1760 to delicacy, sentiment, and amiability, why was Smollett's novel so popular a decade later? Why did so learned a man consciously reject the theories of Voltaire, Hume, Smith, Rousseau, Steuart, and others? Why in several places did he claim to perceive the collapse of British civilization in the pallor of London bread? And why does he often seem a vestige of an earlier generation of English satirists? It is on the broad middle ground of Smollett's conscious attitudes that the elements of this study converge.

Standing together, tradition, age, author, and work take on a significance each lacks when separated, and the light cast upon one illuminates
all at once.[22]

Before concluding these preliminary remarks, it is necessary to return
to the place of luxury in Western history. I have assumed that the concept must be approached historically, that though altered it remained
strong into the nineteenth century, and that its meaning remains moot
today. To examine these assumptions is to reply to one of the most
profound objections ever raised against historical research, phrased thus
by Samuel Johnson: "Life is surely given us for higher purposes than to
gather what our ancestors have wisely thrown away, and to learn what is
of no value but because it has been forgotten." In *Humphry Clinker*
Smollett gives Bramble's attacks upon the luxury of Bath and London
a discursive quality, a cogency growing out of immediate indignation
and careful reflection—a quality familiar to readers of his earlier work.
In such passages luxury is held responsible for two related kinds of disorder in contemporary England, in public life and in personal behavior.
Of the first Bramble cites careless architecture and shoddy construction,
narrow pavements, crowded houses, "noise, tumult, and hurry," "confusion, glare, and glitter," rampant commerce and high prices, oppressive assemblies and entertainments, vulgarization of Ranelagh and Vauxhall, great increases in the numbers of country houses, town houses,
servants, black cattle, and horses, wine and tea drinking, "folly and
extravagance," "fraud and sophistication," but great decreases in the
total population. Of the second he notes the insolence of merchants
and tradesmen and servants, debauchery of farm boys, large increases
in the numbers of thieves, sharpers, and highwaymen, idleness of the
poor, mixture of classes and sexes, drunkenness, "ignorance, presumption, malice, and brutality," "stupidity and corruption."

To show that Smollett's conception of luxury varies significantly
from nineteenth-century usage, one need go no further than the turn of
the century to find several authors for contrast. Yet for an effective
contrast a later decade would be preferable, one that demonstrates that
the issue of luxury had been settled and that the rough quarrels over
meaning of the previous century had receded into a nostalgic past.
Ideally the demonstration would involve a mid-century novelist, one
with a shared sense of his society's values, and one who was nearly as
fascinated by luxury as Smollett had been. Indeed either of the authors
who leap to mind, Dickens and Thackeray, would serve. Thackeray is
particularly apt. He was one of Smollett's greatest admirers, and his
esteem for *Humphry Clinker* remains unsurpassed. A recent study of
his major fiction by Barbara Hardy is entitled *The Exposure of Luxury:
Radical Themes in Thackeray* (1972).[23] And his account of the age of

George III in *The Four Georges,* written in 1856, is valuable for our purposes, for it seeks to capture the flavor of Smollett's own time—re-creating it in what Thackeray assumed was its own terms. Although he was a careful reader of Smollett and acknowledged his indebtedness to him, the contrast in meaning between the two novelists is virtually complete.

The axis of the opening half of Thackeray's description is itself a studied contrast between the aristocratic culture of latter eighteenth-century England and the middle-class culture of the Victorian age. For illustrations of social life after 1760, he selects from the published letters to George Selwyn. "As one reads the Selwyn letters—as one looks at Reynolds's noble pictures illustrative of those magnificent times and voluptuous people—one almost hears the voice of the dead past. . . . How fine those ladies were, those ladies who heard and spoke such coarse jokes; how grand those gentlemen!"[24] He seeks, in his choice of adjectives, an initial sense of nostalgia that he will proceed to qualify, an atmosphere he wishes to capture in order to banish.

> I fancy that peculiar product of the past, the fine gentleman, has almost vanished off the face of the earth, and is disappearing like the beaver or the Red Indian. . . . In the days when there were fine gentlemen, Mr. Secretary Pitt's undersecretaries did not dare to sit down before him; but Mr. Pitt, in his turn, went down on his gouty knees to George II.: and when George III. spoke a few kind words to him, Lord Chatham burst into tears of reverential joy and grati-tude; so awful was the idea of the monarch, and so great the distinctions of rank. . . . At the accession of George III., the patricians were yet at the height of their good fortune. Society recognized their superiority, which they themselves pretty calmly took for granted. [Pp. 63–64][25]

Where Bramble saw only insubordination and plebeians bent upon in-sulting their betters, Thackeray perceives servility and flatterers. Reverence for the patrician world, Thackeray thinks was well-nigh uni-versal: "To Smollett, to Fielding, even, a lord was a lord: a gorgeous being with a blue ribbon, a coroneted chair, and an immense star on his bosom, to whom commoners paid reverence" (pp. 64–65). And in Selwyn he finds that world displayed in easy dishabille, "the real original men and women of fashion of the early time of George III." Inspecting a new club or abroad on the Grand Tour, at court or at home in the country, English high life compelled fascination and wonder.

Having conceded the attraction of the latter part of the eighteenth-century, Thackeray proceeds to bring it to judgment. Citing one of Selwyn's correspondents, the chaplain Dr. Varner, he finds its religion lukewarm, shallow, and politic. Citing Lord Carlisle, he finds the management of public affairs frivolous at best, corrupt at worst: "one of the English fine gentlemen who was well-nigh ruined by the awful debauchery and extravagance which prevailed in the great English society of those days. Its dissoluteness was awful" (p. 67). To Thackeray Carlisle is significant as a representative of an aristocracy rendered impotent and dissolute by luxury. "Besides the great London society of those days, there was another unacknowledged world, extravagant beyond measure, tearing about in the pursuit of pleasure; dancing, gambling, drinking, singing; meeting the real society in the public places (at Ranelaghs, Vauxhalls, and Ridottos, about which our old novelists talk so constantly), and outvying the real leaders of fashion in luxury, and splendour, and beauty" (pp. 67–68). But compared with many of his fellow patricians, Carlisle's sins of luxury were venial and temporary; he had caught the distemper of the times. "He found himself, in the midst of a dissolute society, at the head of a great fortune," was forced into luxury, suffered, and repented (pp. 68–69).

The point is clear. Although Smollett and Thackeray agree that luxury is idleness, extravagance, and dissolution in society, and both look for it at Ranelagh and Vauxhall, they disagree radically on its social locus. Thackeray leaves no doubt that luxury is a vice indigenous to the ruling classes: "If, in looking at the lives of princes, courtiers, men of rank and fashion, we must perforce depict them as idle, profligate, and criminal, we must make allowances for the rich men's failings, and recollect that, we, too, were very likely indolent and voluptuous, had we no motive for work, a mortal's natural taste for pleasure, and the daily temptation of a large income. What could a great peer, with a great castle and park, and a great fortune, do but be splendid and idle?"

> It is to the middle class we must look for the safety of England: the working educated men, away from Lord North's bribery in the senate; the good clergy not corrupted into parasites by hopes of preferment; the tradesmen rising into manly opulence; the painters pursuing their gentle calling; the men of letters in their quiet studies; these are the men whom we love and like to read of in the last age. . . . Their minds were not debauched by excess, or effeminate with luxury. [Pp. 70–71]

To Thackeray luxury is a vice of limited scope. Although a pervasive tendency among the predominant classes, it *could not* cause or account for all the many and various breaches Smollett sees. It could not, that is, cause shoddy architecture, impudence in workingmen, or an increase in robberies. Indeed on the issue of building and architecture their concepts are openly contradictory. For Thackeray, luxury would tend to produce buildings that were magnificent, grand, and fine: great wealth squandered where simplicity at less cost would have sufficed. For Smollett, in contrast, luxury produced buildings that were cheap in both senses, inexpensive as well as tawdry and inefficient, overly vulgar rather than overly refined. For the one man, luxury as a vice could not, by definition, reach down to the lower levels of English society; it was a vice of the rich. For the other, luxury had nothing to do with the idleness of a Carlisle or the sycophancy of a Varner. It could not, by definition, directly touch the behavior of royal, noble, or gentle society; it was a vice of the middling and poorer sort of Englishman. Between their respective uses of the same concept there is not only logical contradiction, but also social tension. Between 1771 and 1856 one of the basic principles for understanding the relationships within a society underwent fundamental transformation. That much is certain. Yet one is still left with the question so often asked during the eighteenth century— with irony by Mandeville, curiosity by Hume, and exasperation by Adam Smith. What does this chameleon of a concept *mean?*

Part One

A HISTORY OF MEANINGS

*Luxury . . . turns men into greedy brutes.—Lycurgus,
according to Plutarch*

*Luxury is the source of this female insurrection.
—Cato, according to Livy*

Luxury is the abandonment of nature.—Seneca

*Luxury is as the thirst of a man who has a fever . . . which is in
no degree like the thirst of a man who is in health.—Epictetus*

Luxury . . . the fount and origin of all evil.—Sallust

Luxury is slavery.—Ambrose

*   *   *   *

*. . . this ambiguous term, Luxury. There is no word more
inconstantly used and capriciously applied to particular actions.
—Warburton,* The Divine Legation *(1737)*

*Luxury is a word of uncertain signification, and may be taken in a
good as well as a bad sense.—Hume,* Political Discourses *(1752)*

*Few writers, when they treat of luxury, ascertain the idea of it
in a proper manner.—*Critical Review *(1765)*

*There is scarce any subject that has been more frequently
treated by political writers than that of luxury, and yet few have
been treated in a more vague and superficial manner.
—*Monthly Review *(1772)*

One

NECESSITY AND HIERARCHY: THE CLASSICAL ATTACK UPON LUXURY

In the beginning was the Word, and for Western man the essential words of early history had the dual function of revealing God's Law and accounting for the human condition. While not the earliest source for the criticism of luxury, the story of Adam and Eve in Genesis 2–3 is a natural starting point for a survey, for it contains the simplest definition of luxury: *anything unneeded.* To understand the initial intertwining of luxury with human destiny, one must recall the elaborate Hebrew conception of history. What is distinctive to it is the conviction that it is God and not the world that is fearsome to man. Like the garden of Eden, the historical world of the Old Testament is the sacred and magnificent work of God's creation. It is Yahweh himself whom men must fear, for while he is the source of all good, he is also the source of terrible punishment. The world is but the ground upon which Yahweh works.

For the Hebrews the world is cultic and nonrational, governed only by the rules of Yahweh, the Law. The injunction to Adam is thus entirely consonant with the remainder of Mosaic Law: it is arbitrary, inviolable, and immutable. It seeks not moral perfection, but legal righteousness. It asks not choice, but obedience, for there can be no mitigating circumstance for disobedience. It is satisfied only by resignation, continually demonstrated, to the will of God. Out of this conception grew the conviction that luxury represented a changeless, eternal violation of God's Law.

The archetypal luxury of Adam and Eve involved five elements ever present thereafter. The first is the legislator, Yahweh, who defines the limits of necessity and thereby the threshold of luxury; it is an arbitrary distinction comprehensible only in terms of the will of the legislator. The second is the object of testing or temptation. In Genesis the fruit of the forbidden tree is by definition inessential to sustenence and comfort, for before it had been created "every tree that is pleasant to the sight, and good for food." It is present to fulfill not human happiness, but the conditions of the Law. Third, there is the tempter, an agent either external or internal which seeks to thwart the Law. The serpent appears as an external tempter, a force attempting to betray man's state of innocence, almost an anti-God, intent as its reason for being upon frustrating God's will.

The fourth element is imperfect human nature, incarnate as subject to the Law and victim of the tempter. Initially the sin of luxury is committed by "the woman." It is significant to all later interpretations of luxury that Adam's helpmeet is not named until after the Fall and just before the Expulsion, in Gen. 3:20. In the language describing the Fall itself (3:6) there is indication of a remarkable agreement of opinion. As much for early Jewish commentators as for the Jacobean translators of 1611 and political orators a century later, luxury is a single process: thought arousing desire impelling action. In the King James Version the process is expressed in a single sentence: "And when the woman saw that the tree was good for food, and that it was pleasant to the eyes, and a tree to be desired to make one wise, she took of the fruit thereof, and did eat, and gave also unto her husband with her; and he did eat." Punishment is the final element, a movement from enjoyment of all good things to enjoyment of few or none, a translation from arbitrary happiness to arbitrary grief.[1]

For Christian writers the lesson of Genesis was sufficient. But for the Hebrews it told merely the first half of the story of luxury. The Deuteronomic writers interpreted the Fall as an event of philosophic reconciliation, an explanation of Creation by an all-perfect God, on the one hand, and the predicament of the Israelites on the other. If no

further, historical lapse into luxury had occurred, then the Israelites as
a nation would have lived on earth with the same peace and security
enjoyed by Adam and Eve before their violation. The Deuteronomic
writers were speculating retrospectively, however, after the second great
lapse and the consequent Diaspora. Recorded in the four successive
books of Samuel and Kings, the latter half of the Hebrew account of the
ravages of luxury is the most mordant chapter of Old Testament
history and the type of subsequent devolutionary national histories,
amplifying the social and political meaning of luxury: *anything to
which one has no right or title*. Samuel and Kings recount the rise and
fall of the nation of Israel, from the elevation of its first king to the
period of infamy when a ruler of the southern kingdom would be slave
to the king of Babylon. From 2 Samuel onward it is a tale of almost
unrelieved calamity, six centuries of whoring after strange gods. On a
deeper level, it is the story of human happiness forever squandered, a
state of luxury becoming a state of accursedness. As in Genesis, only
when the accursed thing has been expelled and isolated will God renew
his blessing upon the Hebrews.[2]

The conflict of the whole arises at the outset, between the judgment
of Samuel and the collective will of the people. Samuel has been a wise
and just interpreter of the Law, but the people would throw off the
rule of a moral judge in favor of a warrior king. He warns that a
monarchy will subvert the Mosaic ideal of a theocratic nation in which
God and God alone is the source of power, wealth, and authority. He
warns, that is, that the object of testing is now the fundamental design
of the Hebrew world. When the Israelites demand a king, they persist
in the most serious of human errors: they yearn for something they do
not need and may not claim, something that cannot profit or deliver.
And when they place the power of God in the hands of an earthly ruler,
it is to be expected that the ruler too will want, and take, what he does
not need. With Saul begins the chain of misdeeds that decimate the
ruling house, the domestic evils afflicting the monarch becoming the
political evils afflicting the Israelite nation. Each of the leaders of Israel
is perverted by luxury: to denial of the source of his authority, to neglect of the Lord, to unjust and unnatural wants. Saul's pride will not
brook God's admonitions and impels him to apostasy, attempted assassination, and civil war. David's sense of justice is turned aside to lust
and murder. Once satisfied, Amnon's desire for Tamar is transformed
into disgust. Absalom's anger leads to fratricide, attempted regicide,
and greater revolt. Solomon's wisdom is twisted to lechery and idolatry.

After Solomon, individuals are of less importance than the general
pattern of punishment in national degeneration. From 1 Kings 12, the
Deuteronomic writers present a rapid panorama of catastrophe: purges,

massacres, usurpations, barbarities, and assassinations. The second fall and destruction of Jerusalem mark the physical dissolution of the nation of Israel, as the enslavement of Jehoiachin, its last king, marks the spiritual. For the royal house and the people of Israel alike, the wages of luxury are death and desolation.

Throughout these pages of moralized history the guilt of a leader of Israel comes to envelop his people: "his sin wherewith he made Israel to sin." (1) Luxury is shown to be an *active* sin. It cannot be merely avoided or ignored. Since it is rebellion against the Law, it must be confronted, conquered, eradicated. (2) Luxury is a *generic,* cardinal sin. From it follows general immorality and impiety. It is a violation of divine order, upsetting the relation not only of man to God but also of man to man. (3) Given the Jewish conception of history, luxury is necessarily a *political* crime as well as a violation of Law. By the time of Samuel and Kings it is something far more than an abstract theological vice; it is a palpable, irrational presence, a folk devil. (4) Luxury is a *national* sin, in which the folly of the people is transmitted to their leaders and then refracted in aggravated form to the nation as a body. When monarch and subject together pursue God's will, the nation is secure, satisfied, and prosperous. Yet, in an example of divine irony, when security, satisfaction, and prosperity are pursued as ends in themselves, then monarch and subject alike are devastated. Samuel's words are equally admonition and prophecy: "And turn ye not aside: for then should ye go after vain things, which cannot profit nor deliver. . . . Only fear the Lord. . . . But if ye shall still do wickedly, ye shall be consumed, both ye and your king."[3] (5) Luxury becomes associated with *original* sin. When the Hebrews move from monolatry to monotheism, the desire for luxury is transformed from a national failing to a universal one, the human malaise. Presence of this desire is taken as a sign of corruption of the whole species, and the prohibition of luxury henceforth extends to all of mankind. When the frailty transmitted from Adam reaches the kings of Israel, it destroys the nation but not itself. In obscure fashion, luxury has passed beyond the chosen people to infect the whole Gentile world as well. The Old Testament account of luxury has come full circle.[4]

Because the history of luxury is immense and complex and the purposes of this chapter are limited, it may be of use to review its elements at the outset. Already for the Hebrews the concept of luxury is what Lovejoy would call a complex idea, a fabric rather than a thread. It conveys the most decisive response possible to the human condition, a theory of entropy that explains as it describes how men, singly or collectively, lose vitality and fall from grace. For individuals it bears a theory of ethics, for nations a theory of history. Yahweh's Law is singular and establishes the moral unity of the Hebrew testament. All values are one, subsumed by obedience; the antithesis of luxury is not simplicity but obedience, the beginning and end of morality. Love is obedience. Virtue is obedience. Happiness is obedience. Freedom is obedience. Wisdom is obedience.[5] Within the Creation such unity is immutable and indivisible. But the Fall is a breaking of faith, a fracture perpetuated in the divisions that beset mankind. In retrospect the oneness of Creation can be analyzed, for with its loss came the manifold ruptures of human society. The entire raison d'être of human law, religion, and philosophy is to regain, as far as humanly possible, the harmony of Creation, to restore the principles of Necessity and Hierarchy that sustained it.

The Law of Genesis expresses the priority of natural law, antedating civil law in its founding of moral obligation within divine creation. As Aristotle, Cicero, Grotius, and Aquinas were to phrase it, natural law defines that which it is man's nature to observe. Thus it is also reason's law, plain to all rational creatures—nature's simple, universal plan. It ordains Necessity. As Necessity is made explicit by the Law, so too is Hierarchy. Eden is Yahweh's creation, not Adam's. Its perfection is that of divine plenitude, not human aspiration. Within the terms of the divine mandate Adam is free; he is free as Evangelus, steward to Pericles, is free, to enjoy the pleasures of his master's estate in the course of his duties, but not at their expense. Because he comprehends Eden, Yahweh is the legislator who determines all ramifications of the Law. Emphatically and repeatedly in Samuel and Kings, Yahweh demands submission to hierarchy; for the luxury of a secular ruler the Israelites pay with their sorrow and their children's sorrow. It was their duty to accept theocratic authority as they had accepted the bondage imposed by the Egyptians. Since all men are God's slaves, social and political relations among men are nugatory.

The Israelites fell as Adam and Eve did. They would have that for which they had no need and to which they had no claim. Luxury in the Old Testament begins in the neglect of necessity and the forgetting of one's place in the hierarchy. The Law teaches that one must be indifferent to personal and social condition. Only God's favor will ease pain, shatter physical bonds, and liberate the soul from mundane constraints. God permits the Israelites to enslave other nations and even each other; he does so to demonstrate that spiritual shackles alone are real. Hierarchy makes palpable for human understanding the unfolding of the Law. It declares who is the legislator, what is the object of testing, who is the tempter, who is subject to the Law, and how violators will be punished. Hierarchy determines, in ordinary terms, who gets what and who makes that decision. As it determines what one may covet, so it decides what one may love. The Israelites may not covet the form of government of their neighbors; a slave may not love freedom—or a free woman. Clear to all rational creatures is a natural relationship of legislator and subject, superior and inferior, master and servant.

The perfect subject of the Law is a person at one with the legislator, someone who fulfills his nature by becoming an instrument of the legislator's will. Since his nature is defined by the terms of the Law, he is the type from which particular models may be drawn: for example, the good child, wife, tradesman, soldier, servant, or slave. But the paradigm will hold merely in the abstract, in the perfection of the Law, for human nature is deficient. The attractions of luxury multiply, moreover, and the tempter grows in cunning. Because of his weakness the subject inevitably becomes the victim, first of the tempter and then of the sanctions prescribed by the Law. As luxury is the most heinous of sins, its punishment may be justly fierce, extending to enslavement and execution. In Genesis the dishonor of Ham brings perpetual bondage upon his descendants; in Kings Yahweh punishes the pride of the rulers of Israel with servitude to the Babylonians. Whether poor sinner or mighty nation, those who fall victim to the tempter will fall victim to the ineluctable Law.

Between the Hebrews and eighteenth-century England there is a demonstrable continuity in the conception of luxury—a continuity of form, the persistence of what I have called its five elements and their use in sustaining Necessity and Hierarchy. Since Englishmen inherited their sense of luxury not from the Old Testament but from classical Latin writers and the Christian church, such continuity is itself remarkable. (Historians of the language have traced the term to two Latin nouns: *luxus,* dative *luxu,* "sensuality, splendor, pomp"; and its derivative, *luxuria,* "riot, excess, extravagance."[6]) Yet it is not altogether surprising. Given the generalizing habit of moralists and jurists, often drawing upon the exact phrasing of their predecessors, the concept could remain relatively uniform over time and geography. To note this fact, however, is to distinguish between luxury as an intellectual entity and its concrete effects upon people and institutions. As slaves could not write about slavery as freely as their masters, so the subjects of the Law left far fewer records than the legislators. An important consequence is that we know much more about luxury in the abstract than we do about its influence upon people's lives. We do know enough to declare that it was never negligible. Philosophers, princes, and judges were able comfortably to shape their applications to their own ages and requirements. The power of legislators fluctuated over time, as did the type of punishment they would wield; objects of testing were construed one way by the Greeks, another by the church fathers. Spartans considered Athenians tempters, Cato suspected all Greeks, Augustine denounced Greek and Roman alike, Calvin blamed the pope. And while the injunctions of the Law might be virtually identical over three thousand years, its primary subjects could be quite diverse—from Athenian slaves and the widows of wealthy Romans to Tuscan apprentices and London merchants.

To simplify somewhat, one might say that both Smollett and Thackeray retain the Hebrew conception of luxury but apply it differently, particularly in deciding who is subject to its commands. For the significance of luxury is to be found not so much in a unique proper meaning as in the history and variety of its many meanings, a history in which inveterate elements are given a distinctive pattern in each succeeding age. Within a context of nominal identity and conservation of tradition, moralists made large changes and drew material distinctions in their application of the idea. Over centuries such changes came to express quite different and (usually) unrecognized alterations in experience and circumstance. While widely employed and universally accepted, it was kaleidoscopically fluid and demonstrably complicated, one aspect sometimes seeming to negate or contradict another. It could mean many things to many people because its content could be infinitely distended and adjusted. With such dynamic and generative possibilities, it was an idea to be used, not defined.

THE SEARCH FOR RATIONALITY IN GREECE AND ROME

The Greek view of luxury is a secular and rational complement to the Hebrew view. Luxury was as threatening to the Apollonian ideal of *sophrosyne* as to the Hebrew ideal of obedience. The Apollonian tradition exhorted men to recall that necessity and mortality set strict limits upon individuality and that pleasure and happiness were subject to the constraints of rationality. Luxury was therefore regarded as a retreat from order, a violation of harmony, and the introduction of chaos into the cosmos, preventing the individual and the community from realizing their natural ends. Theoretically, as in Hesiod's *Theogony* or Plato's *Timaeus,* luxury is an ever-present threat to the unity of the *cosmos;* concretely, as in Herodotus or the *Republic,* it is an immediate threat to the polis.

In Plato and Aristotle the temptation to luxury is described not as an anti-God seeking to frustrate the divine will, but as a constant drive of man's psychological nature. Later, in the church fathers, the two views will be joined even more closely, reconciled in the belief in both an external satanic tempter and a corrupted inner nature. For the Greeks

the vice cannot be eradicated but must be suppressed. In that conviction originates the practice of defining putative instances of luxury with
juridical precision, a process greatly accelerated by the Romans.
Throughout the *Republic* Socrates speaks of the luxurious man as a man
of mere appetite, in whom the lowest part of the soul predominates, a
creature of impulse and passion unable to distinguish necessary from
unnecessary desires. The luxurious man cannot be eliminated, for in the
workaday world it is he who does the labor of the polis and produces
the commodities essential to its existence. He can be controlled, however, by segregation, severe laws, and increased labor.[7] Punishment must
be harsh, since the vice is like a disease whose contagion, particularly
to those of some wealth, makes it the lethal enemy of the state.

The just and healthy state Socrates proposes—like Augustine's City of
God and Hobbes's Christian Commonwealth—enforces two related
principles. Man's needs are few, and incipient luxury is incipient
anarchy. When Glaucon insists that the state ought provide for its
citizens' wants as well as their needs, Socrates enunciates the classical
Graeco-Roman indictment against luxury (2. 372c–373c). Quoted here
in full (but without Glaucon's short statements of agreement), it makes
plain that for Plato all men are subject to the Law and that all items
of comfort and refinement are potentially dangerous; from personal
adornment through warfare, the depredations of luxury are so well
known that they may not only be seen but also foreseen.

> Yes, I said, now I understand: the question which you would
> have me consider is, not only how a State, but how a luxurious
> State is created; and possibly there is no harm in this, for in such a
> State we shall be more likely to see how justice and injustice
> originate. In my opinion the true and healthy constitution of the
> State is the one which I have described. But if you wish also to see
> a State at fever-heat, I have no objection. For I suspect that many
> will not be satisfied with the simpler way of life. They will be for
> adding sofas, and tables, and other furniture; also dainties, and
> perfumes, and incense, and courtesans, and cakes, all these not of
> one sort only, but in every variety; we must go beyond the neces-
> saries of which I was at first speaking, such as houses, and clothes,
> and shoes: the arts of the painter and the embroiderer will have to
> be set in motion, and gold and ivory and all sorts of materials must
> be procured.
>
> Then we must enlarge our borders; for the original healthy State
> is no longer sufficient. Now will the city have to fill and swell with
> a multitude of callings which are not required by any natural want;
> such as the whole tribe of hunters and actors, of whom one large

class have to do with forms and colours; another will be the votaries of music—poets and their attendant train of rhapsodists, players, dancers, contractors; also makers of divers kinds of articles, including women's dresses. And we shall want more servants. Will not tutors be also in request, and nurses wet and dry, tirewomen and barbers, as well as confectioners and cooks; and swineherds, too, who were not needed and therefore had no place in the former edition of our State, but are needed now? They must not be forgotten: and there will be animals of many other kinds, if people eat them.

And living in this way we shall have much greater need of physicians than before?

And the country which was enough to support the original inhabitants will be too small now, and not enough?

Then a slice of our neighbors' lands will be wanted by us for pasture and tillage, and they will want a slice of ours, if, like ourselves, they exceed the limit of necessity, and give themselves up to the unlimited accumulation of wealth?

And so we shall go to war, Glaucon. Shall we not?

Then, without determining as yet whether war does good or harm, thus much we may affirm, that now we have discovered war to be derived from the causes which are also the causes of almost all the evils in States, private as well as public.

[Trans. Benjamin Jowett]

Here and in the memorable attack upon the luxurious quality of democracies (8. 555b ff.), Socrates poses the central question of Platonic order. Will the disordered and irrational multitude, driven by evanescent passions, be permitted to wield human destiny? Who will preserve necessity against "insolence and anarchy and prodigality and shamelessness"? Natural law furnishes the only satisfactory answer. As the body is subordinate to the mind, the appetitive part of the soul to the rational, and the servant to his master, so must subjects be ruled in all things by the guardians of the state.

The *Laws* makes yet clearer that for Plato only the intellectually superior partake of the rational and divine, possess the soul of gold, and thereby attain freedom. For the many, reckless and bewildered, the proper role is submission to the will of the virtuous guardians. It is luxury and a violation of order for a bondsman to seek freedom, a woman to rule a household, or a mechanic to govern an estate. It is luxury to seek that for which one has neither capacity nor understanding. Freedom belongs to the truly rational. All the rest is luxury.[8]

Plato's reshaping of the elements of luxury perforce affected the principles of necessity and hierarchy. To the former he added a theory of politics. If the syndrome of luxury is so plain in history, it will be as plain in the present and future. It will explain, that is, the contemporary rivalries of faction or party that erupt whenever groups seek to defend their present luxury against virtue and the law and to contend for more. To the latter he added a system of dualisms that divide humankind into those assumed to be virtuous and those whose capacity for virtue is doubtful. Thus the immediate division between the few legislators and the many subjects. Aristotle surpassed Plato not in presenting new arguments against luxury—found primarily in the *Ethics* and the *Politics,* they are elaborations of Plato—but in his specificity in defining necessity and hierarchy.

In the *Rhetoric* and the *Politics* Aristotle deduces the forms of authority from the primitive household. Nature, custom, and reason—whose union creates virtue—testify that as members of the house are subject to the father, so most persons must be subject to the dominion of the legislator. The child may wish to rule the father, but like the slave coveting freedom the desire is illusory and destructive, for he cannot govern even himself. Domestic hierarchy gives rise to social and then to political hierarchy—all from natural differences in moral-intellectual capacity. "From the hour of their birth," runs his memorable assertion in the *Politics,* "some are marked out for subjection, others for rule." To legislators he commends the arts of coercion and warfare, that they may with ease master "those who deserve to be enslaved." As contemporary legal entities, the estate and the nation are distinctive; yet they represent the kind of community where, because of economic dependence upon the master, all members are assumed to be united by common interest. And while involuntary servitude is mandatory for the wants of the community, such dependence marks a narrowness of soul and a deficiency of intellect.

For thinkers as late as Blackstone, Aristotle had established the inviolable distinctions between necessity and luxury, virtue and sin. No longer the arbitrary test of Yahweh, that distinction was seen as an a priori component of all nature. The frame of Law had been demonstrated: moral, paternal, and agrarian. The natural legislator had been identified in the man of the land whose birth, wealth, and intellect had elevated him to independence of other persons. All other human beings were subordinate to his will, which was codified in the laws of custom and the state. The ground of testing had been affirmed to be the complete spectrum of human activity. The virtue of dependent persons, necessarily of a lower and mechanical sort, was to be determined by the degree of their union with the rationality of the legislator, their ability to anticipate and satisfy his will; the most virtuous were those whose individual wills had been expunged. In the fulfillment of function lay the rationality of dependent mortals; in its neglect lay their luxury—strictly defined and rigorously punished. Aristotle's purpose was to harmonize nature and society. His accomplishment was to identify dependent persons as potentially luxurious and thus potentially subversive. His depreciation of women—that the rational part of woman's soul is impotent—is well known; among others without the deliberative faculty he placed servants, tradesmen, artisans, mechanics, freedmen, slaves; the immature, the illiterate, the weak; and such outsiders as non-citizens and foreigners. Within such groups legislators would discover the enemies of the state. At their best they might prove loyal; yet they were predisposed to be lazy, moronic, rebellious, irresponsible, and sexually dissolute.[9]

Without the explicit injunction of God that guided the Hebrews, Plato and Aristotle grounded their attack upon luxury in what they considered the universal norms of nature, which they associated with origin and birth as well as a presumptive primeval state. Paradoxically, the most thoroughgoing assault upon luxury came from men who repudiated the Platonic sense of hierarchy but extended much further the principle of necessity. Utter rejection of luxury is the foundation of Cynic, Sophist, and early Stoic philosophy, for it was regarded as the abiding impediment to self-sufficiency. Yet their adherents refuse to identify the legislator with secular power, placing it instead within the individual conscience. Unlike Plato and Aristotle, they did not assume that nature and society were—or could be—harmonized. Universal reason, they held, revealed that men of all ranks were consumed with blind craving for what they did not need—fame, wealth, possessions. It likewise revealed that extant social institutions were mere conventions or, worse, active restraints upon individual liberty. Philosophical dissidents, they sought truth and freedom in independent reason and independent conduct. Distinctions between old and young, male and female, rich and poor, citizen and alien were but accidental and superficial, irrelevant to the true principles of natural law. Every person might gain rational freedom from the passion and prejudice of luxury, at least from the omnivorous desire for things. Diogenes said that the true slaves of the world were everywhere to be seen walking free, men in rich robes enslaved by fleeting desires; things were their masters; things alone were self-sufficient. In the world they observed about them, Antisthenes, Crates, Zeno, Diogenes Laërtius, Chrysippus, and Panaetius saw the great majority of men enfeebled by luxury, a multitude that, lacking moral discipline, could not conceivably achieve virtue and rationality. Hence they regarded luxury as even more pervasive than did Plato and Aristotle. And while they rejected the philosophical validity of hierarchy, they accepted it as being as ubiquitous as ignorance. Putting the case more forcefully, Diogenes held that slavery was a tolerable convention so long as neither master nor slave was depraved by the relationship. He and the others taught individual, not social, reformation; toward society they taught indifference. They provided the perspective for uncovering luxury in *every* man, even the most exalted legislator; for the Roman historians' search for national decadence; for the joining of Hebrew and Christian social teachings; and for the intellectual theme we have come to call primitivism.[10]

From the middle Stoa of Panaetius through the late Stoa of Seneca, Greek philosophy was adapted to the practical ends of Roman statesmen and soldiers; so modified, it was the first postulate of countless Roman attacks upon luxury. Seneca himself, while elaborating the doctrine that the soul cannot be diminished by external circumstance, certainly seeks a practical civic virtue different from Zeno's social disdain. Luxury he terms the abandonment of nature, a perversion of both personality and politics that age by age has been growing stronger in Rome. Upon the nation it is like acid, dissolving the natural bonds that form men into a community and turning them from mutual fellowship to mutual plunder. In his own time he sees men slashing and bruising each other not over essentials but over luxuries. Intellect has been made slave of vice.[11] In the pseudo-Senecan pastiche *Octavia*, the Senecan indictment of the present is given mythic elaboration as the writer joins history, politics, and philosophy in his description of the birth of luxury. The character Seneca has described the Golden Age, the intermediage ages, and has now come to his own time.

> But another breed less gentle then appeared. A third race arose, cunning in new arts, yet holy. Soon came a restless race which dared pursue the wild beasts in the chase, to draw out fishes in nets or by the light rod from their hiding places in the waters, to catch birds, or with wicker stockades to fence in the fat cattle, to master fierce bulls by subjecting them to the yoke, to dig the earth, until then immune, with the wounding plough, earth who hid her fruits deep in her sacred womb. But this degenerate age dug into its mother's bowels; it dragged forth heavy iron and gold, and soon armed its savage hands. Boundaries marked out divided kingdoms, and new cities were built. Men defended their root-trees with their own weapons, or, threatening plunder, invaded the dwellings of other men. Astraea the Virgin, great glory of the stars, neglected, fled from the earth and the savage ways of men and hands polluted by gory slaughter. Desire for war grew and hunger for gold. Throughout the whole world the greatest evil arose, luxury, an

alluring plague, to which the long lapse of time and grievous error gave strength and power. All these many vices, heaped up through long ages, now overflow on us. We are crushed beneath the heavy burden of an age in which crime rules, mad impiety rages, violent lust dominates in shameful love, and triumphant luxury has long since seized the huge wealth of the world with greedy hands, only to lose it. But lo! with thundering step and savage countenance Nero comes. I shudder in my mind at what he may bring.

[Trans. Lovejoy and Boas]

Like Seneca and most Roman moralists, Cicero assumed that the origin and nature of luxury had been established beyond dispute. It was understood, yet for generations it had been allowed to spread unabated. What was wanted was not more analysis but more rhetoric, of the kind that compels effective law and public administration. Cicero is remarkable for the sheer volume of his calls for suppression of luxury and for his dexterity in applying diverse arguments to contemporary conditions in Rome. He is as willing as Seneca to censure the luxury of the mighty, at least among his political adversaries. And his debt to the Stoics is everywhere visible in his demands for thrift, self-denial, sobriety, and simplicity. He writes, for instance, in *Pro Roscio Amerino:* "The city creates luxury, from which avarice inevitably springs, while from avarice audacity breaks forth, the source of all crimes and misdeeds. On the other hand, this country life . . . teaches thrift, carefulness, and justice" (27, trans. John Henry Freese). But his sense of simplicity is less that of Diogenes of Sinope than Trimalchio of the *Satyricon.* In *De officiis* he attempts to define the qualities of the good life and feels the need to distinguish the various occupations available to the man seeking it (1.150–51).[12] He immediately dismisses money-lending and the collection of harbor taxes, then all labor for wages, since the wage is a warrant of slavery. All crafts and most trades are too mean. (He specifies fishmongers, butchers, cooks, poulterers, fishermen, dancers, and music-hall performers, but does not mention miners or servants; these are too mean even to dismiss.) He calls teaching, medicine, and architecture reputable occupations, for they call for some intellect and "are respectable for those whose status they befit." Domestic trade is mean, foreign is reputable. "But of all things from which one may acquire [wealth], none is better than agriculture, none more fruitful, none sweeter, none more fitting for a free man."[13]

What this passage suggests is that Cicero's denunciation of urban luxury and praise of rural austerity are in large part rhetorical conventions. *De officiis* belongs to a tradition running from Xenophon's *Oikonomikos* in the fourth century B.C.—and including Cato's *De agri cultura,* Varro's *Rerum rusticarum,* Columella's *De re rustica*—to Charlemagne's ninth-century *De villis* capitulary. No more than Cicero does any of these champions of agriculture concern himself with the specific tasks or techniques of farming. Like many other scourges of urban luxury—Seneca, Sallust, Apuleius, Atticus—they are very wealthy men, of the class Defoe in his *Tour* would have called Great: not farmers, but masters or managers or gentlemen farmers. For them agriculture means the ownership of land—the best possible occupation since it entails no occupation at all. For them and their followers in eighteenth-century England—like Pope, Swift, Bolingbroke, Fielding, and Smollett's Matthew Bramble—occupational categories are not (in the modern sense) economic, but moral. The rustic, virtuous simplicity Cicero commends is not a life of frugal fare and rigorous toil. It is a life of comfortable leisure, free from labor. It is the mean who must labor and labor meanly.[14]

Cicero represents one of the Roman contributions to the history of luxury, the impulse to purge the disorder—by draconian legislation if necessary—from every phase of Roman life, a practical approach that preoccupied most European nations until the middle of the eighteenth century. The wit and invective of the literary attacks by Horace and Juvenal represent another.[15] In the most important, historians of the late Republic treated luxury not as object but as subject, discovering in it an essential, causative factor in the narrative of national calamity they were obliged to impart. They were telling again the Deuteronomic story of national disaster without resort to divine intervention and recasting the plot of *Octavia* with specific dates, events, and persons; and they were searching in accounts of the confusion of the second century B.C. for the origins of first-century corruption. The result was an account that has fascinated readers to the present day and that indelibly linked luxury to the demise of republican greatness. Of all the moralists Sallust was the most systematic and highly reputed. To the younger Seneca, Martial, and Tacitus, Sallust was the foremost of the Roman historians, a classic and a model. Jerome and Augustine revered him as much as they did Cicero and Vergil. Erasmus recommended his work over that of Livy and Tacitus, Milton called him a sublime moralist, Johnson praised him as "the great master of nature," Arthur Murphy and others provided fresh eighteenth-century translations. In the wealthier parishes of London, historically minded clergymen made his name a commonplace.[16]

Roman history as Sallust viewed it took on an immediately visible pattern, and as identifiable as the pattern of the whole was the line of degeneration into *luxus* and *luxuria.* Described in the prologues to *Bellum Catilinae* and *Bellum Jugurthinum,* Sallust's thesis can be briefly stated. Rome prospered when it possessed *virtus* and sought *gloria.* This, the ancient way, kept the Republic secure as well as virtuous, but was undermined about the time of the destruction of Carthage.[17] The event marked the advent of *luxus,* which brought with it ambition, pride, avarice, and luxury, and these in turn overwhelmed justice, honesty, industry, and sobriety. In the *Catilinae* itself he outlines the major events. Rome was founded when a disparate and contentious mob was transformed into a group of citizens by the action of *concordia.* Kings ruled the city until they fell victim to the lust of domination. With their expulsion and the establishment of the Republic, Rome enjoyed a long era of *virtus* and *concordia maxima,* an era that ended with the sacking of Carthage. Avarice was then preeminent until the furthest stage of corruption, that of *luxuria,* was reached in the age of Sulla. Luxury was brought to Rome from Asia by Sulla's returning army, and in a short time it consumed the city, leaving little of the old values and bringing the Republic, in Sallust's own day, to the edge of moral, social, and political ruin. In the interim, Rome was filled with every species of vicious luxury, a city fit only for a Catiline. In the *Jugurthinum* he elaborates upon certain of these elements, particularly the role of party politics. Both parties, the *nobiles* and the *populus,* craved luxury, but the appetites of the aristocrats were insatiable and their superior resources gave them the instruments of oppression: the luxury of the few enforcing the poverty of the many and private opulence standing alongside public indigence.[18]

From the time of Sallust through the life of Macrobius in the fifth century after Christ, historians of Rome were to give luxury a causative role in the tale of republican decline. Although they do not agree on its dating, the historians are virtually unanimous that a moral crisis of profound significance occurred during the second century B.C.[19] For Sallust, *luxuria* appears comparatively late, but for most writers its appearance was the beginning of the process of devolution. In the annalistic tradition represented by Livy, luxury enters the bloodstream of Rome with the return of a victorious army from Asia in 187 B.C., as the material wealth and luxurious debauchery it brings with it form *luxuriae peregrinae origo* and *semina futurae luxuriae.* As Shakespeare's Romans see Antony corrupted by Egypt and eighteenth-century moralists were to see the decadence of France as the wellspring of luxury, so the Roman historians looked to the rankness of the East as the source of national ills. Livy marks the spread of luxury in the city itself with a long oration by Cato against the extravagance of women, many of whom were demanding the repeal of several sumptuary laws. To capitulate to the demands, Cato declaims, would be to allow the passions to rule over reason, to abandon masculinity, and to relinquish proper subordination in society—themes to be reiterated for the next eighteen centuries. For Plutarch too, Cato is a model of the upright Roman legislator, as Lycurgus is of the Spartan. Both had used eloquence and legal sanctions to combat a national disease; Lycurgus was successful; Cato, given the virulence within Rome, could not be.

Tacitus uses senatorial debates in the *Annals* to disclose how corruption reached the highest precincts of the Republic. He describes with contempt how the *nobiles* maneuver to write laws that will not apply to themselves and reports the argument of their spokesman, the infamous Gallus Asinius:

> In household establishments, and plate, and in whatever was provided for use, there was neither excess nor parsimony except in relation to the fortune of the possessor. A distinction had been made in the assessments of Senators and knights, not because they differed naturally, but that the superiority of the one class in places in the theatre, in rank and in honour, might be also maintained in everything else which insured mental repose and bodily recreation, unless indeed men in the highest position were to undergo more anxieties and more dangers, and to be at the same time deprived of all solace under those anxieties and dangers.
>
> [2, trans. Alfred John Church and William Jackson Brodribb]

This argument, turning upside down Socrates' reasoning in the *Republic,* so enrages one senator, Lucius Piso, that he will endure no more. The city is so replete with luxury, Piso declares, that it is no longer fit for the habitation of honest men (precisely the charge to be brought later against Bath and London). Luxury is daily corrupting the courts, bribing the judges, and hiring false witnesses. For him the only honorable option is to fly to a distant retreat.[20] When Tacitus summarizes the course of luxury from Tiberius through Vespasian, he introduces a note of generosity unusual among Roman moralists and anticipates Hume's comments in 1752 upon the progress of English commerce and the "new men" of the middle order. The passion for luxury was not exhausted, Tacitus notes, until large numbers of great families were themselves exhausted. "The new men who were often admitted into the Senate from the towns, colonies and even the provinces, introduced their household thrift, and though many of them by good luck or energy attained an old age of wealth, still their former tastes remained." Also anticipating Hume is his vague optimism (as rare among writers of the late Republic as among those of the earlier eighteenth century) and his unwillingness to concede all to the ancient position: "possibly there is in all things a kind of cycle, and there may be moral revolutions just as there are changes of seasons. Nor was everything better in the past, but our own age too has produced many specimens of excellence and culture for posterity to imitate."[21]

CHRISTIANITY: SYNTHESIS AND ACCOMMODATION

One of the first lessons Augustine seeks to teach in the *City of God* is that prosperity begets luxury and then avarice, and to that end he cites Sallust (at great length), Seneca, Cicero, Aristotle, and Plato. In the writings of the church fathers from the second century onward, the ravages of luxury recounted by the Roman historians are stated as indisputable fact and often cited seriatim. The Stoics held that all men possessed the inner resources to lift themselves from the mire of worldly things; yet in calling attention to the discrepancy between the capacity of the whole and the achievement of the very few, they raised more questions than they tried to answer. For Christians the answers were present throughout the Gospels, as when Jesus asserts that freedom lies in bondage to the Lord (John 8:31–35). The practical clarity of this position makes it more than a restatement of the Stoic paradox. All men are by nature enslaved, yet all men have the choice of master—God or mammon. Bondage is inescapable, but it may be the ennobling kind that brings redemption or the luxurious kind that brings corruption. Like Moses, Jesus places the legislator beyond individual consciousness; for him the Law is fixed and immutable and antedates human creation. Whereas the Stoics generally see the natural man as virtuous and free of social contamination, Jesus sees him as a slave to luxury, a sinner. For Hebrews and Christians alike, that is, the alternative to luxury is not Stoic primitivism, but obedience. As Paul wrote, the sinner seeks freedom from righteousness, while the saint seeks bondage to righteousness (Rom. 6:15–23). Or as a seventeenth-century Christian has Abdiel express it,

Unjustly thou deprav'st it with the name
Of *Servitude* to serve whom God ordains,
Or Nature; God and Nature bid the same,
When he who rules is worthiest, and excells
Them whom he governs. This is servitude,
To serve th' unwise, or him who hath rebell'd
Against his worthier, as thine now serve thee,
Thy self not free, but to thy self enthrall'd.

[*Paradise Lost*, 6.174–81]

A distinction there is, but it lies elsewhere. In the books of the Old

Testament and the Apocrypha—especially Samuel, Kings, Proverbs, Job, Ecclesiastes, Ecclesiasticus, and the Wisdom of Solomon—the motive for the renunciation of luxury is adherence to God's will, not denial of self. In the New Testament, however, this distinction is not maintained. When Jesus calls the disciples, "whosoever will come after me, let him deny himself, and take up his cross, and follow me" (Mark 8:34), he is yoking the negative message of self-abnegation to the positive one of obedience. The Evangelists often repeat the double injunction (e.g., Matt. 10:38, John 12:25) and on occasion advocate the abandonment of all material possessions (Matt. 19:21, Mark 10:28, Luke 9:57–62) and perpetual chastity (Matt. 19:12). To the Deuteronomic writers, earthly prosperity flows upon the Israelites as a direct consequence of their righteousness. To the Evangelists earthly reward is needless and even suspect.[22] The former treat luxury as a threat to the destiny of the Israelite nation as a whole, using it as a theory of history; the latter regard it as the curse of individual souls—a theory of ethics. Perfect virtue and freedom come only in absolute conformity to the will of the Lord. Neither king nor serf can slip God's shackles. What the Christian emphasis and synthesis does effectively, Lecky has observed, is to raise the moral stature of servitude. For the Greeks and Romans, servility was synonomous with vice; for Christians, fidelity, humility, obedience, and resignation are among the cardinal virtues.[23]

About necessity, therefore, early Christians were as stringent as Diogenes, about hierarchy as respectful as Aristotle. And to recognize that Christianity absorbed the classical attack upon luxury is, in effect, to understand why the concept seemed so vital for so long to European moralists. The Christian virtues were essential in service to God and valuable in service to temporal authority. The early Christians demanded revolution in spiritual aspiration, not in social hierarchy. Because all men were brothers in Christ, secular status was of no moment. In God's plan one man's temporal condition was no better—or worse—than another's, and a herdsman could be as devout a servant of the Lord as a king. Christian faith was one thing, material dependence another; no tension need exist between the two realms so long as the dependent believer served his master "as unto Christ."[24]

Given the teachings of the New Testament, then, luxury was *ex hypothesi* condemned by the leaders of the early church; given their preoccupation with individual morality, it was often associated with physical self-indulgence. Yet in noting this preoccupation, one must also recall that *luxuria* was never simply a minor taint but was the seed of all vices of the will and the flesh. Tertullian delivered a scathing denunciation of the luxury of his age in the *Apology,* and in *De cultu feminarum* analyzed "this vice of women," the source of corruption and effeminacy. Clement of Alexandria in the *Paedagogus* and Origen in the *Exhortation to Martyrdom* cite and use Stoic ideas in arguing that the denial of all forms of luxury is a needful preliminary step in the purification of the soul, an element of spiritual psychology much elaborated in the third century. In the *De officiis ministrorum*, Ambrose asserts with Epictetus that a luxurious man is not really a man, but a slave to vice and anxiety. And it was to become a central teaching of the Fathers of the Desert and the founders of monasticism in the fourth century. All the major figures argue that virtue is confined to no station. Clement and Augustine indeed maintain that the rich are more liable to luxury, for their wealth allows them to exercise their inherent vanity and sensuality. Since all of the secular realm is subject to the injunctions of the Law, the poverty and distress of the lowly may be viewed as valuable discipline of the spirit.[25]

In the *City of God* appear what came to be regarded as the definitive patristic condemnations of luxury, accepted without apparent reservation by Albert, Aquinas, and Bonaventure in the thirteenth century. Augustine was of two minds about luxury, and Christian Europe through the Renaissance generally preserved the different but related views he proposed. On the one hand, he did more than any other early Christian writer to keep alive and vivid the classical Platonic and Stoic condemnations.[26] In turn, Christian theologians, political theorists, and legislators would cite him as the source of their belief that the appearance of luxury signaled the onset of the death fever of civilization. The *City of God* is his treatise against the vice, inasmuch as it rules the enemy, the earthly city. While the heavenly city has put off the old man and put on the new, the earthly city continues its wicked and licentious course. The implication is that Christians must learn well "the calamities which befell Rome and its subject provinces" through luxury and impiety. In the opening five books he rehearses the decline of Rome and other ancient kingdoms. Book 1.30, entitled ''That those who complain of Christianity really desire to live without restraint in shameful luxury,'' is in essence a paraphrase of Sallust, arguing that contemporary pagans threatened the Christian world as sottish libertines did Neronian Rome.

> First concord was weakened, and destroyed by fierce and bloody seditions; then followed, by a concatenation of baleful causes, civil wars, which brought in their train such massacres, such bloodshed, such lawless and cruel proscription and plunder, that those Romans who, in the days of their virtue, had expected injury only at the hands of their enemies, now that their virtue was lost suffered greater cruelties at the hand of their fellow-citizens. [Trans. Marcus Dods]

A "nation corrupted by avarice and luxury" is a nation mired in original sin, where tyranny and injustice are commonplace (1.30). Yet even where luxury reigns, the Christian can free himself; misery and submission expiate as well as manifest sin. Even where unjust, hierarchy can act as a check upon the crooked wills of the dissolute. No man may complain of utter injustice, he remarks, for no man is utterly innocent (19.15).

On the other hand, Augustine was absorbed with the proselytizing mission of the young church and came to stress luxury as the carnal lust of individual men—a lust that could be fought successfully only through the divine grace dispensed by the church. In consonance with earlier patristic emphasis upon the ideals of virginity and asceticism, he subsumes the meanings of *luxus* under those of *luxuria* and uses the latter to mean individual self-indulgence in general and lechery in particular. In the *Confessions,* the *Homilies,* and the later parts of the *City of God,* he concentrates not on the political effects of luxury but on the psychological. Especially in books 9 through 14 of the *City of God,* he recasts the Stoic psychology of luxury in Christian form. In the life of Jesus, he declares, Christians have found the perfect model of renunciation. A man must be judged by what he loves. The upright man loves God, but the luxurious man pledges all his love, his desire, and his energy to the world. Luxurious man is spurred by vain ambition and by concupiscence of the eyes and the flesh. He is fallen man, a worldly man; his punishment for disobedience to God is disobedience to himself. Since he has willed *not* to do what he could do, he now wills to do what he cannot. He has fallen, indeed, to the level of the beasts.[27]

The age of Augustine in all likelihood marks the time when the condemnation of luxury became practically universal in Western Europe. With a partial shift in emphasis to the personal, the classical attack had been embraced by the church and its secular instruments. Luxury was no longer a sin of abhorrent kind, as it had been for the Hebrews, but was remade into one of abhorrent degree, loathsome yet still pardonable through the offices of the church. Something vivid and concrete, it was no longer the concern, primarily, of the educated, but was brought into the daily lives of ordinary Christians. Although there were several others, the main popular vehicles were the soul drama and the deadly sins, depicted together or independently.[28] The pattern of the soul drama, as described by Samuel Chew, is relatively consistent. Man has forfeited immortality through Sin and must pass into the World of Time, ruled by Fortune. Here he will be faced with the Two Paths. If he chooses aright the strait and narrow, he will be beset by the Deadly Sins but will also gain the assistance of the Cardinal Virtues. At the end of his journey-struggle he will confront Death; yet with the courage of purity in his heart he will realize he is about to enter the City of God. According to Morton Bloomfield, the allegory arose from the homilies, late apocrypha, Latin poetry, and Prudentius; it passed over into the visual arts, and about the time of Aquinas into vernacular literature, dramatic and nondramatic. It is to be found, for instance, in most of the morality plays, Huon de Mari's *Le tournoiment de l'Antichrist,* Chaucer, Langland, Alanus's *Anticlaudianus,* and the *Cursor mundi.* Later versions appear in Spenser, Cervantes, Bunyan, and Goethe. A secularized variant is present in eighteenth-century fiction, certainly in the stories of Bramble, Jery, Humphry, and Lismahago in *Humphry Clinker,* in varying degrees in *Moll Flanders, Pamela, Clarissa, Joseph Andrews, Tom Jones, Amelia, Rasselas,* and the Gothics.

The soul drama motif suggests that early Christianity accepted the Hebrew view of Eve's Fall as a single process, then analyzed that unity into the infernal trinity and again into the seven (or more) deadly sins. From the Fall came, in Chaucer's rendering of 1 John 2:16, "the thre enemys of mankinde, that is to syn, the Flessche, the Feend, and the World," and thereafter the group usually composed of Luxuria, Superbia, Avarita, Gula, Ira, Accidia, and Invidia. That is, by the Middle Ages Christian writers had not only made luxury as familiar and repugnant as a folk devil, they had also rendered it virtually omnipresent. In its pilgrimage the soul must encounter luxury in three forms. In the beginning it is the cause of the primal Fall. Then it is the fundamental carnality that unites the world, the flesh, and the devil against God's Law. Augustine, Gregory the Great, and Aquinas all agree that luxury can be seen as: (1) the visible sign of the presence or activity of the devil, (2) the comprehensive sin of humanity and the worldly state, and (3) the devil's strongest type of temptation, which binds the flesh to the world and thereby to himself. And finally it is among the most formidable of the mortal sins. In iconographic terms the three forms of luxury came to be represented by three figures: Eve, Worldly Temptation (or Fleshly Pleasure), and, in her own garb, Dame Luxury. Furthermore, Dame Luxury threatens the pilgrim soul not once but at least twice, for it is vulnerable to her charm at two stages of life, in youth, when the delights of the flesh are most insistent; and later in maturity, when worldly power is most attractive. This presumed vulnerability of youth is of course very influential in the careers of most of the young men in English literature, but has particular application to such eighteenth-century figures as Lovelace, Joseph Andrews, Tom Jones, Rory Random, Pery Pickle, Rasselas, Humphry Clinker, and Jery Melford.

In the vast amount of literary and visual material dealing with the soul drama and the deadly sins, spanning 1,500 years, there is naturally little uniformity in many things. The ages of man depicted in the drama vary from three to twelve. The name, number, and position of the sins often change from writer to writer, illustrator to illustrator, century to century. About luxury, nevertheless, there is an arresting degree of agreement. In the early lists of cardinal sins influenced by John Cassian, luxury is usually placed first, regarded as primary in the sense of generative. Later ones, probably derived from Gregory the Great, place it last and refer to it as the ultimate sin, the culmination of all others. The lists also often switch the places of luxury and pride. When luxury is put first, pride is last and vice versa, suggesting a dread circularity of luxury evolving into pride and pride manifesting itself in luxury. And while it is usually identified with physical lust, it is often used by learned writers to stand for lust in figurative senses. Thus they often associate *luxuria* with lust for revenge, lust for worldly goods belonging to others, and lust to retain material possessions. In such instances the sin of luxury encompasses wrath, envy, avarice, and pride, as well as lechery. A popular parallel is revealed in didactic retellings of the Fall, with Eve guilty of pride, Adam of lechery, wrath, envy, and avarice all together.

There is moreover more consistency in the personification of luxury than with any other chief sin. With the major exception of the *Faerie Queene,* almost all personifications of luxury are feminine. Prudentius in the *Psychomachia* depicts Luxuria as a beautiful woman astride a splendid chariot. She has perfumed hair, graceful and languishing airs; her car is made of gold, silver, and precious stones. In her train come Amor, Jocus, and Petulantia. Unlike the other vices, she enters battle unarmed, violets and rose petals her only defense; and against her alone the virtues seem confused. At last Sobrietas steps in front of the chariot with the sign of the cross, the horses rear, the car upsets, and Luxuria falls groveling in the mire, to be killed by Sobrietas with a single blow.[29] Thereafter the portrayal of Luxuria as a lustful woman is continued in Jean de Meun, Langland, Dante, and Chaucer. In *Doctor Faustus*, Marlowe makes luxury the only female sin. The personification became a favorite device of Romanesque sculptors in the south of France and was carried over to the great Gothic cathedrals of France, Germany, and England, and later, in a figure by Cellini, into the ducal palace of Venice. In early illustrations of the *Roman de la rose,* as in the windows of Notre Dame, Chartres, and Amiens, she appears carrying the comb and mirror of cupidity and self-love; in some places she also holds a scepter to mark her omnipotence and sexual domination over men. Elsewhere she is less attractive. In the churches of Toulouse, Moissac, and Braisne, she is a nude figure being attacked at breasts and genitals by snakes or toads. In some illustrations she is a semidraped figure exuding sulfur to kindle the flames of delight. As though the point required underscoring, several medieval and early Renaissance depictions carry beneath the name a subtitle, "The Power of Woman." Some combination of these types was to remain in the visual arts through the Renaissance.[30]

Medieval theological speculation is brought to a climax with Aquinas. Taking Augustine's teaching as his ground, he provides an analysis of luxury that is narrow but deep, the most thorough examination of luxury as sin before the eighteenth century. Like the Roman jurists, Aquinas is a consolidator, and in retrospect the decisive point is that he does unify, rather than diminish, neglect, or deny. He was not in Augustine's position, impelled to accommodate the political structure of the Roman world. For now the church was itself powerful, and its teaching was always potentially subversive of the classical suppositions about necessity and hierarchy. Did it not preach the equality of all men under God, and the existence of a world of spirit in which all men were free? Slavery was gradually disappearing in western Europe, moreover, and some of the most brutal forms of subjugation were being ameliorated. The repeated eruption of egalitarian—and heretical—sects demonstrated that some Christians were accepting as literal the fraternal teaching of the church. Why then did not the egalitarian ideal of Christianity overmaster its previous practical compromises? David Brion Davis's study of slavery suggests some answers. The first is the potent legacy of two millennia that associated luxury with original sin and divinely conceived necessity and hierarchy. Second, to challenge the traditional conception of luxury would be to question fundamental Christian postulates about God's purpose and man's nature. For if luxury was to be accepted or redefined, then why had God enjoined it in Scripture and every nation enjoined it in law? If the attack upon luxury did not possess a divine function and instead violated a natural law of equality or a divine law of brotherhood, then whence the authority of state, legislator, landowner, and social arbiter? The tensions within Christianity are many and complex. It is enough here to note that for several centuries after Aquinas they were held in conservative equilibrium.[31]

Far from denying them, Aquinas emphatically reasserts the traditional principles of necessity and hierarchy. He argues that original sin is to be understood as luxury, the penchant for needless, temporal things. Once tainted, Adam and Eve and all subsequent parents transmit the sin to their children as a genetic predisposition for sensuality. (Aquinas thus retains Augustine's union of metaphysical and physical luxury while seeming to distinguish them; only with Adam and Eve is the distinction philosophically or historically meaningful.) Luxury is the enemy of chastity, for in contrast to the chaste man, the luxurious man is unable to contain his passion for self-aggrandizement, especially his sexual desires. He is precisely dissolute, for luxury leads to a general dissolution of personality. Having sinned against reason, he eventually loses his reason and intelligence, and reality is lost, hidden by blinding desire. And as the luxurious man has lost reason, so too he begins to lose will. He becomes rash, headstrong, and quarrelsome. Since he is closed to religious joy and the pursuits of the spirit, only the gross and the foolish have power to move him. In its most advanced form, luxury entails sin not only against reason, but also against nature. This stage, which might be termed the Neronian, culminates in bestiality, unnatural acts, and setting oneself in opposition to God who has ordained the nature of things.[32]

Perceiving the true nature of things, the godly man transcends worldly needs in order to find fulfillment in God, to recognize his place in the harmony of divine creation. And for Aquinas the plenitude of creation represents a monumental series of progressive hierarchies rising to several classes of angels in heaven. Before the Fall man was unfettered, but now he is obliged to preserve his proper place and function. The rationality of creation is manifest in plenitude and gradation, human rationality in recognizing an eternally fixed order of being. Luxury would undermine that order and disrupt the rational processes of nature (1.2.71–82, 96). To higher authority the Christian relinquishes both his will and his body. Regarding luxury, then, Aquinas is more Augustinian than Augustine and brings the patristic and scholastic traditions into essential accord. It was to be an important union, augmenting the church's concern for matters of individual morality and sexuality, while reaffirming her involvement in the governance of public affairs. It is reflected in the works of Boethius, Berchorius, Thomas à Kempis, Guido Faba, and Robert Holcot, and not altered in any significant way by either Luther or Calvin.

The major writers of the English Renaissance for the most part retain the medieval emphasis upon lust in their use of the term. Spenser writes of "lustfull luxurie and thriftless wast," Marlowe of "unchaste luxury." Webster has Ferdinand address the Duchess of Malfi: "Marry? they are most luxurious / Will wed twice."[33] A principal villain of Tourneur's *Revenger's Tragedy* is the young lecher—whose "heat is such were there as many concubines as ladies he would not be contained"—named Lussurioso. Almost all of Shakespeare's sixty or so uses of the term are in lascivious contexts, as in "he most burnt in heart-wish'd luxury," and "She knows the heat of a luxurious bed." In *Henry V* Pistol calls a French soldier a "damned and luxurious mountain goat"; in *Hamlet* the ghost terms Gertrude's bed a "couch for luxury and damned incest."[34] Probably the most memorable of Shakespearean uses is Lear's cry of despair:

> Let copulation thrive; for Gloucester's bastard son
> Was kinder to his father than my daughters
> Got 'tween the lawful sheets.
> To't, luxury, pell-mell, for I lack soldiers.   [4.6][35]

In other seventeenth-century poets, however, luxury is connected less exclusively with lust and more with all the deadly sins together. Donne in the second Satyre writes of the lawyer "spying heires melting with luxurie, / Satan will not joy at their sinnes, as hee." Milton, returning to Old Testament and Roman sources, returns also to their associations. Using the story from the book of Samuel, he has luxury appear in the wake of Belial,

>   who fill'd
> With lust and violence the house of God.
> In Courts and Palaces he also Reigns
> And in luxurious Cities, where the noise
> Of riot ascends above thir loftiest Tow'rs,
> And injury and outrage.   [*PL,* 1.495–500]

Book 4 of *Paradise Regained* contains Christ's denunciation of the Romans, a once virtuous people, "just, frugal, and mild, and temperate." Now they are guilty of

>   lust and rapine; first ambitious grown
> Of triumph, that insulting vanity;
> Then cruel, by thir sports to blood inur'd
> Of fighting beasts, and men to beasts expos'd
> Luxurious by thir wealth, and greedier still,
> And from the daily Scene effeminate.   [4.137–42][36]

SOME THEORETICAL AMBIGUITIES

The narrowly physical aspect of the concept—the "foule lust of luxurie" of Chaucer, Spenser, and Shakespeare—was not one that eighteenth-century writers chose to emphasize. For reasons to be adduced in the next chapter, their sense of luxury was more Roman than scholastic. As for Smollett, at no point in his writings from 1756 have I been able to discover an exclusive identification of luxury with lechery. Bramble acknowledges without remorse that he has left bastard children scattered about England and Wales. And while Smollett did see Britain menaced by the forces of luxury, lechery was not numbered in their lists. However, the survival of medieval attitudes into the sixteenth, seventeenth, and even eighteenth centuries does indicate something of the protean—not to say colossal—quality of the vice and does explain the readiness with which ordinary Englishmen came to associate it with base and ignoble human conduct. The 1707 edition of *Glossographia Anglicana Nova* indeed gave "carnal Pleasure" as the basic definition of the word. More learned or abstract associations might escape them, but from ballad or sermon they knew what they knew.

This brief survey serves to indicate part of what Englishmen in the early eighteenth century "knew" about luxury. Since all of the nuclear ideas included in that conception had been present long before the birth of Christ, its continuing and growing place in European thought might be accounted for in different ways. From the point of view of stern moralists, the charge of luxury was the most incisive criticism that could be directed against Western civilization. But on a more popular level, the idea was a *crambe repetita* for writers of varying and conflicting interests. In either case luxury had become a fluid and complex concept in which moral, religious, economic, and political attitudes were mixed into a vague and sometimes contradictory amalgam. From at least Cato onward, writers had devoted much attention to elaboration, little to definition. Assuming that their readers knew what luxury meant, they could begin their discussions with what was essentially a conclusion. Such a beginning, in turn, logically precluded any neutral or value-free discussion. Thus conventional usage demanded that when the issue of luxury arose it was for rhetorical or polemical purposes—to be denounced as sin and as a matter of course.

These assumptions and conventions can be reduced to three interrelated suppositions about the nature of luxury. In the first place, the pursuit of luxury, however considered, was viewed as a fundamental and generic vice from which other, subordinate vices would ensue. In the Old Testament, where it is equated with disobedience to God, it is *the* cardinal sin of the Israelites. In Plato and Aristotle, the Cynics and the Stoics, it is the first and most important violation of nature and reason. For the Roman historians, it is the primary factor in the dissolution of the Republic. For the Christian theologians, it is prima facie evidence of both disobedience to God and love of a degraded world. For all of these systems, from the Hebrews through the Protestants, luxury represents the starting point of historical or philosophical speculation. In ethical systems it is an index of human sinfulness and moral or intellectual deficiency, calling forth the requirement for inner regeneration and self-surrender. In the social realm it is an index of chaos and irrationality in the workings of public affairs, calling forth the demand for order, discipline, authority, and hierarchy (and, implicitly, self-surrender and self-sacrifice). All of these theories, moreover, make luxury a generic vice in another sense, using some metaphor like contagion to describe the movement of its corruption from the one to the many. When it strikes a man, it has the fatal power to dissolve his character and to destroy his estate—that is, his social position and financial well-being. When it has struck a sufficient number of individuals, luxury will sap a nation's economic and military strength and subsequently bring down the nation itself.

Second, while the vicious nature of luxury was regarded as immutable, its manifestations were viewed as virtually infinite. One way to explain this assumption is to assert with Diogenes that the objects of man's illicit desires are numberless. Each change in station or fashion or aspiration brings a concomitant set of new wants. Indeed on the level of simple desire all men are equally rich, bound only by the capacity of their imaginations. Another explanation is that few writers distinguished nicely between cause and effect, between a disposition toward luxury and the manifest consequences of that disposition. Socrates hypothesizes a luxurious man accumulating wealth and material goods, then banding together with others of his kind in order to preserve and extend his possessions. When completed, the process would encompass social division, economic competition, political corruption, war, rapine, and conquest. And at each stage of this series, Socrates seems to see luxury—not simply its operation. For Sallust, the rich spoils taken by Sulla's army are luxurious, as are the diverse uses to which that booty is put. Gilt swords, ivory daggers, and purple robes are luxuries, but so equally are drunkenness, prostitution, and pederasty. To Suetonius practically everything Nero touched turned to luxury, from costly rings to fair-haired boys. Augustine and Aquinas speak of physical lust as luxury at least as often as they do the more general trait of self-indulgence. Yet another explanation is that many writers included, on occasion, items of their own dislike or disapproval in their castigation of luxury. Diogenes had no use for baths, Seneca for cold drinks, Cato for the laughter of slaves. Less obvious but possible examples might be the frivolous dress Socrates sought to banish, the intellectual pertness of women that offended Cicero, the speech and manners of the patricians that repelled Sallust and Tacitus. What is certain, amid these possibilities, is that each of the major critics of luxury believed that in his own time its manifestations were increasing at an accelerated rate.

Third, to explain the relative absence of information about many native American tribes, some cultural anthropologists have proposed that happy people leave no history. If the obverse is also true, that unhappy people readily chronicle their woes, then the concept of luxury reveals a history of deep and bitter division. Throughout Western history men have called upon tradition to account for the terrors and surprises of the unknown and the irrational. For Hebrews and Christians the Fall became a cogent symbol of the corruption of mankind, and the major Greek philosophers agreed that not all men and not all of nature were subject to the order of reason. Roman writers frequently referred to their world as an *urbs deis hominibusque communis*—a household common to gods, men, beasts, all living things—yet they too felt required to explain why this household was often in open rebellion against itself. At virtually every point in the history surveyed here some figure could be found to warn that his society was in danger of degenerating into barbarism or hardening into tyranny. When a people or its leaders felt themselves the victims of misfortune they regularly saw in luxury the enemy that caused it. Ancient writers describe three main types of crisis: divine anger, political disturbance, and natural catastrophe. Luxury was interpreted as the direct source of the first two, and to the extent that a writer like Herodotus or Augustine would see in a plague, drought, or military defeat the sign of God's wrath, then it would account for all forms of disaster. Luxury was thus an absolute, a natural reflex of mind that could explain the new, the dissonant, the disturbing. The very durability of the concept suggests that it was psychologically satisfying, consolidating while it was dividing.

Luxury readily accommodated, even encouraged, belief in a historical division of mankind into a virtuous "we" standing against a luxurious "they." In a psychological sense, it *proved* the existence of lower, corrupted, imperfect humanity, whether called Gentile, pagan, plebeian, heterodox, or damned. In this vague sense of abhorrence and negation, luxury is akin to insanity as described by Michel Foucault in *Madness and Civilization,* to heresy in Frederick Heer's *Intellectual History of Europe* and *God's First Love,* to savagery as treated by the authors of *The Wild Man Within,* to racial inferiority as studied by Winthrop D. Jordan, Roy Harvey Pearce, Gary B. Nash, and others. Each of these concepts has a distinct history, and there are probably as many differences among them as similarities. Yet all represent conditions of almost universal reprobation among all strata of society. All stand for persons, thoughts, and behavior that have been branded as unacceptable. Individually and collectively, all represent "the Other"—that which is beyond the pale.[37]

Like insanity, heresy, and savagery, luxury was probably an idea born of psychological necessity. The men who defined it did so in order to describe the unspeakable, to classify the abhorrent, to name the vile. One might say it was named specifically to be abhorred. It provided its users with a powerful measure of self-worth, for it identified all they *were not*. It thus became a mode of self-justification and, by negation, of self-definition. There were of course other ancient theories of entropy, such as that of the Book of Esdras: "So you too must consider that you are smaller in stature than those who were before you, and those who come after you will be smaller than you, for the creation is already growing old ... and past the strength of youth" (2 Esdras 5:54-56). But these comprehend a universal condition allowing no exceptions. Luxury, on the other hand, permitted Tobias Smollett, like thousands of moralists before him, to declare in effect, "A perfect man I am not, but assuredly I will not countenance luxury in any of its forms." Ordinary Europeans even might not be able to say precisely what made them good or normal or frugal or orthodox citizens, yet they could at least testify that they were not luxurious.

Foucault's *Madness* supplies an apt analogue, with one significant difference. Laws could not easily be drawn to prevent or punish insanity, but certainly were so drawn regarding luxury. The mere existence of such legislation indeed ensured that a great proportion of Europeans would consciously consider, if not fear it. It evolved into a concept difficult to ignore with impunity. In practical political terms perhaps the closer parallel would be heresy. Although there is no military campaign against luxury to compare to the wars of the Reformation, it is certain that men and women were ostracized, fined, beaten, imprisoned, and executed for instances of alleged luxury. Such punishments do not equal any single act of war, yet over centuries they were as deadly.

The concept of luxury can be seen as much as a cluster of symbols as it can as a cluster of ideas, sustaining one type of code while rejecting another. Augustine could admit the strength and attraction of the earthly city, yet be certain of its doom. God punishes the luxurious. The ruling groups of societies as distant as those of Israel in the eighth century B.C. and England in the eighteenth century A.D. alike tried to exercise their authority by convincing the majority that only they possessed the possible and legitimate means of satisfying human needs; all other methods were luxurious, anathema.

SUMPTUARY LAWS AND THE POLITICAL CONVERGENCE

In retrospect, the issue of luxury seems to have been almost perpetually surrounded by controversy. Part of that history of dispute can be traced, as we have seen, to logical or theoretical ambiguity. Yet perhaps a larger part derived from *practical* ambiguity. All the philosophical systems or theories noted thus far have taken as self-evident man's pursuit of pleasure and satisfaction; the most rigid Stoic admitted that, in the world he saw about him, every man was as luxurious as he was able to be. The condemnation of luxury was therefore an admonition that touched everyone. To recall Voltaire, although all men condemned luxury, all men practiced it. How could this contradiction be resolved in the everyday world of men?[38]

The practical answer to the inconsistency of precept and practice was government intervention. Because luxury had always been regarded as a primary threat to the state, the state was obliged to defend itself through sumptuary laws and similar measures. The institutes of Lycurgus, Solon, and Demosthenes are far from being the earliest, and such legislation absorbed the attention of the English Parliament as much as it did the Roman Senate. Two consequences flow from government regulation of luxury. It brought the concept from the empyrean of philosophy, theology, and abstract ideas down to the forum of institutions, politics, and power. In that forum, so ruled by compromise, there evolved a tacit double standard regarding what actually was luxury. Legislators in general drew a sharp distinction between the immoral and illegal lust for false wealth and station that corrupted men and nations, on the one hand, and the natural and admirable expression of position and self-interest that produced genuine value, on the other. In theory all men were subject to the prohibitions of luxury; in reality persons of authority were free to do as they pleased. To the philosophers as well as to the powerful, the contradiction was illusory. For man in his primal state was vicious, a slave to his passions, and thus of necessity subject to the laws of state and church. As Aristotle had put it, "No man can practice virtue who is living the life of a mechanic or laborer." The cultivated man, refined by wealth and education, could be assumed to be virtuous, hence subject to no authority other than his God or his conscience. While Epictetus, himself once a slave, argued that women and the young needed protection against luxury, the Senate actually drafted laws protecting the state against women and young people. Whereas Seneca wrote eloquently of the corruptions of wealth, many rich senators united to combat the luxury of the poor. The rabble was the greatest threat to the empire, these senators held, for, lacking everything, it coveted everything; not freedom or possessions but the lack of them signaled luxury. Had Seneca written the sumptuary laws, all men might have been in jeopardy; but, as Tacitus shows, the laws were actually made by the kind of men Seneca most distrusted. Seneca's own life was hardly the perfect expression of Stoic virtue. First tutor then advisor to Nero, he accumulated a vast fortune through political "gifts" and usury. A longtime opponent, Publius Suilius, attacked him publicly as a "hypocrite, an adulterer, and a wanton, a man who denounces courtiers and never leaves the palace; who denounces luxury, and displays 500 dining tables of cedar and ivory; who denounces wealth, and sucks the provinces dry by usury." Two monarchs renowned in their own times for extraordinary enforcement of laws against luxury were Nero and Louis XIV; they were vigorously opposed to the luxury *of others*. And Sallust, the arch-foe of extravagance, was known to his contemporaries as a man who had become immensely wealthy in politics and had then built himself a living monument, the *horti Sallustiani,* which would be coveted by Nero, Vespasian, Nerva, and Aurelian. Like many great contradictions, those enveloping the control of luxury could be absorbed into a higher unity: wise and virtuous authority ruling the irrational forces of the world. The aversion to luxury inherited by the eighteenth century had been incorporated into not only one or two, but the whole range of Western institutions.

Seldom can the historian of a seemingly lost world of ideas point to thousands of palpable monuments to its once incontestable vitality. Yet the plethora of European laws drawn to combat luxury represents just that, standing to the concept of luxury as, say, the Linear B tablets do to Mycenaean Greece. They are available, what is more, in abundance for almost every age and region of Europe from archaic Greece to industrial England. Despite their virtual ubiquity, they have been little studied and are often referred to as minor, paternalistic regulations of dress and spending.[39] A mere glance at the history of sumptuary legislation, however, discloses that they are certainly much more than that. All the moralists surveyed thus far attacked luxury in order to preserve their measure of necessity and hierarchy. Granting the negative quality of such attacks and the negative thou-shalt-not quality of Western law, the major philosophers were perforce de facto lawgivers.[40]

Fundamental to every attack has been the statement of the Law, and over three thousand years there was little disagreement over the general features of that Law. Xenophon's *Oikonomikos* is a useful gloss on the way Greek statutes incorporated those features. The sort of work standing between the richness of Socratic dialogues and the bleakness of legal codes, it is amateur philosophy, a collation of platitudes that would be unexceptionable to its audience—gentlemen landowners like its author— the type of what I have called the legislator, for whom ethics, politics, economics, and farm management are indissoluably one. Xenophon holds as a fact of nature that the good life is the free life and that, to obtain the freedom to which he is entitled, the legislator must cultivate the practical art of governing his inferiors, those who labor in his behalf. Right to the good life is certainly his; yet to reap its fruits he must carefully train and manage his slaves, servants, children, and wives. The *Oikonomikos* bore for centuries the reputation of a charming and reliable conduct book, telling clear truth clearly. It was cited admiringly by Plato and Aristotle, translated by Cicero and others, and quoted often by eighteenth-century philosophers like Francis Hutchinson (and sometimes by men who were truly interested in the techniques of farming, like Jethro Tull and Arthur Young). Smollett gives Xenophon's view of natural law clear voice in *Humphry Clinker* through one of his most sympathetic characters, one who will himself become a gentleman farmer, when Lismahago says he hopes he shall "never see the common people lifted out of that sphere for which they were intended by nature and the course of things."

With Xenophon, Greek writers equated citizenship and its attendant rights with the ownership of land, and the Romans certainly elaborated the equation. Most people in antiquity lived off the land; for the few who were owners this meant no labor; for the many, incessant labor. As the philosophers deduced the sources of moral and material good from the land, the legislators framed laws that would ensure full enjoyment of that good. Since such mundane burdens as taxes drastically limited the enjoyment of landowners, the law allowed them to pass the burden on to their dependents. The possession of wealth and status carried with it the right to preserve wealth and status.

By the very arbitrariness of his injunction, Yahweh sought to create order out of Law. Seeking rationality, the Greeks and Romans reversed the process, attempting to create Law out of the social order. The model of civil polity became agrarian, paternal, and hierarchical. Politically the nation was associated with the hierarchy of the household, economically with that of the estate. At its apex were the all-powerful masters, those who possessed the land, *potestas, manus,* and *dominium,* who according to Aristotle were economically independent and hence truly free; all other persons were inferior and dependent. Masters were ordained for political rule, for only they were free to pursue other than basic, physical needs. Their birth granted independence, their education confirmed it. From independence flowed leisure, which led to responsibility for government, a central function of which was to ensure that the great majority of persons remained dependent and continued to perform the essential and involuntary labor that sustained the legislators' independence.

Founded upon slavery and other forms of involuntary servitude, the economy of the ancient world gave rise to a society of orders and status. P. A. Brunt has observed that in Rome this hierarchical structure was even more aggravated by continued warfare, with its concomitants of conscription, confiscation, and ever more harsh and demanding laws.[41]

Indeed several of the most comprehensive Greek and Roman sumptuary codes were enacted after the outbreak of war and retained when the fighting ceased—thus accumulating crisis upon crisis. They could be enacted quickly and retained permanently because they were directed against those traditionally regarded as dissolute, unpatriotic, and un-reliable—specifically those groups, that is, who were excluded from government. In the context of universal history, M. I. Finley calls compulsory labor the norm, not the exception. To understand a society founded upon legally defined status, Finley recommends the metaphor of a spectrum, but one that removes the polar extremes of total free-dom and total lack of freedom. Between the two extremes falls the range represented by ancient Greece and Rome, where status and rights were defined simultaneously.

> A person possesses or lacks rights, privileges, claims and duties in many respects: he may be free to retain the surplus of his labour after payment of dues, rents and taxes, but not free to choose the nature and place of his work or his domicile; he may be free to select his occupation but not his place of work; he may have certain civil rights but no political rights; he may have political rights but no property rights so long as he is . . . *in potestate;* he may or may not have the right (or obligation) of military service, at his own or public expense; and so on. The combination of these rights, or lack of them, determines a man's place in the spectrum, which is, of course, not to be understood as a mathematical continuum, but as a more metaphorical, discontinuous spectrum, with gaps here, heavier concentrations there.[42]

Although intended to clarify the societies of Greece and Rome, Finley's metaphor does much to bring clarity to all the European sumptuary laws accumulated over three thousand years. They may be national, as in England and France; municipal, as in the cities of Germany and Switzerland; written into published ordinances; discretionary, upon the judgment of monarch or ruling council; enforced by secular govern-ment or by the church or by both together.[43] Yet all are designed to effect the legislators' sense of necessity and hierarchy, to place all subjects within the spectrum. More concretely, all are designed to ob-tain by coercion a person's labor (or service or property) and proper conduct; and further, to establish by law some form of social and psychological discrimination among groups of people.

   To ancient legislators the model of a properly ordered society was what it was for Xenophon: a great estate, where it was assumed that only persons of the same goals and values were admitted and where status was patent and fixed by type of labor. Here tempters, strangers, interlopers, and foreigners could be easily excluded. Here value for all could be dictated from above, by the master. The worst kind of place by this standard would be one where tempters were many and diverse, where the population was heterogeneous and (in the sociologist's sense) unintegrated, and where goals, values, and masters were various. In short, a city. Keeping workers on the land was the first function of the laws; the second was controlling social behavior in places without the hierarchy of farm labor—the market towns and the cities. At the latter the obvious badges of farm labor would be missing or cunningly disguised, and subversive persons—artisans, mechanics, servants, women, and young people—might congregate in numbers. Hence the gravity of laws defining status and costume in Athens and Rome and later in Genoa, Venice, Paris—and London.

Jurists assumed that the lower orders were tempted with ease and with ease turned tempters themselves. With Aristotle they held that the lower forms of humankind corrupt the higher and must therefore be classified and separated. From this assumption followed the immense profusion of legal terms required to define status. To cite but a tiny fraction: there would be substantial differences in the quality of life among the *ptochos,* the *penēs,* and the *plousios* in Greece; the *sclavii, adscripticii, vasii, coliberti, coceti, servi,* and *coloni* in Rome; and the slaves, villeins, serfs, clients, agents, tenants, debt-bondsmen, and vassals in medieval Europe. In death there was segregation; a Roman law of the second century B.C. ordered the maintenance of separate common ditches for burial of the lowly. For the living multitude many outward signs of status were available: identification tablets, shorn heads, uniforms, brands, tattoos, and bonds (for foot, ankle, wrist, or neck). Although dress and outward marks were the most common devices for designating status, less visible means were as numerous and important, including the ability to enter apprenticeship and a guild, to travel or reside in a parish, to use weapons, to marry across status lines or to marry at all, to rear one's children, to enter into a contract, to appear before a magistrate, and so on.[44] To select an example from the Christian era, Gratian in the fourth century declared that any servant or slave charging his master with a crime (other than high treason) would be burned alive regardless of the validity of the accusation.[45]

Such legislation was viewed as a simple means to a very difficult end. Trying to persuade the lower orders to restrain their desires was as futile as trying logical argument upon imbeciles. A single law properly drawn, however, could impose discipline upon people who would otherwise have been ruled by impulse to fleeting gratification. It could assign a man to a specific kind of labor, regulate his general conduct, and visibly fix his status. To the legislator it conserved necessity and hierarchy and was humane as well as useful. It permitted his subjects to exercise their own peculiar form of virtue, the fulfillment of an assigned function. Subjects had no independent sensibility, philosophers and jurists concurred, for the whole of their beings was predicated upon the use the legislator had for them. Everything not mandatory, it could be assumed, was forbidden.

Subjects to the law could be regarded as things—the slave is merely the extreme example—who possessed no rights, no family, no name even unless granted one by the legislator.[46] In their elaborate codes the Romans were consolidating systematically the practice of many earlier societies when they defined the position of laborers. They merely made explicit what the Greeks and Hebrews took for granted: a dependent laborer is not free *not* to enter the work force, and once in it is not free to withdraw. When the empire was dissolved, its legal influence was maintained through the concrete institutions of servitude—in England, for example, through the continuance of large-scale slavery until the thirteenth century. It was reasserted in written form once French jurists recovered the Justinian Code and became the basis for Bracton's work, the poor laws, for villenage, and for feudal law generally.[47] Sumptuary legislation drawn specifically to meet English conditions dates from the fourteenth century, and significant extensions occurred during each succeeding century. Major codification of existing laws came in 1463, further legislation was passed in 1533, and the Act of Precedence —which sealed the social order in law as if in amber—followed in 1539.[48] The culmination of these efforts was the act known commonly as the Statute of Artificers of 1563. With it Parliament sought to preserve England, socially and economically, as a permanently agrarian nation, enjoining persons who sold their labor from shifting from one trade to another (the seven years' apprenticeship already enforced in some trades was made mandatory for all), one district to another, one social order to another, and one kind of apparel to another.[49]

The Statute of Artificers, to look no earlier, suggests that the legal means devised to maintain necessity and hierarchy were becoming as complicated as their ends. It was not especially hard for legislators to translate the agrarian ideal of Xenophon, Aristotle, and Cicero into the juridical matrix of feudal Europe. But it was another thing altogether to hold an altered economy within those legal bounds. English law attempted to keep laborers on the land even when feudal service was economically obsolete. By the sixteenth century villenage had largely given way to rents, contracts, and monetary payments, yet the law continued to add circumstances—that is, crimes—for which a man could be placed in bondage for the rest of his life. The tensions that resulted were present well into the eighteenth century. Landowners who entered into contracts with laborers were among the legislators who prohibited such agreements; legislators became divided amongst themselves, and individual legislators were divided between their practice and their principles. Subjects too were thus divided between the growing number with indulgences and those without. Bolingbroke attempted to reduce the chance for division with the Landed Qualification Act of 1711, proposing that no man represent a shire in the House of Commons unless he held land in annual value of £600, or, for a borough, £300. Then the laws themselves seemed to require closer guarding and greater severity. Beyond church and Parliament, surveillance and enforcement were in the hands of mayors, baliffs, sheriffs, aldermen, justices of the peace, and committees of selected citizens. The number of offenses against property classed as capital quadrupled during the eighteenth century, from about fifty to more than two hundred. The Waltham Black Act of 1723 not only provided capital punishment for vandals, poachers, and the like, but also encouraged landowners to supply their own punishment in the form of mantraps and spring guns. According to Leon Radzinowicz, the measure standing alone constituted a complete criminal code: "There is hardly a criminal act which did not come within the provisions of the Black Act; offences against public order, against the administration of criminal justice, against property, against the person, malicious injuries to property of varying degree—all came under this statute and all were punishable by death."[50] By one count Radzinowicz finds 50 distinct offenses punishable by death under the act; by another, stricter interpretation (which takes in accessories, second and third principals, etc.), he discovers between 200 and 250. Men like Pope, Swift, Fielding, Goldsmith, Smollett, Boswell, and many others reviled the movement of laborers away from the land and called for more laws to keep them put. What we can see in retrospect is that legislators were not lax, that laws did what they could to preserve the sanctity of the country estate.

Subjects to the sumptuary laws included all persons whose labor was required or whose dependence was undenied. While all were burdened, women were triply so. Because natural law was interpreted as barring them from office as legislators, they were necessarily reduced to subject-victims. When by chance a woman like Elizabeth was elevated to the role of legislator, the anomaly was explicable in terms of a male legislator's requirements of inheritance. The law first stipulated their dependence, irrespective of birth, fortune, or education, then regulated their conduct according to sex and again according to status. Aristotle's contempt for feminine reasoning had already been codified in classical Greece. Early Athenian law prohibited the erection of memorial steles to women, and Solon in the sixth century B.C. promulgated laws controlling their walks, dress, food, drink, and holidays; he established the conditions under which women were allowed to marry and approved the sale into slavery of a ward or daughter not a virgin. Demetrius in the fourth century B.C. followed Aristotle's advice directly and founded boards of "regulators of women," men who would censor all aspects of feminine conduct. The Oppian law (215 B.C.) confiscated for the state virtually all the wealth held by Roman women. It restricted to one-half ounce the amount of gold a married woman could hold and expropriated all the wealth of wards, widows, and single women. Roman law determined what woman was fit to ride in a chariot, on a horse, a pack animal, an ass, or not to ride at all. (English law followed suit, distinguishing among the honorable, gentle, worthy, and several orders below common; for each respective order was mandated length and material of coat and dress, number of flounces, width of lace, length of shoe points, height of bonnet, and so on.)[51] In Greek and Roman law women were regarded as a national resource, to be specially cultivated like the land during periods of war and natural calamity. Reasons of state dictated if and when women might marry or remarry and bear children; only during times of war were citizens legally required to rear their daughters, an obligation never relaxed regarding sons. Graeco-Roman sumptuary codes also enforced the principles of woman as "in-house slave," *partus sequitur ventrem,* and feminine incapacity for public affairs.[52] From early Christianity came an ambivalent conception of woman: holy–threatening, passive–active, AVE–EVA. Mary was to be honored, but the ordinary daughter of Eve was another case, Chrysostom in the fourth century calling her a "necessary evil, a natural temptation, a desirable calamity, a domestic peril, a deadly fascination and a painted ill." Aquinas said that woman could legitimately be considered "defective and misbegotten," for she produces the mere matter of humanity while man produces the essential form, and that, moreover, she was not part of the original creation, having been generated not from divine material but at one remove, from Adam. And in a sermon preached before Elizabeth, Bishop John Aylmer described woman as "in every way doltified with the dregs of the devil's dunghill."[53]

The preservation of sumptuary legislation into the Christian era was but the outward sign of Christian acceptance of the attack upon luxury. No less than the Deuteronomic writers, Aristotle, or Seneca, the church fathers wished to impose virtue upon the recalcitrant masses. In the Old Testament the concept of luxury formed an implicit link between spiritual discipline and social control. The decision in favor of a warrior-king is unwise both religiously and politically. It alters not only the moral atmosphere of Israel but also its mode of government. In the classical Greek and Roman authors the connection between religious and secular realms is made explicit, and after the novel synthesis of the New Testament that connection would remain fast for nearly 1,800 years. Plato, Critias, Isocrates, Polybius, Scaevola, Varro, Cicero, Livy, and Vergil were among the many thinkers who, although themselves skeptics, argued that religious dogma must be maintained in order to control the masses. In the *Republic* Socrates defends the habit of rulers' "lying for the public good." In the *Histories* Polybius argues that the fickle and violent multitude can be held in check only by the piety and terror of religion devised by the rulers of the state, a religion that, while without a claim to truth, would be politically useful. Luxury allied patriotism with religious devotion and cloaked the management of the multitude in the worship of Mars, Jupiter, and Minerva.[54]

As a social issue, luxury is no less blatant within the Christian era, and no less effective. With its emphasis upon the universal but individual nature of sin, early church theology could decry all men as sinners yet honor extant social distinctions.[55] Even without such accommodation, there need be no philosophical contradiction between moral absolutism and legal-political relativism. For Greek and Roman philosophers as well as Christian theologians found means to come to terms with the imperfections of the world. For many of the Cynics and Stoics, the state of the present world had degenerated irretrievably from some earlier condition, usually identified with the Golden Age. For Tertullian, Augustine, and Aquinas, the nature of fallen man rendered his works inevitably degraded. From the perspective of either the Golden Age or the City of God, that is, human history and human society were of course fatally flawed. Luxury could no more be eliminated than could mortality. On the level of doctrine, therefore, pagan and Christian alike taught a kind of indifference to history and society that amounted to silent toleration of luxury. True freedom involved self-transcendence and disengagement from one's immediate environment. The world meanwhile could be expected to continue its guilty course, and the men in charge of secular affairs could not be expected to be any better than they had ever been.[56]

On the level of concrete, day-to-day existence, moreover, still more direct compromises with the world became prudent. As the Christian church survived the presumptive millennium and saw the need to accommodate itself to a sturdy world, it came to accept the institutions of the state as valuable instruments for doing God's work and extending its own influence into secular affairs.[57] Several studies have revealed that on many issues church and state of the Middle Ages moved to a relationship not of mere accommodation but of mutual support and encouragement. Luxury was the hub of such agreement, for the concept could be made to comprehend any sort of behavior—social, political, economic, or moral—that seemed to undermine the authority of the present order. The church, on its side, devoted increasing attention to canon laws that served to reinforce extant civil legislation, as in the protection of property (including slaves) and the stipulation of status. Civil government gradually but increasingly assumed some of the moral functions and proscriptions of the church, as in the prosecution of "victimless crimes" such as profuse spending, drunkenness, swearing, and gambling. Together they evolved the doctrine of "consumption by estates" under which standards of conduct and comfort were fixed according to social rank; liberty and magnificence were reserved for the highest rank but prohibited to all others, and so on down the great chain of social being. Until the nineteenth century it was customary for sumptuary laws to be read from the pulpit in every church at least once a year—a daunting task, since ordinances regarding dress alone often ran more than one hundred duodecimo pages. Until the Reformation the legislation against luxury enacted by secular European governments was administered by ecclesiastical courts (on the Continent called consistories); thereafter the clergy retained several places on the court. In seventeenth-century Germany and Switzerland the courts were called *Reformations-Kammer* or *Reformations-Rath*.[58] The reformation intended by such bodies was not of theology but of morals and conduct, and when influential men in London, many clergymen included, decided that the sumptuary laws were being neglected, they formed in 1692 a Society for the Reformation of Manners that became the model for similar societies begun in other cities throughout the eighteenth century. A parallel organization explicitly uniting the church with the call for stronger sumptuary codes was established in 1698 (and flourishes today) as the Society for Promoting Christian Knowledge. The Society for the Reformation of Manners did not attempt to police the whole spectrum of luxuries or even the whole of southeast England. Nevertheless, it claimed responsibility for 91,899 arrests by 1725.[59]

A final example: in the 1590s, while Shakespeare was using luxury as a synonym for lechery, civil and ecclesiastical leaders were maintaining its widest application. In June of 1592 the bishop of London and various other church officials joined the lord mayor and council of London to condemn the riotous and luxurious behavior of apprentices at the playhouses. Boys and young men were temporarily forbidden the right of free assembly, and the Rose was closed for three months. A similar reaction occurred in the summer of 1595, when the London price of certain staples, including eggs and butter, doubled and often more than doubled. When the young and the poor protested violently, church and state again cried out in one voice against luxury and insolence. Prices remained high, martial law was invoked, and those agitators who could be found were hanged, then drawn and quartered on Tower Hill.[60] Englishmen of the eighteenth century owed their understanding of luxury more to the bishop and lord mayor of London than to Chaucer or Shakespeare. Like religious and secular authorities 160 years earlier, Smollett and his contemporaries came to fear the discontented mass of the London poor. Particularly when spurred by allegedly unscrupulous politicians, the poor seemed always on the brink of collective insurrection. They seemed to represent a potent threat to property and status and that nexus of political power implicit in the ownership of property. Such was the protean inner logic of an idea used to decry the barbarities of a Nero that it could be brought to bear, at the height of England's quest for empire, upon the poorest of the poor.

Two

LEGISLATORS DIVIDED:
THE ATTACK UPON LUXURY
IN THE EIGHTEENTH CENTURY

Every society has a right to preserve public peace and order, and
therefore has a good right to prohibit the propagation of opinions
which have a dangerous tendency . . . no member of a society
has a right to teach any doctrine contrary to what society
holds to be true.—Samuel Johnson

When Smollett's type of the natural legislator, Matthew Bramble, revisits several English cities after long absence in Monmouthshire, he is shocked to discover how deeply luxury has eroded the habits, manners, and institutions of Old England. In London he finds the management of public affairs in the hands of base and incompetent men, the result, he says, of "luxury and corruption"; he thereupon advances the proposition that all institutions arranged in a "democratical form" will soon "degenerate into cabal and corruption." In Bath and again in the metropolis he is jostled and insulted, cheated and confounded by tradesmen and their wives and by common people who are surly, insolent, and restless in their station; all of which he terms the working of "luxury and insubordination." At the end of his travels, Bramble observes that these related forms of luxury have turned the natural order in England upside down.

The subversion of necessity and hierarchy in government and every-day life—corruption and insubordination, in contemporary shorthand—which so exercises Bramble in a novel of 1771 had outraged writers throughout the earlier part of the century and became, for readers with appetite enough, the weekly fare of those common rooms of public philosophy, the political papers and pamphlets. Corruption of the civil polity was the incandescent charge brought in almost every number of the *Craftsman*. In one example, the pseudonymous editor Caleb d'Anvers rehearses the parlous state of English affairs, then draws an ominous parallel: "This was the Case of the *Roman Common-wealth* of old, and of others of much later Date. Luxury and Profuseness led the Way to Indigence and Effeminacy; which prepared the Minds of the People for Corruption; and Corruption for Subjection; as they have constantly succeeded one another, and will do so again, in the same Circumstances, in all Countries, and in all Ages" (no. 56 [29 July 1727], 2:73). Later d'Anvers turns from history to fable to draw his moral, describing a dream-visit to an island Edenic in its native liberty and prosperity. As long as its inhabitants can remember, d'Anvers learns, the island has been happy and fruitful. Then suddenly, a dark tree shoots forth, grows with amazing velocity, and envelopes the entire land in the shadow of its branches. "I saw it put forth a vast Quantity of beautiful Fruit, which glitter'd like burnish'd Gold, and hung in large Clusters on every Bough. I now perceived it to be the Tree of Corruption, which bears a very near Resemblance to the *Tree of Knowledge*, in the Garden of *Eden*, for whoever tasted the Fruit of it, lost his Integrity and fell, like *Adam*, from the *State of Innocence*" (no. 297 [25 March 1732], 9:53). The fruit of corruption bears inscriptions that identify it with the national debt, stockjobbing, and the moneyed companies. An obese little man perched in the tree tosses the poisoned fruit into the crowd, which is beguiled, then sickened with the new diet. Soon the island is fouled and blighted, and no healthful food remains. From the once-happy island now arises a general lamentation, relieved only by the sinister chortle of the fat man and his minions.

Attacks upon the intransigence of the common people became common about mid-century and found their way even into the pages of relatively nonpolitical periodicals like the *Gentleman's Magazine*. During the autumn and winter of 1757–58, for example, the *Gentleman's* carried a heated and lengthy series of letters from members of the provincial gentry. With more vigor than was usual in the regular letters column, they wrote of their indignation at the crimes committed in their shires and towns by the forces of luxury. Various as their complaints were, they agreed that the laboring poor had become so licentious as to be no longer manageable. When, for the major example, the price of common grain had been increased, large numbers of laborers had refused to pay the new price or to buy an inferior grade. After demanding a return to the previous level of prices and being refused, many laborers rioted. Food riots, sporadic but common in the summer of 1757, provided landowners with what seemed to them cogent instances of the depravity of the times. Their letters summarize popular notions of luxury in the 1750s and indicate how easily disparate events could be explained by a single concept. One of the most revealing of the letters assumes that the evil forces have been condemned sufficiently, but that practical action has been lacking. Printed under the heading "The Mob Must be Conquered," it argues that, unless the luxury of "the lower sorts of people" is suppressed, Britons will lose the property, "laws, religion, and natural blessings of our country."[1]

Reflecting a sense of anxiety rising to alarm, such correspondence echoed current debates in the House of Commons and was carried in many English periodicals during the 1750s and well into the 1760s.[2] For more than a decade the *London Magazine* was a regular outlet for anguished protest against the enveloping tide. In the issue for September 1754, "Civis" writes that, "Amongst the many reigning vices of the present age none have risen to a greater height than that fashionable one of luxury, and few require a more immediate suppression, as it not only enervates the people, and debauches their morals, but also destroys their substance" (23:409). He denounces in particular the rise of the fashion among the lower orders and calls for speedy enforcement of sumptuary laws against urban laborers. In January 1756 another correspondent notes that, while he usually disapproves of "those common place declamations against the degeneracy of the present times," he now believes that luxury has increased so prodigiously as to "threaten the undermining of our constitution and the downfall of our state. . . . Our riches may perhaps be greater than formerly, but I am sure that our virtue is less" (25:15-16). Two years later, in May 1758, "Britannicus" seeks to describe in detail "to what degree this pestilence hath spread itself through the nation" and to forewarn readers of the certain ruin facing England if it is not eliminated (27:223). Although the storm of denunciation had moderated by 1764, occasional outbursts persisted, and in December "Aurelius" writes: "A little rational consideration will enable us to discover the kindred links between luxury, rapine, meanness, extravagance, misery, idleness, vice and guilt; for they are of one family, as scandalous as pernicious, and alike fatally destructive in their effects" (33:620).[3]

These letters represent a mere droplet in the last great wave of public condemnation to sweep England during the eighteenth century. For the period of Smollett's lifetime, 1721–71—roughly the time between the enlarged edition of the *Fable of the Bees* and the *Wealth of Nations*—the British Museum and London School of Economics possess more than 460 books and pamphlets in English that discuss luxury; for the whole century the number would nearly double. This estimate includes works, like Hume's *Political Discourses,* of which only part is devoted to luxury. But it does not include the vast number of comments in periodicals. If comments of all types during the century were counted, the number would be several thousand. Although not a matter to be ascertained with statistical certainty, the controversy over luxury probably reached its highest pitch in British history in the years 1756–63. These are also the terminal years of the Seven Years' War and of Smollett's active involvement in polemical journalism. When the novelist and three other "gentlemen of approved abilities" issued the first number of the *Critical Review* on 1 March 1756, armed conflict with the French had already been under way for months. His tenure as editor and probably sole writer of the pro-government sheet the *Briton* ended 12 February 1763, two days after the war had been officially concluded. The coincidence of these circumstances is not fortuitous.

As the previous chapter has indicated, cries against luxury have been loudest when a people is under unusual stress. From at least the time of the Philistine attacks upon the Israelites through the War of the Spanish Succession, public dispute over the issue was the visible sign of a sense of crisis. When war or domestic discord appeared to threaten important interests and values, then old theories were respun to clothe new situations. Luxury arose time and again, for it could account for any unwanted or unforeseen shift in the scales of military, economic, social, political, moral, and even literary forces. The specific occasion might be sudden outbreaks of crime, violence, and immorality, or fierce partisan quarrels in politics (often over the goals and tactics of war), a lost battle, bad harvests, interruptions in foreign commerce, high taxes, or unexpected financial reversals (as in the South Sea Bubble). Most often, all these events occurred together. In all cases, men of civic spirit demanded explanation and resolution: the sources of discontent had to be discovered, the traitors identified. So it was in eighteenth-century England, and Smollett's anxiety over luxury was a normal one for his contemporaries.

To understand the particular nature of the controversy over luxury during the century, it is useful to turn first to the best summary of contemporary ideas, provided by Mandeville:

> It is a receiv'd Notion, that Luxury is as destructive to the wealth of the whole Body Politic, as it is to that of every individ-

ual Person who is guilty of it, and that a National Frugality enriches a County in the same manner as that which is less general
increases the Estates of private Families. . . . What is laid to the
Charge of Luxury besides, is, that it increases Avarice and Rapine:
And where they are reigning Vices, offices of the greatest Trust
are bought and sold; the Ministers that should serve the Public,
both great and small, corrupted, and the Countries every Moment
in danger of being betray'd to the highest Bidders: And lastly, that
it effeminates and enervates the People, by which the Nations
become an easy Prey to the first Invaders.[4]

Thus the received notion of luxury near the beginning of the eighteenth
century was essentially what it was in Old Testament times and in Rome
of the first century B.C. The first portion of Mandeville's definition
reveals that luxury continued to express a theory of value, an ethic for
both individuals and nations; the second, that it remained a theory of
history, an explanation of both personal and collective decline in the
past. One needs to go beyond Mandeville, however, for an explanation
of the complex mutations the concept had undergone by Smollett's age.
Several related questions require at least tentative answers: Why the
attack upon luxury remained as important to the English as it was to
the Romans, why it was not met by countervailing or competitive
theories of national history, why it was applied so massively after 1688,
why it fit partisan polemics so well, why in common parlance "corruption" and "insubordination" acquired such special significance, and
what kinds of challenges were at work. In fine, what was old in the
eighteenth-century situation, and what new. Although full justice to
the situation is not possible within the limits of a chapter, present
purposes can be served by an overview, drawing upon major studies of
English society by J. G. A. Pocock, Peter G. M. Dickson, and Isaac
Kramnick, followed by an account of the main phases or periods of
debate over luxury.

The primary answer is that what is new is a congeries of economic,
political, and social circumstances, while what is old is the way those
circumstances are perceived. The seventeenth century gave rise to a new
series of relationships among Englishmen as well as to new relationships
between them and their principal institutions. It carried English
thought, according to Pocock, from its post-medieval to its early modern stage. What was involved in this transition was a willingness to look
more closely, to analyze more exactly the flux of history. Change could
be seen as something more particular than the sheer disorder Herodotus
or Augustine observed; now it could be seen "in terms of intelligible
social and material processes." But while a century of revolution could
induce attention, it could not compel approval. The conceptual universe

of early eighteenth-century England remained essentially what it was for the ancients—a universe bound by a "rigorously limited epistemology of the secular," in which particular events and their causes were ill understood. This universe of ideas obliged men to interpret change negatively, as a subversion of the divinely and naturally ordained principles of necessity and hierarchy and as a degeneration from grace, virtue, stability, and rationality.[5] Since the Hebrews, the concept of luxury had possessed the capacity to communicate those values and to describe the consequences of their violation. Hence it was one of the very few traditional concepts in which aspects of change were inherent. Embodied in holy Scripture, in the works of the great philosophers and theologians, and in the corpora of Hebrew, Greek, Roman, and Christian law, it provided a reflexive doctrine upon which opponents of any instance of change might base their misgivings or resentment. At once, luxury accommodated change, absorbed it, explained it, and judged it. Regarding the concept of luxury, the classical world extended from the rule of Moses to that of George III.

Second, with ample documentation Dickson calls the years 1688–1756 the period of "financial revolution in England," the Bloodless Revolution standing as watershed between the older agrarian England and the newer commercial nation. The new financial order encouraged a trend toward a more urban and bourgeois society, more centralized economic and political institutions, and became the requisite ground for the industrial revolution to follow.[6] Over this congeries of changes, the eighteenth-century battles of luxury were fought. For to adherents of the classical conception, a vocal if not overwhelming majority for much of the century, the Revolution of 1688 was a Pandora's box setting loose a spirit of luxury the natural order could not contain. To them the world was spinning not only beyond control, but almost beyond comprehension. Luxury was fast begetting new, false, and artificial wealth, a new and noxious economic order, and a new and sinister breed of men whose sole office was to multiply by some nefarious means the new man-made values. Taxes, credit, public funds, stock-jobbing, a standing army—all of these misbegot, from nothing, the innovators, the moneyed men who set out to break the nation to their own ways. They bought influence with cash and political power with corruption; they used them solely for subversion—of the constitution, the machinery of government, the spirit of the country, the morals and manners of its people. With loud anguish Bolingbroke phrased the situation in his *Dissertation upon Parties* (1733–35): "THE POWER OF MONEY AS THE WORLD IS NOW CONSTITUTED IS REAL POWER."

Third, as it accounted for devolutionary change and the genesis of corruption, so the concept of luxury described the character of the agents, the actual human beings engaged in the destructive process. To the Hebrew sense of degradation, it conjoined the Greek sense of natural duality. Luxury was not the sole theory of entropy available to the ancient world, but it was the most attractive, I believe because it allowed (or required) the exclusion of exceptional men from the devolutionary course. As we have seen, the legislators—the men who in Greece, Rome, and feudal Europe wrote the laws, sermons, histories, and philosophical treatises—felt themselves proof against the dread temptations of luxury. Lesser beings would succumb, but the natural legislator was held aloft—by his land, his wealth, his birth, his education, his status—in eighteenth-century terms, by his estate. From Plato onward it was assumed that humankind was divided between the legislators and the subjects, the select few and the ignorant multitude, the men of honor and everybody else (including, with significant emphasis, the men of profit). It was further assumed that legislators would be united and act as one, for they tended to be males of similar background, training and philosophy; indeed they were to use the Law to atomize their subjects, to guarantee industry, and to prevent insubordination. If Birth was their throne, Law was their sword.

But in eighteenth-century England, throne and sword had been thrust apart. Power was no longer the exclusive prerogative of the natural legislators and sometimes fell into the hands of what was to them a bastard simulacrum. In the illegitimate world ushered in by the financial revolution, men of mere profit were in the ascendancy. Now place and power were divided between natural and unnatural claimants. The situation was sufficiently grave for the men of honor to sound alarum, to rouse themselves to wrest control from the venal. They, Aristotle's independent men, possessed the right to rule, not the moneyed men who were natural subjects, who had no virtue themselves and who led a herd of blind mercenaries. They, noble of birth and noble of character, alone had the right to determine necessity and hierarchy for England. Hence the decades-long cry of corruption: luxury as it threatened the constitution. Men like Pope, Swift, and Bolingbroke had been forced to discard belief in the monarch as sole or even chief upholder of the constitution. Now they were being goaded to explain how that role had devolved upon mere subjects—those of the middle orders against whom Greek and Roman law had been written. The Deuteronomic writers would tolerate no usurers, bakers, confectioners, or the like. Socrates, Cato, Cicero, and Augustine agreed. Sumptuary codes had for centuries suppressed or limited their numbers and activities. Now they were claiming influence in government, a certain sign of corruption of the civil polity. They were guilty of what in civil law was termed jactitation, a claim falsely made, and as yet stood unpunished. Again Bolingbroke puts the case succinctly, in his *Letter on the Spirit of Patriotism* and again in the *Idea of a Patriot King* (both 1749): "THE LANDED MEN ARE THE TRUE OWNERS OF OUR POLITICAL VESSEL; THE MONEYED MEN, AS SUCH, ARE NO MORE THAN PASSENGERS IN IT."

Despite Bolingbroke's capitals, the usurpers continued to thrive, not only diluting the power of the natural legislators, but succeeding even in sundering them from it. Perhaps the most galling aspect of Opposition strategy during the 1720s and 1730s was that it had to be extra-parliamentary, forged mostly outside the arena of power. For a generation before Walpole's rise and nearly a generation after his fall, many leaders of the great families echoed Bolingbroke's anguish. Here, they cried, was an infernal paradox born of the corruptions of luxury: they were intended by the nature of things to guard the constitution, that part of natural law deduced specifically for the governance of England; yet they could not get into the ministry. Isaac Kramnick has argued persuasively that to the Opposition Walpole's cardinal sin was moral, in the sense that the sumptuary codes were moral, delimiting moral capacity as well as legal culpability. By reducing government to administration and mediation, Walpole appeared to have reduced politics to an acquired skill. But to most of the Opposition, statecraft was a thing of the spirit, requiring proper birth and classical education, social grace and rhetorical eloquence. A skill might be learned by anybody, when to be anybody was to be nobody. The concept of luxury and the workings of natural law, on the other hand, dictated that only the men of land and family could observe necessity and hierarchy. Kramnick writes:

> To Bolingbroke, Walpole's political corruption was the symbol of a much larger corrupt society. . . . The financial revolution of 1690–1740 was, then, the most meaningful social experience in the lives of Bolingbroke and the others in his circle . . . it informs all their writing on politics and society, and it feeds their gloom, their satire, and their indignation. They saw an aristocratic social and political order being undermined by money and new financial institutions and they didn't like it.[7]

Fourth, division among eighteenth-century legislators and the concomitant vituperation of attacks upon luxury appear in retrospect to have been unavoidable. The pattern of argument after 1688 suggests that all of the conflicts inherent in the classical concept were aggravated in the growth of a more fluid and complex society. What is revolution to men on one side of the wheel is devolution to those on the other.

Where European society had been relatively static, as in rural areas of medieval England, the authority of the natural legislator went largely unchallenged. However, in the market towns and the capital, where expansion was the desideratum for legislator and merchant alike, challenges were frequent, and the law was called into play to enforce order. Where the law was neglected or rescinded, the apparent cause was the new power won by the middle orders. "Stadluft," the Germans claimed, "macht frei." A process visible in imperial Rome, Renaissance Venice, and seventeenth-century Paris was asserting itself once again in London, as several forces marched together: prosperity and aspiration on one side, resentment and attacks upon luxury on the other. By the middle of the eighteenth century, London was the largest city in Europe and contained the greatest proportion of national population—one in ten. She was also the greatest port, the largest center of international trade, and the largest center of ship-owning and shipbuilding in the world. Through these enterprises she eventually became the world center of banking, finance, and insurance.[8] One consequence of this concentration was that the city exercised an enormous influence over the British economy. Defoe called her the great octopus that sucked to itself the vitals of the nation's trade, and Hume noted that "[Our] national debts cause a mighty confluence of the people and riches to the capital, by the great sums levied in the provinces to pay the interest." Another was that she evoked an enormous amount of envy and suspicion, suggested by Defoe and Hume and voiced loudly by the societies bent upon reforming city manners and by those who identified with the provinces. The lines of division are indicated by the host-narrator in the opening chapter of *Tom Jones:* "we shall represent Human Nature at first to the keen appetite of our reader in that more plain and simple manner in which it is found in the country, and shall hereafter hash and ragout it with all the high French and Italian seasoning of affectation and vice which courts and cities afford."

The sumptuary codes of the ancient world testify that societies ordered by juridical status were usually fragile and insecure, alert subjects continuously seeking new privileges, alert legislators continuously seeking new restrictions. In Rome, M. I. Finley has noted, as the empire prospered, the number of slaveholders grew, as did the number of slaves. A worried Senate responded with additional controls over slaves and slave owners. A similar dilemma faced the natural legislators of England. They could try either to halt the new prosperity or to find means to control it. The former course was futile, for even before 1688 commercial expansion was virtually irrevocable. The latter was at best difficult, for with their influence diluted in court and Parliament they could not hope to institute the drastic measures required to renew the old model of necessity and hierarchy. Throughout English history the disturbance of any kind of national equilibrium was likely to be followed by fresh condemnations of luxury. This reflexive offering of a placebo recurred because verbal tirade was, it seems, virtually the only method accepted for solving inveterate problems. Especially after 1688, when numerous types of equilibrium were being violated, the very tenacity of such problems insured that luxury grew not less important, but more. For when effective means to resolve difficulties were unknown or unacceptable, then ineffective ones were pressed with greater insistence—if only to allay popular anxiety. Changes in English society had been growing apace for decades, most of them set off by deliberate decisions of the traditional natural legislators. By the eighteenth century such changes had created serious human problems, principally for women, the poor, and the urban middle orders. When enclosure or poor harvests or other pressures pushed a farming family toward the city, for example, the family became enmeshed in an obvious double bind. If it remained in the country seeking a new site for old labor, it was accused of truculence and insubordination. If it sought new work in the city, it was decried for indigence and restlessness. As with the occupational roles of the poor, so with the social roles of educated women and the financial roles of merchants and tradesmen. In each instance English traditions generated serious difficulties, and English traditions condemned whatever solutions were sought. And in each instance the leaders of Old England could issue their denunciations of luxury with genuine satisfaction. A campaign of moral rearmament, they could assume, had been opened. The enemy had been identified and located; victory would follow shortly. Thus the concept of luxury again served its consolidating function, and the discovery of luxury among the laboring poor became the social equivalent of detecting French agents concealed in St. John's Woods.

Victory did not usually follow, however. By the late seventeenth century Englishmen were certainly aware of land, labor, capital, and raw material as the ingredients of a commercial economy. This much at least is revealed by the adventures of the Mississippi Company in Paris in 1718 and the South Sea Company in London two years later. But economic theory hobbled behind economic reality. Johnson wrote justly that "There is nothing which requires more to be illustrated by philosophy than trade does." Not until the last quarter of the century did a prolegomenon to such a philosophy appear in Smith's *Wealth of Nations*. Until the 1760s there seemed little hope of reconciling the buoyant, optimistic proponents of material progress who were translating economic power into political power with the dubious, pessimistic observer of material decay. No longer could a man of the land rise with the confidence of a Roman born to wield power, assert the harmony of nature and society, and deduce the unity of all values. Arguments questioning traditional authority were surfacing in treatises and even appearing weekly in the papers. If it was toppled, the whole edifice surrounding the conception of luxury might follow.

Fifth, that edifice seemed to be under siege on several fronts at once. To the natural legislators the most insidious threats were also the most predictable. Centuries of experience had prepared them for the guile of foreign enemies and the unbridled middle and lower orders. Such tempters were expected to act with cunning, for they represented inveterate resistance to natural virtue, resistance that it was the design of law and government to contain. Although it was quite clear by the time of Walpole's Robinocracy that those controls were no longer working, a change of administration might bring about their renewal. What was not so predictable was the apparent treason of some philosophers and writers, men who were the normal allies or servants of the traditional order. Hobbes was a fervent ally, but a dangerous one; for his reduction of necessity and hierarchy to issues of fear, power, and self-interest had stripped natural law of its divine sanction.[9] Locke was an equally dangerous foe, for his redefinitions of legitimate authority seemed to cast natural law away from its ancient agrarian center. Some mercantile writers, it is true, continued the attack upon luxury in a classical way. Others however were not so careful and suggested that the economic order was best governed by its own laws. These held that economic behavior was of itself morally neutral; luxury could be justified if it provided a market for the nation's goods and increased the circulation of money.[10]

Besides Locke and the economic writers, the important figures symbolic of national division were Defoe and Mandeville. The one challenged the classical notion of hierarchy in his defenses of women, laborers, pauper children, and the commercial interests. In scores of exuberant, commonsensical works he ventured to say that the new freedoms won by the middle orders could never reasonably be called luxury. The other, an audacious conservative who because of his conservatism sought to jettison the old taboos against luxury, flatly denied the classical notion of necessity. Neither Defoe nor Mandeville had any real power, yet each possessed enough notability to be branded infamous. Neither was at all radical—as, say, Milton and the Levellers had been. Both were intent upon strengthening extant English society by clearing it of the detritus of patent contradiction.[11] But to the natural legislators such mediation was pointless and uncalled for—indeed, exacerbating. They would brook no talk of contradiction, because their most abiding anxiety lay, it seems, in the fear that their supremacy was being undermined by a dark and demonic force that they could sense but not comprehend. To face the moneyed men on their own terms in the political arena was one thing, and a familiar one. But to be told that they were facing the impassive workings of a relentless social and economic process—that was another, and a damnable one.

The hostility that greeted Defoe's and Mandeville's social writings suggests that rancor and tension were as much a part of eighteenth-century controversy as division. They were bridge figures attempting to reconcile the past to the present and calling attention to the fact that English society—in our terms, the field of testing—had been thoroughly secularized. Their reception showed how desperate and controversial the issue of luxury remained and indicated that such contradictions as they found would persist. As much as Defoe and Mandeville, the defenders of necessity and hierarchy were obliged by momentous events to emphasize the secular workings of luxury—in philosophical basis as well as everyday articulation. Moral arguments, whether Platonic, Augustinian, or Calvinist, were certainly used, but mainly in passing. Even churchmen came to concentrate upon the putative economic and political consequences of luxury; even they were more alarmed over its predicted effects upon the nation than upon the individual soul. In practice, that is, they grasped for the same sword wielded by Hobbes and their adversaries, making economic and political theory the fount of moral norms. And they found it double-edged. They were not trying to say something novel about the vice; indeed nothing new or significant was added to the classical attack during the century, not even by Rousseau. Instead, the traditional arguments were culled for their collective and economic implications. A domestic hurricane was raging, and any text in a storm. What original thinking about luxury did occur during the century was carried out by men who rejected some part of the classical attack. Men like Defoe, Mandeville, Hume, Johnson, Kames, Ferguson, and Smith were not attempting to betray the values of European civilization. Rather they were arguing that the ancient dogma of luxury was not essential to those values.

Sixth, the protean quality of the classical attack upon luxury—informing every traditional institution and judging the conduct of every subject—insured that its spirit would persist in many forms. At any particular moment, the number of Englishmen bold enough to challenge it was relatively small. In the popular mind at least, it would be generations before the traditional horror would be moderated or redirected. Beyond all questions of philosophy and historical movement, therefore, there remain complicating habits in usage. Mandeville demonstrates that luxury entered two distinct levels of usage. On one it is, for men like Bolingbroke, Hume, Harris, Ferguson, and Smollett, a nuclear and organizing concept in an elaborate social and political system. Swift, for example, supplements his philosophical quarrel with luxury by claiming, in the *Proposal for Correcting . . . the English Tongue* (1712), that the vice is responsible for debasement of the language. On the other level, a vulgarization of the first, it has passed into general currency as a commonplace element in various kinds of dispute. Many anonymous pamphlets could be cited to illustrate this popular level of usage, tracts that hold luxury responsible for a multiplicity of circumstances: for both high prices and low, prosperity and hardship, crime and discourtesy, brutality and effeminacy, martial weakness and unsuccessful diplomacy. As a springboard for vulgar controversy, the idea was of enormous utility, for it was inherently polemical and customarily vague. Popular discussions of economic topics reveal this tendency in the extreme, often totally neglecting such elemental distinctions as those among necessities, conveniences, and comforts— all of which were changing during the century. Numerous writers of the first rank, moreover, who generally possessed a learned view of luxury, on occasion also utilized popular senses of the term—for example, as a synonym for physical indulgence or sexual immorality. Similarly, writers felt free to excoriate the presumed dissipation of every class and sector of society but their own. Men of the middle orders rejected out of hand the argument that their claims upon government were luxurious. But many were willing to entertain the same argument directed against the working poor. William Temple of Trowbridge, friend of John Wilkes and defender of City causes, was at once a voluble supporter of the commercial interests against charges of luxury and a fierce enemy of the luxury of laborers. Nathaniel Forster criticizes oligarchs like the Walpoles and the Pelhams for insensitivity toward the privations of the poor. Horace Walpole derides the extravagances of Clive and other nabobs. Clive is shocked by the luxurious apparel of servants in London.[12] In the *Travels*, Smollett finds occasion to ridicule many instances of French and Italian luxury, but he is incensed by the absence of comfort in his own lodgings; these are not luxurious enough. For Bramble, the comforts of Lord Queensberry savor of refinement and hospitality; those of Squire Burdock reek of dissipation and bad taste.

Variations in usage were natural and common throughout the century, for luxury probably *was* the greatest single social issue and the greatest single commonplace. The situation apparently posed no extraordinary difficulties to contemporaries, but it is bedeviling to modern students. Elizabeth Gilboy's comments upon luxury are not altogether compatible with those of Norman Sykes; each is regarding only part of the concept, and that from a specialized perspective. Smollett's contempo-

raries, particularly among major intellectual figures, were no more confused in their discussions of luxury than modern writers are in their
analyses of, say, liberalism or communism or democracy.[13] As men
brought the concept to bear upon the whole spectrum of human
activity, luxury became an increasingly centrifugal constellation of
ideas. To note this evolution is merely to recast the distinction between
luxury as form and luxury as content. Thus, while Greek, Roman, and
Christian arguments of a general sort persisted through much of the
century, specific examples or manifestations continued to accumulate—
at an increasing rate. On the one hand, a writer would tend to repeat
the maledictions of his predecessors while adding a few uniquely his
own. On the other, each new social disturbance—from the South Sea
Bubble and the '45 rebellion to increased prices of porter and the
decline of education at Oxford—could provide further instances of the
reign of luxury. Critics of the *Estimate of the Manners and Principles
of the Times* chided John Brown not for his relatively narrow view of
the nature of luxury, but for his restricted perspective of its consequences. They accordingly extended Brown's list of grievances with
contributions of their own. Bramble's "catalogue of London dainties"
and his list of English affectations are closely related in motive and
form to earlier strictures against luxury.

A final complication should be noted as a caveat. The issue of luxury
was volatile and political, the period one of rapid and drastic change.
The coincidence of these circumstances made for controversy that is
overblown and division that is too schematic. When a flaming political
issue is raised and a simple answer required, many men will respond
who would ordinarily remain silent or venture a cautious "maybe."
Such probably was the case during the eighteenth century, else the
flames of dispute would have continued burning as high after 1763.
Ordinary Englishmen probably were not as certain of their own minds
as the philosophers and lawmakers of previous centuries. Our understanding must take into at least tacit account the tepid, the dubious,
and the confused. The division, moreover, could not have been throughout the period a simple one of gentlemen versus merchants, since well
before 1750 there were several fine gentlemen who were merchants and
as many merchants who considered themselves fine gentlemen. And
political combatants, as is their wont, routinely shifted sides. Defoe,
the famous example, could write for one side, then the other, and later
for both at once. He could—and in fact did—write a fiery pamphlet in
October refuting a fiery pamphlet he had published in July. With John
Trenchard, Thomas Gordon produced the scathing *Cato's Letters;* yet
about 1724 he accepted a place from Walpole and thereafter became
foremost government writer. Journeying in the other direction was the

Earl of Bath, William Pulteney. After breaking with Walpole over a position in the ministry, he joined the Opposition and produced some of its more effective pieces of polemic. Such examples are too extreme to represent the ordinary Englishman, but they do reveal the danger of interpreting character entirely through politics. The issues of a great debate can remain consistent, but most human participants cannot.

STAGES IN THE ATTACK

Despite such complications, the bases of the attack upon luxury through 1763 are relatively clear. The upholders of traditional privilege sought first to remind England of the Law known from antiquity that set limits upon what most men *may* do by defining the limits of what they *can* do, and which condemned categorically all forms of luxury. From that law they deduced their own status as guardians and legislators, the embodiment of the law and its interpreters. They argued that the very essence of English nationhood was endangered and represented the immediate field of moral testing—challenging legislators and subjects alike to unite in the effort to reestablish the natural order of virtue. The new moneyed men and their many imitators, they held, were at best rebels acting out of pride and greed and falsely claiming privileges to which they had no right; at worst these men were tempters, witting or unwitting agents of infernal destruction. The series of crises and disruptions the nation had undergone since the previous century they viewed as decisive instances of the punishment that follows violation of the law. Conflict was implicit in each of these positions, for few of their opponents—their reluctance to defend luxury notwithstanding—were willing to grant their title to dominion, far less all of their premises. The ensuing controversy appears to have followed the political temperature in England. During relatively normal times, there issued a seemingly constant flow of attacks upon luxury, usually along familiar moral and religious lines; in 1794 two pamphlets were published each of which asserted it would deliver the final answer to Mandeville. This constant base was increased and aggravated whenever political emotions grew fevered, and at least five phases or periods of aggravation can be distinguished. The earliest occurred about 1698–1702 during the Court and Country debates over a standing army. The next is represented by the last four years of the reign of Queen Anne, when Whig fought Tory over the direction of government policy. Responses to Mandeville and the South Sea Bubble of 1720 dominated the third; a few were elicited by "The Grumbling Hive" of 1705, most to editions of the *Fable of the Bees* of 1714, 1723, and 1728. During the latter 1720s and 1730s the

terms of the debate were widened with the superaddition of Tory
theories of history and politics to older criticism of luxury. Luxury here
became a weapon in the serious paper battles against Walpole and his
supporters, and a banner of attack for the Opposition. In the final
phase, from about 1750 to 1763, the controversy widened once more
to include a concerted attack upon the habits of the laboring poor.
During this last stage, in which Smollett was a prominent figure, previous arguments against luxury flowed together and raised the tide of
condemnation to its highest crest in English history.

The first period centered on the writings of a group of men—John
Toland, John Trenchard, Walter Moyle, Andrew Fletcher, and Charles
Davenant—often referred to as the Commonwealthmen.[14] Their resistance to a permanent army was the manifestation of a larger reaction
against the drift of English politics. Luxury, not patriotism, was guiding
public affairs, they feared, and the result was a loss of moral and political stability. In his *Discourse of Government with Relation to Militias*
(1698), Fletcher asserted that nothing of the old order remained except
"the ancient Terms and outward Forms," and that "the generality of
all Ranks of Men are cheated by Words and Names" (p. 5). He perceived luxury besetting Europe in strength about the time of the Renaissance, in the wake of the new learning, new inventions, new wealth, and
new trade. As Pocock has shown, he opposed a standing army and the
new version of patriotism it represented because he saw a substitution
of money values for feudal duty. The men of this latter kind of army
were not faithful vassals rallying to their lord's call, but mercenaries
whose services had been purchased. Where once service was owed, now
it was bought, and all essential elements of life were measured by
monetary value.

> By this means the Luxury of Asia and America was added to that
> of the Antients; and all Ages, and all Countries concurred to sink
> Europe into an Abyss of Pleasures; which were rendered the more
> expensive by a perpetual Change of the Fashions in Clothes, Equi-
> page and Furniture of Houses.
>
> These things brought a total Alteration to the way of living,
> upon which all Government depends. 'Tis true, Knowledg being
> mightily increased, and a great Curiosity and Nicety in every thing
> introduced, Men imagined themselves to be gainers in all points,
> by changing from their frugal and military way of living, which I
> must confess had some mixture of Rudeness and Ignorance in it,
> tho not inseparable from it. But at the same time they did not
> consider the unspeakable Evils that are altogether inseparable from
> an expensive way of living. [Pp. 12-13]

By expensive way of living, Fletcher means one absorbed with money and its concomitant values. By unspeakable evils, he means the loss of station and function, of the social harmony implicit in the ancient order. By frugality, he means the absence of choice, the coincidence of duty and station. Now luxury has enabled many men to choose what they would do; if they would not fight, they can hire others to take their places. The innovations of luxury have weakened the warrior quality of subjects and legislators equally.

Fletcher was alarmed over the physical and psychological corruption the financing of war produced. Davenant was appalled by the new breed of men who did the financing, men "whom peace would have left in their original obscurity, in troublesome times shine forth; but they are like portentous meteors, threatening ruin to the country that is under their malevolent aspect."[15] In his *Discourse on the Public Revenue and on the Trade of England* (1698), Davenant held that as it had corrupted Rome, so luxury was corrupting England. Everyone was money-grubbing, and the worst were merely those grubbing the most. Not only did the bankers, stockjobbers, and moneyed companies control the destiny of the nation during war, they also sucked it dry during peace. *The True Picture of a Modern Whig* (1702) is his portrait in dialogue of the projectors and financiers who care only about cash. Tom Double, spokesman for the modern Whigs, boasts that in 1688 he was shoeless, but after fourteen years as a stockjobber is worth £50,000. To anyone attracted to his party, he is ready with counsel: "In general, detract from and asperse all the men of quality of whom there is any appearance that either their high birth, or their great fortunes, or their abilities in matters of government should recommend them to the future administration of affairs. . . . It is our interest to humble the ancient gentry because they know our originals and call us upstarts and leeches that are swollen big by sucking up the nation's blood" (4:179). Davenant gives plain statement of the source of England's ills in the *Essay upon the Probable Methods of Making a People Gainers in the Balance of Trade* (1699):

> Trade, without doubt, is in its nature a pernicious thing; it brings in that wealth which introduces luxury; it gives rise to fraud and avarice, and extinguishes virtue and simplicity of manners; it depraves a people, and makes way for that corruption which never fails to end in slavery, foreign or domestic. Lycurgus, in the most perfect model of government that was ever framed, did banish it from his commonwealth. But, the posture and condition of other countries considered, it is become with us a necessary evil. We shall be continually exposed to insults and invasions, without

such a naval force as is not to be had naturally but where there is an extended traffic. However, if trade cannot be made subservient to the nation's safety, it ought to be no more encouraged here than it was in Sparta. [2:275]

The next period serves in part to demonstrate the vitality of classical attitudes toward luxury. From 1711 to 1714, the *Spectator* commented upon luxury a half-dozen times or so, suggesting that the vice did not loom so large to writers of Whiggish bent. Taken together, they provide useful contrasts in tone to the acrid polemics of Tory and Country journalists, for all are written with a temperate reasonableness spiced with wit. Addison's no. 55 is the earliest, longest, and most important, offering a fable of modern times in which Luxury and Avarice, once enemies, now unite to despoil the world. Quoting Persius and Sallust, he asserts that luxury was responsible for the demise of Rome and could devastate Britain. In nos. 260 and 294, Steele calls luxury a harking after fashion, the chief way the wealthy waste their money. Budgell, in no. 331, asks sardonically if the growing of beards will not become another fashion to advance the luxury of the times. Steele returns to satire in no. 478, arguing that tradesmen favor luxury because it and all other forms of folly increase their business. Finally, in no. 574, Addison declares that, contrary to ordinary thinking, luxury cannot bring happiness. Persons who succumb to its temptations are victims of artificial wants and, unable to satisfy themselves, are in a continuing state of artificial poverty.

Direct responses to Mandeville were mainly of two kinds. More learned writers like John Dennis and William Law reiterated Platonic and Stoic ideas. Law's riposte, founded on the necessity for reason and order, is contained in *Remarks upon a Late Book, Entituled the Fable of the Bees* (1724). In *Vice and Luxury Publick Mischiefs* (1724), Dennis finds luxury threatening on grounds of both fact and reason. He finds the evidence incontrovertible that the vice was responsible for the falls of Sparta and Rome and for the present exorbitant size of the English national debt. Passion and vanity are the sources of luxury, and these must be quelled or all civil order will be lost: "Reason will approve of just so much of them [dress, furnishings, housing] as is requisite for the Distinction of Rank, and the keeping up of that Subordination, which is absolutely necessary to Government" (p. 54). Again, "Where Luxury once prevails and becomes habitual, the Passions have entirely got the upper Hand of Reason, have banished all consideration, and ruin'd all Oeconomy" (p. 73). Unlike Law and Dennis, however, most of Mandeville's adversaries did not sense the existence of a genuine intellectual issue. Pope's reply appears, in effect, in the "Epistle to Bathurst":

What Nature wants (a phrase I much mistrust)
Extends to Luxury, extends to Lust:
And if we count among the Needs of life
Another's Toil, why not another's Wife?   [11.25-28]

Instead they saw an outrageous threat to the normal order of things.
Representative of many such replies is George Blewitt's *An Enquiry
whether a General Practice of Virtue tends to the Wealth or Poverty,
Benefit, or Disadvantage of a People?* (1725):

> The Dearness of Labour of all sorts, the Largeness of Wages and
> other Perquisites of Servants, their Idleness and insolence are all
> the effects of Luxury; of which . . . though the Example arise
> among idle Persons, yet the Imitation is run into all Degrees, even
> of those Men by whose Industry the Nation subsists. To this we
> owe the Scarcity of Servants where they are *really* wanted; and
> from hence arises the prodigious loss to the Publick, that Draught
> of lusty and able-bodied men from Husbandry or Country Busi-
> ness, to add to the magnificence of Equipages: *A sort of idle and
> rioting Vermin, by which* (we are told) *the Kingdom is almost
> devoured, and which are everywhere become a public nuisance.*
> [P. 208]

From Mandeville's point of view, the received notion of luxury
amounted to an intellectual cliché, the bogeyman of the educated. It
had retained the pattern and weight of great menace, but not the
substance; it was an anomaly, like an old toad that lives on though
buried under a stone. Thoughtful men at least should not regard it
seriously, he argued. Mandeville and his critics did share one piece of
common ground: luxury definitely was useful as a generalized theory
of history. The distinctive use of the concept during the 1730s, however, is as a *specialized* theory of contemporary English history. Reviewing events of the past half-century, various writers of Tory inclination
reported finding in luxury the source of a nefarious process that had
robbed them and their patrons of their accustomed rank, power, and
privilege. In sermon and treatise, broadside and history, they elaborated
a series of indictments against the men who had profited from the
events of 1688, especially those who were without birth, breeding,
formal education, or history of family involvement in government. In
the Glorious Revolution, they attempted to demonstrate a sharp break
in the continuity of English history, a devolution from the high
standards of Old England, a subversion of the English constitution, and
a deterioration in the quality of English life and art. In the new Whigs
and the moneyed interest, they sought to expose a group guilty of the
rankest usurpation and insubordination.

For more than a generation, writers articulating either the gentry position or the somewhat narrower one of the Opposition held that the course of contemporary English history was precisely that foretold by countless ancient philosophers. They wished, as Pocock has said, to subsume particular modern events under the vocabulary of the ancients. The workings of luxury they saw as congruent with the movement of history. The sense of decline explicit in such identification accurately reflected the disconsolate temper of the times. A progressive theory of history was available through continental—particularly French—writers, yet it could have little appeal for men who felt acute grievance. To such men only two conceptions of history could possibly accommodate their experiences: one of cumulative deterioration, the other of cyclic rise and fall. Luxury fitted both. When considering the past, furthermore, Whig and Tory alike were searching for practical lessons in ethics and politics, and once again luxury provided specific examples. One of Bolingbroke's central theories concerned the pragmatic uses to which historical writing and thinking should be put, as a guide to political and ethical truth. In the eight letters of the *Study and Use of History* (1735–36), he disdains the erudition of the annalistic tradition, proposing instead the drawing of "political maps." As an example of the kind of writing he favors, he includes a sketch of European history from about 1500, which incidentally vindicates by reference to "general laws" Tory principles and his own career.[16]

On the professional level, this view is represented by Smollett's histories, written largely amid the slough of despond stimulated by the unsuccessful early stages of the Seven Years' War and by Gibbon's preoccupation with the dismemberment of Rome. Popularly, it can be seen in numerous pamphlets even before the 1730s, especially those condemning the War of the Spanish Succession and the South Sea Bubble. An anonymous work published the year after the Bubble, *An Essay Towards Preventing the Ruin of Great Britain* (1721), blames the spread of luxury for the debacle and possesses the tone of angry despair Smollett was to recreate in his histories. The author calls the Bubble a visitation from God, a lesson intended to show the fatal effects of the nation's luxury, corruption, and folly. National reformation is necessary; religion, industry, subordination, public spirit, and patriotism must be reinstated in men's hearts. England could regain genuine wealth and prosperity only through the natural and traditional means of agriculture and trade. It could never be regained through the public gaming table where "money is shifted from hand to hand in such a blind fortuitous manner, that some men shall from nothing in an instant acquire vast estates with the least desert; while others are as suddenly stript of plentiful fortunes" (p. 5). While luxury is the natural cause of national decay and ruin, national and personal virtue is the strength and sustenance of the body politic. The lessons of Rome are going unattended, and the English are rapidly becoming corrupt and impotent, drowning in luxury. All persons in the kingdom have been tainted with the corruption; so all persons must renounce their obsession with private interest.

> The south sea affair is not the original evil or the greatest source of our misfortune; it is but the natural effect of these principles which for many years have been propagated with great industry. And as a sharp distemper by reclaiming a man from intemperance may prolong his life, so it is not improbable but this public calamity that lieth so heavy on the nation may prevent its ruin . . . if it should turn our thought from cousenage and stock-jobbing to industry and frugal methods of life; in fine if it should revive and inflame that native spark of British worth and honor which hath too long lain smothered and oppressed. [P. 25]

The fourth great wave of protest against luxury took place between approximately 1726 and 1742, terminal dates that coincide with Bolingbroke's return to active engagement in politics (and the founding of the *Craftsman*) and Walpole's resignation. In the emphasis upon luxury as a divisive political issue, Bolingbroke is apparently the foremost figure—as theorist, financier, and spokesman for the opposition to Walpole.[17] And although it was not used massively until the later 1720s—compare a tract by Fletcher or Davenant with a number of the *Craftsman*—this highly polemical interpretation of the concept probably had its source in the violently partisan strife between Whig and Tory earlier in the century, between 1710 and 1714. These bitter years were the seedtime not only of Bolingbroke's theories but also of Tory attitudes toward expansionist wars—attitudes voiced most persistently later by Tobias Smollett.

The Tory government led by Harley and Bolingbroke, which ruled between the Sacheverell incident and the death of Anne, had two principal goals: destruction of its opposition and conclusion of the war with France. For Harley and Bolingbroke, the objectives of the war had been already achieved in the containment of Louis's power in the Netherlands and Italy. But for the Whigs, the Dutch, and the Duke of Marlborough, the war would have to be continued until the French were driven totally out of Spain. In order to discredit the Whigs and "their war," the government launched a vast paper war which sought to make three points: that the war enriched only the moneyed interest and proportionately drained the landed interest; that England had already contributed enough to a continental campaign that benefited only the

Dutch and the Austrian emperor; and that Marlborough and other leaders of the Whigs had made fortunes by corrupt management of war moneys. These were the themes Swift sounded in the *Examiner* and in his highly successful *Conduct of the Allies* (1711). In the latter he wrote: "We have been fighting to raise the Wealth and Grandeur of a private Family [Marlborough's]; to enrich Usurers and Stock-jobbers; and to cultivate the pernicious Designs of a faction by destroying the Landed-Interest." Names changed, these are the staple arguments and phrases Smollett used against the City in the years 1756–63.

Enveloping the specific goal obtained in the Treaty of Utrecht, however, was a deeper complex of Tory grievances. The Glorious Revolution had been only the visible beginning of change. The Revolution Settlement, to the extent that it reconciled Anglican and Purtian, Tory and Whig, to that same extent compromised the material and political interests of traditional high Tories. The Act of Settlement of 1701 then settled the reversion of the English crown upon the Protestant Electress of Hanover and her children, jettisoning Tory claims of divine right and hereditary succession. Opposition to the war with France was therefore merely one sign of that mixture of fear and anger with which Tories regarded "the Modern Whigs." There was the Whig lust for commerce: expansion, inventions, new manufacturers, new trading centers, the movement of economic and political power from the land to the cities. Then there was the new financial order erected to support commerce: land taxes, national debt, stockjobbing, moneyed corporations, foreign alliances, the Bank of England, and the East India Company. All of this and more convinced the Tories that the traditional structure of Old England—the structure that had upheld them for so long—was being undermined. In his open Letter to Sir William Windham, written in 1717, Bolingbroke reflected upon the political campaign begun in 1710:

> We looked on the political principles which had generally prevailed in our government from the Revolution in 1688 to be destructive of our true interest, to have mingled us too much in the affairs of the continent, to tend to the impoverishing of our people, and to the loosening of the bonds of our constitution in church and state. We supposed the Tory party to be the bulk of the landed interest, and to have no contrary influence blended into its composition. We supposed the Whigs ... to lean for support on the presbyterians and other sectarians, on the bank and the other corporations, on the Dutch and the other alllies.[18]

The most vexing characteristic of the new moneyed middle class was its social inferiority. As Swift wrote in the *Examiner* for 2 November 1710: "Let any man observe the equipages in this town, he shall find the greatest number of those who make a figure, to be a species of men quite different from any that were even known before the Revolution."[19] The most dangerous was its growing influence in Parliament, and both Country and Court deplored its concomitant financial and political prosperity. While the landed gentry carried the full weight of national expense, Bolingbroke wrote, the moneyed men reaped huge profits but "contributed not one bit to its charge." (This is another accusation reiterated by Smollett in his polemical writings and by Bramble in his first letter from Bath.)

The complex of conservative attitudes evoked by the events of 1710–14 and provoked afresh by the Hanoverian Succession lay behind what has been termed the gloom of the Tory satirists. It also informs much of the power of the *Dunciad,* the *Beggar's Opera,* and *Gulliver's Travels.* Part 3 of Swift's masterpiece, published in 1726, is a valuable guide and bridge to both periods of Tory polemics, reflecting the atmosphere of 1710–14 and anticipating the issues of the 1730s. Chapter 8 of the voyage to Laputa and other places makes three charges that would be developed at length in the pages of the *Craftsman.* First, Gulliver remarks upon the *recent* introduction of luxury into England, a comment cast in the form of an observation upon Roman history: "I was surprized to find Corruption grown so high and so quick in that Empire, by the Force of Luxury so lately introduced."[20] Second, Gulliver voices his rejection of events of the recent past and of the writing of history, concluding with a thinly veiled reference to the revolution of 1688:

> I was chiefly disgusted with modern History. For having strictly examined all the Persons of greatest Name in the Courts of Princes for an Hundred Years past, I found how the World had been misled by prostitute Writers, to ascribe the greatest Exploits in War to Cowards, the wisest Counsel to Fools, Sincerity to Flatterers, Roman Virtue to Betrayers of their Country, Piety to Atheists, Chastity to Sodomites, Truth to Informers. How many innocent and excellent Persons had been condemned to Death or Banishment, by the practising of great Ministers upon the Corruption of Judges, and the Malice of Factions. How many Villains had been exalted to the highest Places of Trust, Power, Dignity, and Profit: How great a Share in the Motions and Events of Courts, Councils, and Senates might be challenged by Bawds, Whores, Pimps, Parasites, and Buffoons: How low an Opinion I had of Human Wisdom and Integrity, when I was truly informed of the Springs and Motives of great Enterprizes and Revolutions in the World, and of the contemptible Accidents to which they owed their Success.

Third, Gulliver expresses acceptance of the degenerative theory of history, finding occasion for "melancholy Reflections" upon "how much the Race of human Kind was degenerate among us, within these Hundred Years past." Luxury and corruption had altered the English countenance, shortened physiques, "unbraced the Nerves, relaxed the Sinews and Muscles, introduced a sallow Complexion, and rendered the Flesh loose and rancid." Surrounded by degeneration, Gulliver yearns for a return to simple, virtuous Old England:

> I descended so low as to desire that some *English* Yeomen of the Old Stamp, might be summoned to appear; once so famous for the Simplicity of their Manners, Dyet and Dress; for Justice in their Dealings; for their true Spirit of Liberty; for their Valour and Love of their Country. Neither could I be wholly unmoved after comparing the Living with the Dead, when I considered how all these pure native Virtues were prostituted for a Piece of Money by their Grand-children; who in selling their Votes, and managing at elections have acquired every Vice and Corruption that can possibly be learned in a Court.

In chapter 10 the point is underscored, Gulliver noting "the several Gradations by which Corruption steals into the World" and the "continual Degeneracy of human Nature so justly complained of in all Ages."[21]

For the Opposition, the special utility of the concept of luxury was to explain not so much how they fell as how the unworthy Whigs rose. In this respect Bolingbroke and his group offer an elaboration of the arguments of 1698–1702 and lay the immediate ground for those of the 1750s. From the earliest essays of the *Craftsman*, the coalition of "Patriots" made prosecution of luxury the paper's predominant philosophical theme, uncovering the vice nearly everywhere and insisting upon the foreboding parallel with Rome. The ideal polity for the Opposition was largely what it was for Aristotle and Cicero: a derivation of the natural, traditional social order, where the masters of the land are the masters of the nation. In a "genuine" polity—as opposed to the "bastard" polity of contemporary England—Bolingbroke finds the emblem of "a free people" in the patriarchal family, where all values are set by the father. Birth, rank, and independence are the marks of the natural legislator—"Men of the *highest Dignity,* the *most acknowledg'd Wisdom,* and *try'd Integrity,*" in Pulteney's words—without which the civil polity is inevitably debased and unnatural.[22] Bolingbroke distinguishes between "subjects" and "tutors and guardians"; between "the multitude designed to obey, and . . . the few designed to govern." Since the design in question is both divine and natural, the *Craftsman* is a clarion call to all genuine leaders. In its number for 10 January 1730 appears a representative exhortation:

> As for you, *Gentlemen,* who are possessed of *large Estates* and a *natural Interest* in the Counties, where you live, I think there can be no Occasion for many Arguments to excite you to a Conduct, which is now happily become both your *Duty* and your *Interest.* Whatever Attachments you may have to *this* or *that Party;* whatever Engagments you may be under to *particular Men;* or by whatever *Names* you may distinguish your selves; you will certainly unite, as one Man, in this common Cause, and support each other against the Incroachments of *Stock-jobbers,* or *beggarly Tools of Power,* who are sent amongst you, without any Recommendation of Merit or Virtue, to supplant you in the Esteem of your Tenants, Neighbours and Dependants; and to get themselves chosen, by indirect Means, as well as for vile Purposes, to be your *Representatives.* [No. 184, 6:10-11][23]

Under its natural leaders, England would regain its inherent unity and rid itself of factious diversity. Calling luxury the *fons et origo mali,* Bolingbroke identified it as the root source of individual corruption and the original sin of nations; money, he wrote, had become "a more lasting tie than honour, friendship, consanguinity, or unity of affections."[24] Division into parties was a visible sign that personal gain had replaced national interest and that individual independence was no longer valued. To him, as earlier to Shaftesbury and later to Smollett, the model politician was an independent country gentleman drawing his virtue and freedom from the land, wise enough to join other natural legislators in ruling the nation, brave enough to resist tyrannical crown or executive. To Walpole, on the other hand, the ideal politician was a sycophant. Quoting *Cato's Letters* the *Craftsman* frequently advised, "Forget . . . the foolish and knavish Distinction of *High-Church* and *Low-Church,* of *Whig* and *Tory;* Sounds, which continue in your Mouths, when the *Meaning* of them is gone, and are now only used to set you together by the Ears, that Rogues may pick your Pockets." Wedded to such counsels were arguments over place bills and demands for new sumptuary laws.[25]

With ancient history as his text, Bolingbroke could foresee only disaster for Britain. When Sparta, Athens, and Rome fell under the spell of mean men, they lost all capacity for virtue and public valor. As they fell, so "will the people of Britain fall, and deserve to fall." The present situation was indeed more serious, for superimposed upon ancient luxury were the monsters introduced with the financial revolution—the national debt, stockjobbing, and moneyed companies—simultaneously instances of luxury and constant temptations to new forms of corruption. For the Opposition the model of economic polity was the great estate; it followed that such an unholy trinity would ruin the nation. No estate could withstand a huge debt, a division of management, and a piecemeal parceling out of ownership.[26] As the alleged panderer of impending catastrophe, Walpole was the Lucifer of Bolingbroke's demonology. He was seen as guilty of two types of political crime. On the one hand, he was supposed cynically and resolutely to have subverted English morals in order to achieve his personal aggrandizement. To this end he, like Mandeville, called luxury useful and perhaps necessary. On the other hand, he was seen as the progenitor of faction, selfishness, and insubordination, forces that were now remolding English society. To the Opposition the most bitter proof of Walpole's venality was that he had given a voice in public affairs to men "whose talents would scarce have recommended them to the meanest offices in the virtuous and prosperous ages of the commonwealth," men "who had not, either from their obscure birth, or their low talents, or their still lower habits, the least occasion ever to dream of such elevation."[27]

Like Fletcher and Davenant a generation earlier, Bolingbroke was convinced that England was depraved beyond redemption. With luxury the reigning standard, the arts and the professions could only lapse into dullness and stupidity; wit, learning, good sense, and public spirit declined together. The *Idea of a Patriot King* was to be his political testament, providing his catalog of the forms of luxury obtaining in the nation and his final prescription for unity and reform: rule by a single great man who stood above all divisions and differences. This, his ultimate statement that legislators were now hopelessly divided, cited Cato, Sallust and the Roman historians, and Machiavelli to demonstrate that when luxury cannot be abated by normal means, only the great man can uphold the general welfare.

Bolingbroke's political despair was to be echoed frequently during the 1750s, and the similarities between Opposition and later attacks upon luxury are many. Both identify the issue as economic and political. Both locate a historical watershed in the recent past. Both contrast the older virtuous order of birth with the newer degenerate values of an order dominated by money. Both assert the death of patriotism and public spirit and the omnivorous vitality of riot, faction, self-interest, and insubordination. Both declare the corruption of most politicians and call for some form of moral rearmament. Both are deeply pessimistic about the future of Britain. The main distinction lies in the broad scope of later attacks. In the 1750s and 1760s writers included both the middle and lower orders in their campaigns against the vice. Bolingbroke earlier concentrated his hostility upon his immediate political opponents, the wealthy Whigs and their mercantile supporters. Toward the lower orders he seems a benevolent patron, writing in the "Fragments, or Minutes of Essays" that for the masses luxury could prove a benefit. If defined as added comforts of life, he writes, luxury would be valuable to the majority of men, as an increase in the amount of "physical good" possessed by mankind. When he wrote of the corruption of luxury, he was referring to the comparatively limited condition: the influence upon public affairs of new men and new money.

> That luxury, which began to spread after the restoration of king Charles the second, hath increased ever since; hath descended from the highest to the lowest ranks of our people, and is become national. Now nothing can be more certain than this, that national luxury and national poverty may, in time, establish national prostitution. Beside this, it is to be considered, that the immense wealth of particular men is a circumstance which always attends national poverty, and is in a great measure the cause of it. . . . Now, as publick want, or general poverty, for in that sense I take it here, will lay numbers of men open to the attacks of corruption; so private wealth will have the same effect, especially where luxury prevails, on some of those who do not feel the public want; for there is imaginary as well as real poverty. He who thought himself rich before, may begin to think himself poor, when he compares his wealth . . . with those men he hath been used to esteem . . . far inferiour to himself. . . . Thus may contraries unite in their effect, and poverty and wealth combine to facilitate the means and the progress of corruption.[28]

Although the partisan controversy over luxury appears to have abated immediately upon Walpole's fall, the campaign waged by the Opposition had made an indelible impression upon the minds of many Englishmen. Attacks upon luxury would continue to grow for at least another generation, and the Opposition version of that attack would be absorbed into the body of older criticism. Hence, by the middle of the century the condemnation of luxury was practically unanimous among the traditionally privileged groups of England. While such opposition did little to define one's position, it did signify one's quarrel with the present age. It therefore appealed to very disparate persons: Jacobites, Tories, political "outs" of many varieties; Catholics and Puritans; monarchists, primitivists, and classicists; philosophers, moralists, and ecclesiastics; pessimists and malcontents; those who had lost rank and fortune and those who had rank and fortune to lose. Even so generous a man as Henry Fielding found cause in 1749, in *A Charge delivered to the Grand Jury . . . of Westminster,* to exclaim: "The fury after licentious and luxurious pleasures is grown to so great a height, that it may be called the characteristic of the present age." What is distinctive in the polemics of the period is, as Samuel Johnson saw, the new animus directed against the English poor. Surveying this last and most relevant period in the controversy over luxury, the immediate context of Smollett's own writings, one notices not so much the voice of argument as the cacophony of curse and threat. Whatever their political stripe, eighteenth-century legislators were largely united in a policy of firm control over labor—an element of national well-being thought to be as essential as control of the prices and quantities of goods. Domestic social and economic policy could thus be subsumed under the attack upon luxury, combating idleness, mobility, insolence, and prosperity among the common people. Population could be considered the source of national wealth only if it was productively and profitably employed, with the definitions of *profit* and *productivity* left to employers. Many writers earlier in the century had identified the luxury of the poor with idleness. Some cited the notion of the utility of poverty to demonstrate that any wage above bare subsistence, even in times of abundance, was a contribution to luxury. Some, like Defoe in *The Great Law of Sub-ordination Consider'd* (1724), complained that the habits of the rich had corrupted the poor by making them discontent. Some, like William Wood, used all three ideas: "where riot and luxuries are not discountenanc'd, the inferior rank of men, become presently infected, and grow lazy, effeminate, impatient of labour, and expensive, and consequently cannot thrive by trade, tillage, and planting."[29] There was a liberal contribution to this argument, but a weak one. When certain writers held that luxury invariably reduced population, increased unemployment, raised the price of food, and ruined poor families, they presumed to be speaking for the national interest and not for special privilege. Yet they could summon no conclusive empirical corroboration for their position, and later evidence, like the census of 1801, found it untenable or misleading. Studies of sumptuary and related laws, it should be recalled, record thousands of warnings, arrests, and convictions during the seventeenth and eighteenth centuries in England. But not one, so far as I can discover, was directed against a person of noble or gentle birth. As Adam Smith noted, many writers could grant freedom and prosperity to England only by denying them to Englishmen.

What is clear is that during the 1750s and early 1760s fear and anxiety brought forth by national and international conflicts nourished the conventional criticism of luxury. Rising crime, grain riots, and general increases in the price of staples were among the social and economic factors that gave fresh impetus to the pamphlet-writers. Upon the outbreak of war at mid-decade, writers found additional grounds for alarm, lest luxury should drain national resources and hasten national defeat. Fielding's *Enquiry into the Cause of the late Increase of Robbers* (1751) is significant in this context, for it reveals the extent to which the Opposition's method of social analysis had become normal. As journalist and as magistrate, Fielding had seen closely the miseries and dislocations of the city; the experience led him to make luxury the major premise in his attack upon the effects of social change.

His starting point is economic:

> nothing hath wrought such an Alteration in this [the lower] Order of People, as the Introduction of Trade. This hath indeed given a new Face to the whole Nation, hath in great measure subverted the former State of Affairs, and hath almost totally changed the Manners, Customs, and Habits of the People, more especially of the lower Sort. The Narrowness of their Fortune is changed into Wealth; the Simplicity of their Manners changed into Craft, their Frugality into Luxury, their Humility into Pride, and their Subjugation into Equality. [P. xi]

His principal argument is that luxury, not poverty, is the immediate cause of crime among the poor:

> I think that the vast Torrent of Luxury which the late Years hath poured itself into this Nation, hath greatly contributed to produce among many others, the Mischief I here complain of. I aim not here to satirize the Great, among whom Luxury is probably rather a moral than a political Evil. But Vices, no more than Diseases will stop with them . . . in free Countries, at least, it is a Brand of Liberty claimed by the People to be as wicked and as profligate as their Supperiors. . . . It reaches the very Dregs of the People, who aspiring still to a Degree beyond that which belongs to them, and not being able by the Fruits of honest Labour to support the State which they affect, they disdain the Wages to which their Industry would entitle them; and abandoning themselves to Idleness, the more simple and poor spirited betake themselves to a State of Starving and Beggary, while those of more Art and Courage become Thieves, Sharpers and Robbers. [P. 3]

Like Smollett, Fielding senses a dangerous insubordination among the "Dregs of the People" and urges, as a short-run measure, their exclusion from all places of amusement—a proposal Smollett repeated. For the longer range he seeks to establish "How far it is the Business of the Politicians to interfere in the Case of Luxury." He recommends two types of action, both involving sumptuary laws. The first and more important is legislative, "effectively to put a Stop to the Luxury of the lower People, to force the Poor to Industry, and to provide for them when industrious" (p. 126). The second is judicial, the rigorous and universal application of comprehensive laws.[30] His half-brother, John, seconded his call for strong laws to combat dissipation:

> Time is the Labourer's Stock in Trade; and he that makes the Most of it by Industry and Application is a valuable subject. A Journeyman can no more afford to give or throw away his Time than a Tradesman can his Commodity; and the best Way of preventing this useful Body of Men from this species of Extravagance is to remove from their Sight all Temptation to idleness: and however Diversions may be necessary to fill up the dismal Chasms of burdensome Time among People of Fortune, too frequent Relaxations of this Kind among the Populace enervate Industry.[31]

The interrelationship of luxury, population, and labor was among the common topics of political and economic works. Josiah Tucker, in *Reflections on the Expediency of a Law for the Naturalization of Foreign Protestants* (Bristol, 1751), asks rhetorically: "Was a Country *thinly* populated ever rich?—Was a populous Country ever *poor*?" (p. 19). His negative answer is supported by William Horsley in *The Universal Merchant* (1753), which argues that the ideal laborer for the British economy is a poor man with a very large family: "Herein consists the Marrow of that Maxim, *that Numbers of People are the Wealth of a Nation:* as where they are plenty, they must work cheap, and so Manufacturers are encouraged for a foreign Market, and their Returns is a Wealth of a Nation, which numbers thus procure."[32] Since it threatened to eliminate large families, luxury was attacked as a menace to the whole nation. The presumed decline in national spirit appeared all the more dangerous with the outbreak of war. Among the many alarmist pamphlets published within a few months was the anonymous *The Parallel; or, The Conduct and Fate of Great Britain in regard our present Contest with France; exemplified from the Histories of Macedon and Athens* (1756). Reviewers drew the same point from Thomas Leland's translation of *All the Orations of Demosthenes* (1756). They held luxury the primary cause of Athenian defeat and selected from Leland extracts that seemed to support their charge.[33] The urgent need for discipline and a rejection of luxury were central to Francis Fauquier's *Essay on Ways and Means for Raising money for the Support of the Present War without increasing the Publick Debt* (1756) and the anonymous *The True National Evil* (1756). The latter, a sermon, used as its text a paraphrase of a line from the seventh chapter of Joshua: "There is an accursed thing in the midst of thee, O Britons." In the anonymous *Trial of the lady Allured Luxury* (1757), the *lady* is a notorious foreign spy, convicted of every charge brought against her, who is rescued by the fools and knaves of England.

Insofar as the ferment over domestic and foreign problems could be epitomized in a single work, the work would be John Brown's *Estimate of the Manners and Principles of the Times,* the first volume of which appeared in 1757. The *Estimate* is basically a bill of indictment against the English people, particularly the commercial classes, and supplies a catalogue raisonné of the evils of luxury. In this respect it follows a pattern familiar after Bolingbroke, but it is more concise and more concrete than anything done by him. It was also one of the most popular works of the decade, the first volume running through seven authorized and pirated editions in the first year, far surpassing any comparable work and calling forth an extraordinary response from correspondents and reviewers in the periodicals.

What immediately distinguished the content of the *Estimate* from dozens of other works of the fifties was the breadth and particularity of Brown's indictment. Where other writers had railed in abstruse or historical terms, Brown offers pungent details and contemporary names. He laments that the inconsequential essays of Hume are preferred to the substantial achievements of Bolingbroke and Warburton. Opera and pantomime have driven Shakespeare off the boards. Military officers, politicians, and clergymen all neglect their high callings in favor of self-gain. Cowardice, hypochondria, and suicide are but various symptoms of the same national disease of luxury. In the current period of crisis only a total reformation will preserve the nation. Honor, religion, public spirit, and renunciation of self-interest must be returned to their traditional places in English life. Otherwise the disciplined French will overrun the plains of Salisbury as they have overrun the plains of America.[34]

For the evils of his age, Brown blames the *new* commercial interests, as ominously novel to Brown in 1757 as they had been to Bolingbroke in 1710 and Davenant in 1698. He writes, "The spirit of Commerce, now predominant, begets a kind of regulated Selfishness, which tends at once to the Increase and Preservation of Property" (1:22). And, "the Spirit of Trade in its Excess, by introducing Avarice, destroys the Desire of *Rational Esteem*" (1:173). Since the interplay of economic forces must not be left to determine British affairs, firm moral and political regulation is required. Increased wealth at this stage brings not order, but "superfluity, avarice, effeminate refinement, and loss of principle" (1:157-58, 195-96).

It was from a vantage very similar to this that Smollett judged the effects of economic change. He certainly concurred with Brown's estimate of the weakness of human nature: "Humanity neither improved nor controlled, is always defective and partial; and may be very dangerous in its effects" (2:38). For both men the source of a "National Spirit of Union" lay in a strong monarchy, Brown claiming that strength and unity are to be gained most easily in absolute monarchies. In "free Countries," unity is continually threatened by selfishness, faction, and "Freedom of *Opinion* itself" (1:105). Like Smollett, he saw the liberty of the press outrageously abused. For its critical short-range exigencies, Britain needed government by an elite, "whose Superiority is approved and acknowledged . . . who have been so unfashionable as to despise the ruling System of Effeminacy: and [who have] *laboured* and *shone* in a College" (1:77).[35]

Again like Smollett, Brown has no high regard for the common people:

> the Manners and Principles of the common People will scarce find a Place in the Account. For though the Sum total of a Nations immediate Happiness must arise, and be estimate, from the Manners and Principles of the Whole; yet the Manners and Principles of those who *lead,* not of those who *are led;* of those who *govern,* not of those who are governed; of those, in short, who *make* Laws or execute them, will ever determine the Strength or Weakness, and therefore the Continuance or Dissolution, of a State.
>
> For the blind Force or Weight of an ungoverned Multitude can have no steady nor rational Effect, unless some *leading Mind* rouse it into Action, and point it to it's proper *End:* without this, it is either a *brute* and random Bolt, or a *lifeless Ball* sleeping in the *Cannon:* It depends on some superior *Intelligence,* to give it both *Impulse* and *Direction.* [1:24-25]

The masses of people, moreover, do not gain materially from increased national wealth and may be left comparatively poorer. Luxury thus begets more "Murmurs, Sedition, and Tumults." His distress is almost apocalyptic: "Or what can come forth from such Scenes of unprincipled Licentiousness, but Pick-pockets, Prostitutes, Thieves, Highwaymen, and Murderers! These are your Triumphs, O BOLINGBROKE, TINDAL, MANDEVILLE, MORGAN, HUME" (2:86).[36]

Within a year and a half of the publication of volume 1, the *Estimate* had prompted a vast amount of commentary. Almost all the periodicals of the day reviewed it, many correspondents offered their opinions, and answering pamphlets appeared. Perhaps because Brown had criticized so many of his contemporaries and had severely rebuked the weekly and monthly journals, its reception was mixed and sometimes ambiguous. Yet there could be little doubt that Brown had written what many others had been thinking. Reviewers found his arguments against the periodicals unfounded, and clergymen thought his remarks on their profession too harsh, but few challenged or contradicted his censure of luxury. Rather he was chastised for misjudging its nature, not identifying all its manifestations, or not citing all its consequences. The upshot was a new round of popular debate and self-castigation. The *World* deplored the liberalism of the British constitution; the *Grand* rejected as vain all hope for honest government. The *Universal* lamented the depravity of human nature, and the *New Royal* called for ruthless measures by the government. The *Universal Visitor* said that reliance upon trade destroyed the customs and stability of English society. All seemed to agree, however, on the need for immediate action. In the words of a correspondent to the *London Magazine:*

> The time of war, when people are obliged to contribute largely for its support, and consequently cannot spare so much for superfluities, seems the fittest to suppress luxury; for experience shows, that peace always promotes it: And indeed, if men will be luxurious, when in distress and under pressures of war, there can be little hopes of their leaving it off in times of peace, and when their circumstances are more affluent.[37]

The year the *Estimate* appeared also saw the widespread anxiety over the provision and price of grain indicated earlier. By 1760 some forty pamphlets had been published condemning either the adulteration of bread or the general high prices of grain. The discussion of high prices, in fact, lasted more than a decade. Many of the writers related their arguments to the current excitement over luxury; among these were James Manning, *Poison Detected; or, Frightful Truths* (1757); *The Causes of the Present High Price of Corn and Grain* (1758); *A Modest Apology in Defense of Bakers* (1758); and *A Dissertation on Adulterated Bread* (1758). Bramble's letter of June 8 from London, it will be recalled, included adulterated bread in the "catalogue of London dainties" produced by luxury. "The bread I eat in London," Bramble wrote, "is a deleterious paste, mixed up with chalk, alum, and bone-ashes; insipid to the taste, and destructive to the constitution." The same charge had been made in 1758, in *An Essay on Monopolies; or, Reflections upon the Frauds and Abuses Practiced by Wholesale Dealers in Corn and Flour.* The author holds "the vain and luxurious" responsible for the existence of such monopolies.

After all that has been urged on this subject, we are obliged to acknowledge one melancholy truth, that *mistaken luxury* and *general folly* have laid the foundation, and afforded incitements to all these frauds. We know that a few years ago a fancy prevailed amongst persons of elegance, to paint all their wainscots with a dead white; but why that should be the colour of their bread, too, is not easy to be accounted for, as it certainly is a very unnatural one. . . . There is known to be a yellowish cast in the best and purest flour, especially when mixed with yest; but it is a matter of astonishment, that people who boast of taste, should merely for the sake of a colour, exchange the sweetness, elasticity and consistence, of a pure home-made loaf, for a harsh, dry, and crumbling composition of, *they really know not what.*[38]

Anxiety of a less material sort preoccupied many writers for several years after 1757. In a comparative flood of sermons, pamphlets, and books, they warned of a national malaise of disturbing proportions, a sickness of which luxury was both cause and symptom. The whole of Goldsmith's *Enquiry into the Present State of Polite Learning* (1759) reflects this view. Wherever he looks, Goldsmith sees avarice controlling behavior and policy. Learning and culture have been debased by "luxurious affluence" to the point that vulgarity alone finds applause. The course of his inquiry leads him "to deduce a universal degeneracy of manners, from . . . the depravation of taste; . . . as a nation grows dull, it sinks into debauchery . . . vice and stupidity are always mutually productive of each other" (pp. 195–96).

Historical precedents for the current crisis were presented in a tone of urgency. One of the lessons of Thomas Leland's *History of the Life and Reign of Philip King of Macedon* (2 vols., 1758) was that luxury had corrupted Persia in the time of Xerxes: "When Princes, either through inattention, defect of judgment, or want of virtue, suffer their subjects to sink into all the excesses of effeminate luxury; from such subjects they are not to expect generous sentiments, or great and gallant actions. Ruin and slavery [are] the necessary and natural consequences of such corruptions" (2:104). Edward W. Montagu interrupted his *Reflections on the Rise and Fall of Ancient Republics* (1759) to attack Mandeville and the corruption of English life he had ostensibly endorsed (p. 159). The anonymous *Additional Dialogue of the Dead* (1760) seems written for the specific object of comparing the Athens of Pericles and the Britain of Pitt. Aristides at one point asks:

> *Arist.* . . . suppose that, by the excess of commerce, and overflow of wealth, or by any other cause, a pernicious *luxury* should creep in, and steal unperceived on the highest ranks . . . and suppose this political *venality* should, in fact, creep in along with luxury; what consequence should you expect?

Pericles. You terrify me by the representation. I behold the state on the brink of *ruin*.[39]

Similar omens were further identified in M. P. Macquer,*A Chronological Abridgment of the Roman History* (1760); *The History of the Roman Emperors from Augustus to Constantine* (1760); *The Private Life of the Romans* (1761); volume 3 of N. Hooke's *Roman History* (1763); and John Mill's third volume of *Memoirs of the Court of Augustus* (1763).

Many economic tracts meanwhile broadcast the demoralizing effects luxury had upon the laboring classes. Two anonymous pamphlets, *Populousness with Oeconomy the Wealth and Strength of a Kingdom* (1759) and *A Letter to the Right Hon. Sir Thomas Chitty* (1760), dwell upon the dangers of depopulation and demands for higher wages. *A View of the Internal Policy of Great Britain* (1763) maintains that only the resettlement of poor families in uninhabited areas could insure a steady flow of "hardy industrious people." Other works contended that those of the laboring population who had settled in the city—the resort of sickness, laziness, and libertinism—were already lost, for they had succumed to a fashion that ruined the constitution and prevented healthful reproduction. The coordinate issue—the relationship of luxury, idleness, and insubordination—is explored in James Ridley's *The Schemer* (1763); *Remarks on the Present State of the National Debt* (1764); and *North Briton Extraordinary* (1765). Containing an otherwise commonplace argument, the *Remarks* reveal one sign of a decided shift in popular notions concerning luxury: its author regards only idleness among the poor as *dangerous* luxury; all other forms are mere refinement or innocuous luxury. Later in the century William Cobbett was to insist that in his own lifetime the attitudes of the rich had become much harsher, a deterioration reflected in common language. By the time of the *Rural Rides* the old term "the commons of England" had given way to "the populace," "the pesantry," and "the lower orders."

Religious objections to luxury continued to be offered in a traditional vein, but increasing emphasis was given to its political effects. In *Sermons on Public Occasions* (1761), Charles Bulkey declares that Christianity and patriotism stand together against the vice.[40] Thomas Cole's *Discourses on Luxury, Infidelity, and Enthusiasm* (1761), which was highly praised in at least three periodicals, makes the same point at greater length. Cole devotes much of the first half of his work to a repudiation of Mandeville; the latter half is an attempt to prove that luxury has been and will always be "the utter ruin of every nation where it prevails." Within a period of five years, another clergyman, Edward Watkinson, published seven sermons and tracts attacking luxury. One, *An Essay upon Oeconomy* (1762), which saw three editions its first year and eight within five years, held that "the *Glory* of a Nation was never founded on the *Luxury* of the People. . . . *Luxury* always relaxes the Sinews of Government" (p. 34). Another, *An Essay upon Gratitude* (1764), calls discontent a blameworthy kind of envy and states that it is a *religious* duty for Englishmen to feel affection and gratitude toward their government. Samuel Cooper's *Definitions and Axioms relative to Charity* (1764) finds vicious only the luxury of the poor; the pleasures of life are permissible when confined to the "middling and higher orders of people." Cooper's chief practical proposal is the prohibition of "plays and shews of every kind" before an audience of laborers.

Such jeremiads continued beyond the Treaty of Paris, although with declining frequency and with less absorption in immediate crises. Samuel Fawconer's *Essay on Modern Luxury* (1765) is a summing up of the concerns of the 1760s, as Brown's *Estimate* had been of the previous decade. Assured of England's military survival, Fawconer wishes to uproot the social manifestations of luxury that persist despite the imprecations of wartime. His language and point of view have the added interest of anticipating Bramble's attacks upon Bath and London in *Humphry Clinker.* His main target is the aspiring middle orders, particularly their fashions in dress, amusement, equipage and retinue, and their "new and unprecedented" claims for inclusion in public affairs. Such concerns, he says, are properly the exclusive domain of rank and wealth. Encroachments upon that domain can lead only to chaos and insubordination. The crises weathered by government and constitution followed directly from faction, sedition, and riot spawned by luxury. For the aspirations of the middling sort of people, he has only ridicule; though they are ridiculous, they do pose a threat to national order, especially in London. He is horrified by the state of life in the capital, likening it to an overgrown head, whence luxury moves to the rest of Britain like a "distemper," a "frenzy," and a "madness."

Fawconer reveals that for some Englishmen the Aristotelian principles of necessity and hierarchy still held fast. For natural legislators splendor and elegance is fitting, for,

> it may be right for people of family and fashion to live up to their quality and fortune: as it gives mankind an opinion of their dignity and opulence, and promotes the circulation of the materials of happiness. But here lies the danger: luxury is of that assimilating insinuating nature, that its infection, like a pestilence, runs thro' every order of the community, from the throne to the cottage. And, whether tempted by inborn pride or seduced by the power of all-prevailing fashion, every impertinent inferiour treads

on the heel of his betters. This emulation of pomp and parade is not confined to equals in point of rank or fortune, but extends itself to the most distant degrees in both. [Pp. 4-5]

(Six years later, the letters of Bramble would twice return to the image of ignorant and impertinent plebeians treading on the heels of their betters.) Suitable laws would have prevented such abuses of liberty, but they were not enacted: "Hence it is that so many make a figure in the eye of the world, and keep up a farce of grandeur without anything to support it. Like an *ignis fatuus,* they shine and glitter for a while, and in a moment disappear" (p. 6). For the same reasons as Bramble, Fawconer finds London oppressive:

it is observable, that luxury generally abounds, in proportion to the populousness of the capital city. It is become a fashion for every body to crowd to the metropolis, to spend part of the year in town, for the sake of its pleasures and diversions. . . . And, where the exteriors form our judgment of the man, and appearance in the vulgar eye passes for the only criterion of true worth: every one is ready to assume the marks of a superior condition, in order to be esteemed more than what he really is. [Pp. 6-7]

Nor is this the only inconvenience that is suffered in a city, whose inhabitants are continually on the increase. For these temporary inmates must be accommodated with lodging . . . there is reason to apprehend, that this overgrown metropolis must in a few years be crushed with its own weight. Already the head is too large for the body. The prodigious increase of inhabitants raises the price of provisions to an exorbitant height. The additional consumption is so large, that the produce of the neighborhood is unequal to the supply. And when the necessaries of life are procured from a distance, they must fall into the hands of dealers and factors: who are too often led, by this temptation, to monopolies and combinations, to make their own advantage of the necessities of others. [Pp. 8-9]

Spreading outward from the capital, the distemper had infected all parts of Britain. Spas are now "public marts of folly and misery"; what was once a center of recreation has become the seat of "public riot and dissipation, the place of general resort for the sick, and idle, and people of fashion and fortune; and persons of figure without any pretensions to either" (p. 10).

For the fashionable entertainments of the present age are the

most empty and trifling that can possibly be imagined; arguing not
the want of good taste only, but even of common sense. And this
must always be the consequence, whenever sensual pleasure is suffered to assume the empire over our rational faculties. [Pp. 10-11]

In his discussion of luxury in dress and furnishings (pp. 13-21),
Fawconer urges an alliance of religion and government to suppress the
vice, for it is dishonest and reprehensible for a person to dress or live
above his station and thereby undermine hierarchy. Persons of rank
and fortune are degraded, Fawconer argues, when their inferiors are
permitted to dress, speak, or behave like them.

> The custom of all civilized countries, hath regulated some general
> standard of dress, as most convenient to discriminate one from
> another in point of sex, age, and quality. The propriety and
> necessity of such a regulation, is evident from the mischiefs that
> could ensue from the want or neglect of it. For on whatever
> levelling principle the reasonable distinction of merit and degree
> is confounded, the order of government is broken in upon and
> destroyed. [Pp. 16-17]

Having ruined the health, property, fortune, and family of individuals,
luxury then subverts the foundations of national economy and government: "O luxury! Alas! patriotism!" (p. 24 n).

LATER DEVELOPMENTS

Within a decade of the unprecedented attention given Brown's *Estimate,* the concept of luxury had lost much of its power instantly to
arouse indignation and partisan fervor. After several generations of
expanding the concept to fit new social and financial situations, Englishmen began to reconsider its uses. Luxury had become so cumbersome,
it appears in retrospect, that in order to become manageable once again
it had to be redefined and hence renewed. Pocock has argued well that
the history of political ideas is also a history of political language. Both
concept and language became ambiguous when English legislators concentrated upon the use and consumption of *things*—when they were
constrained to give luxury a primarily economic construction. An
emphasis upon hierarchy subverted their position on necessity, and vice
versa. If imported foods or textiles were dangerous in and of themselves, why were they not as dangerous to legislators as to subjects?
Tiberius found a way to square that circle; George III did not try.
Pocock writes:

Because men in speaking commit themselves to a load or fabric greater than they can control, it is possible for others in reply to employ the same words to convey the loads of meaning they desire to select. Communication is possible only because it is imperfect. Because we affect one another's most intimate behavior by the spins we impart to words as they pass to and fro between us, it is possible for the linguistic polity to synthesize conflict with the recognition of interdependency. Politics is a game of biases in the asymmetrical universe of society. What we have called paradigms are linguistic constructs recognized as carrying increasingly complex loads in excess of what can be predicted or controlled at a given moment.[41]

The political games played over the idea of luxury would never again be quite the same.

The history of luxury from about 1763 to the end of the century proceeds along three lines: strict continuity, moderate redefinition, and radical change. The *Essay on Modern Luxury* is interesting as a prelude to Smollett, and it would be notable among dozens of attacks published at the outbreak of the Seven Years' War. Appearing as it does nearly a decade later, however, Fawconer's pamphlet is noteworthy as an example of a declining genre, reflecting a diminution in both the number and the intensity of attacks upon luxury.

Such changes were neither sharp nor consistent. The *Fable of the Bees* continued to evoke outraged replies through the 1790s. Edward Watkinson's *Frugality and Diligence* (York, 1766) reproduces without significant modification the religious argument common to the seventeenth century. And like Richard Price, in *Observations on . . . the Population* (1779) and *An Essay on the Population of England and Wales* (1780), writers continued to worry over the relation between luxury and the supply of labor. Persistent disquiet among the laboring population, moreover, continued to prompt warning against luxury. As Arthur Young wrote of his *Eastern Tour* (1771), "every one but an idiot knows, that the lower classes must be kept poor or they will never be industrious" (4.361).[42] To men like these, a large majority in 1750 but a minority fifty years later, luxury remained an absolute vice, to be suppressed or eradicated.

Yet another and growing trend attempted to moderate between old attitudes and new situations, arguing that luxury represented an inevitable condition of English life, to be understood and if necessary controlled. It is to this latter development of thought that Goldsmith refers, in hyperbolic terms, in his dedication to the *Deserted Village* (1770):

In regretting the depopulation of the country, I inveigh against
the encrease of our luxuries; and here also I expect the shout of
modern politicians against me. For twenty or thirty years past, it
has been the fashion to consider luxury as one of the greatest
national advantages; and all the wisdom of antiquity in that particular, as erroneous. Still however, I must remain a professed ancient
on that head, and continue to think those luxuries prejudicial to
states, by which so many vices are introduced, and so many kingdoms have been undone. Indeed so much has been poured out of
late on the other side of the question, that merely for the sake of
novelty and variety, one would sometimes wish to be in the
right.[43]

Goldsmith's judgment is doubly revealing. Elsewhere, in the *Citizen of
the World,* he had voiced approval of certain forms of luxury. He also
attributes its defense to "modern politicians." The implication, supported by other evidence, is that with the successful conclusion of the
war luxury ceased to be an incendiary social and political issue. British
imperial conquests, with the increased commerce they implied, together
became translated into a new popular acceptance of "the commercial
vice." Even writers for the *Critical Review,* formerly arch-foes of luxury
in any form, expressed themselves in reasoned, judicious tones. Two
years after Smollett left the journal, the reviewer of a French work
declares:

Few writers, when they treat of luxury, ascertain the idea of it
in a proper manner. Some of them . . . comprehend profusion and
intemperance, and therefore declaim against it as inconsistent with
the maxims of Christianity and the welfare of society. Others . . .
mean costly furniture, magnificent buildings, splendid equipages,
elegant entertainments, and other things of the nature, and
agreeably to this notion, maintain, in opposition to the first, that
it promotes the circulation of money and the advantage of the
community. On both sides there is truth; and each party would
allow, were they mutually to explain the meaning of the expression, that they differ more in appearance than in reality.

Luxury, (this author) observes, is contrary or favorable to the
enrichment of nations, according as it consumes more or less of
the produce of their soil and of their industry, or as it consumes
more or less of the soil of foreign countries; and it ought to have
a greater or a less number of objects, according as these nations
have more or less wealth. With such an extensive commerce as now
prevails, with so universal a spirit of industry, with such a multitude of arts brought to perfection, it would be a vain scheme to

think of bringing Europe back to her ancient simplicity, which
would be only bringing her back to weakness and barbarism. The
only point should be to give luxury a proper direction, and then
it would contribute to the grandeur of nations and the happiness
of man kind.[44]

More concisely, a later writer for the *Monthly Review* repeats the point:
"There is scarce any subject that has been more frequently treated by
political writers than that of luxury, and yet few have been treated in a
more vague and superficial manner. The generally received opinion is,
that luxury has proved the ruin of the greatest empires, and that, in
whatever state it prevails, it must in the end be fatal to it; and on this
topic orators, moralists, philosophers, and divines are eternally declaim-
ing."[45]

Boswell provides an illustration of the new judiciousness in a conversation between Johnson and Goldsmith dated 13 April 1773. Goldsmith seeks to draw Johnson "on the common topick, that the race of
our people was degenerated, and that this was owing to luxury." Johnson doubts the fact of degeneration and also denies that luxury could
ever cause it. He asks consideration of a contrary, indisputable fact:
"how very small a proportion of our people luxury can reach. Our
soldiery, surely, are not luxurious, who live on sixpence a day; and the
same remark will apply to almost all the other classes. Luxury, so far
as it reaches the poor, will do good to the race of people; it will
strengthen and multiply them. Sir, no nation was ever hurt by luxury;
for, as I said before, it can reach but to a few." In the *Decline and Fall
of the Roman Empire* Gibbon also distinguishes between harmless and
harmful luxury, along the same lines as Johnson and Adam Smith. Discussing the age of the Antonines in chapter 2 (published in 1776), he
remarks that "in the present imperfect condition of society, luxury,
though it may proceed from vice or folly, seems to be the only means
that can correct the unequal distribution of property." While the rich
strive to enjoy every possible type of pleasure and refinement, the mass
of the people must labor incessantly to provide them. In this process,
which Gibbon sees as occurring in all ages, luxury acts as "a voluntary
tax" paid to the poor by the possessors of land. However, when luxury
has so pervaded a society that no other pursuit is possible, as occurred
in Rome under Theodosius, then the situation has altered entirely.
Luxury is no longer a distributive tax, but "that indolent despair which
enjoys the present hour and declines the thoughts of futurity." When it
reaches the army it is "a secret and destructive poison," under whose
influence the infantry lays aside its heavy armor, later to be overwhelmed "naked and trembling" by the cavalry of the enemy (chap.
27, 1781).

In Scotland, where Enlightenment views on luxury were more warmly received than in England, several major writers were also challenging the received opinions of men like Arthur Young. Beginning in the 1750s a group of writers on social theory began to portray social development as directly related to means of subsistence. This group—including Dalrymple, Ferguson, Kames, Smith, and Smith's student John Millar—proposed that all societies pass through successive stages of hunting, pasturage, agriculture, and commerce, each stage possessing its own distinctive complex of values and institutions. Flowing from this four-stage theory were a more favorable view of commerce, an assertion of modest progress in human affairs, and a criticism of primitivist theories.[46] In his chapter on luxury in the *Essay on the History of Civil Society* (1767), Ferguson attempts to remove the concept altogether from the arena of polemics. Following an argument put forward by Hume in 1752, Ferguson suggests that luxury possesses a positive and important meaning directly related to the material progress of a society: the capacity to use the accommodations and conveniences the age has developed. He largely reduces the question of visible luxury to one of mere changing tastes; Smollett four years later was reducing visible changes in taste to a question of dangerous luxury. In a direct challenge to attacks upon the luxury of the poor, Smith argues in the *Wealth of Nations* (1776) that if the effects of British trade are economically beneficial, they should also be socially welcome. The economy *required* the free exercise of self-interest. Indeed the economic, then social, benefits that filtered through to the mass of laboring people returned to the nation as multiplied economic security:

> The common complaint that luxury extends itself even to the lowest ranks of the people, and that the labouring poor will not now be contented with the same food, cloathing, and lodging, which satisfied them in former times, may convince us that it is not the money price for labour alone, but its real recompence, which has augmented.
>
> Is this improvement in the circumstances of the lower ranks of the people to be regarded as an advantage or as an incoveniency to the society? The answer seems at first sight abundantly plain. Servants, labourers and workmen of different kinds, make up the far greater part of every great political society. But what improves the circumstances of the greater part can never be regarded as an inconveniency to the whole. No society can surely be flourishing and happy, of which the far greater part of the members are poor and miserable. It is but equity, besides, that they who feed, cloath and lodge the whole body of the people, should have such a

share of the produce of their own labour as to be themselves tolerably well fed, cloathed and lodged.[47]

It was the redefinition of the concept, which had been attempted long before 1763 and will be discussed in the following chapter, that eventually led to a complete reversal in its conventional usage and thence to Thackeray's and the modern sense of luxury. Perhaps most influential in the process of redefinition was Hume's *Political Discourses* of 1752. Hume had at least three incisive criticisms against contemporary, all-embracing uses of the term. Philosophically, such uses were frequently untenable, based as they were upon vague or unspecified assumptions. Historically, they were inaccurate, founded upon a reading of ancient and modern history for which there was no evidence. And socially, they were very biased, defending the few against the many. In calling attention to the political and social animus contained in the theory of luxury, Hume distinguished between luxury as criterion of value and luxury as vehicle of prejudice. His views had little effect upon the young Scottish writer who had just published his second novel or upon the Scottish nobleman about to begin the education of the future monarch. But they were influential upon the work of two other Scots, Ferguson and Smith, who together delivered the intellectual coup de grace to the more blatant political purposes to which the idea of luxury had been put. Yet because luxury was far more than an intellectual construct, the arguments of brilliant minds alone would not alter it greatly.

It is important that Hume was not the only reputable Tory to help dissolve its social animus. Another staunch conservative, undeservedly regarded as extreme in his political views, began a number of the *Literary Magazine* in 1756 with the assertion, "The time is now come, in which *every* Englishman expects to be informed of the national affairs, and in which he has a right to have that expectation gratified." Thus Johnson at the opening of the Seven Years' War, at the conclusion of which Smollett was yet arguing the contrary position. It was also Johnson who understood better than most "the maxims of a commercial nation": "To entail irreversible poverty upon generation after generation only because the ancestor happened to be poor, is in itself cruel, if not unjust, and is wholly contrary to the maxims of a commercial nation, which always suppose and promote a rotation of property, and offer every individual a chance of mending his condition by his diligence." And perhaps his most pertinent comment in the review of Soame Jenyns: "The shame is to impose words for ideas upon ourselves or others." A third notable Tory, although somewhat equivocal about luxury, included in his novel *The Vicar of Wakefield*, published five years before *Humphry Clinker* and written earlier, a chapter extolling the virtues of the English middle class and especially its contributions to domestic trade and domestic liberty. Echoing Hume, Goldsmith calls that class of which he and Johnson were members:

> that order of men which subsists between the very rich and the very rabble; those men who are possest of too large fortunes to submit to the neighbouring man in power, and yet are too poor to set up for tyranny themselves. In this middle order of mankind are generally to be found all the arts, wisdom, and virtues of society. This order alone is known to be the true preserver of freedom, and may be called the People.[48]

English success in the war accelerated acceptance of this view, for political change was needed before a political concept would be altered. In the mid-1750s Horace Walpole had often evoked a genuinely desolate mood: "Between the French and the earthquakes, you have no notion how good we are grown; nobody makes a suit of clothes now but of sackcloth turned up with ashes." The tone of his metaphors in 1757 had not lightened: "It is time for England to slip her own cables, and float away into some unknown ocean." Yet with the Treaty of Paris his sense of English greatness had more than returned: "Throw away your Greek and Roman books, histories of little peoples." Walpole's allusion seemed apt, for with the peace had emerged the second and greater British Empire. His elation, too, reflected a common sentiment. "French superiority . . . received a death-blow on the heights of Abram," wrote Leslie Stephen, "and Englishmen, finding that they had not become cowards, forgot the alarm or remembered it only as a good jest." Modern historians have perceived the same response. "The British . . . were overtaken by hubris after 1763," Ian R. Christie has written; "Everywhere the theme was expansion."[49]

Expansion presumed cooperation between government and commercial interests; put in the terms of those interests, expansion presumed that industry and commerce would operate on a grand scale, as part of a concerted national policy. English victory seemed to indicate that at least one kind of human progress, the commercial, was attainable. (In the paper war of the early 1760s, the *Critical Review* continued for a time to warn against luxury in situations where the *Monitor* saw only "commercial progress.") French defeat provided a complementary lesson upon the vulnerability of an empire held by force of arms alone. What befell the French colonial armies could easily recoil upon the English (and in the American colonies soon did). Far better to found a trading empire bound to England by shipping routes and self-interest, not by chains and fear. While Burke came to regret that an age of "sophists, economists, and calculators" had succeeded the age of chivalry and that "the glory of Europe is extinguished for ever," he nevertheless saw Adam Smith as a new Moses, declaring: "The laws of commerce are the laws of nature, and therefore the laws of God." Once Smith's views had found a solicitor, they would soon find a singer; and in the fourth book of *The Progress of Civil Society: A Didactic Poem in Six Books* (1796), Richard Payne Knight provides a redaction into verse of the lessons of the *Wealth of Nations:*

> Each found the produce of his toil exceed
> His own demands, of luxury or need;
> Whence each the superfluity resign'd,
> More useful objects in return to find:
> Each freely gave what each too much possess'd,
> In equal plenty to enjoy the rest.
>
> Hence the soft intercourse of commerce ran,
> From state to state, and spread from clan to clan;
> Each link of social union tighter drew,
> And rose in vigour as it wider grew.   [Pp. 77–78]

By 1780 two events of symbolic importance had occurred. James Watt, who once wrote bitterly that the gentry treated him as a mechanic no better than a slave, had joined Matthew Boulton in the production of steam engines for industry—science and invention entering into partnership with manufacturing. And for the first time in English history Parliament found it worthwhile to levy a tax upon retailers' shops. Within the decade every statistical measure of production turned sharply upward; the revolution in commerce and industry was visibly upon England. The popular counterpart of these changes is the history of John Bull: a figure of ridicule in Arbuthnot's pamphlets of 1712, a commonplace of political caricature until the late 1750s, and the typical, *good* Englishman from the 1770s onward.[50]

The dispute over high prices to be described below will demonstrate that in learned works of the early 1760s luxury could be turned 180 degrees, loosed from its aristocratic moorings, and set against the bastions of the rich. In Addison, Steele, and Defoe we have already witnessed the penchant of Whiggish writers to turn an argument against luxury into an indictment of the upper orders, a tendency continued in Gray's association of luxury with pride and wealth in the *Elegy* (1751), in Churchill's location of luxury exclusively at court in book 1 of *Gotham* (1765), and in Burns's attack in *The Cotter's Saturday Night* (1786). It finds a transatlantic parallel in the movement of American Quakers for the abolition of slavery, a movement that inspired the English Quaker Thomas Day to compose the highly influential *The*

Dying Negro (1773).[51] By 1771 the reversal of target in condemnations of luxury was sufficiently acceptable to appear in a popular novel. In *The Man of Feeling,* published in the same year as Smollett's last novel, Mackenzie has a passing stranger explain to Harley how the luxury of the rich harms the poor and corrupts civil government, his comments on education sounding like a gloss on the careers of Jery and Lydia Melford.

> "Indeed, the education of your youth is every way preposterous: you waste at school years in improving talents, without having ever spent an hour in discovering them; one promiscuous line of in-struction is followed, without regard to genius, capacity, or proba-ble situations in the commonwealth. From this bear-garden of the pedagogue, a raw unprincipled boy is turned loose upon the world to travel; without any ideas but those of improving his dress at Paris, or starting into taste by gazing on some paintings at Rome. Ask him of the manners of the people, and he will tell you, That the skirt is worn much shorter in France, and that every body eats macaroni in Italy. When he returns home, he buys a seat in parliament, and studies the constitution at Arthur's.
>
> "Nor are your females trained to any more useful purpose: they are taught, by the very rewards which their nurses propose for good behaviour, by the first thing like a jest which they hear from every male visitor of the family, that a young woman is a creature to be married; and when they are grown somewhat older, are instructed, that it is the purpose of marriage to have the enjoyment of pin-money, and the expectation of a jointure.
>
> "These indeed are the effects of luxury, which is perhaps insep-arable from a certain degree of power and grandeur in a nation. But it is not simply of the progress of luxury that we have to complain: did its votaries keep in their own sphere of thoughtless dissipation, we might despise them without emotion; but the frivolous pursuits of pleasure are mingled with the most important concerns of the state; and public enterprise shall sleep till he who should guide its operation has decided his bets at Newmarket, or fulfilled his engagement with a favourite-mistress in the coun-try."[52]

Similar charges were to be repeated in a series of important works in the middle of the decade. The year 1776 saw not only the publication of the *Wealth of Nations,* but also Paine's *Common Sense,* Bentham's *Fragment on Legislation,* and Richard Price's *On Civil Liberty;* it also brought the first comprehensive proposal for parliamentary reform.

The wide social gulf between the nobility and gentry, on one hand,

and the merchants on the other certainly persisted alongside such signs of change. Writing of London around 1780, Archenholtz records the suspicion and jealousy existing between the groups, and though Smollett would have quickly recognized the sources of the hostility the foreign visitor describes, he might have been surprised by its terms of expression.

> This difference which holds even in the hours of eating and drinking, in the kind of amusements, the dress and manner of speaking etc. has given rise to a degree of mutual contempt by the inhabitants of each of these quarters for the other. Those of the city reproach them of the other end for their idleness, luxury, manner of living, and desire to imitate everything that is French: these in their turn never mention an inhabitant of the city but as an animal gross and barbarous, whose only merit is his strong box . . . this mutual dislike is sung in the streets, it is introduced upon the stage, and even in parliament it is not forgotten.[53]

Smollett's total and uncompromising classical denunciation of luxury in 1771, then, is anachronistic. It is wholly consistent with his earlier pronouncements on the subject, but it is less consistent with the development of British attitudes after the Treaty of Paris. Rather than the confidence of the end of the 1760s, *Humphry Clinker* reflects the doubt of the beginning of the decade, supporting the contention that in the novel Smollett is returning with gusto to some of his earlier political quarrels. In his many attacks upon luxury, the novelist is returning also to an ancient rhetorical mode, and *Humphry Clinker* must be read in the light of its traditions. He seeks no novelty or conscious originality for his arguments. On the contrary, his strength sustains itself upon ancient convention, invoking the familiar and the commonplace in order to reflect the patterns of truth and experience. The burden of controversy taxed that strength, demanding that he deny economic arguments in favor of luxury in order to express his social and political antipathies. In this respect he could be called the last Patriot.

Three

SUBJECTS RAMPANT: DEFENSES AND REDEFINITIONS OF LUXURY IN THE EIGHTEENTH CENTURY

Hume's essay "Of Luxury," among the *Political Discourses* of 1752, is a devastating commentary upon the type of thinking outlined in the previous chapter. Yet only eight years later, while gathering his essays for a new collection, Hume altered the title, substituting the word *refinement* for luxury. Confident that his own view of the matter would soon hold the day, he was willing to forego at least part of the taunting edge of his earlier position. His aplomb is, for us, both revealing and deceptive. It certainly was prescient, for his general estimate of luxury stands as the usual one today, when leisure and convenience are meant. But for the English world of ideas it was also quite premature. A generation later, in 1776, Johnson was still correcting Boswell: "Many things which are false are transmitted from book to book, and gain credit in the world. One of these is the cry against the evil of luxury. Now the truth is, that luxury produces much good." Hume's recasting of the concept, like Johnson's defense of its effects, is an example of a rare genre. It is a liability of progressive treatments of intellectual history that to the twentieth century the best-known discussions of luxury are those of the few heretics rather than the many true believers.[1]

For the first three-quarters of the century there are probably fewer arguments in support of luxury than there are defenses of deism or greater democracy. Traditional condemnations were so widely accepted during most of the century that few writers were bold enough to meet them frontally. For writers in every field—with the partial exception of political economy—the classical attack upon luxury amounted to precious orthodoxy. There is a real paradox in this. For if one accepts the view of the commonwealthmen, then the reign of luxury began with William and Mary and should have received concerted support thereafter. If one takes another view, making Walpole the serpent of the British Eden, then defenses should have flowed massively from hired pens after 1720. Yet little of this did follow. In fact, Walpole's party journalists usually responded to Bolingbroke's charges not with approval of luxury but with counterattacks upon the motives and integrity of the Opposition. Whether defending George II, Newcastle, Pitt, or Beckford, later writers sought as a matter of course to shift the terms of dispute from luxury to a more immediate, concrete political issue. Even those men audacious enough to voice approval of some aspect of luxury—a group that includes some of the foremost intellectual figures of the period—generally did so obliquely: Mandeville with irony and epigrammatic sallies, Johnson in conversation, Steuart, Ferguson, Smith, and others as part of comprehensive revaluations of social and economic theory or policy. The essential issue was of course not moral courage, for no defense of luxury however straightforward would have entered a favorable climate of opinion much before 1763. The situation is clearest with those writers of the 1750s and 1760s who tried to defend the poor against charges of debauchery. They wished to initiate debate over the material evidence of luxury in English society, especially in the lives of the homeless and miserable. In a few instances they received replies ostensibly couched in terms of manifestations of luxury: empirical testimony and the corollary comparison of life past and present. For the most part, however, they were answered only with repetitions of the original charges. Their opponents were not much concerned with logic and evidence, and the basic difference between the two groups was not merely descriptive or empirical but was of a more profound sort. Rather than a learned disagreement over the course of social and political change, the controversy reflected a collision over the ancient principles of necessity and hierarchy—whether they represented the sole expressions of ultimate virtue.

So long as the leaders of England, of all sorts, adhered to the traditional conception of luxury, it possessed the power of religious dogma: self-sustaining, self-confirming, and invulnerable to internal contradiction or even argument. Precisely how and why it lost that support cannot be answered with certainty. The development of British Protestantism, frequently remarked by students of the century, no doubt acted as a cultural catalyst. A fully secular social philosophy, an ethic of benevolence spurring liberalism, sentiment, and tolerance; a socially powerful evangelical movement: these and other forces prompted some Englishmen to ask anew the ancient questions of what people needed, and where, socially, they belonged. What is clear is that the reaction, when it arrived, came from outside the normal context of English beliefs—in new social, economic, and political relationships, international as well as domestic, signaled by division among the legislators. Internal arguments against traditional attitudes did not simply prevail by virtue of intellectual force. Rather they were left holding the field as older positions were abandoned. To account fully for the transition, one would need the kind of grand cultural analysis provided by Kuhn in *The Structure of Scientific Revolutions* or Foucault in *The Order of Things*. (One could contend, for example, that in its setting it represented as complex a change, with sources as diverse, as the Reformation.) More modestly, one can note that by the end of the century the traditional concept no longer satisfied many of England's intellectual and political leaders. Political economy had come to emphasize the latter half of the phrase as much as the former, and here writers discovered not only demonstrably new knowledge about the economic mechanism, but also what was perceived as a new economic structure itself. Under such circumstances luxury as it had been viewed for centuries underwent a lasting devaluation: from a myth to a fiction, from an ethic to a prejudice, and from an essential, general element of moral theory to a minor, technical element of economic theory.

In what might be called the "macroeconomic" sense, the modernizing of luxury of course passed beyond Smollett's comprehension. But on the "microeconomic" level of palpable month-to-month changes in political and economic relationships, he was more aware of what was happening in England than most of his educated fellow countrymen. And most of what he saw he did not like. The present section is intended as a clarifying interchapter, indicating some of the sources of eighteenth-century controversy as well as present-day thinking about luxury and relating the general criticism of luxury sketched above to Smollett's own, traced in following chapters. There is no need here fully to recount the flux of argument that sustained the controversy outlined in the previous chapter. At each stage of the attack, there were

a few writers able in some manner to respond. Of these the most interesting—including Mandeville, Defoe, Walpole's party writers, and Hume
—were also the most influential, at least in the sense that they could not
be wholly ignored. Those of the novelist's contemporaries who in some
fashion defended luxury were surely important to him and were perhaps
also influential in shaping *Humphry Clinker*. More obviously, they
provide two gauges of his antipathy toward luxury: indirectly as
exponents of the theories of society that were available to him but that
he either tacitly rejected or publicly repudiated; directly as targets of
severe criticism in the pages of the *Critical Review,* particularly during
debates over the high price of food.[2] Less obviously, they probably
altered the classical form of the condemnation of luxury. From ancient
times this condemnation had expressed codes of religion and morality.
Eighteenth-century defenders of luxury, on the other hand, chose
to deemphasize morality in favor of economics, arguing in the main
that luxury could increase and redistribute wealth and was therefore a laudable trait in a society. Whatever its moral blemishes, they
said, luxury served a needful economic function. To meet this new
challenge at least partway, traditionalists needed to reshape their
tirades, at a minimum to glance briefly at the actual economic condition of the nation as a whole.

Historically the men who in some measure commended luxury were
harbingers of "classical" economic theory, were instrumental in dis-
mantling the older mercantile system, and represented a thoroughgoing
challenge to the classical principle of necessity. In comparison with the
critics of luxury, they are far fewer in number, more recondite in treatment, more cautious in language, and more empirical in approach.
Unlike the critics, they analyzed both the causes and the effects of
luxury in order to isolate its various elements. Some, like Mandeville,
went further, arguing in anticipation of Adam Smith that causes and
effects could not in practice be separated at all. If trade was accepted as
a beneficial activity for the nation, then a rise in the consumption of
luxuries would necessarily be a part of those benefits. Recognizing with
Johnson that "every state of society is as luxurious as it can be," most
of these writers couched their defenses or redefinitions of luxury in
terms of the expansion of industry, employment, and population. Two
corollary arguments were also advanced. The first held that a state of at
least partial luxury had always been a precondition of liberty, education, and refinement. The other—treated here with the controversy over
prices—held that the improvement of men's lot through the extension
of physical luxury was a laudable end in itself.

The influence of the *Fable of the Bees* upon this tradition would be
difficult to overestimate. Mandeville's argument, or a distorted version

of it, was still under attack by pamphlet writers as late as 1794, and at least fourteen appeared during the 1760s with the stated intention of answering his position once and for all.[3] We have far more evidence than Johnson's that Mandeville was at the heart of part of the controversy during the century. In the face of orthodox classical and Christian denunciations of luxury, he assumed that men were proud, egoistic and governed by their passions, and therefore he posited three theses that in this context were relatively novel. (1) National frugality—the contemporary term for necessity—is a vice, not a virtue, since prodigality, among other things, redistributes wealth and provides for the whole of the population. (2) Luxury is a concomitance of, perhaps even a prerequisite to, national greatness: it is inevitable. (3) The pursuit of individual self-interest normally redounds to the prosperity of the state. It was indeed the increased prosperity of the state that he sought ultimately to release. He had no moral objections to the extant economic structure of England—indeed he was more conservative than most of his apparent adversaries—but he wished to point out that by traditional standards the whole of that structure would be called immoral. The notoriety of the *Fable* derived from Mandeville's unmistakable statement that Englishmen said one thing but, fortunately, did another.[4]

Mandeville was very much a part of the fevered quarrels outlined in the previous chapter, the "Grumbling Hive" being a response to several political poems of the turn of the century, and the 1714 edition of the *Fable* answering several Tory attacks of Anne's reign.[5] He was aware that his critics objected not so much to the wealth generated by trade as to the men who acquired that wealth. Such critics routinely associated luxury with pride, proof to him that they saw vice and hypocrisy only in those they considered their social inferiors. If they wished to brand as luxury all the changes English society was undergoing, Mandeville said, so be it: let them rest content with *verbal* victory and *moral* satisfaction:

> Thus every Part was full of Vice,
> Yet the whole Mass a Paradise . . .
> Such were the Blessings of that State;
> Their crimes conspir'd to make them great.

In addition to challenging conventional assumptions about society, Mandeville sought to clarify both the issues and the language informing the concept of luxury. To the current attitude that said luxury must be a vice because frugality, its supposed opposite, was a virtue, he answered that frugality had never been a *national* virtue. Historically it had rather been a mere necessity, avoided whenever possible. To the other dominant attitude, which held that luxury, by corrupting a nation and wasting its resources, was economically dangerous, he responded that the charge had no historical foundation. In fact luxury was necessary for economic prosperity and had always been found together with it. He therefore ridiculed the careless way most men used the concept.

> If everything is to be Luxury (as in strictness it ought) that is not immediately necessary to make Man subsist as he is a living Creature, there is nothing else to be found in the World, no not even among the naked Savages; of which it is not probable that there are any but what by this time have made some Improvements upon their former manner of living.
>
> . . . if once we depart from calling everything Luxury that is not absolutely necessary to keep a Man alive . . . then there is no Luxury at all; for if the wants of Man are innumerable, then what ought to supply them has no bounds. [1:107–8][6]

Similarly, he spurred five generations of sermon-writers, usually to indignation, with his perception of moral paradox: "It is the sensual Courtier that sets no limit to his Luxury; the Fickle Strumpet that invents new fashions every Week . . . the profuse Rake and lavish Heir . . . : It is these that are the Prey and proper Food of a full grown Leviathan. . . . He that gives most Trouble to thousands of his Neighbours, and invents the most operose Manufactures is, right or wrong, the greatest Friend to the Society" (1:355–56).

The next major philosophical defender of luxury was Smollett's contemporary and fellow historian, Hume. But in the years between the *Fable* and Hume's *Political Discourses* (1752), Mandeville's argument, though usually not Mandeville himself, earned a certain modicum of intellectual respectability. Without granting it anything approaching universal applicability, writers could allow its usefulness in understanding the undisciplined members of mankind. The dissolute, the weak, the unorthodox—all indeed who did not behave according to strict principles—all these could be seen as driven by the desire for luxuries to harder and more efficient work. Thus surrounded by a host of proper qualifications, luxury might be viewed as an independent force in the scales of national production, one capable of increasing labor by energizing laborers.

Yet the men most responsible for capturing the new energies abroad in Britain were of a more humble cast than the great Hume. Represented by Defoe and Walpole's party writers, they wrote largely for the moment. But the abundance of that moment earned them an enduring stature; in Pocock's words, they were among "the first intellectuals on record to express an entirely secular awareness of social and economic changes going on in their society, and to say specifically that these changes affected both their values and their modes of perceiving social realities."[7] By intent, Defoe was neither defender nor redefiner of luxury. He was not, like Locke or Mandeville, a philosopher of the new commercial age. Rather he was, as G. D. H. Cole has said, its poet laureate. And Walpole's stable, although it included several able minds bestirred at times to philosophy, was designed to protect a ministry, not a stoa.

Defoe wrote nearly as much and as often about luxury as did Smollett. The resemblance, however, ends there. While Smollett stayed fast within the classical tradition, Defoe, two generations earlier, was closer to the moderns Dickens and Thackeray. Violations of necessity and hierarchy he certainly sees everywhere about him, but the usual notions of these principles he curtly dismisses. In a series of consecutive issues of the *Review,* beginning with no. 9 for 18 January 1706, he describes the corruption that disturbs him: "the Luxury and Vanity of a Court, and the Extravagances of the Gentry." In no. 10 he reports that his readers object to such a construction of luxury; he will therefore elaborate his position and show that the "Luxury and Extravagancies of the *English* Nobility, have been the Advantage of the Common People." The "Ancient Nobility and Gentry" have brought "Havock and Destruction" upon themselves and are fast losing their ancestral estates. Where have the estates gone? They have "been swallow'd up, by the Commonalty and Tradesmen, who are now Richer all over the Nation." He thus turns on its head the argument used by Fletcher and Davenant earlier, Bolingbroke and Pulteney later. They held that the luxury of the common people threatened the great families and thereby the constitution. He holds that the luxury of the great families harms only themselves, encourages trade, redistributes wealth, and thereby strengthens the nation as a whole.

Over thirty years of polemical writing, Defoe's consistency on the matter of luxury cannot be of the letter-for-letter variety. He is acutely aware of the complex of customs and attitudes branded luxury, especially their use in political thinking. Hence he tries to accomplish two quite different ends: to use luxury himself as a political weapon against the landed interests; and, alternatively, to insist that luxury must be considered dispassionately without recourse to immediate political point-scoring. In no. 34 of the *Review* he notes that the freedoms, "Pleasures and Conveniences of Life" that all men should have are commonly stigmatized "in that ill-natur'd Term Luxury." At least thirty numbers of the paper say luxury is beneficial to trade; at least five, that it is harmful. For twelve consecutive numbers starting 7 February 1706, he argues that what is "a Vice in Morals, may at the same time be a Virtue in Trade"—but only so long as tradesmen and laborers are not caught up in it. His ambivalence is plainest regarding the working poor, toward whom he seems to feel both sympathy and suspicion. Numerous times in the *Review* and several times in the *Tour,* he rejects the charge that a decent wage is a luxury. Laborers, he says, have the right to as much leisure and as high wages as they can get, for these amount to "the vast Hinge on which the Wealth of the Nation turns." But far more frequent, in the *Review* as well as in his work of the 1720s, is his own charge that the poor are sexually loose, shirk their work, waste their wages, spend their time on backs and bellies, and generally live a "Riot of Luxury."[8]

Luxury for Defoe is associated with idleness, and he is often uncertain who is more morally luxurious, the garishly rich or the dismally poor; neither meets his measure of necessity. About the middle orders, however, he admits no serious doubts, and his major nonfictional works of the 1720s are strenuous defenses of the commercial interests against the prevailing attack upon luxury. What he will continue to defend to the end of his life, that is, is not luxury, but those men interminably accused of it. *The Complete English Tradesman* (enlarged ed., 1727) is the manifesto of a new and ascendant social order, the *trading* gentry. To landed men, tradesmen are mostly vile and mean wretches; to Defoe they are sturdy, vigorous men of sense and dignity. Most important, they are productive and industrious, not idle like the men of land. If they will avoid the luxuries that have sapped the old legislators, they will gain power and recognition proportionate to their merit. They have done more than transform England into a trading country, for it is now the greatest trading nation in the world. The transformation they have worked upon commerce they can work upon society and government (pp. 304-19). Written about 1728-29 but not published until 1890, *The Compleat English Gentleman* is a companion volume, a plan for reform of English education. Most in need of genuine education, Defoe feels, are the youth of the great landed families, since they are at present vain, weak, idle, and ignorant. Indeed for long they have not possessed the virtue, learning, and ability that the title of gentleman originally implied; elsewhere he calls them the victims of luxurious fathers, "bred boors, empty and swinish sots and fops." Now that title more properly belongs to the tradesman, the man who is great because of personal achievement, the *novus homo.*

Some of the earliest numbers of the *Review* allege that Tories will remain enemies of unfettered trade, for such trade carries with it the new liberties that so revolt the landed interests. This argument remains, twenty years later, at the heart of his strategy for a robust international power, *A Plan of the English Commerce* (1728). The classical sense of luxury and concomitant notion of fixed hierarchy he dismisses out of hand, as "Family Jargon, for it is no more."[9] History read aright, he says, teaches that tradesmen were nearly as important in antiquity as they are today. The ancient division of peoples into "Gentry and Commonalty" he calls nonsense born of false pride (p. 4). His own division is between a landed gentry who are truly luxurious, since they live off rents and the labor of others and have mere pride of purse, and the manufacturers who are truly virtuous, since they live off their own industry and possess pride of achievement (pp. 37–38). This, he says, is the crux of all quarrels surrounding luxury and trade: "Employment is Life, Sloth and Indolence is Death." When commerce expands, the purse-proud lose relatively, the industrious gain. Hence present attacks upon luxury, which any man of sense could expect and dismiss:

> Trade is the Wealth of the World; Trade makes the Difference as to Rich or Poor, between one Nation and another; Trade nourishes Industry, and Industry begets Trade; Trade disperses the national Wealth of the World, and Trade raises new Species of Wealth, which Nature knew nothing of. [P. 51]

For fifteen years Defoe had been Walpole's man, but far from his only man. Throughout Walpole's administration, government writers met Opposition charges of luxury with arguments of their own (though drawn in large part from Locke), some of which had the effect of moderating the classical attack. First, natural law was not what the Opposition supposed. All men are equal in the state of nature. To their persons and the property they might honestly acquire, no other man may lay claim a priori. Government derives from a voluntary relationship intended for security, not subordination; it was not designed to shackle dependents to masters, but to provide life, liberty, and property for all.[10] Second, where the Opposition saw 1688 as the engine of England's climactic devolution, Walpole's press saw it as the inauguration of her glory. The *London Journal* called the Glorious Revolution the nativity of national freedom, the end of tyranny, and the beginning of true progress in, for example, representative government, a responsive economic system, and a distribution of power suited to the range of English talents.[11] Third, the Opposition called parties a pernicious division within what was by nature a family united by paternal authority and mutual interest. The Whig papers responded with the proposition that, since all men could not concur over the national interest or even their own self-interest, political divisions were inevitable and wholesome. Better to express disagreement through parties than to suppress them through tyranny; it was the intent of the Glorious Revolution to permit such differences. Parties were like the two sides of "an express contradiction"; they could be stated but, short of blood-shed, not reconciled.[12]

Finally, to the charge that Walpole ruled by luxury and corruption, they made several responses. It was not the duty of a magistrate to dictate how people may dispose of their persons and property so long as they injured no one else, they argued in a version of Locke's call for tolerance and a limited government. Similarly but rarely, they held that few of the habits and freedoms the Opposition called luxurious deserved such stigma. What Bolingbroke and his coterie sought was to limit the opportunities of persons other than themselves, "under a pretense of preventing luxury."[13] They admitted that Walpole used Treasury funds, but denied that such use was corruption. Rather it was patronage, the reward of service in government as much as in the arts; if placemen were examples of luxury at work, then the vice was innocuous enough.[14]

In approach Hume is more distant than the ministerial press could afford to be. In three of the essays (and parts of three others) of *Political Discourses* (Edinburgh, 1752), he attempts to refute all the long-standing objections to luxury. "Of Commerce" replies to the charge that trade subverts political liberty. "Of Luxury" argues against previous definitions of the concept. And "Of the Populousness of Ancient Nations" challenges current thinking on depopulation. Taken together, his discourses amount to an all-encompassing reappraisal of mercantile society. On major points he assumes a position antithetical to the tradition embraced by Smollett. Whereas the novelist deplored the rapid growth of the cities, Hume approved it, arguing that people gathered in urban areas to receive and communicate knowledge, thereby increasing their humanity. Smollett writes often from the common assumption that luxury leads to venality and corruption in government and the demise of political liberty. Hume, by contrast, sees a parallel growth in luxury and commerce, on the one hand, and humanity and sympathy on the other. Where Smollett stresses the authority of tradi-tional morality, Hume emphasizes its flaws. The existence of such a contrast is in itself instructive, for Smollett in 1771 was repeating most of the objections to luxury that Hume in 1752 saw himself as answer-ing. Hume moreover regarded his position as a moderating one, one about which men of unprejudiced common sense might gather. The fact that Smollett found this position too moderate indicates much about his own social and political attitudes, particularly with regard to the role of merchants and their representatives in English affairs.

Hume's study of English and European history yielded his funda-mental premise: the rise of materialism, individualism, and economic power outside the court had stimulated political freedom and parlia-mentary government. Indeed the increase of European power and grandeur during the previous two hundred years was directly attributable to the fruits of luxury. In contemporary England, the interests of the class of tradesmen and merchants, "the middling rank of men," had had a liberating influence upon the policies of the House of Commons. As a group they were "the best and firmest basis of public liberty." "These submit not to slavery and meanness of spirit; and having no hopes of tyrannizing over others, like the barons, they are not tempted, for the sake of that gratification, to submit to the tyranny of their sovereign. They covet equal laws, which may secure their property, and preserve them from monarchical, as well as aristocratical tyranny." This phenomenon is furthermore a universal feature, to be found in every society whose economy is evolving from primitive agriculture to sophisticated manufactures.

> A state is never greater than when all its superfluous hands are employ'd in the service of the public. The ease and convenience of private persons require, that these hands should be employ'd in their service. The one can never be satisfied, but at the expense of the other. As the ambition of the sovereign must entrench on the luxury of individuals; so the luxury of individuals must diminish the force, and check the ambition of the sovereign. [P. 6]

> If we consult history, we shall find, that in most nations foreign trade has preceded any refinement in home manufactures, and given birth to domestic luxury. [P. 16]

Hume ascribes the controversies surrounding luxury to the absolutist sense in which the term is used. Few writers consider the all-important relative factors of nation, time, and condition of individuals.

> Since luxury may be consider'd, either as innocent or blameable, one may be surpriz'd at those preposterous opinions, which have been entertain'd concerning it; while men of libertine principles bestow praises even on vitious luxury, and represent it as highly advantageous to society; and on the other hand, men of severe morals blame even the most innocent luxury, and represent it as the source of all the corruptions, disorders, and factions incident to civil government. [P. 24]

The remainder of the discourse "Of Luxury" is an attempt to correct and mediate between the men of libertine principles like Mandeville and those of severe morals like Dennis and Law. Hume's argument is threefold. (1) Far from being reprehensible, the ages of innocent luxury and refinement have in fact been the happiest and most virtuous in world history. (2) When luxury is excessive, it must be recognized as "the source of many ills," but it becomes a vice only when "pursu'd at the expence of some virtue, as liberality or charity." (3) Even a society tolerating vicious luxury is preferable to one entirely without luxury.

Hume's method is no less distinctive than his conclusion, for he is one of the few writers to speak with both authority and sympathy of ordinary laborers. Luxury was a continual spur to working men, Hume held, because initially it led them to work, then gave a sense of liveliness to its performance, and finally provided pleasure at its completion. From such private or individual happiness flowed the more public happiness of industry, knowledge, and humanity. As the laborer gains satisfaction in the mechanical arts, so the larger society acquires the liberal arts. While industry is increasing order and discipline, understanding is diminishing ignorance and superstition. Although moralists persist in advocating "the monkish virtues," it is luxury that renders "the government as great and flourishing as [it renders] individuals happy and prosperous" (p. 28).

What has chiefly induc'd severe moralists to declaim against luxury and refinement in pleasure is the example of antient *Rome,* which joining, to its poverty and rusticity, virtue and public spirit, rose to such a surprising height of grandeur and liberty; but having learn'd from its conquer'd provinces the *Grecian* and *Asiatic* luxury, fell into every kind of corruption; whence arose sedition and civil wars, attended at last with the total loss of liberty. All the *Latin* classics, whom we peruse in our infancy, are full of these sentiments, and universally ascribe the ruin of their state to the arts and riches imported from the East: insomuch that Sallust represents a taste for painting as a vice no less than lewdness and drinking, and so popular were these sentiments during the latter stages of the republic, that this author abounds in praises of the old rigid *Roman* virtue, tho' himself the most egregious instance of modern luxury and corruption. . . . But it would be easy to prove, that these writers mistook the cause of the disorders in the *Roman* state, and ascrib'd to luxury and the arts what really proceeded from an ill model'd government, and the unlimited extent of conquests. Luxury or refinement on pleasure has no natural tendency to beget venality and corruption. [Pp. 32–33]

To the charge that British government since 1688 had been corrupt and venal, Hume replied that nothing could "restrain or regulate the love of money but a sense of honour and virtue; which, if it be not nearly equal at all times will naturally abound most in ages of luxury and knowledge" (pp. 33–34).

The house of commons is the support of our popular government;

and all the world acknowledge, that it ow'd its chief influence and consideration to the encrease of commerce, which threw such a balance of property into the hands of commons. How inconsistent, then, is it to blame so violently luxury, or a refinement in the arts, and to represent it as the bane of liberty and public spirit. [P. 36]

Compared with his rebuke of stern moralists and disappointed politicians, however, his answer to advocates of libertinism is rather weak. Referring directly to Mandeville, he comments that, "it seems, upon any system of morality, little less than a contradiction in terms, to talk of a vice, that is in general beneficial to society" (p. 39).

Hume nevertheless concludes his discourse on luxury strongly, affirming that there is no just alternative to the function of luxury. Whereas Smollett and others said that fear of punishment and starvation was sufficient motive for labor, Hume favored a more positive stimulus, the anticipation of reward and pleasure.

Luxury, when excessive, is the source of many ills; but is in general preferable to sloth, and idleness, which wou'd commonly succeed in its place, and are more pernicious both to private persons and to the public. When sloth reigns, a mean uncultivated way of life prevails amongst individuals, without society, without enjoyment, and if the sovereign, in such a situation, demands the service of his subjects, the labour of the state suffices only to furnish the necessaries of life to the labourers, and can afford nothing to those, who are employ'd in the public service. [P. 40]

The discourse "Of the Populousness of Antient Nations" assumes a related agnostic position. Just as the critics of luxury have no evidence for the corruption of English life, so there is no valid evidence concerning luxury and depopulation. In the first place, Hume writes, there exists no reliable information about size of population in any nation of classical or medieval times. In the second, if such evidence existed and if it did show a trend toward depopulation, then luxury still could not be held responsible for the situation. The same trend could easily have been caused by some other factor or group of factors. Hume thus dismissed the common luxury-degeneracy-depopulation argument as specious, founded as it was on unsupportable assertions.

The *Discourses* have a threefold significance for the study of luxury and Smollett. They answer directly many of the charges the novelist raised against the temper of his times. By 1771, Hume and Smollett had been friends for perhaps longer than a decade. Smollett had an obvious respect for his abilities and called him "one of the best men, and undoubtedly the best writer of the age."[15] Hume's essay on population, moreover, elicited an anonymous pamphlet that anticipates the major distinctions between England and Scotland that Smollett makes in *Humphry Clinker*. The author of *A Dissertation on the Numbers of Mankind in Antient and Modern Times: In which the Superior Populousness of Antiquity is maintained . . . and some Remarks on Mr. Hume's Political Discourse of the Populousness of Antient Nations* (1753) is content to repeat the assertions Hume attempted to discredit.[16] He contends that Egypt, Palestine, Greece, Italy, Sicily, and Gaul were better populated, particularly after being converted to Christianity, than contemporary Europe. In earlier times the simple, frugal, Christian life prevailed; at present an irreligious life of luxury dominates. Beginning with Alexander the Great and continuing during the Roman Empire, luxury destroyed simplicity and fertility.

> The magnificence and splendor, shows and diversions, excesses and debaucheries of the courts of princes, would allure vast numbers [of rural folk]. By all these methods, the world daily declined in temperance, frugality and virtue, and of course the people were continually diminished. . . . Nor indeed has the world ever recovered the antient taste of frugality and simplicity, but is either barbarous . . . or corrupted by luxury and false refinements.
> [P. 197]

As the most relevant example of this idyllic, primitive state, simple, frugal, and happy Scotland is contrasted with vain, luxurious, debauched, and unhappy England. In Scotland the author finds that "the most humble virtues are found to be not only consistent with, but greatly conducive to the populousness and grandeur of society" (p. 198).

Later, Joseph Harris and Oliver Goldsmith followed Hume in arguing that luxury increased happiness by allowing men to produce and consume freely. Harris, in *An Essay upon Money and Coins* (1757), is careful to exclude the objects of vanity from his defense of luxury. "The word *luxury* hath usually annexed to it a kind of opprobrious idea; but so far as it encourages the arts, whets the inventions of men, and finds employment for more of our own people, its influence is benign, and beneficial to the whole society" (p. 30). Luxury achieves these benefits by increasing trade, industry, and efficiency. As these rise, the mechanical arts are perfected and production grows. At each stage of the process wealth increases faster than population: owners receive higher profits, more workers are employed, and taxes can be reduced. In letter 11 of *The Citizen of the World* (collected ed., 2 vols., 1762), Goldsmith gave voice to a point of view quite different from that of the earlier *Enquiry into the Present State of Polite Learning*. His letter-writer finds luxury leading to refinement and meditation.

Certainly those philosophers, who declaim against luxury have little understood its benefits; they seem insensible, that to luxury we owe not only the greatest part of our knowledge, but even of our virtues. . . . The more various our artificial necessities, the wider is our circle of pleasure; for all pleasure consists in obviating necessities as they rise; luxury, therefore, as it encreases our wants, encreases our capacity for happiness. [P. 35]

Examine the history of any country remarkable for opulence and wisdom, you will find they would never have been wise had they not been first luxurious; you will find poets, philosophers, and even patriots, marching in luxury's train. The reason is obvious; we then only are curious after knowledge when we find it connected with sensual happiness. The senses ever point out the way, and reflection comments upon the discovery. [P. 35]

Politically, luxury is no threat, for "the greater the luxuries of every country, the more closely, politically speaking, is that country united" (p. 36). Hence Goldsmith's conclusion is favorable.

In whatsoever light, therefore, we consider luxury whether as employing a number of hands naturally too feeble for more laborious employment, as finding a variety of occupation for others who might be totally idle, or as furnishing out new inlets to happiness, without encroaching on mutual property, in whatsoever light we regard it, we shall have reason to stand up in its defense, and the sentiment of Confucius still remains unshaken: *that we should enjoy as many of the luxuries of life as are consistent with our own safety, and the prosperity of others, and that he who finds out a new pleasure is one of the most useful members of society.* [P. 37]

During the two decades before *Humphry Clinker* appeared, a few further works were published that gave qualified support to certain aspects of luxury. William Temple of Trowbridge, in *A Vindication of Commerce and the Arts* (1758), for instance, says luxury is benign so long as it is an incentive to risk-taking and free spending. Adam Anderson, in *An Historic and Chronological Deduction of the Origin of Commerce* (2 vols., 1764), concludes that in the major European cities luxury is the inevitable concomitant of commerce. To weaken one is to weaken the other. Yet these works are overshadowed in significance by another group that, even though they did not treat the question of luxury directly, are perhaps more central to an understanding of England and Smollett.

This latter group of writers was concerned over the recurring crises brought about by fluctuations in the price of staples. More particularly, they sought some way to alleviate the sufferings of the laboring class that invariably followed a rise in prices. In comparison with the majority of writers cited previously, they entered the controversy over luxury almost inadvertently, since they were generally addressing themselves to the economic position of laborers. In varying degrees they dissented from the normal economic attitude and practice of the century: that the wages a worker received should provide for only slightly more than mere subsistence. They argued rather that higher wages and an improved standard of living should be ends in themselves. Beyond this heretical tenet, most of them made one or more of the following observations: (1) Few laborers were actually idle or dissolute. (2) Idleness, when it did prevail, was largely beyond the laborers' control. (3) The standard policy of wage depression was deplorable, destroying incentive and reducing workers to despair. (4) Higher wages would reward labor and spur the demand of laborers for goods. (5) Increased spending by laborers could create a more stable and equable society. Such attitudes led the writers to a position extraordinary, if not paradoxical, for the time. To different extents, they condemned the luxury of the rich, while redefining or defending the luxury of the poor. Although this body of material is too large to treat adequately here, a brief outline of it is needed further to define Smollett's attitudes. It is a position with which Smollett was certainly acquainted, for the *Critical* reviewed several works containing it while he was editor and afterward. These reviews, furthermore, were consistently hostile toward plans for assisting the laboring poor. The pattern of such hostility becomes even clearer when one compares reviews of the same works in the *Critical* and in the *Monthly*.[17]

Besides Hume and Harris, writers who were sympathetic to the plight of the poor during the period 1750–70 included W. Hazeland, Malachy Postlethwayt, William Mildmay, Nathaniel Forster, James Steuart, and, surprisingly, Soame Jenyns.[18] Three of the most famous of these, Forster, Steuart, and Jenyns, merit specific notice. Forster's *Enquiry* attacks luxury almost exclusively from the point of view of the poor majority of Englishmen. Forster condemns as "as false, as it is inhuman" the doctrine that "the poor will be industrious only in the degree that they are necessitous" (p. 55). Oppression leads not to increased production, but to "desperation and madness." "I cannot but think it is as good a general maxim as ever was advanced, that the sure way of engaging a man to go through a work with vigour and spirit is, to ensure him a taste of the sweets of it" (p. 60). At the same time that he carefully redefined the "necessaries" required by the poor, saying they too needed luxuries, Forster called the luxury of the rich both the immediate and long-term cause of high prices.

> Articles of luxury are of no consideration in comparison to the necessaries of life. Nothing but a plenty of these [last] can make the people tolerably happy, or at all increase their numbers. A nation, therefore, cannot more fatally mistake its own interest, than in giving the least encouragement to luxurious productions, when they are in any degree inconsistent with such as are necessary to general subsistence.

After granting Hume's point that luxury should be a stimulus to industry, Forster says it cannot possess such motivating force in contemporary England. For it is not permitted the poor and certainly has no effect upon the rich; they are not stimulated even to work, much less to work harder (pp. 37–39). At present, luxury serves only "more and more to widen the fatal gap between the very rich, and the very poor" (p. 42). "They that work the hardest live too the hardest. And it seems to be looked upon by some as an act of generosity, that they, who have naturally the best right to live, are suffered to live at all" (p. 191).

Most of the *Enquiry* is devoted to minute and learned examination of the effects luxurious fashions have upon the poor. One chapter is given to bread, another to cattle, a third to horses. Regarding horses, Forster says that the fashion for personal horses and equipages has hurt poor farmers by taking away tillage land from cattle, replacing useful animals with useless ones, driving many farmers off the land, and sending up the prices of hay, straw, and oats. Since Forster's attack upon luxury is presumably from the opposite end of the political spectrum from Smollett's, it is perhaps surprising to find Bramble in his letter of May 29 from London complaining that, "The incredible increase of horses and black cattle, to answer the purposes of luxury" has driven men from the farms. It is, in any case, one of Forster's purposes to show the process by which food and animals which are necessities for the rural poor are, through increases in prices, transformed into luxuries for the urban rich.[19]

Steuart's *Inquiry* is far broader and much more theoretical than Forster's book. Like Hume, Steuart identifies luxury with commerce and calls for control rather than suppression. So long as trade and luxury support the national economy, they are to be encouraged. And while his defense of luxury is more neutral than Forster's, he advocates the extension of prosperity to English laborers. In the section on trade, he seeks to distinguish between moral and economic issues.[20] The narrow moralist sees luxury as self-indulgence and excess. The descriptive economist, however, views it as the inevitable consequence of the introduction of money. Once money dominates economic organization, then a desire for luxury is the main motive for industry and one of the main regulators of production and consumption. It is precisely because luxury is so central to economic activity, Steuart says, that it must be controlled. An exporting nation must control its domestic luxury lest foreign competitors undersell the same products. Discussing the position of laborers, Steuart says an improved standard of consumption for the poor majority is a precondition for economic progress, and he warns of an economic as well as a social danger in a very unequal distribution of wealth. If prices continually outstrip wages, production will fail; but deserved increases in wages will yield greater production.

Jenyns's short pamphlet *Thoughts on the Causes and Consequences of the Present High Price of Provisions* is in at least one respect the most unusual of all the works arguing for more humane treatment of laborers. Half of it appears to be a conventional diatribe against all forms of luxury, in whatever class it is found. Jenyns wants everyone to be frugal, especially the government. Yet in the second half, when he seeks to particularize his grievances, he finds that luxury, like taxes and the national debt, enriches only a few already wealthy individuals. As the few grow richer, the many grow poorer. The present exorbitant price of all staples is but one sign of the wretched position of the laboring classes. While rejecting such a solution as unlawful, he admits that the only permanent answer would be a more equable division of the country's wealth (p. 23).

Forster, Steuart, and Jenyns are but a small sample of the heterogeneous group of writers who defended laborers against charges of idleness and luxury. In addition to preparing the ground for the *Wealth of Nations*, they served partially to untangle the knot of issues labeled luxury, rebutting such charges as Fielding's of the criminal luxury of the poor. In effect, they argued that insofar as luxury was good, the poor must be extended its virtues; insofar as it was bad, the poor were incapable of its vices. Addressing the immediate situation of high prices, they made three observations. (1) Wages should be proportionate to prices. (2) Wages should be sufficient to provide for marriage, self-improvement, occasional leisure, and unpredictable need. (3) Unless unemployment or underemployment were general in the country and encouraged by the government, higher wages would prompt faster and more careful work and would discourage idleness. This perspective upon luxury was available to Smollett, but in his signed work he either rejected or ignored it. Yet the *Critical*, because of its reviewing policy, could not ignore it altogether.

Writing in 1767, a reviewer for the *Critical* said that at least five hundred pamphlets had been published during the past ten years on the high price of provisions. However accurate this estimate, the review was highly selective in its notices, extracts, and comments. In the period from the spring of 1765 to the winter of 1767—during which the works of Forster, Steuart, and Jenyns were appearing—the *Monthly Review,* its rival, noticed sixty books or pamphlets on the subject. The *Critical,* meanwhile, was giving notice to twenty-one. And of this small fraction of a voluminous controversy, the only ones to which it gave space and praise, so far as I can discover, were those that condemned the working poor for their luxury and insubordination. The issue of April 1765 carried an extract and comment upon the anonymous *Considerations on taxes . . . also some Reflections on the General Behavior and Disposition of the Manufacturing Populace of this Kingdom* (1765). Its author is quoted as believing that taxes on necessaries are not, as others think, too high. Rather they are much too low and must be higher if Britain is to retain its advantages in foreign trade. The manufacturing populace is also so idle and debauched that they will not work when the price of provisions is low; only fear of starvation will force them to work: "'*taxes on the necessaries of life* tend to enforce general industry, to restrain idleness and debauchery, to improve our manufacturers, and to make labour cheap a *variety of ways*'" (19:308). The reviewer then remarks that the author's argument is strong because of "the habitual indolence of the English common people, who will not work half the week if they can possibly subsist without it" (19:310). He is assured that there is no validity behind the current clamor over the high price of wheat: "We are of the opinion that the facts [the author] has brought to support this are true, and that the principle is therefore irrefragable. The publication is the more useful on account of the public discontents that are so artfully propagated on its subject" (19:310).

In November 1766 the periodical highly recommended the anonymous *Some Observations upon setting the Assize of Bread* (1766) as a work containing "several matters of the highest importance to the poorer of our fellow-subjects" (22:386). In the long extract the *Critical* printed, the author of the pamphlet calls the dispute over prices of bread exaggerated and malicious. From political and disreputable motives, evil persons voiced the cry; it was heard because of "'the universal clamour and tumult raised throughout the kingdom, chiefly among the poor (the vagrant, the idle, the dissolute, not the industrious poor) and either through ignorance, ostentation, false popularity, or some worse motive, so fatally countenanced . . . by persons of every rank'" (22:387). (This latter charge of false motive Smollett leveled against Pitt in the *Briton* and against all those who solicited votes in the *Briton* and in *Humphry Clinker.*) In the following issue the *Critical* noticed two more anonymous pamphlets on the topic. Of the first, *Political Speculations; or, An Attempt to discover the Causes of the Dearness of Provisions, and high Price of Labour, in England* (1766), it printed a short extract that blamed the idleness of laborers and the lack of severity of the poor laws (22:461). The second, *Reflections on the present high Price of Provisions* (1766), took up the raging argument over monopolies. Hazeland, Forster, and many others had called upon the government to act against the grain monopolies that had forced prices even beyond the critical level. The grain cartels were charged with allowing distillers first and complete choice over the harvest, setting exorbitant prices, regardless of supply, and sending English grain abroad while Englishmen starved for want of it. About the new work, the reviewer for the *Critical* wrote: "The author's professed design in this pamphlet, which is sensible, and written upon generous public-spirited principles, is to show, that the free currency of buying and selling both among ourselves and with other nations, will always prove the most effectual expedient for removing a public scarcity, and that the laws against forestallers, regulators, etc., are as unjust and ridiculous as those formerly in force against witches and wizards" (22:462).

Equally revealing is the treatment the *Critical* accorded Forster, Steuart, and Jenyns. On Forster's *Enquiry*—which such modern economic historians as Furniss, Gilboy, and Coats have called one of the most important tracts of the time—the reviewer in the April 1767 issue begins with an attack upon Forster's presumption, in writing on a topic about which everything has been said, and criticizes the work for lack of learning, taste, and observation. He continues:

> We cannot think ourselves greatly edified . . . because it contains no more than what has appeared in different shapes, within these 10 years, in at least 500 other pamphlets. The author's observations on luxury are equally unimportant, and principally drawn from Montesquieu and certain flimsy French writers, who, whatever they may pretend, are ignorant of the British constitution; and whose maxims never can be applicable to the English manners and interests. [23:305–6]

With the *Inquiry* of Sir James Steuart the periodical was not so curt. It devoted twenty-three pages to the work, all but a few paragraphs being extract or paraphrase. Yet it was highly selective; from the lengthy work it extracted the least controversial and most conventional of Steuart's analyses. His definition of luxury is summarized in one sentence, his defense of it in another. After the latter, the reviewer says he respectfully disagrees (23:323). About Steuart's recommendation that the government step in to ensure equilibrium between prices and wages and to promote a more equal division of wealth, the reviewer comments:

> The author, we hope, will pardon us in saying, that we can have no idea of any statesman interfering in the commercial concerns of a free country. They are too delicate to be touched even by an assembly of statesmen. . . . Nothing ought to appear more uncontrouled, or can be more permanent, than the principles of commerce; and nothing ought to be so independent of a statesman, because they are self-evident; and, as they spring from mutual necessities, they never can be mistaken. [23:411]

Jenyns's *Thoughts* received similar treatment in the December 1767 issue. One paragraph of the work—on the need to lower taxes if prices are to be reduced—is quoted, with the comment that the author's argument is rational. Jenyns's remarks on the poor are ignored.[21]

For the *Critical,* then, as for Bramble and Lismahago, luxury remained a negative concept, in social reality an unalloyed evil to be identified and eradicated. Against this backdrop of evolving attitudes toward luxury, Smollett's position can be seen, in one aspect, as entirely static. *Humphry Clinker* is at least as vehement in opposition as were the *Complete History* and the early volumes of the *Critical* fifteen years earlier. The arguments of Hume, Goldsmith, Harris, Forster, Steuart, Jenyns, and others had no perceptible influence in modifying Smollett's attitude. But seen from a second aspect, Smollett's position had indeed developed. In the *Complete History* he traces the turmoil in the nation during his century to the luxuriousness of the middle classes, especially the merchants and tradesmen of London. But in his later writings he sees unrest among the poor as another, equally dangerous manifestation of luxury. If a wigmaker from Stepney challenged the structure of English society when he shoved his way into the Pump Room at Bath, then a tenant farmer from Derby did so even more forcefully when he demanded higher returns or lower prices, or both at the same time. Thus those writers who favored or redefined luxury may have influenced Smollett indirectly by demonstrating that national economic and political issues—and not religious or moral ones—lay behind the discontent of the laboring poor. As Hume, Harris, and Forster argued for more concern and compassion for laborers as a group, Smollett may have seen the need for increased severity and vigilance, especially so during the early 1760s when wigmakers occasionally supported the demands of tenant farmers. And as he had always worked from a panoramic form, he may have seen the desirability of extending it as far socially as he had geographically, to include not only the customary lords, squires, and merchants, but also an occasional and representative farmer or laborer as well. Such indeed is the difference between the earlier volumes of the *Complete History* and the later *Travels, Present State, Atom,* and *Humphry Clinker.*

Part Two

SMOLLETT AND LUXURY

THE POLITICAL HISTORY OF
LUXURY: THE *COMPLETE HISTORY*
AND OTHER WRITINGS

We must consider how very little history there is; I mean real
authentick history. That certain Kings reigned, and certain battles
were fought, we can depend upon as true; but all the colouring,
all the philosophy, of history is conjecture. — Samuel Johnson

Chancing upon a classical attack upon luxury, a twentieth-century
reader would, I think, find the text mute. He would meet hard nouns
and fevered adjectives but be left in doubt over the intense human
experience they strain to express. Where, exactly, was the plague
Socrates tried to stem? What, exactly, were the crimes Cicero called
loathsome? Who, exactly, were the jaded sinners Tertullian sought to
reform? Some parts of the long history of classical attacks are doubtless
beyond recovery; yet to follow Smollett through the copious work of
his last decades is to answer comparable questions for much of the
eighteenth century. It is in fact to grangerize the final, climactic chapter
of the history. Of his time he was representative in both senses, leader
and example. He is as explicit as anybody as to the substance of the

Law, the identity of legislators, subjects, and tempters, and the nature of tests and punishments. He is always ready to inform his contemporaries about what they need and where they belong. And through the potency of his art he has preserved the classical tradition, creating in *Humphry Clinker* a book that is very much alive today.

For Smollett luxury is a hanging matter. From 1756 through 1771 he treated it as a capital crime against British civilization and as the unresolved issue upon which the future of that civilization depended. Given their diversity of form, purpose, and occasion, the nonfictional works of his last sixteen years possess a remarkable singleness of vision. The *Complete History of England* (1757–58), its *Continuation* (1760–65), the *Critical Review* (1756–), the *Briton* (1762–63), the *Modern Part of the Universal History* (1759–65), the *Travels through France and Italy* (1766), the *Present State of All Nations* (1768–69), and the *History and Adventures of an Atom* (1769) reveal the novelist organizing and controlling his material according to a small number of principles. Although the exposure of luxury is but one of these, it is the most prominent and pervasive. In the *Travels* he inquires to what extent France and Italy are more luxurious and decadent than England, and in what ways. In the *Present State,* less concerned with details, he asks how far each nation has been able to defy luxury and retain its necessity and hierarchy. The political arguments of the histories, the journalism, and the *Atom* are complex, for here he also stresses related concepts, using them normally as subordinate to luxury, sometimes as coordinate. On certain issues Smollett was a man of adamantine constancy, and his nonfictional works contain several hundred references to luxury. This chapter will trace his theory of the introduction of the vice to England, given in the *Complete History,* and demonstrate the persistence of the theory in two quite different works, the *Travels* and *Present State.* Chapters 6 and 7 will deal with the *Critical, Briton,* and *Atom,* works that represent his attempts not only to describe the manifestations of contemporary luxury but also to eradicate them.

The seventy volumes Smollett wrote or edited during his later career represent the most sustained attack upon luxury of the period and bespeak the continuity of previous attitudes into the 1750s and 1760s. His opposition to luxury is stated in language that is strongly traditional. He either dismissed or ignored new concepts introduced into discussions of economics in general and of finance and technology in particular. He apparently believed, for example, that all economic problems could be solved by monetary policy, that a mathematically exact balance of trade was necessary from month to month, and that a nation increased its wealth by no other means than did a private individual. His standards for judging his world were semifeudal, paternal, agrarian, mercantilist, and Augustinian. He regarded land and its resources as the ultimate economic units of a society. And his view of human nature was decidedly dark, developing into the belief that the conduct of the great majority of his fellow Britons must be strictly controlled. He supported the landed interest politically as well as socially, and like Bolingbroke called for a return to the conditions obtaining before the Glorious Revolution. Finally, his arguments are virtually all rationalistic, calling for support upon custom, authority, and tradition rather than upon empirical evidence.

Smollett's political writings of this period are of interest on several grounds. They have the attraction of all of his prose: he knows how to charge his words with effective meaning. And they articulate the social and philosophic suppositions of a large portion of educated England. To Smollett politics meant something far wider than mere electioneering, extending to everything that shapes the national character. As the previous chapter sought to show, in ideas he was nothing if not representative. His originality lay in his fictions and his combination of forms; in politics novelty was something he abhorred. In these writings he was to conservative Englishmen what Paine was to rebellious Americans—a passionate logician, a speaker of vigorous common sense. His basic texts were very different from Paine's, as his lessons were antithetic. He courted the authority of the ages while Paine appealed to the instincts and experiences of his readers. He would have fled scandalized from the men and the experiences Paine sought to touch, and Paine would have thought wasted the energy Smollett spent trying to goad the gentry into action. Yet each sought assurance from what he thought to be the fundamental force of political life.

From the beginning to the end of this period Smollett insisted that the spread of luxury carried with it profound political implications. It is therefore not surprising that in his last novel he should include about forty overtly political references, characters, and situations and should frequently link them to the effects of luxury. Most of his writing, it should be remembered, is political and historical, and luxury was a basic criterion by which he judged the movement and tendency of British society from the great historical watershed of 1688 until his own day. When brought to bear upon the events of his day, this habit of approach, I contend, provided him with specific targets for his attacks upon luxury in the novel. If in the English portion of *Humphry Clinker* Smollett is describing the political world of England during the later 1750s and early 1760s, then he is recalling and repeating parts of his earlier campaign against the City Whigs. When placed in this immediate mid–eighteenth-century context, even the most olympian judgments of a Bramble or a Jery or a Lismahago assume a different coloring.

Exactly when and how Smollett became fervent and partisan in his political thinking we do not know. However, we do have one of his own comments on a related matter: when and how he came to repudiate the Whigs. After the publication of the last volume of the *Complete History*, on 2 January 1758, he wrote to Dr. Moore:

> The last Volume will, I doubt not, be severely censured by the west country whigs of Scotland; but for you and other persons of sense and probity, I desire you will divest yourself of Prejudice, at least so much as you can, before you begin to peruse it, and consider well the Facts before you give Judgement. Whatever may be its defects, I protest before God I have, as far as in me lay, adhered to Truth without espousing any faction, though I own I sat down to write with a warm side to those principles in which I was educated. But in the Course of my Inquiries, the whig ministers and their abettors turned out such a Set of sordid Knaves that I could not help stigmatizing some of them for their want of Integrity and Sentiment. [*Letters*, p. 65]

Yet signs of Tory inclination are present from at least as early as 1756, and they increased to the determined partisanship of the *Briton* and the acidity of the *Adventures of an Atom*. In his nonfictional works, such committed advocacy gives Smollett's language a distinction certain to endure. Boldly and vividly he brought into focus the ruthless, disruptive effects of unbridled commercialism nearly a century before Carlyle. There can be no doubt of Smollett's foresight into the ravages of an industrial England. No one who knows Dickens or Mayhew, Engels or the Hammonds can believe Smollett exaggerated the social effects of unreformed capitalism. To this task he brought not only the mind of a Tory believer, but also the heart of a satirist and the eye of a novelist. It was probably to this achievement that Moore referred when he said Smollett was at his best depicting "the inferior societies of life." When trying to describe the larger forces at work in the present and immediate past of his country, however, he relied upon a conventional idea already worn smooth by writers of sermons. Used as a neutral metaphor for the effects of increasing affluence in portions of a society, the idea of luxury could be brilliantly suggestive—as it was in Mandeville, Hume, and Forster. But as a social touchstone it was burdened with theoretical and practical difficulties. For Smollett, nevertheless, luxury was apparently never a neutral or a complex issue, and he accordingly became one of those described by Hume as "men of severe morals [who] blame even the most innocent luxury, and represent it as the source of all the corruptions, disorders, and factions incident to civil government." For this pertinacity five reasons may be suggested.

First and most obvious, luxury was one of the very few social and political ideas current in Smollett's time that was generic or encompassing enough to include all the things the novelist opposed. He saw England menaced by chaos, faction, corruption, insubordination, and lack of patriotism—and only luxury could account for all of them. Second, he had a basically imperious approach to social complexities, an imagination drawn to severe diagnoses and drastic solutions, impatient of compromise. Third, his polemical métier was negative and critical. He was most vigorous and engaged in social criticism, in the politics of status and privilege, and in the defense of tradition against the onslaughts of the vulgar. About matters of actual day-to-day political policy and their repercussions he was less interested and less confident. And when called upon to be positive in his assessment of government maneuvers, as for many months in the *Briton,* his usual force declined notably.

Fourth, as a thinker Smollett was, by his own admission, not deep or systematic. His acceptance of the traditional arguments against luxury therefore gave to his thinking and writing an intellectual cohesion and confidence they might not otherwise have had. It made his writing more vivid, more complete, more immediate, more intelligent. With it he could point a moral as well as adorn a tale. Indeed it provided the intellectual frame essential for anything beyond mere hackwork: a historical perspective, the rudiments of social and political philosophy, and even something of a view of social psychology. For his work in the *Complete History,* the *Continuation,* and the *Modern Part of the Universal History,* it furnished a means both to measure and to evaluate historical change. For his articles in the *Critical Review,* the *Briton,* and the *Present State,* it supplied similar standards with which to judge contemporary affairs in society and government. It gave him grounds to criticize and to predict the behavior of the middle and lower classes, armed as he was with a panoply of historical portents and analogies. It provided a key to the base designs of the City Whigs and to the purposeless depravity of the mob. It suggested that political opposition could often be regarded in terms of status—the attempt by vain, greedy, and overweening men to overtop their betters. It revealed in imitation the source of working-class insubordination and in inspiration by treacherous men the source of popular discontents. It provided, in short, much that was of practical necessity to a hard-pressed writer who was, on the one hand, a proud, thin-skinned Scotsman of conservative and aristocratic bent impelled to make his way in Whiggish, ever-changing London; and, on the other, one of the most active and prolific writers of the 1750s and 1760s, always working but often ill, seldom having enough money, and never, at least from 1756 until 1763, with leisure for random study.[1]

The fifth and overarching reason was Smollett's deep sense of loss in

English social cohesion. He saw himself within a period of devolutionary social change and in effect echoed Aristophanes: Zeus was gone and Whirl was king. He strongly distrusted the effects of such change upon the social fabric and especially upon political institutions. The desire for luxury was for him the root of change, threat, and destiny, goading men of low birth and no breeding to covet the power, the station, the social perquisites of their superiors. Such covetousness had been raging unabated since 1688. The Glorious Revolution, Walpole, the buying of Parliaments, and the South Sea Bubble were among its early symbols. Moreover, its contemporary manifestations—unrest, rioting, demagoguery, Mr. Monitor, the City Radicals, Wilkes—all proved that rather than flagging, covetousness had grown epidemic. In "a vile world of fraud and sophistication," as Bramble calls London society, Smollett must have felt increasingly isolated, by his awareness of its moral squalor and by his adherence to an older and purer aristocratic ideal.

Among his historical works, Smollett introduces the ideas of luxury and national decline in, significantly, the same place—at the opening of the fourth and final volume of the *Complete History*, in his discussion of the reign of William III. Whereas in previous volumes he had not treated any portion of the sixteenth and seventeenth centuries as a golden age of English life, he seemingly regarded the social relations of those centuries, civil war apart, as embodying a vital, organic society lost to his own time. However indefinite and ahistorical this pre-1688 condition may have been to Smollett, it was of decided value to his thought and is present at least by implication in virtually all his works— even *Humphry Clinker,* where it is represented by Brambleton Hall, which Bramble describes (MB, June 8) as the seat of all that is virtuous and harmonious in British country life and a vestige of the older ideal. This last volume, covering the years 1688–1748, contains, by way of Smollett's regular commentary, his one extended treatment of national luxury and its influence on English politics. Although written near the beginning of his career in polemical journalism—it was completed by June 1757 and published in January 1758—the volume, Smollett felt, reflected a mature and independent view of English history, representing as it did the culmination of fourteen months of arduous work on the *Complete History*. It certainly shows him essaying more than the recounting of sixty years of military and parliamentary affairs. Rather, he was tracing the continuity of present and past, discovering the source of contemporary ills in the parliamentary victory he disdained to call glorious.

The notion that history should be useful, an admonition to its readers, is one of the apparent assumptions of Smollett's historical works. It follows from the belief that history is cyclical or otherwise repetitive:

that every government or nation is constantly declining toward corruption and must be rescued periodically by a revitalizing of its constitution and first principles. The historian can assist in this critical process by bringing his knowledge and judgment to bear upon important events and situations. Like Plato and Hobbes, Smollett desires a nation at one with itself, unified inwardly as much as outwardly. He would encourage unanimity of beliefs and sentiments through the identification of subjects with their government. Although his histories stand apart from the major achievements of European historiography of the seventeenth and eighteenth centuries, his concern with the consequences of luxury led him to broaden the usual narrative of political events to include social phenomena. Signs of discontent and mediocrity could be neither isolated nor ignored, for they exemplified a challenge to the unity and authority a nation must possess.

It could be argued that the *Complete History* and *Continuation* are fundamentally unhistorical. Like Smollett's other historical writings, they appeal to a tacit version of natural law, that in essential matters men are always and everywhere the same, and that contrasts between ages are apparent and superficial. He would probably have agreed with Hume's remark that "History's chief use is only to discover the constant and universal principles of human nature." Since genuine, cumulative progress would therefore be impossible, Smollett could account for the vicissitudes of English history only in terms of the quality of the country's leaders. Hence political strife, though deplorable, is made inevitable in times of incompetent leadership. Natural law is qualified further in his account of the very recent past. Deliberately or not, he indicated that, while progress was illusory, deterioration was an accomplished fact. During his own lifetime, he felt, England had been brought low by paltry leaders and greedy factions, so low in fact that her survival was in doubt. This sense of the significance—uniqueness even—of the present contradicts an underlying assumption of the histories at the same time that it gives his writing a sense of involvement and urgency. An immersion in the present, if it can be said to detract from the histories, gives Smollett's fiction its characteristic flavor. A generation earlier than Burke, the novelist was seeking to forestall the moment when the age of chivalry would pass and the glory of Europe be extinguished forever.

Specifically how the evil influence of luxury penetrated English institutions that were basically sound is not a question Smollett addresses. Instead he treats luxury as a spirit that enters the nation from the Continent about the time William and Mary assume the throne. Thereafter it is always associated with money, and the implication is strong that it was imported by merchants bent upon financial gain, an abnormal excrescence attached to England by brutal and avaricious men. In any case the revolution of 1688 becomes an irreparable fracture in the cincture of Old England, and luxury descends upon the nation not with the infinite (or historical) slowness of a stalactite, but with the overwhelming onrush of a torrent. Discussing the Whig merchants, faction, corruption, the South Sea Bubble, the Walpole era, and the position of the common people, Smollett views luxury as "an irresistible tide," "an impetuous current," "a delerious flood," "a deluge," "a torrent" overwhelming morality and tradition—precisely those metaphors to which he returned in *Humphry Clinker.* The prime movers of the revolution and those who most profit by it are the arrogant Whig merchants, the "Moneyed-Interest," and Smollett reflects thus on the state of England in 1692:

> Intoxicated by this flow of wealth, they [the Moneyed-Interest] affected to rival the luxury and magnificence of their superiors; but being destitute of sentiment and taste, to conduct them in their new career, they ran into the most absurd and illiberal extravagancies. They layed aside all decorum; became lewd, insolent, intemperate, and riotous. Their example was caught by the vulgar. All principles, and even decency was gradually banished; talent lay uncultivated, the land was deluged with a tide of ignorance and profligacy. [4:93]

No evidence accompanies this identification of luxury with the merchants and the common people, but in substance the charge is repeated about thirty times in later works. Throughout the reign of William III, Smollett writes, luxury continues to flourish: the interests of the kingdom are sacrificed to "the interests of money," the constitution and public weal are weakened, and public spirit is sacrificed to faction. An unmistakàble sign of national decline is given when positions of leadership pass from men of learning and virtue to men born "to serve and obey." Men of low birth, no abilities, and gross habits could so rise not by merit, but only by fraud and corruption. Meanwhile men of true substance—"men of landed substance," *not* "mere moneyed men"—go into exile or retirement.

Hope for reform is strong at the accession of the Electoral House, for the country by this time is in a perilous, vulnerable position. National degeneracy has proceeded so far, however, that George I is unable even to slow its pace. A steady decline in public spirit and governmental integrity has made England prey to an unscrupulous faction. Smollett writes of George I as "extremely well disposed to govern his new subjects according to the maxims of the British constitution," but the monarch unfortunately fell victim to the machinations of the Whigs and the moneyed interest. It was during the reign of George I that there occurred the single most important event that the novelist associated with the new economic order. In his description of the South Sea Bubble of 1720, he displays an intense disgust, seeing in the economic collapse a damning symbol of the social chaos ensuing whenever established ranks and distinctions are weakened. The bubble is for him an apt symbol of the abettors of luxury—with their sinister innovations, their companies, projects, funds, debts, and stockjobbing:

> The South-sea scheme promised no commercial advantage of any consequence. It was buoyed up by nothing but the folly and rapacity of individuals, which became so blind and extravagant, that [Sir John] Blunt, with moderate talents, was able to impose upon the whole nation. . . .
> Without entering into the details of the proceedings, or explaining the scandalous arts that were practiced to inhance the value of the stock, and decoy the unwary, we shall only observe, that by the promise of prodigious dividends, and other infamous arts, the stock was raised to one thousand; and the whole nation infected with the spirit of stock-jobbing to an astonishing degree. All distinctions of party, religion, sex, character, and circumstance, were swallowed up in this universal concern, or in some such pecuniary project. Exchange-alley was filled with a strange concourse of statesmen and clergymen, churchmen and dissenters, Whigs and Tories, physicians, lawyers, tradesmen, and even multitudes of females. All other professions and employments were utterly neglected; and the people's attention wholly engrossed by this and other chimerical schemes, which were known by the denomination of Bubbles. . . . The nation was so intoxicated with the spirit of adventure, that people became a prey to the grossest delusion. [4:484–85] [2]

The Bubble of 1720 was a portent. Smollett felt that, since national catastrophe was always imminent in a time of luxury, the seeds of economic collapse or political revolution were germinating in his own time.

Since political venality is the twin of economic folly, so by the advance to the throne of George II in 1727 the Whigs had rationalized their policies "by establishing a system of corruption, which at all times would secure a majority in Parliament." Luxury had thus,

> prepared the minds of men for slavery and corruption. The means were in the hands of the ministry: the public treasure was at their devotion: they multiplied places and pensions to increase the

number of their dependents: they squandered away the money of the nation without taste, discernment, decency, or remorse: they enlisted an army of the most abandoned emissaries, whom they employed to vindicate the worst measures, in the face of truth, common sense, and common honesty; and they did not fail to stigmatize as Jacobites and enemies to the government all those who presumed to question the merit of their administration. [4:518-19]

In the *Continuation,* Smollett often remarks that the concomitant growths of luxury and commerce endanger the spirit of the nation. On the state of affairs after the treaty of Aix-la-Chapelle in 1748, he writes:

Commerce and manufacture flourished again, to such a degree of encrease as had never been known in the island: but this advantage was attended with an irresistible tide of luxury and excess, which flowed through all degrees of the people, breaking down all the mounds of civil polity, and opening a way for licence and immorality. The highways were infested with rapine and assassination; the cities teemed with the brutal votaries of lewdness, intemperance, and profligacy. [1:56]

On events of the year 1752, his reflections are similar.

The tide of luxury still flowed with an impetuous current, bearing down all the mounds of temperance and decorum; while fraud and profligacy struck out new channels, through which they eluded the restrictions of the law, and all the vigilance of civil polity. New arts of deception were invented, in order to ensnare and ruin the unwary; and some infamous practices, in the way of commerce, were countenanced by persons of rank and importance in the commonwealth. [1:128]

Indignation against Whig methods of controlling Parliament, especially Walpole's, Smollett raised to the level of doctrine, to be reiterated in at least three other works, including his final novel.[3] In the *Continuation* he laments:

The extensive influence of the c——, the general corruptibility of individuals, and the obstacles so industriously thrown in the way of every scheme contrived to vindicate the independency of p——ts must have produced very mortifying reflections in the breast of every Briton warmed with the genuine love of his country. He must have perceived that all the bulwarks of the constitution were little better than buttresses of ice, which would infallibly thaw before the heat of m——l influence, when artfully concentrated . . .

and that, after all, the liberties of the nation could never be so firmly established, as by the power, generosity, and virtue of a patriot king.

A few years later, in the *Present State,* his language is not so neutral.

> The constitution of England, though said to be as perfect as human wisdom could suggest, and human frailty permit, yet, nevertheless, contains in itself the seeds of its own dissolution. While individuals are corruptible, and the means of corruption so copiously abound, it will always be in the power of an artful and ambitious prince to sap the foundations of English liberty. . . . The crown being vested with the executive power, the command of the forces by sea and land, the prerogative of making treaties and alliances, of creating peers and bishops, to secure a majority in the upper house, and being reinforced by a venal house of commons, may easily acquire and establish an absolute dominion. [2:165–66]

In his historical works Smollett's normal technique is to associate luxury with the most shocking crises and excesses of the post-1688 period.[4] Yet within this pattern he weaves a further design. He represents luxury as the source of venality, ambition, fraud, corruption, faction, envy, insolence, insubordination, riot, and other similar evils, then identifies each with the practices of the Whigs. On the one hand, luxury leads to venality which leads to fraud which leads to corruption . . . which leads to the tyranny of the Whig oligarchs. On the other, luxury also leads to envy to ambition to insolence to demagoguery to insubordination to riot and finally to the sedition of the metropolitan Whigs. The careful reader is thus able to trace the major portion of Whig policy and practice during the eighteenth century to the hateful influence of luxury. The reviewer of Brown's *Estimate* for the *Critical Review,* if not Smollett himself, could have had Smollett's history mentally before him when he wrote of "the lowest and vilest of mankind" as those who profited from that "inelegent luxury . . . which attended the revolution."[5]

As luxury had created certain political evils, so it had exacerbated others. Writing of the condition of the common people of England, Smollett uses luxury in a sense approaching the modern, of excess. Luxury here is the relaxation of strict control, of the breach of traditional barriers (the same sense, that is, in which he uses the term when condemning commerce). In describing the effects of luxury upon the multitude, he appears almost swept away by his own language. He writes that the example of the Whig merchants "was caught by the vulgar," that "the whole nation was infected" by the South Sea scheme and "All distinctions of . . . sex, character, and circumstance, were swallowed up in this universal concern," and that a generation later commercial affluence was a direct cause of murder on the highways. While Smollett used his metaphors of inundation with conviction and wished his readers to understand that they clothed an irrefutable truth, modern historians have nevertheless demonstrated that few eighteenth-century Englishmen could have engaged in social competition or would have been aware of, far less affected by, stock operations in 1720. His habits of overgeneralization do however reveal his adamant belief that luxury had broken the traditional and necessary barriers between classes. The merit of social distinctions is one of the recurring themes of his writing: *Roderick Random* and *Peregrine Pickle,* like the later *Travels* and *Humphry Clinker,* record worlds of minute social discriminations, where a man can—or should—be *known* by his dress and manner.

The comingling of classes for mere business or amusement would appear moderately harmless did it not signal another, deeper disorder. Smollett is particularly scandalized by the mingling of both classes and sexes. Exchange Alley during the bubble drew "a strange concourse of statesmen and clergymen, churchmen and dissenters, Whigs and Tories, physicians, lawyers, tradesmen, and even multitudes of females." The Paris of the *Travels* reveals itself as the hub of continental luxury and dissipation in its confusion of the places of men and women.

As individuals the submerged majority of Englishmen lie outside the pale of the *Complete History.* As in *Humphry Clinker* and especially the *Atom,* they are nameless and faceless. Yet they are very much within the scope of Smollett's thinking, for in his way he was as much concerned with humiliation, crime, and evil as Dickens. His characteristic habit is to assign the poor and the déclassé to the distant confines of a category. Later English novelists were to be as hostile to the working-class "mob" as he—Dickens in *Barnaby Rudge* and Conrad in *Under Western Eyes,* for example—but they were to see the mob as a union of individualized men caught up in mass action. There is no one in Smollett to approach a Sim Tappertit or a Joe Gargery, however, for he appears to have been what modern sociologists term an essentialist, someone who believes that social status is fixed and immutable and that any attempt to breach the barriers between classes is both unnatural and wicked. He certainly relaxes his powers of narration and description into a mere flow of adjectives whenever his subject is the activity of the lower orders. Moreover, he is led to occasional lapses of consistency. He regards individual benevolence as the locus of morality, especially in dealing with one's inferiors. The deserving poor are to be encouraged by individual, infrequent, and arbitrary acts of generosity.

But their undeserving brethren are to be discouraged by organized, collective, and systematic acts of punishment and control.

The multitude, the common people in the aggregate, of Smollett's historical and fictional writing have few if any redeeming features. No warm and humane face looks out of the crowd toward Bramble the traveler or Smollett the historian. Indeed one might say that the crowd possesses no human, individual characteristics at all. In places of social resort it may be derisory and ridiculous. But luxury has made it dangerous as well as foolish. When aroused by seditious persons to meddling in matters of economy and politics, it becomes, in Bramble's words, "The mob . . . a monster I never could abide."[6] The mob does not attract Smollett's serious attention until the five volumes of the *Continuation,* where in examining the years 1748 to 1765 he makes its conduct one of the main forces in English political events and one of the great threats to the constitution. Yet, as described occasionally in the final volume of the *Complete History,* the mob is already monstrous. Or, rather, it is asserted to be so, for Smollett does not usually describe or specify the conduct he indicts. The following comments on his treatment of the common people, although based upon volume 4 of the *Complete History,* find their fullest substantiation in the *Continuation.* First, Smollett's language is normally one of deprecation or revulsion. When he notes the physical presence of a crowd in a lane or a square, his common metaphors are "drunken," "intoxicated," and "inebriated," continuing the liquid imagery of his passages on luxury. The following is a partial list of the adjectives used to portray the behavior of the common people: absurd, low, indelicate, vicious, depraved, insensible, lewd, corrupt, mean, intemperate, venal, gullible, insolent, mercenary, clamorous, riotous, lunatic, intractable, indecent, wretched, licentious, ignorant, loose, savage, profligate, dissolute, slavish, abandoned, tasteless, idle, brutal, drunken, fierce, debauched. Such a list does more than indicate the vigor of Smollett's language, for no comparable list of even a few neutral or favorable terms can be gathered.

Second, his portrayal of the life of the common people during the eighteenth century is strangely incomplete. He devotes a full six volumes (of nine in the original editions) to events since 1688, and in the *Continuation,* where he is narrating events into 1765, he is increasingly concerned with the activity of the masses. Yet nowhere, so far as I can discover, is there an attempt to anlayze the abiding condition of the great majority of Englishmen. He laments the depopulation of Midland farms but is silent on the plight of the dispossessed farmers. He speaks of the desperate men besieging the roads but says nothing of the sources of their despair. He does not distinguish between the position of the laboring poor and that of the unemployed. The seasonal agricultural laborer is not distinguished from the London apprentice. He passes over times of acute shortage as periods of discontent and faction: gin riots and grain riots are equally pernicious. In short, he does not display that understanding of the miseries of the multitude one finds in Fielding, Hume, Johnson, Goldsmith, or Adam Smith. The most sympathetic passage in all of his historical works regarding the poor presents at the same time the belief that they are ineluctably degraded. Writing in the *Continuation* of a measure proposed in 1759 to amend a law regarding debtors, he says:

> A man, who, through unavoidable misfortunes, hath sunk from affluence to misery and indigence, is generally a greater object of compassion than he who never knew the delicacies of life, nor ever enjoyed credit sufficient to contract debts to any considerable amount: yet the latter is by this law intitled to his discharge, or at least to a maintenance in prison: while the former is left to starve in gaol, or undergo perpetual imprisonment amidst all the horrors of misery, if he owes above one hundred pounds to a revengeful and unrelenting creditor. . . . Wherefore the legislature should extend its humanity to those only who are the least sensible of the benefit, because the most able to struggle under misfortune? And wherefore many valuable individuals should, for no guilt of their own, be not only ruined to themselves, but lost to the community? are questions which we cannot resolve to the satisfaction of the reader. Of all imprisoned debtors, those who are confined for large sums may be deemed to be most wretched and forlorn, because they have generally fallen from a sphere of life where they had little acquaintance with necessity, and where altogether ignorant of the arts by which the severity of indigence are alleviated. On the other hand, those of the lower class of mankind, whose debts are small in proportion to the narrowness of their former credit, have not the same delicate feelings of calamity. They are inured to hardship, and accustomed to the labour of their hands, by which, even in a prison, they can earn a subsistence. Their reverse of fortune is not so great, nor the transition so affecting. Their sensations are not delicate; nor are they, like their betters in misfortune, cut off from hope, which is the wretch's last comfort. It is the man of sentiment and sensibility who, in this situation, is overwhelmed with a complication of his pride, his ambition blasted, his family undone, himself deprived of liberty, reduced from opulence to extreme want, from the elegancies of life to the most squalid and frightful scenes of poverty

and affliction; divested of comfort, destitute of hope, and doomed to linger out a wretched being in the midst of insult, violence, riot, and uproar. . . . He scorns to execute the lowest offices of menial services, particularly in attending those who are the objects of contempt or abhorrence. [3:34–36][7]

Third, Smollett was clearly appalled by the general violence of common life in England. He feared what he considered ever-increasing riots and ever-increasing crime and was disgusted by the sources of recreation favored by the vulgar: hangings, gin-drinking, boxing women, bear-baiting, cockfighting. At their height the gin shops of London numbered about 17,000 and crimes classed as capital 250; "Scarce can our fields, such crowds at Tyburn die, / With hemp the gallows and the fleet supply," was Johnson's view. But Smollett's essential, conscious anxiety was political. Luxury, he came to believe, had changed the traditional submission of the common people into envy, discontent, insolence, and insubordination. His historical study, he felt, demonstrated that in their ignorance the common people were attracted by only *false* examples and *destructive* leaders.[8] Easily aroused by faction and popular incendiaries, they seemed to him a senseless mass covetous of active political power. It was at this point that his parallel suspicions of the Whig middle classes and the poor converged. Under the sway of a vulgarizing, emotional demagogue, a gullible crowd could easily be turned into a mob bent upon destroying hallowed English institutions: insubordination spurred to violent sedition. Smollett thus tends to see the machinations of political opportunists—never identifiably of the Opposition—behind quite diverse examples of potential or actual rioting: for gin and against "crimping," for popular heroes and against wage-cutting, for public executions and against high prices. He tends furthermore to see riots in the context of false issues or grievances. That is, he tends to reject the possibility that rioting arises from either legitimate grievance or random aggression. His linking of the leaders of faction to the mob gives the impression of an English third estate, ranging from Alderman Beckford to Welsh smugglers. At the least, his attitudes toward rioting possessed considerable acumen. He evidently realized what many of his contemporaries, like the Fieldings, did not—that the lower orders were not the only groups to riot. Among the rioters were often many merchants, craftsmen, and tradesmen who not only expressed their own grievances on such occasions, but also articulated the grievances of their less eloquent fellows.[9]

A comparison of the *Complete History* and *Humphry Clinker* suggests that Smollett's regard for the quality of English political life did not change greatly between 1757 and 1771. He seems to have retained with some tenacity the attitude toward luxury and its effects he had developed more than a decade earlier. Although we do not have enough direct information about Smollett's social and political ideas before the 1750s to call his later position a conversion, in one respect at least he is like T. S. Eliot after 1932. In their later careers both concentrated with increasing rigor upon the implications of their acceptance of an older ideal, an ideal honored if at all in its transgression. Martz has accounted for the concreteness of observation in *Humphry Clinker* by calling attention to Smollett's labors with encyclopedic compilations. One may cite the further and probably prior and greater influence of his political engagement. In the first three volumes of the *Complete History,* for example, Smollett assembled from various sources the "factors" of English history. In its last volume and in the *Continuation* he was writing *felt* history—specific heroes and villains, virtues and vices replacing the more abstract and impersonal forces of the preceding volumes. Bramble's later catalogs of intolerable conditions at Bath and London can also be seen as the result of Smollett's controlled observation, his inquiry into the effects of luxury and degradation in his own time.

The *Travels* and the *Present State* are useful comparison pieces for both the *Complete History* and *Humphry Clinker.* In the form of international tours, they reveal Smollett a decade after the *Complete History* continuing to use social status as his divining rod in the search for luxury. In the *Travels* part of his intention is chauvinistic—to display for English readers the follies and degeneracy of the French and Italians and, by contrast, the wholesomeness of their own country. He organizes his comments according to social order, describing "the noblesse or gentry, the burghers, and the canaille" of each town he visits (letter 4). He can find only the middle and lower ranks guilty of luxury. Letters 6 and 7 are devoted to a general description of the extremity and absurdity of French luxury: "France is the general reservoir from which all the absurdities of false taste, luxury, and extravagance have overflowed the different kingdoms and states of Europe. The springs that fill this reservoir, are no other than vanity and ignorance" (letter 7). The luxury of French women carries "human affectation to the very farthest verge of folly and extravagance" and serves as "plain proof that there is a general want of taste, and a general depravity of nature" (7). In one of many examples of overgeneralization, Smollett declares that *every* poor woman is likewise infected by luxury: "That vanity which characterizes the French extends even to the canaille. The lowest creature among them is sure to have her ear-rings and golden cross hanging about her neck" (5).

The luxury of the bourgeois is normally ludicrous, and Smollett describes the parvenus of Nice as he does those of Bath, by means of a satiric listing: "One is descended from an advocate; another from an apothecary; a third from a retailer of wine; a fourth from a dealer in anchovies; and I am told, there is actually a count in this country, whose father sold macaroni in the streets" (17). But at other times they are disgusting. At Boulogne tradesmen have napkins on every cover, silver forks, and stamped linen; but their homes are filthy, "Indeed they are utter strangers to what we call common decency" (5). The artisans and shopkeepers of Nice are lazy, awkward, and greedy, for the city, "being a free-port, affords an asylum to foreign cheats and sharpers of every denomination" (20).

In city after city, village after village, Smollett finds the commonality idle and dishonest. Of the French he declares, "I have a hearty contempt for the ignorance, folly, and presumption which characterize the generality" (7). One sign of their presumption is that they wish to travel as comfortably as their betters (9). Another is their impertinent attitude toward strangers: "The natives themselves are in general such dirty knaves, that no foreigners will trust them in the way of trade" (20, cf. 28). More than once he finds them turning into a mob and behaving like barbarians (34), and at St. Remo he reacts with horror upon being invited to sit in a "common room among watermen and muleteers" (25). He is most sympathetic when he finds them exercising proper subordination, as in Nice:

> All the common people are thieves and beggars; and I believe this is always the case with people who are extremely indigent and miserable. In other respects, they are seldom guilty of excesses. They are remarkably respectful and submissive to their superiors. The populace of Nice are very quiet and orderly. They are little addicted to drunkenness. [20]

Throughout the *Travels* Smollett strikes the attitude of a meritocratic *noblesse de robe* jealous of his accomplishments and ready to unite with the *noblesse d'épée* against the comic but dangerous Third Estate. The *Present State of All Nations,* published in the same year the *Encyclopedia Britannica* began to appear, is for the most part a more factually descriptive work. In seven of the eight lengthy volumes in the series, Smollett and his writers resort only four times to the concept of luxury in their analyses, finding the vice to be the major cause of meanness and poverty in Denmark, Asia, Paraguay, and Peru (1:156; 7:4; 8:394, 417). In the remaining volume, for which the novelist was personally responsible, however, luxury is an important part of the discussion.[10] Indeed he opens the introductory plan of the series with an attack, recalling those of Brown and Goldsmith, on the intellectual consequences of luxury: "In this frivolous age, when the powers of the understanding are all unbraced by idleness, and the mind (as it were) overborne by tides of vanity and dissipation, it requires some address to reclaim the attention to subjects of real utility, and to render the voice of instruction agreeable to the votaries of pleasure" (1:iii). Smollett's main task thereafter is the description of England and Scotland. As Martz has pointed out, the *Present State* was apparently designed for English readers, and Smollett withheld virtually all criticism of their country, reserving it for use in *Humphry Clinker*. The manners and morals of the nation receive almost fulsome praise; the places of amusement in London, Bath, and Bristol are held up as models of urban recreation. Smollett in fact permits himself only one rather mild reproof of English life. In the section on diseases, he notes that illnesses due to luxury and gross intemperance "are rife in England, especially in the great towns" (2:222). A smaller deviation might also be noted, censuring not the mainlanders, but the natives of the Isle of Jersey: "Those of the inhabitants, who are temperate, live to a great age; but luxury being more prevalent here than formerly, has brought in distempers unknown to their ancestors" (3:328).

The section on Scotland, which immediately precedes that on England, is in two respects a striking contrast. Smollett does not reprove the English for their luxury, but for obvious reasons neither does he applaud their frugality. Yet in at least eight instances—and in the manner anticipating the Scottish half of *Humphry Clinker*—Smollett explicitly praises the Scots for being *strangers to luxury*.[11] The following, for example, are his comments on the inhabitants of the Hebrides and St. Kilda:

> [The people of the Hebrides] are, in general, strong, vigorous, and healthy, their constitutions being steeled with labour, and preserved by temperance. Happy in their ignorance of luxury and ambition, they live without pride, avarice, and almost without contention, enjoying the hard-earned necessities of life. . . . Perhaps these people might be justly deemed the happiest of mortals, were not their felicity invaded by the horrors of superstition. [1:431-32]

> With respect to their manners [the people of St. Kilda] are a model of innocence and simplicity; and perhaps the happiness of the golden age was never so much realized as in St. Kilda. Unknown to envy and ambition, ignorant of luxury and vice . . . they obtain the necessaries of nature without money, of which they are wholly destitute. [1:451]

Furthermore, whereas Smollett is generous toward English institutions but not toward Englishmen, here his tactic is the reverse. His descriptions of Scottish institutions are generally unfavorable, but he applauds ordinary Scotsmen for their simplicity, industry, and subordination. The majority of his fellow countrymen (in contrast to those of France and Italy) are good laborers because, "a man of the lower class, who has been taught from his infancy to bridle his passion, to behave submissively to his superiors, and live within the bounds of the most rigid economy, will, through the whole course of his life, retain the color of his education" (2:10). Such a laborer will never defy his betters, the law, or any aspect of social decorum: "On the contrary, he will save his money and his constitution: he will pay due deference to those whom fortune hath placed in superior sphere: even when he thinks himself injured, he will rather devour his resentment, than gratify it at the hazard of losing a friend or employer" (2:11).[12]

In a general sense, we need not pass beyond the *Complete History* in order to discover an ultimate source of the opinions voiced in *Humphry Clinker.* In the attack upon luxury Smollett found a form, as well as a theme, that would do him full service for the remainder of his writing career. His discussion of the effects of luxury upon a weakened society in the history can be said to anticipate and account for his portrait of a decadent England in the fiction; his description of the unscrupulous tactics of leading Whig figures is sufficiently angry and inclusive to explain his continued condemnation in the 1760s. Yet to identify the attitudes of the last volume of the *Complete History* with those of the novel would distort the experience that produced *Humphry Clinker.* According to internal evidence, the most probable dates for the composition of the first three-quarters of the novel are 1765–68. That is, the last volume of the history was composed near the beginning of the chaotic and transitional years of the Seven Years' War and the novel some years after its close, with the *Continuation,* the *Present State,* the polemical journalism of the *Critical* and the *Briton,* and the *Atom* intervening. It is likely that the political tone and substance of *Humphry Clinker* were the result of specific political issues and trends of the late 1750s and early 1760s, and, further, of Smollett's disillusionment over his involvement with them.

These issues amount to a calendar of the controversies in which the nation—and consequently Smollett—was engaged between 1756 and 1763. They revolved centripetally about two of his inveterate concerns —the degeneracy and prostitution of an age of omnivorous luxury and the dangerous conduct of the City Whigs and their myrmidons in the metropolis, both in the immediate context of the tactics and purposes of the war with France. The long years of war seemed to many contemporary Englishmen a time of ever-shifting domestic crises: the death of one monarch and the accession of another, the transfer of power from one political group to another, the fall of four ministries, increased agitation by the middle orders for a voice in policy-making, and controversies over the royal prerogative, colonial trade, food prices, standing armies, German alliances, and the costs of war. For the politically inclined, the times compelled increased activity, reassessment, and realignment. For Smollett they brought forth the occasion and the audience for his two journals of political commentary—the *Critical Review* and the *Briton*.

THE POLITICS OF WAR:
THE *CRITICAL REVIEW*

For my part, I cannot bear the tumult of a populous commercial
city.—Smollett, Travels

I saw a Parcel of People caballing together to ruin Property,
corrupt the Laws, invade the Government, debauch the People, and
in short, enslave and embroil the Nation; and I cry'd Fire.
—Defoe on the function of the Review

Smollett's histories amply demonstrate that his objection to luxury
was not pure like a theorem, but concrete and personal like an indictment. In this respect he came prepared to the bruising world of metropolitan journalism. By the time he began the *Critical Review,* some
forty eighteenth-century periodicals had already carried out prolonged
crusades against luxury. Many editors had already explained their
motives in terms of the highest patriotism. Thus Fielding in the *True
Patriot* (no. 7): It was the duty of every Briton to combat luxury, for its
presence aborted all virtue as it spawned all vice. With precedent and
principle established, a political paper could settle into its real business,
to identify and denounce that "Parcel of People" bent upon corrupting
the nation. Smollett broadcast his indictment of luxury in nearly everything he wrote, but he delivered its bill of particulars in the *Critical* and

the *Briton.* Many Englishmen in each decade—certainly the more in-fluential ones who financed and wrote the papers—regarded luxury as not only the curse of the age, but also the threat of the very hour. Like many writers before him, Smollett used the opportunities of his month-ly and weekly journals to mark the movement of that hour. Here the roles of social critic and political commentator were one, and here luxury could be exposed at its source—in the antics of unprincipled politicians, fatuous tradesmen, and a swinish mob.[1]

It is significant to an understanding of Smollett's temper that the world of journalism he entered in the 1750s was altogether different from that of later centuries. He began his career, not like Dickens, in the scrupulous verification of factual detail, but in commentary upon men, books, and events. Almost his entire experience in journalism was as editor and polemicist, his realm that of opinion and controversy. The pattern of his journalistic writing becomes the pattern of the later *Travels, Atom,* and *Humphry Clinker:* he takes notice of the large, incontestable fact—the book *was* published, the Louvre and the British Museum *are* there, the war is *still* on—and proceeds quickly to what interests him more, his own judgment of the fact and its circum-stances. The political tumult of the 1750s encouraged this pattern, for it reflected two levels of crisis—one caused by major changes in domes-tic and international affairs, the other brought about by the failure of older theories adequately to explain these changes. The visible result was a period of inflamed debate, burning with such intensity that many Englishmen were convinced that the ultimate destiny of their country hung in day-to-day balance. Public commentary, especially on the con-duct of the war, subsisted on a pinch of fact, a pound of opinion. The *Critical Review* could not observe the flow of national affairs without also altering it. It became, itself, a new weight in the balance of contend-ing forces. And the attack upon luxury of the *Complete History* was applied, as it had been from Plato to Bolingbroke, to events of the pres-ent and predictable future and thus became a politics.

In the early stages of the war the *Critical* attempted to bring down the Newcastle administration, condemned the Whigs as inveterate rabble-rousers almost as often as they attacked the French, and repudi-ated mercantile arguments in favor of the German alliance. As the war was entering its third and fourth years without a sign of eventual vic-tory, Smollett and his writers raised a chorus of deprecation against the presumed evils of the age and most particularly against the evils of their political opponents. They resumed the offensive later when victory did appear assured, with attacks upon those who opposed an early peace. In the *Briton* Smollett was himself called upon to praise the terms of the peace treaty as well as the characters of George III and the Earl of

Bute and to disparage their adversaries among the City Whigs. What remains constant through the entire length of these many-sided campaigns is not so much the language or the logic or the argument or even the immediate political position of Smollett's periodicals. Rather, it is the object of attack—the independent Whigs of the London middle class. Indeed, of the twenty-five or so journals that flourished during the period, Smollett's are the most adamant and complete foes of the City Whigs.[2]

Although we do not know the full extent of Smollett's contributions to the *Critical,* we do have sufficient evidence to say that he dominated the review from its inauguration in March 1756 to his departure from England in June 1763.[3] In the first place, his public and especially his enemies—it is significant that he attracted more decided enemies than mere opponents—identified him as its presiding genius, to the extent that a preface was attached to the sixth collected volume (1759) asserting that Dr. Smollett did not write all of the articles in the review.[4] Furthermore, in a list he composed of his published works he added "Great Part of the Critical Review," and he had earlier indicated that he approved virtually everything that went into the journal. In addition, he described himself in a letter written in 1762 as "proprietor" of the *Critical,* although in such a context as to suggest he may not have been sole proprietor.[5] Finally, a copy of the first volume marked with the names of reviewers suggests Smollett as its main author, Knapp surmising that both his editorial control and the number of his reviews increased in succeeding years. After surveying Smollett's work for the *Critical,* Knapp speculates that he was "the leading reviewer in London for the period from 1756 to 1763."[6] During this period the political point of view of the journal remained relatively constant: a consistency reflected in the fact that the first, and rather feeble, defense of luxury ever to appear in the *Critical* was not published until two years after Smollett relinquished active involvement in it.

France and England were already in armed conflict in North America when the first issue of the review appeared. The coincidence was not altogether happy, for Smollett and his writers were deeply suspicious of combat over trade rivalries in the colonies. Of all the major issues the *Critical* confronted during Smollett's editorship, it was on only this initial one that it seemed confused and ambivalent. Always hostile toward the French, it was nevertheless nearly as hostile toward the men who supported the war and its aims: the merchants and tradesmen, the newly affluent, the optimistic and hearty. Some of the journal's early critics accused it of a belligerent antimetropolitanism and an antagonism toward commercial expansion. Others meanwhile perceived in its attitude a primitive, agrarian, and peculiarly Scottish defiance of English policy, whatever its direction.[7] Yet the review was in something of a dilemma. It had announced in a preface to the first volume its patriotic intention to combat sedition and to join controversy. As rapidly as it became a brutal fact, however, war with France faded as an issue of dispute. By mid-1756 Smollett and his writers were faced with a problem that, with historical hindsight, can be summarized thus: How could a new review very much devoted to public affairs survive during a period of war if it were simultaneously isolationist on international issues and aggressive on domestic matters? The practical answer the *Critical* evolved was a three-sided attack not upon the war itself, but upon the Whigs and their handling of the conflict, the effete temper of the times, and "popular" demands upon government. Such a compromise was equally imaginative and successful: while the *Critical* not only survived but prospered, this compromise remained a fundamental feature of its position during Smollett's active editorship.[8]

In one of the earliest examples of the policy, articles attributed to Smollett led an assault upon Newcastle's administration after Admiral Byng's retreat from Minorca.[9] When the incident first became known, the *Critical* joined in the public consternation expressed against the admiral himself, but eight later reviews attempted to deflect indignation onto the duke and his ministers, charging them with deficiencies in experience, leadership, and preparation. These reviews, appearing as judgments of the many pamphlets by ministerial and antiministerial writers, also contained a second theme, that both ministerial and opposition Whigs were rousing the mob with scurrilous and irresponsible rhetoric—a charge Smollett would repeat many times and in many circumstances during the next eight years.[10] The review's vituperative tone in challenging Newcastle and Smollett's later defense of Byng in the *Continuation* reveal that the actual target of the dispute was the old minister himself and not his unfortunate admiral.[11] The flavor of this campaign against Newcastle can be justly gauged in the *Briton,* which although written later represents Smollett's writing alone. In no. 32 of the *Briton* Newcastle is depicted as a "superannuated original" scurrying about madly, "as usual in a sea of absurdity." Yet more harsh is the portrait in no. 38 of him as a senile fool in "the vineyard of sedition": "an old pilot conveyed through the public streets upon an ass, his face turned to the tail, with a cap and bells upon his head, a slavering bib under his chin, and a rattle in his hand."

To the *Critical,* Newcastle was merely the leader of a political faction and the temporary favorite of the fickle multitude—a gloss upon Smollett's use of the term. During the Byng affair the *Critical* was part of the faction opposing Newcastle, but to this group the review gave the title "patriots." As defense of the royal prerogative became much more significant to Smollett and his writers under George III, so they allowed the "popular voice in public affairs" its due when it removed Newcastle but vigorously deplored it when it sought to bring down Bute.

Perhaps because he saw an end to the power of the Whig junta, perhaps because he foresaw a rapid end to the war, Smollett welcomed the elevation of Pitt, Newcastle's successor as principal minister. While opposing many of his plans for conducting the war, the *Critical* termed Pitt "the most venerable character of our age" and called abuse of him in the press "invidious and unjust."[12] Smollett had paid personal tribute to Pitt in a handsome dedicatory statement prefaced to the *Complete History*. Yet the *Critical's* support of the minister was relatively brief and did not extend, even in moderated form, beyond 1759, after which he was regularly denounced by Smollett and his writers. They deplored the continental campaigns and argued with equal vehemence against naval ventures. They likewise opposed all German alliances and the increased influence being assumed by the City interests, who urged an expansion of the aims of the conflict. So long as the nation appeared united behind Pitt and no Tory alternative seemed practicable, the *Critical* attacked his policies but not his leadership.[13] When the terms of that unity were altered in 1760 by signs of eventual victory and by the death of George II, however, the review again became partisan in opposition. It recalled earlier grievances and soon came to call Pitt's ministry "the most despotic that ever reigned in England . . . he resigned because he could not retain his despotism."[14]

Thus it was that in his writings of the 1760s—especially the *Briton* and the *Continuation,* but also *Humphry Clinker*—Smollett was to repudiate his earlier praise of Pitt. His themes were two: Pitt had enkindled faction, and he had sought support among the dregs of the people. In the *Continuation* he wrote that Pitt's resignation "savoured of disgust and resentment, and implying a disapprobation of the k——g's measures, acted as a ferment upon the ill humour of the people. Such a commotion could not fail to clog the wheels of government, obstruct the public service, and perhaps have some effect in alienating the affections of the subjects" (4:333-34). He charges Pitt with responsibility for the "heats and dissentions which inflamed and agitated the nation." In a similar vein, he discloses his attitude toward Pitt's followers when he comments upon a tribute made him in October 1761 by the London common council:

> Whether this resolution was not in fact an arrogation of right to decide upon the merits of a minister, the particulars of whose conduct they could not sufficiently distinguish; and implied a

disapprobation of their S——n and his council, because they had
not implicitly surrendered their own faculties of perception and
reflection, to the ideas of one man; nay more, because they had
not complied with the violent measures he proposed, in diametrical
opposition to their own sentiments and judgment; posterity will
be candid enough to determine, when those clouds of prejudice
which now darken the understanding, are dissipated, and all the
rancour of personal animosity is allayed and forgotten. [4:335]

The *Briton* contains many of Smollett's most vitriolic comments on
Pitt, as upon other topics and figures. He is disparaged in no. 3 for
alleged ingratitude toward George III; in no. 5 as a man "who raised
himself into a colossal idol of popularity"; in no. 7 as greedy but undeserving of a royal pension; in no. 15 as a man without principles, a
man "who changed his party as often as he changed his cloaths." Two
other attacks are notable for their similarity to Bramble's remarks in
Humphry Clinker and for their double condemnation of the minister
and the groups he supposedly led. In no. 37 Smollett rejects a comparison between Pitt and Scipio Africanus because the latter did not "climb
upon the shoulders of the mob to the first offices of the state . . . nor
use the lowest arts of popularity to play upon the passions of the vulgar,
and raise the most dangerous spirit of discontent among his fellow-
citizens." This is precisely Bramble's position when he decries gentlemen who stoop to the level of the mob. In a longer statement of this
theme, the *Briton* no. 11 presents a portrait of Pitt that, although no
doubt unjust and malicious, anticipates the technique Smollett used
with so much skill in *Humphry Clinker*. In the guise of a letter-writer,
the novelist identifies Pitt with one Luca Pitti, a Florentine demagogue
of the fifteenth century. This letter, significant enough to be quoted
in full, fully utilizes the devices of fiction and grasps the novelistic
opportunity to create memorable and convincing details of Pitt's tyranny. It thereby presents a substantial case, with concrete evidence,
something Smollett could not or would not do in his other non-fictional
writing against the elder Pitt. It also contains the simile of the minister as a political comet, to be used again in the novel.

Smollett opens the letter with a straightforward statement of one of
his fundamental political assumptions: "A wise man will scorn alike the
censure and applause of the multitude; the first as an impotent attack
which virtue cannot avoid, and innocence has no cause to fear; the last
as a contemptible bubble, without solidity or duration." In *Humphry
Clinker* Barton restates this position in order to explain Newcastle's
periods of popular support. The letter in the *Briton* then proceeds with
the evidence of history.

There are some examples on record, of good men and great patriots sacrificed by popular frenzy; but I could fill a whole volume with instances, both from ancient and modern history, of men without real merit, whom the mob, without reason, has raised into idols, worshipped for a season; and then their adoration changing into disgust, abandoned to contempt and oblivion. Reverses of this nature might be found in the annals of this country, even within my own remembrance: but as such a review might be displeasing to some persons still living, whom I have no intention to offend, I shall select one remarkable instance from a foreign republic, the case of a famous demagogue in Florence, called *Luca Pitti,* who flourished, and fell in the fifteenth century. He was a plebeian of a bold and turbulent spirit, who sought to gratify the most aspiring ambition, by courting the favour of the populace. This, he found no difficulty in acquiring, possessed as he was of a natural flow of eloquence, perfectly adapted to the taste and understanding of the vulgar. By dint of exerting this talent in the council of the state, and espousing the cause of the multitude on all occasions, he raised himself into such consideration among the lower class of citizens, that nothing was heard but the praise of Pitti. When he appeared in public, the mob rent the air with acclamations; and every mechanic of any substance, presented him with some valuable token of his esteem. Cosmo de Medicis the first, the wealthiest and the best subject of the republic, who knew his disposition, and was well acquainted with his aim, employed his influence in such a manner, that Pitti was chosen gonfalonier of justice; and then his real temper appeared without restraint. He no longer kept any measures with his fellow-citizens. He treated his superiors with insolence, and his equals with contempt: he fleeced the people without mercy: he granted protection and encouragement to the most abandoned profligates, who were endued with any art or talent which could be turned to his private advantage; and the multitude, which he had formerly courted and caressed, he now held in the most mortifying subjection. Afterwards, when the family of Medici was supposed to aspire to sovereign power; when the people were alarmed for their liberty; when opposed factions were on the point of drawing the sword, and his country was threatened with the horrors of a civil war: in this emergency, when certain patriots entreated him to interpose his influence towards an accommodation, or declare himself in favour of those who wished well to the constitution; he shrunk from the service of his country in the day of danger and distress, he lent a deaf ear to all their solicitations; and wrapt himself in the shades of inglorious retirement, at a critical juncture, when public freedom was at stake, and his country in an especial manner demanded the full exercise of his faculties and interest. His behaviour on this delicate occasion, though palliated by a few hireling emmissaries, provoked his former adherents to such a degree, that their attachment was changed into hatred; their applause into reproach. The gifts they had formerly bestowed with rapture, they now recalled with disdain: not one gold box or trinket was left as a testimony of his former credit! Their indignation, however, gradually subsided into contempt. *Luca Pitti,* who had appeared like a comet in politics, now set, never to rise again. He passed the evening of his life in disgraceful solitude, and died in utter oblivion. It must be owned, however, in behalf of this man, that when he quitted the helm, he was quiet. He did not attempt to disturb the operation of that machine which he would no longer manage; and if he did not exert himself to the utmost of his power, for the service and advantage of the public; so neither did he employ or countenance a set of desperate incendiaries, to kindle the flames of civil dissention in the bowels of his country. If any turbulent *Pitti* is living at this day, he will do well to take warning from the fate of this Florentine; or should such infamous partisans be at work, I hope every good man will think it a duty incumbent upon him to detect and expose them to the detestation of their fellow-subjects.

During Smollett's years of intense political involvement, Pitt was not only a formidable opponent, but also the foremost representative of a succession of related forces the novelist found threatening. As a purposive cause standing beyond immediate appearances, luxury was ever in the background of Smollett's political purview. In the midst of an arduous and unpredictable war which he felt might well end in calamity, in the years 1756–60 Smollett apparently came to see luxury as having depleted a once-proud nation he honored under the rubric of "Old England." It had weakened both its men and its institutions; it had squandered land, food, animals, raw materials, and other national resources. The enervation begun in 1688 seemed to be nearing its fateful climax. Especially during the *Critical's* period of support for Pitt, but also as early as its first issue, it was denouncing "the age of shopkeepers" in terms at least as harsh and as comprehensive as John Brown's in the *Estimate* and Goldsmith's in the *Enquiry into the Present State of Polite Learning in Europe.* Many of its pages indeed provide the corroborative tone to Bramble's cheerless nostalgia for better times past. In *Humphry Clinker* Smollett is certainly reviewing this mood when he has Bramble ask rhetorically:

whether the world was always as contemptible, as it appears to me at present?—If the morals of mankind have not contracted an extraordinary degree of depravity, within these thirty years, then I must be infected with the common vice of old men, *difficilis, querulus, laudator temporis acti;* or, which is more probable, the impetuous pursuits and avocations of youth have formerly hindered me from observing those rotten parts of human nature, which now appear so offensively to my observation. [MB, June 2]

The answer, in fact, comes immediately: "We have been at court, and 'change, and every where; and every where we find food for spleen, and subject for ridicule." As evidence that Bramble is not being merely peevish, we have Smollett's own even more savagely pessimistic observation in the *Continuation:*

From the frivolous pursuits of the people, the rage for novelty, their admiration for show and pageantry, their ridiculous extravagance, their licentious conduct, their savage appetite for war and carnage which they had for some time avowed, and the spirit of superstition with which they began to be possessed, one would be apt to believe that the human mind had begun to degenerate, and that mankind was relapsing into their original ignorance and barbarity. [4:19]

The *Critical's* crusade against luxury was as fierce as that of the *Craftsman* had been twenty years earlier. It conceded only once through 1766, in a review already cited, that its effects would not be devastating to the nation, retaining Smollett's policy of condemnation for at least four years after his resignation from the review.[15] Seven aspects of its comments on luxury merit particular attention. First, the *Critical* gave considerably more notice to works decrying luxury than did the other leading review, the *Monthly Review.* Second, it was highly selective in the notice it gave works that discussed social conditions, a tendency already noted with regard to rising prices. Reviewing a book that called for both higher productivity and higher wages, for example, it would report or extract only the former position, ignoring the latter. Third, more than once its writers held that the most dangerous form of luxury was the idleness or insubordination of the poor. Fourth, it gave the most curious of all reviews of John Brown's *Estimate of the Manners and Principles of the Times,* deploring its alleged appeal to mass emotions. The same review reiterates the charge that luxury came to England in the wake of William III and the Whig moneyed interest. Fifth, it chose to extract from the many volumes of the *Modern Part of the Universal History,* which was edited by Smollett, those portions that

describe the vicious effects of luxury in other nations. Sixth, it anticipated one of the major themes of *Humphry Clinker* by twice attempting to establish that the poverty of Scotland was directly caused by the
luxury of England. Finally, it renewed the Opposition's contention that
the liberal arts and graces of England had been dissipated by the forces
of luxury.

In the preface to the first volume of the *Critical Review,* Smollett
wrote that the periodical was determined to combat the seditious tendencies then obtaining in England. He and his fellow writers apparently
viewed luxury as among the foremost of such seditious trends, since
they used virtually every issue to attack it. With so many books and
pamphlets being published on the topic, occasions for comment were
manifold. Thus by either direct statement or approbation of the opinion
of others, writers for the periodical summoned up practically all the
arguments against luxury cited in chapters 1 and 2. On the abstract
level, luxury was held responsible for political faction, social chaos,
economic decline, popular discontent, and national degeneracy. More
specifically, it was regarded as the root of depopulation, crime, high
prices, grain riots, losses at war, and an unfavorable balance of trade.[16]
Instances of luxury were condemned as vain, silly, sinful, vicious, and
unpatriotic. Arguments against luxury, one reviewer said, must be
repeated as often as possible, however old or unoriginal they may be.[17]
Perhaps it was this belief that led Smollett and later editors to give so
much attention to sermons denouncing luxury. The *Critical* occasionally
chided clergymen for straying into matters of commerce and science,
but it was generous with its space and its praise when the clergy damned
luxury.[18]

As an indication of editorial policy, luxury was continually made a
political issue. In the issue of August 1756, one writer warns that
individual resistence to luxury will be inadequate, for "the best
endeavours of virtue will be vainly exerted to save us from ruin, should
indolence, luxury, and corruption become the sole ends of the administration" (2:84). Another, writing in the same issue, concludes a discussion of the luxury and effeminacy of Athens with the comment: "Few
of our Readers, we imagine, will be able to pass over this character of
the degenerate *Athenians* without an application, but too obvious, and
some melancholy reflections on the striking resemblance between *them,*
and a nation *now subsisting,* sunk into universal corruption and
depravity, and perhaps on the very brink of ruin" (2:2). Foreseeing
English defeat in the war with France, a third, in December 1756, saw
luxury as the source of national weakness: "We are become a most
venal and mercenary people,—that there is little or no public virtue left
amongst us—that selfish regards have swallowed up all true social

affection—" (2:460). Even in less fearsome times, the periodical continued to see luxury as a political evil. Writing in March 1761, a reviewer called luxury the central issue of the forthcoming parliamentary elections. He therefore recommended a particular sermon against luxury "to the electors of Great Britain at the present important juncture, when the love of our country is so immediately necessary towards the making of a proper choice of their representatives in the ensuing parliament" (11:201).

This conservative bias, regarding virtually all change as a sign of luxury and degeneracy, is revealed further in the *Critical*'s reviews of economic works. As in the controversy over high prices, the periodical ridiculed or ignored those books and pamphlets (or parts thereof) that called for a more equable treatment for the mass of English people. Nominally reviewing a pamphlet that called for an end to the adulteration of bread, a writer in the May 1758 issue used the opportunity to damn as sedition current popular discontent: "The pipe of self-interest played upon by these wretches [the bakers], has become a trumpet of sedition, arousing the turbulence of popular uproar to revenge their oppressors" (5:443).[19] Similarly, in its reviews of two of Malachy Postlethwayt's books on commerce, the periodical neither mentions nor extracts the author's suggestions for relief of the poor and the better distribution of national wealth. Of Postlethwayt's *Great Britain's True System* (1756) it published sixteen pages of extracts and comments, but those concerned only monetary policy (2:432–48). Phillip Cantillon's *Analysis of Trade, Commerce* (1759) contains several passages calling for changes in attitude toward labor and the structure of society, but the periodical's long notice of the work in March 1759 refers only to the history of money (7:241–49). Indeed this reduction of economic problems to questions of monetary value characterizes the *Critical*'s attitude during the controversy over high prices. Writers who addressed themselves to problems of misery, starvation, monopolies, insufficient wages, restrictive distribution, and unfair division of wealth were perilously close to treason, the journal argued, for the situation "cannot be remedied [by means other] than by preserving an exact and true proportion between gold and silver" (9:469; June 1760).

With other writers, those of the *Critical* increasingly came to identify the idleness and insubordination of the laboring poor as the form of luxury most threatening to the national interest. They rejected, that is, Defoe's contention that luxury was the immediate cause of idleness in all classes. They had identified effect with cause and applied this line of reasoning with special vehemence to one group only: the laboring poor. They also brought mercantilist thinking to bear on the alleged excesses of the poor. Returning to the older proposals for a tax on such luxuries as French lace, they recommended that laborers be taxed when they were unemployed. They criticized the charity schools, as they had been attacked in the 1720s, for placing too much emphasis on reading and writing and not enough on "labour and industry." The idea that the economy depended upon very low wages was likewise put to peculiar use. Demands for higher wages were possible only when laborers felt secure in their jobs. They could feel so only when the number of jobs equaled the number of workers. That, in turn, was possible only when the country had been depopulated. Thus a controversy over wages was a certain sign of depopulation, and both were signs of national luxury. A writer in the July 1760 issue rhetorically asks why it is

> that there is not that order, regularity, and subordination main-tained among the manufacturing poor of this as of other countries; that our poor are in their morals more loose, dissolute, and abandoned; that we daily hear of combinations among journey-men in manufacturing towns to extort exorbitant wages, without ever growing richer; nay, on the contrary, growing more idle, drunken, and debauched, in proportion to increased wages? [10:43][20]

The causes he cites are of course luxury and depopulation.

Yet the most curious demonstration of the *Critical*'s antipathy to the common people of England came in its long review of Brown's *Estimate* in the issue for April 1758. One would have expected the periodical's editors to hail Brown as a welcome ally, for they had attacked the same agents of luxury and shared his uncompromising aversion toward luxury itself. As has been shown, moreover, Smollett's language of condemna-tion often echoes that of the *Estimate*. But rather than praise, the periodical gave Brown stern rebuke. His book was to be deplored and repudiated, the review stated, not so much because of its argument, but because of its appeal to anarchical, mass emotions. Precisely because of its popularity, the work threatened to arouse the public to a degree of irresponsible zeal. At the same time that the *Gentleman's Magazine* and the *London Magazine* were commending Brown as an erudite and patriotic writer, the *Critical* was reacting extremely in the opposite direction. It compared him with Smollett's notorious antagonist, Dr. John Shebbeare, whose *Letters to the People of England* were consid-ered treasonable incitements to riot. And while threatening domestic order, Brown was also giving comfort to England's enemies.

The review first questions Brown's knowledge of the origins of contemporary luxury in precisely the terms Smollett had used in the *Complete History of England* to describe the aftermath of the Glorious Revolution.

The inelegant luxury, the degeneracy of taste, the universal profligacy of manners, which attended the revolution, were owing to causes very different from those which this estimator has assigned. They were the natural consequences of money-corporations, funding, stock-jobbing, and the practice of corrupting p——ts, which began to be reduced into a system in the reign of King William. Deluges of wealth flowed in upon contractors, stock-jobbers and brokers, the lowest and vilest of mankind, utterly destitute of taste, knowledge, or liberality. They were seized with the ambition of rivalling their betters: they substituted expense in the room of elegance, and gave into all the absurdity of extravagance. Their example influenced the common people, who knew their origin and envied their affluence. These began to thirst after the same enjoyments, and scrupled at nothing to attain them. . . . Such was the origin and progress of that degeneracy which we now lament. [5:285]

The effect of the *Estimate* can be only unfortunate.

Our author speaks . . . with a becoming severity of the writers of such books as tend to overturn religion . . . but many will be apt to put a hard question to our author, by asking him, Who is to be looked upon as the greatest pest of society—the writer, who, tho' he attacks the principles of religion, writes only to a few metaphysical readers, or the writer who published a treatise level to all capacities, in which the most hideous picture is drawn of his fellow subjects: the community to which he belongs is libelled without any regard to truth and decency, and held up to the view of the neighboring nations, as lost to every generous, manly, and virtuous principle; a nation of poltroons, and on the very brink of destruction, by our degenerate manners? . . . a character which every true Englishman will read with indignation, and every Frenchman with joy and triumph. [5:313]

And such adverse effects, furthermore, are likely to continue. "The more popular a writer is, the more dangerous, because his efforts are adopted, his falsehoods believed, and the world apt, like *Mirabel* in the comedy, to fall in love even with his faults" (5:319). The periodical expresses approval of only one of Brown's positions, his charge that servants "are now generally left to the workings of unbridled passions, heightened by idleness, high living, and dissolute example." About this passage, the reviewer writes: "What this writer has said concerning the manners of servants in the present age, it is but justice to him to acknowledge, is very fit and proper, and expressed with that warmth

and indignation which their shameful licentiousness so highly deserves''
(5:312).

For some reason not readily discoverable, the *Critical* interpreted the
thesis of the *Estimate* to be democratic and leveling. Yet as we have seen
(and as Leslie Stephen has shown) Brown's position was highly traditional and conservative, depending in part upon Tory ideas on luxury
from the 1720s and arguing for a more nearly omnipotent monarch and
a more elitist Parliament. Although this position was more flexible than
the *Critical's* normal preference for absolute monarchy, it was certainly
not leveling, and Smollett's periodical was alone in seeing it thus. That
the periodical persisted in this interpretation for at least three years is
revealed by its review in June 1760 of the anonymous *Additional
Dialogue of the Dead, between Pericles and Aristides* (1760). From the
beginning the reviewer presumes Brown to be the author and calls
Brown's praise of the Greek ideal of democracy "equally pernicious and
deceptive" (9:466). He continues by arguing, in language almost identical to Smollett's description of the reign of George II in the *Complete
History* and to Lismahago's tirade in *Humphry Clinker* (MB, July 15),
that even the present English form of limited representative democracy
is evil.

> What shall our author say to great, powerful, and civilized people,
> who delegate their rights to a certain number of representatives,
> chosen by themselves! To a people who, void of every idea regard-
> ing public virtue, barter their rights for the mean gratuity given by
> a candidate for a seat in the senate! Who have absolutely reduced
> to system this species of corruption, whereby the price of every
> corporation is exactly ascertained! Who entrust the liberties of the
> nation to representatives, who have wasted their influence in
> soothing, cajoling, corrupting and destroying the morals of their
> constituents? Who are sensible that the broken fortunes of these
> representatives must be repaired by methods inconsistent with
> freedom; that they are assembled in one house under the im-
> mediate eye of a court, rich in lucrative posts and preferments, and
> liberal in pensions, out of the public money? What, shall influence,
> and power of bribes, avail nothing here? [9:466]

The review concludes with a mordant statement of conservative disillu-
sion: "Consult history, consult your own mind . . . there can [never] be
a dependence on the integrity of the people, where luxury and interest
contribute in rendering corrupt, those on whom they have devolved
their rights, and constituted their representatives" (9:467). As in its
review of the *Estimate,* the *Critical's* reaction is peculiar. It alone of all
the reviews saw in the *Additional Dialogue* any signs of liberalizing or

reforming tendencies. The *Monthly Review* for July 1760 termed it a tract on the gullibility and dependence of the masses (13:30); my own reading of it is similar.

While the *Critical* was pursuing its immediate opponents, it also sought to ensure that the presumed historical consequences of luxury were kept before its readers. One of its methods was to extract pertinent sections from historical works that blamed luxury for national degeneration. Between 1759 and 1765, the multivolume *Modern Part of the Universal History,* prepared by Smollett and others, was used in this way,[21] the periodical extracting about four hundred pages of the work in all, usually in its lead article. Since the *Modern Part* was a vast survey, extending to sixteen volumes, the editors of the *Critical* had an abundance of material suited to its purposes. Among the extracts they published were discussions of the laudable tax on luxury instituted by the Venetian Republic, the general effects of luxury on European trade, the ways luxury had led to the corruption of various legislative bodies, and the effrontery instilled by luxury in the merchant class throughout Europe.[22]

The *Critical*'s judgments on the economic relations between England and Scotland run parallel to those voiced by Bramble and especially Lismahago in *Humphry Clinker.* In Bramble's letter of December 20, Lismahago denies that the Union has brought a significant amount of benefit to Scotland; rather, the Scots themselves have labored hard for what they have achieved. In a review of Robert Wallace's *Characteristics of the Present Political State of Great Britain* (1758), a writer for the *Critical* in April 1758 says:

> With respect to the riches of North Britain, which seem to be our author's native country, we shall not pretend to dispute. This, only it may be proper to observe, that he, in imitation of all the Whig writers, ascribes the late improvements which have been made in the agriculture, manufacture, and commerce of Scotland, to the union of that kingdom with England: whereas, in fact, it seems owing to the natural progress of trade, which has been increasing in the same proportion, during that period, in other improveable countries. [5:290]

Lismahago holds that Scotland has improved in spite of English policies, not because of them. The reviewer of the Wallace book writes:

> We cannot allow the truth of his assertion that the present trade and wealth of this nation are owing to the security and liberty which the nation gained at the revolution above what they had enjoyed in the preceding period. It is well known, that trade

flourished during that period to a very great extent; that navigation was as free, and commerce much less clogged with duties and
restrictions, than it has been since the revolution; that the subsequent increase of trade was a natural consequence of improvement
and extended industry, assisted by the wretched policy of France,
which by persecuting its protestant subjects, drove them into
England, where they were hospitably received in the reign of
James II, and where they established the manufactures of silk, hats,
toys, etc. to the inconceivable emolument of the kingdom. [5:290–
91]

The echo is yet stronger in the October 1766 issue, in a review of M. V.
D. M. [Mons. Vivand De Mezague], *A General View of England . . .
translated from the French* (1766), which focuses upon the relative
luxury of the two countries. The reviewer disdains the book as a "wild
production" but quotes part of it at length, as Lismahago listens
patiently for a while to Bramble, in their *débat*.

How well informed this very superficial but assuming Frenchman
is, may be gathered from his observations upon Scotland, when
speaking of the benefit which England receives from that country.
"As to the money that the Scotch proprietors may perhaps spend
in England, you are to observe, that Scotland is but a very poor
country: that those landed gentlemen of theirs who come into
England, generally carry back with them more than they brought,
and that the other people of that country, who go into England,
carry little or nothing ever with them, and always carry back something, and often pretty considerable too. It is not the Limousine
that enrich Paris . . . they go thither only, because they are wanted,
in order to carry back with them all that they can save, out of the
wages paid them for their labour. It may be safely affirmed, that
this article, far from contributing to England, swallows up more
than the three millions of livres raised by the taxes levied in Scotland, which, moreover, may be presumed, to have been already
exhausted by the pensions, salaries, and appointments of those,
who are employed in the different branches civil and military, of
the government of that country. Thus then, the territorial income
of Scotland, considered abstractly, from all kinds of commerce,
contributes nothing to England, whereas England may be said to
contribute largely to Scotland."
A Scotchman who understands the present state of his own
country, could inform this writer, that though manufactures and
commerce are of late years incredibly encreased in Scotland, yet
they carry on their trade chiefly, if not wholly, by paper-money;

and that one of the principle reasons for this is, because their great landholders rake together all the specie they can get among their tenants that they may spend it in England from whence they bring nothing down to their own country, but a knowledge of the vices and fashions of the places where they resided.

"It is impossible," continues our author, "that Scotland should contribute the least tittle to the art of trade with England. It is even certain, the balance is greatly in its favour; for, having nothing to sell, to enable it to buy, all its conveniences must arise from its national industry and oeconomy. Its sales therefore are few, and its purchases still less, insomuch, that it dares not venture to purchase the very wheat that it wants; were it to purchase such wheat, it would be forced to go without many other necessary articles, and would soon become more depopulated than it is at present. A great number of its inhabitants content themselves with eating oatcakes, and very often a kind of oatmeal soaked in water. Scotland sends into England nothing but some black cattle, linen, salt herrings, salmon, and a particular kind of coal that is burned in the houses of people of fashion only. It is true, indeed, that Scotland furnishes swarms of lawyers, physicians, surgeons, military officers and soldiers, shopkeepers, artizans, and pedlars, but very few seamen. Now any country that has nothing, or what is next to nothing, can't but be great gainers by trading with a country that has a great deal. It is not France that gets by Savoy; but Savoy certainly gets by France. The only benefit therefore that England reaps by its trade with Scotland, is, first, by drawing from thence a number of men, whose labour and industry comes cheaper to them than that of their own people, which therefore is a great saving to them. Secondly, by drawing men from thence, who serve to replace those that she is continually losing by her luxury, by her trade, by navigation, and by her wars, which necessarily therefore, makes her less subject to depopulation."

Never, perhaps, was such a string of absurdities and mistakes crowded in so few lines as in the preceding paragraph. The Scotch mention it as a melancholy truth, that their luxuries are so much encreased by their trade, and the improvement of their estates, that they purchase the chief articles of their expences (in household furniture especially) from England; that their houses are as elegantly furnished, their attendants as numerous, and even their tavern expences as dear as in any part of England; that the housekeeping of their nobility and gentry is as extravagant; and that all their trade can scarcely supply the demands the English have upon them for the several articles they import. If anything was wanting to show the ridiculous mistake of this author with regard to the poverty of Scotland, we might appeal to that infallible criterion, the price of land in Scotland, which is said to be as high, at this very time, as in England. [22:300–301][23]

Finally, in the arts and sciences, as well as in government, commerce, and trade, the fruits of civilization seemed rotten to the *Critical*.[24] Reason had become corrupted, liberty abused, and "the public" depraved. Nearly every issue contained at least one discussion of "the degeneracy, want of taste, trifling pursuits, and dissipation of the present age," as the issue for April 1759 (7:375) termed the English condition. The review seemed to be preparing its readers for an impending national catastrophe:

> There is not a stronger mark of the corruption and depravity of any state or kingdom, nor perhaps a more certain symptom of its approaching dissolution, than a visible contempt of the arts and sciences, with an universal coldness and neglect in regard to every branch of literature. We have too much reason to think from the love of indolence and pleasure, which distinguishes the age we live in, that this species of degeneracy is every day gaining ground upon us. [4:46; July 1757]

Most of the periodicals of the time, as before noted, at some time and to some degree participated in such national recrimination. Yet the *Critical*'s contributions are distinguishable on a number of grounds. Its repeated calls for English reformation were most insistent and confident and had more obvious social and political biases. It emphasized, in effect, not what *we* can do, but what can be done to *them;* not general responsibility, but particular blame. The review often lamented the lack of *amor patriae* in persons "too cold, indifferent, and mercenary," yet sought to identify itself and its individual writers, Smollett especially, as the "true patriots."[25] Besides denouncing luxury, Smollett and his writers chose to attack what they thought were its particular manifestations. The review of Brown's *Estimate* already cited is a cardinal example of the periodical's habit of turning a general indictment into an occasion for pursuing specific enemies.[26] Unintentionally but rather accurately, Smollett is describing the practice of his own periodical when he has Bramble lament to Dr. Lewis: "I should renounce politics the more willingly, if I could find other topics of conversation discussed with more modesty and candour; but the daemon of party seems to have usurped every department of life. Even the world of literature and taste is divided into the most virulent factions, which revile, decry, and traduce the works of one another" (MB, June 2). The

THE POLITICS OF WAR   173

Critical's demands for reform are in consequence essentially different from the calls for moral and ethical regeneration being made by dozens of other periodicals and pamphlets. It was arguing for a stronger monarchy, a reassertion of traditional controls over most Englishmen, a resumption of power "by men born to wield it."

Such goals went well beyond even those of John Brown and certainly were the antithesis of what the City merchants meant by political reform. When the *Monitor* called for reform, it was asking for a wider franchise and some redistribution of parliamentary seats.[27] To Smollett such calls were in themselves evidence of the degeneracy of the times, and from 1756 through 1763 the *Critical* poured its ample fund of scorn upon them. Reviewing Joseph Warton's essay on Pope, Smollett in 1756 anticipates one of his principal theses in the *Briton* and reveals the characteristic tone of the earlier *Critical:*

> We think the author of the essay mistaken, when he asserts . . . that the sciences cannot exist but in a republic. The assertion savours too much of a wild spirit of Democratic enthusiasm, which some people have imbibed from the writings of the *Greeks.* —. . . it betrays its owner into all the absurdities of an overheated imagination.—The sciences will always flourish where merit is encouraged; and this is more generally the case under an absolute monarchy, than in a republic, for reasons so obvious, that they need not be repeated. [1:233; April 1756]

Two months later, a review of *A Vindication of Natural Society* misses the work's irony and proposes a choice between the status quo and "total anarchy and confusion."

> In regard to our author's arguments (if any argument there be) we cannot but esteem them weak and inconclusive: for although it will very readily be granted, that every species of society and every form of civil government is attended with many evils, and subject to inconveniences and abuses, it will yet, by no means follow, that total anarchy and confusion, which would be the inevitable consequence of (what he terms) *natural* society, are therefore *eligible.* The grievances and imperfections of which he so heavily complains, must always continue whilst men are men, unless he could persuade his friend [Bolingbroke] in the shades to send us one of his *Utopian* patriot kings to govern us, and a better rule than his *first philosophy* to regulate our moral conduct. [1:426; June 1756]

Subsequent issues called the desire for political change "the seed of civil dissension," a disruption of "public order and national tranquility," and a sign of "resistance and opposition."[28] A review in 1760 already cited pronounces an author's admiration for the Greek ideal of democracy "equally pernicious and deceptive" and cautions that merely representative government leads inevitably to "storms of popular faction" and "narrow jealousies of rival merit."[29]

The proximate cause of English degeneracy, the City mercantile interests, Smollett kept constantly in the foreground of his political scrutiny. Of association with them, Pitt was guilty in both person and policy—sufficient grounds alone to disturb the *Critical.* To adapt two of Smollett's metaphors, if luxury was the tide inundating English society, then the City Whigs were the sharp rocks upon which the society would be broken.[30] His hostility toward the City, extending in his nonfictional work from the beginning of the *Critical* in 1756 through the publication of the final volume of the *Continuation* in 1765, was widely publicized on Grub Street. It was the subject of dozens of pamphlets and articles in periodicals. Yet for the twentieth-century reader it is obscured by the apparent vagueness of both Smollett's language and the nature of the City and its goals. Respecting the customs of controversy and the libel laws of his time, Smollett did not normally name names in his attacks, Admiral Knowles notwithstanding. Like most controversialists he instead used obvious and convenient titles like Mr. Monitor, Mr. Addressor, Mr. Alderman, Mr. Freeman, The Old Woman of the Monthly, Liverymen of London, and later, Mr. North Briton and Mr. Patriot. A variant is the type of name he used so often in his fiction, such as Alderman Grog, Freeman Vain, and Yelper. Other references are geographical, to the wards or streets where merchants and tradesmen lived or had their presses, as in "the Shadwell mob," "the mob at Temple-Bar and Guild-Hall," "the worthies of St. George-in-the-East," and "the Monmouth St. reformers." Thus in *Humphry Clinker,* Bramble refers with malice to the "delicate creatures from Bedfordbury, Butcher-row, Crutched-Friers, and Botolph-lane" (MB, April 23). A further category would include such terms of evident disparagement as "cits," "zealots," "rabble-rousers," "republicans," "incendiaries," and that trinity of scorn he used so often—it appears in the *Complete History, Continuation, Critical, Briton,* and *Humphry Clinker*—"contractors, stock-jobbers, and brokers."

Although they would not have answered to such names, City merchants apparently recognized Smollett's contempt and returned it. For decades at the center of the English economy, they had also become, since the early 1750s, a significant factor in national politics. By 1760 the City had a population of about 150,000 and was the undisputed focus of banking, insurance, overseas trade, and the older crafts. At the top of its financial pyramid were "the moneyed-interest," the Whig oligarchy: the governors and directors of the Bank of England, the principal insurance companies, and the great merchant companies like the East India Company. Whig by tradition and self-interest, these men were largely unreformed and a law unto themselves. They were attached by business and taste to the court and the current ministry; they were themselves fashionable and lived in fashionable districts. The actual heart of the City's community and political life, however, was not with the few oligarchs but with the larger, more middling sort—the 8,000 liverymen and 12,000 to 15,000 freemen who belonged to the City's sixty or so companies. From this group, attached to the City by both occupation and residence, came the 236 members of the London Common Council, representing twenty-six wards and one hundred vestries. Such a large concentration of interest and activity made the Common Council a potent political force in its own right and, equally important, a political forum second only to Parliament.[31]

The large measure of unity and experience displayed by the Common Council during Smollett's day came as the result of a traditional division of forces within the City. While the council amounted to the lower house of metropolitan government, the Court of Aldermen, composed of one representative from each of the wards, was the upper. The councilmen normally initiated political action but were often opposed by the aldermen, who tended to be wealthier, more aristocratic, and "better connected." The aldermen, in addition, acted as though they composed a gentlemen's club, were fewer in number, met more frequently, had the decisive vote in such decisions as selections of a lord mayor, and were either more receptive or more vulnerable to manipulation from court. The division between aldermen and councilmen led on the one hand to unrest and suspicion, but on the other to a creative friction that bound the City together as it seemed to rend it. The liverymen and freemen found common interests and kept a continual pressure upon the aldermen, who, in response, were less inflexible than they would otherwise have been. The City was thus a source of political ferment, or at least motion, which to opponents like Smollett appeared subversive, leveling, and radical.[32]

Far from seeking the favor of court or ministry, the City as a whole and the Common Council in particular took great pride in a tradition of independence and usual opposition to Whitehall and St. James. For twenty years a center of steady opposition to Walpole, it became, according to Lucy Sutherland, a major political force during the Seven Years' War. At some point during the latter 1750s its leaders determined that the City should no longer accept the roles the oligarchs had previously set it, as stalking-horse and scapegoat. Among the signs that City interests were restive in their secondary positions was the establishment of their own periodicals of opinion and controversy, like the *Monitor* (founded 1755), the *Con-Test* (1756), the *Patriot* (1762), and the *North Briton* (1762). In their pages, and in a plethora of pamphlets, writers claiming to represent a unified City point of view vociferously supported Pitt and the war, opposed concessions, and reviled the surrender of conquests. Overall, they argued for a greater and more visible share of political power. Yet by far the greatest amount of dispute arose over more specific, month-to-month political and economic issues that fell outside the conduct of the war, especially those raised at election time and as questions or legislation in the Common Council and Parliament. These were items of metropolitan, sometimes even national, interest and captured notice in the newspapers and reviews (Smollett's opportunity for criticism). Representatives of the City, both within and without Parliament, argued that England could not be a great and just nation when fixed and often exorbitant prices subsidized the landed aristocracy at the expense of the needy, when a wealthy junta dominated overseas trade through state monopolies, when national monopoly franchises were granted for manufactures, when the gentry's laissez-faire attitude toward wage rates kept laborers at mere subsistence, and when landed interests virtually controlled commercial policy and set harmful customs and excise taxes. In place of these policies they proposed parliamentary regulation of grain prices, to fluctuate with the size and quality of harvests; independence of trade from the crown and freedom for competition; expansion and competition in manufactures; higher labor rates, to be set by Parliament if necessary; and governance of commerce in the hands of men engaged in commerce. Beyond such largely financial matters, City spokesmen advocated seemingly radical changes in political and social custom, ranging from the publication of parliamentary debates and ministerial decisions to the opening of certain streets and sections of London heretofore closed to tradesmen.

Because they were essentially gradualist and reformist—"true sons of the Glorious Revolution"—members of the Common Council and its sympathizers in Westminster and the Court of Aldermen strove for parliamentary recognition of their contributions to the nation. Hence the movement for parliamentary reform, a repeated issue in the 1750s and yet more so in the 1760s, subsumed many of the other social, political, and economic goals of the City. The movement had its origins in the period of Walpole's dominance and of course found not even partial satisfaction until 1832, but to traditionalists during Smollett's time it often seemed as large a threat as the armies of Louis XV. As elaborated over a number of years, the fundamental demands of the City Whigs were four: (1) shorter (three-year) and more frequent parliaments; (2) stronger and more effective, though nonetheless traditional, means of restraining the power of the crown; (3) elimination of those centers of aristocratic—as well as royal—power, the rotten boroughs; and (4) binding of parliamentary representatives to the wishes of their constituents by means of contractual pledges made at election time. All these points were in the political air while Smollett was writing and receiving his lasting opprobrium—in great measure because both Smollett and the leaders of the City had profound hopes for change at the accession of George III. While the novelist trusted that the young monarch would, with Bute's guidance, repudiate Whiggish principles, the City hoped (with considerably less confidence, however) that he would be persuaded by Pitt to elaborate, extend, and purify them.

Sutherland finds a new phase of City politics opening with the resignation of Pitt in 1761. Disabused of hope for court support or even neutrality, the City appeared to possess much greater self-confidence and political competence, to the extent that it became the dominant partner in its alliance in opposition with the Rockingham group. It was united against Bute and his terms for peace and was determined to press its petitions and its demands for reform. William Beckford, City alderman and lord mayor during the period of the *Briton,* concentrated his parliamentary election campaign in 1761 on the issue of electoral reform, declaring in a speech in March that, "our Constitution is defective only in one point, and that is, that little pitiful boroughs send members to parliament equal to great cities."[33] Pitt's principal lieutenant in the City and the chief backer of the *Monitor,* Beckford resumed his argument in the House of Commons after the election. During a Commons debate in November 1761, he said that the government was not always in harmony with "the sense of the people" and went on to clarify the phrase.

> The sense of the people, Sir, is a great matter. I don't mean the mob; neither the top nor the bottom, the scum is perhaps as mean as the dregs, and as to your nobility, about 1200 men of quality, what are they to the body of the nation? Why, Sir, they are subalterns, I say, Sir . . . they receive more from the public than they pay to it. If you were to cast up all their accounts and fairly state the ballance, they would turn out debtors to the public for more than a third of their income. When I talk of the sense of the people I mean the middling people of England, the manufacturer, the yeoman, the merchant, the country gentleman, they who bear all the heat of the day. . . . They have a right, Sir, to interfere in the condition and conduct of the nation which makes them easy or uneasy who feel most of it, and, Sir, the people of England, taken in this limitation are a good-natured, well-intentioned and

very sensible people who know better perhaps than any other nation under the sun whether they are well governed or not.[34]

For this and earlier campaigns the more active aldermen, councilmen, and their supporters, especially in the press, gained the name, City Radicals, which many of them cherished. Yet during the 1760s they were also known as "the Bill-of-Rights people" because of a famous chain of events in which Smollett played an important part. For more than two years before Bute became chief minister, his allies in court and in the press had been attacking the *Monitor* as seditious and had at least four times threatened government suppression. Then on 25 May 1762, Bute was made first lord of the treasury (and the next day a knight of the garter), and Whig rule was at an end. Within four days Smollett produced the first number of the *Briton,* whose function, that initial number stated, was "to oppose and expose and depose *The Monitor.*" Two weeks later Arthur Murphy was engaged to assist Smollett with a second ministerial weekly, the *Auditor.* Soon thereafter the ministry began intercepting mail to and from important journalists and politicians of the opposition. In November a warrant was issued for the arrest of one of the principal writers of the *Monitor* on grounds of sedition. The City had henceforth another unifying issue of resistance—the suppression of freedom of speech, a freedom, it held, guaranteed by the revolution of 1688. That cause had of course been trumpeted five months earlier in the first number of the *North Briton,* in whose opening lines Wilkes had written:

> The *liberty of the press* is the birth-right of a BRITON, and is justly esteemed the firmest bulwark of this country. It has been the terror of all bad ministers; for their dark and dangerous designs, or their weakness, inability, and duplicity, have thus been detected and shown to the public, generally in too strong and just colours for them long to bear up against the odium of mankind. Can we then be surpriz'd that so various and infinite arts have been employed, at one time entirely to set aside, at another to take off the force, and blunt the edge, of this most sacred weapon, given for the defence of truth and liberty? A wicked and corrupt administration must naturally dread this appeal to the world; and will be for keeping all the means of information equally from the prince, parliament, and people.

Although many in the City itself doubted Wilkes's motives, they were yet more anxious over the government's response to the periodical: further warnings of suppression, a duel, a dozen or so threatened legal actions, a general warrant, and final suppression. Their own eventual reaction, summarizing years of political agitation, was the cry for "Wilkes and Liberty."[35]

Smollett's treatment of the City Whigs in the *Critical,* the *Briton,* the *Continuation,* and *Humphry Clinker* turns inside out the City's conception of itself. Smollett was apparently convinced that, because they had neither judgment nor learning, the men of the City could have no awareness of how foolish and ignorant (and therefore alarming) they appeared to cultivated Britons. A group of men bent upon insulting their betters could expect no quarter from the *Critical* and received none. Within this general policy of disparagement, the review's criticism of the City Whigs had five specific characteristics. First, an immeasurable but probably small part of it derived from a continuing rivalry between Smollett's review and Griffiths's *Monthly Review* (and to a lesser degree between the *Critical* and Scott's *Monitor*). The *Critical* and the *Monthly* were to some extent contending for the same audience, and they frequently assumed adversary positions for the sake of simple opposition as much as for political partisanship.[36] Second, from its inception the *Critical* found little favor and much hostility in the City, and the review typically returned abuse in kind. When in *Humphry Clinker* Newcastle calls his opponents a "pack of rascals . . . Tories, Jacobites, rebels," Smollett is recalling the epithets most often hurled by City writers at the *Critical.*[37] Third, the review's identification of the City Whigs with luxury is almost certainly a function of nationality, politics, and class. That is to say, nowhere in the pages of the *Critical* through 1763 have I been able to uncover any of the following types of (British) persons or causes associated with luxury: Scottish, Welsh, Irish, Tory, noble, aristocratic, gentle. All of Smollett's writings, the *Present State* especially, proclaim that within the British Isles only the English have been infected with the virulence of luxury. Of the English, only persons of inferior birth—the mercantile or middle and lower classes—display its symptoms. And of these, the contagion is most visible in those men who claim to be heirs of the Whig revolution, who are striving, ambitious, mobile, and disdainful of social and political traditions. The Whig oligarchs are pernicious because of what they do; but the metropolitan Whigs are despicable because of what they *are.*

The most obtrusive and positive example of this identification of the City with luxury appears in the *Adventures of an Atom.* This political apologue, Smollett's *Gulliver's Travels,* published twelve years after the *Complete History,* reflects the effects of the journalistic conflicts of 1758–63, with Smollett distinguishing between the two main groups of Whigs and attacking each in turn. It also anticipates his method of invective in *Humphry Clinker,* ridiculing specific Whig aristocrats like Newcastle in extended individual portraits, while condemning the popular Whigs of the City almost exclusively as a group. Early in the work Smollett describes this political division during the reign of George II.

> The two factions that divided the council of Japan [i.e., England], though inveterate enemies to each other, heartily and cordially concurred in one particular, which was the worship established in the temple of Fakku-basi [Whiggism], or the White Horse. This was the orthodox faith in Japan, and was certainly founded, as St. Paul saith of the Christian religion, upon evidence of things not seen.[38]

After depicting the leading members of the junta, Smollett proceeds "to describe many other stars of an inferior order."

> At this board there was as great a variety of characters, as we find in the celebrated table of Cebes. Nay, indeed, what was objected to the philosopher, might have been more justly said of the Japanese councils. There was neither invention, unity, nor design among them.—They consisted of mobs of sauntering, strolling, vagrant, and ridiculous politicians. Their schemes were absurd, and their deliberations like the sketches of anarchy. All was bellowing, bleating, braying, grinning, grumbling, confusion, and uproar. It was more like a dream of chaos than a picture of human life. . . . Here, however, one might have seen many other figures of the painter's allegory; such as Deception tendering the cup of ignorance and error, opinions and appetites; Disappointment and Anguish; Debauchery, Profligacy, Gluttony, and Adulation; Luxury, Fraud, Rapine, Perjury, and Sacrilege; but not the least traces of the virtues which are described in the groups of true education, and in the grove of happiness. [P. 415]

In the *Atom,* as in *Humphry Clinker,* Newcastle and his ilk are marked by extremes of foolishness, guile, and sham. Yet by the nature of things they are immeasurably greater in stature than the mobs of an inferior order who induce anarchy, confusion, uproar, chaos, "Disappointment and Anguish; Debauchery, Profligacy, Gluttony, and Adulation; Luxury, Fraud, Rapine, Perjury, and Sacrilege." The plebeians at Bath expose themselves at the general tea-drinking: "There was nothing but justling, scrambling, pulling, snatching, struggling, scolding, and screaming" (JM, April 30). The political plebeians expose themselves at Whig councils: "All was bellowing, bleating, braying, grinning, grumbling, confusion, and uproar." The nobility can control and improve this mass of anarchy, as Quin says, "as a plate of marmalade would improve a pan of sirreverence."

Smollett's reluctance to identify luxury with the aristocratic Whigs and *all* of the City merchants may seem to argue a confusion or inconsistency of point of view. But, as earlier sections have indicated, very little rigor could be expected in application of a concept that by the 1750s was a polemical convention and at worst a hasty slogan. Given such patterns of usage and the additional exigencies of almost daily political controversy, Smollett was indeed consistent. He observed nice distinctions of class and was yet more certain of the identity of his political adversaries. As discussion of the *Briton,* for example, will show, the attacks upon the licentiousness of the press in *Humphry Clinker* that Smollett places in the context of a universal weakening of moral integrity have their historical basis in his journalistic disputes with the City Whigs. For the only periodicals that carried out a sustained attack upon government policies and personalities in the period 1761–63—and the only ones he denounced by name—were those either sympathetic to, or actual organs of, the City. It is revealing of the social-political divisions of the time that the same writer, Arthur Murphy, was hired to defend the Whig Newcastle against the City in 1756 (in the *Test*) and the Tory Bute against the City in 1762 (in the *Auditor.*)[39]

The fourth major feature of the *Critical's* treatment was the alternately hot and cold language it employed against the City, both styles bearing the same refrain. On the one hand, when the City commented upon matters of great moment, like the conduct of the war, the *Critical* rejoined in tones of righteous alarm. In the early dispute over the German alliance no less than during the later one over the terms for peace, the review argued against a strategy of mercantile expansion, holding that such measures were the desire of only a clique of greedy, selfish, and insubordinate men leading a mindless mob. Of the sixteen review articles condemning the alliance that were printed between 1756 and 1758, a minimum of eight are attributable to Smollett. In one of the earliest he held that: "It is well known . . . how great a clamour was raised, and still subsists, artfully propagated by the enemies of government. . . . But these are clamours which could never have existed, or gained ground, but amongst persons totally ignorant of the views and motives aimed at by the bringing over of Germans" (2:121; September 1756).[40] By statement as well as innuendo, the review insisted upon the existence of sordid and often seditious motives behind the various positions the City Whigs took through the signing of the peace treaty.[41] In effect, the *Critical* said that the arguments of the City should be quickly dismissed, for they merely cloaked the intentions of base and mercenary men.

On the other hand, the City Whigs were base in yet another sense, and

Smollett's periodical used the language of ridicule to expose their vulgarity. When concerned with matters of lesser importance, the *Critical* derided their lack of education and manners, their trades and crafts, and sneered at their competence to hold, much less express publicly, views on art, government, and international affairs. Much of this derision was directed toward the *Monitor,* whose writers, the *Critical* alleged in some of its earliest issues, were narrow, stupid plebeians.[42] But the *Critical's* attitude to the opposition journal depended in most instances upon the current political situation. In January 1759, with George II seemingly well and Pitt seemingly impregnable, it could make the necessary identification of the *Monitor* with faction while also indulging in a measure of relatively tolerant irony: "We should imagine that there is very little occasion for a Monitor, while a *Mentor* stands at the helm of government; while faction and opposition are, in a manner, annihilated; and every individual joyfully acquiesces in the wisdom and uprightness of the administration. What occasion, therefore, is there for this champion, to fight for the Rex or the Grex [?]" (7:22-23). Yet two years later, in May 1761, with a new monarch adamantly hostile to the Commoner, its tolerance had vanished. Speaking of the opposition press, particularly the *Monitor,* a reviewer predicts that "the present times will be distinguished in future ages for political rancour. Every subject of a political nature is debated with as much indecent warmth and animosity as if persons were sworn enemies, though possibly the writers may be entire strangers to each others faces, names, and characters" (11:363). More representative of the *Critical's* raillery is a notice in February 1757 of an anonymous open letter to Pitt on the topic of trade in the colonies.

> The author of this perplexed and absurd letter ["a merchant of the city of London"], begins with this modest assertion; "That as he has been conversant with commercial affairs for upwards of twenty years, in the course of that time he cannot fail to have made such observations and remarks upon our trade and navigation, as may tend, at this juncture, to the advancement of both!" Notwithstanding this claim to infallibility, his whole performance demonstrates the great possibility of failing, and that a bourgeois may be all his life employed in commercial affairs, without being qualified to direct a minister of state even in matters relating to trade and navigation. As the letter is addressed to the r——t h——ble W—— P—, Esq; the public is not immediately concerned in it, therefore we hope the bookseller, upon perusal of the ms, has had the precaution to print a very few copies, which the author may present to his friends at the club, to show that the new ministry

must certainly prosper, as they are assisted by such an able counsellor. [3:186]

This notice might be taken as typical of the majority of the *Critical*'s reviews of works it interprets as Whiggish in intent: it neglects most of the letter's contents, distorts the rest ("claim to infallibility"), and ridicules its author. As men of the City do not know even their own business, so they are by nature incapable of higher refinement. Hence a caricature in the April 1760 issue:

Should it enter into the brain of a phlegmatic alderman to open Pindar, it is probable he would regard the flights of that poet as the extravagancies of a disturbed imagination, and his admirers as the dupes of prejudice and superstitious veneration for antiquity. From the very first line he would conclude him a milk-sop, and prefer the pertness of a *Marriot*, or the solid dullness of a *Richmond Groves*, to the impetuous fire and luxuriant fancy of the Greek. Dead to all sensibility, and the warm emotions of the heart, vainly should we strive to give his tastless soul a relish of the beauties, or convince him that genius ever existed out of the countinghouse, or taste out of Billingsgate and Leadenhall-market. [9:289]

In the period 1761 to 1763, while Smollett was at work on the *Briton*, the *Critical* gave its full support to Bute and his policies. In practice this support meant not only continuing, but substantially increasing its denunciations of the City, Bute's primary opposition, and within its own review format the *Critical* pursued a course parallel to Smollett's own defense of the ministry, a course owing as much to political consistency as to loyalty to its former editor.[43] From the beginning of the war the review had assumed positions nearly identical to those favored by Leicester House and the opposition in Parliament. From the death of George II it had argued with a tone of great urgency for a cleansing of English politics, a new reformation designed to recapture old glories. The issue of March 1761 contains what amounts to a manifesto of the new order. The writer calls for a return to a unified nation under the direction of a strong monarch who would bring an early peace and dispel those clouds of jealousy and faction that too long had oppressed the country. A reassertion of the royal prerogative would necessarily put an end to those claims of influence made by men with no inherent right to opinions in governmental affairs (11:233–37). More than two years later—after Bute's fall and Smollett's departure for France—the review was repeating its call for a powerful monarchy. One example appears in the issue of October 1763, in a review of the collected numbers of the *North Briton*. Number 39 of the *North Briton* had drawn a fairly elaborate comparison between the Treaty of Paris of 1763 and the allegedly infamous Treaty of Utrecht of 1713. Of it the reviewer for the *Critical* wrote: "The 39th number is very arch, and a great part of it very true. But, after all, what is the substance of all our author advances, when digested in the alembic of national interest, or weighed in the ballance against public peace and unanimity?" (16:283).

A final characteristic of the *Critical's* attitude toward the City was its repeated charge that the Popular Whigs were engaged in criminal agitation among the common people. On its surface this charge appeared difficult for Smollett's opponents to credit, for it comprehended mobs and discontent in Shropshire, Warwickshire, and Cumberland, where the City Whigs were not directly or physically present, as well as in London, where their influence was undisputed. Yet, as we have seen, the charge certainly does follow from two of Smollett's assumptions about the nature of luxury. If, as he believed, the mob was a mindless, insensate mass, then its public activity was occasioned by either imitation or instigation. If, as he also believed, opposition to authority was permitted in one place, then it would surely spread to another, the insolence of London plebeians quickly infecting the vulgar of the provinces. In this sense, then, the general unrest of the lower orders followed inevitably from the political opposition of the City. Indeed, Smollett's normal attitudes precluded belief in any other possible source of unrest.

The charge of agitation was most pronounced in the controversy over electoral reform, but was also used by the *Critical* in a variety of other contexts. In the dispute over reform, the review chose to widen the issue considerably. As Beckford and the *Monitor* were at pains to make clear, the City was definitely not urging the inclusion of the masses in the electoral process. Yet the review used the idea of reform to raise a specter of riot, chaos, and drunkenness as "the mob" and "the people" were permitted free expression of their political views. Smollett and his writers foresaw hordes of soldiers, sailors, thieves, smugglers, and whores arriving gaily at polling places.[44] It is notable that not once over eight years, so far as I can discover, did they use the phrase "the people of England" in the favorable (and limited) sense in which it was constantly used by the *Monthly,* the *Monitor,* and the *North Briton.* Indeed in the *Briton* Smollett attacked as illegitimate and outrageous the concept of equality the phrase implied. When laborers in London banded together to resist impressment into the navy and when provincial journeymen united to demand higher wages, the *Critical* saw nefarious schemes to disrupt civil government and the end of all "order, regularity, and subordination."[45] In such pages we can also trace Smollett's attitude toward servants and their "shameful licentiousness," an attitude that led in *Humphry Clinker* to Bramble's instant dismissal of the footman John Thomas, "who is naturally surly," at the servant's first sign of impudence (JM, May 24).[46] As Smollett did in the *Continuation,* the review applauded proposals for closing all places of working-class resort and amusement.

The *Critical*'s attitude toward the Methodists can be seen as parallel to, or a part of, its opposition to the middle-class Whigs. From one contemporary point of view, Methodism represented the challenge of emotion, enthusiasm, and innovation to the bulwarks of reason, tradition, and orthodoxy in religion. Seen in this way the Methodists were religious anarchists but not otherwise dangerous. But from another perspective, which the review seems to have held, the Methodists were but one of many groups of ignorant upstarts assaulting the institutions of English society. For Smollett and his writers, orthodoxy in religion was apparently inseparable from orthodoxy in politics. Such views were clearest in reviews of Voltaire and Rousseau but also appeared in discussions of Methodism.[47] The *Critical*'s demands for orthodoxy indeed placed the City in a position of double jeopardy, since many of the freemen and liverymen were religious dissenters as well as Popular Whigs. In the *Present State* Smollett had noted a parallel instance, writing that members of the middle class in Edinburgh were, "like the burghers of every opulent city, a better kind of vulgar, consisting of merchants and tradesmen, the majority of whom are religionists of the presbyterian leaven, sour and censorious" (2:123). English merchants and tradesmen often seemed to more respectable persons to be engaged in the same activity of stirring up the rabble that characterized the Methodist leaders. Whitefield opened his tabernacle in London about the same time that the *Critical* began publication, and the review maintained a steady denunciation, terming him the grimy "apostle of Tottenham-Court" and lumping him with Wesley as "the false apostles" of the age.[48] Reviewing the collected sermons of a clergyman of the Church of England, a writer in the issue of March 1761 noted: "This is talking like a cool, dispassionate, sensible preacher, who appeals not to the passions, like our ranting hypocritical roarers at the tabernacle, but to the understanding of his audience" (11:200). In October 1763, the review carried an attack upon the characters of Whitefield and Wesley couched in largely the same terms as its invectives against the Whigs.

> The rapid and dangerous progress of *methodism* amongst us, is, to the last degree, astonishing and unaccountable, in a nation so justly and universally esteemed as our own for its good sense, penetration, and sagacity, especially when we consider what poor and contemptible characters figure at the head of it. The fanatics

of the last age, though equally absurd in their doctrines, had men amongst them who were professed of some parts, learning, and capacity; but the leaders of the methodists are a set of the most stupid and illiterate creatures that ever pretended to mislead a multitude. [16:293–94]

In this review Wesley is called a "vehement roarer at the Foundry," and "a true Pharisee" guided by "pride and insolence" who should be "the object of universal contempt and aversion in the eyes of every unprejudiced and impartial man." Two issues later the whole Methodist movement is called "infidelity" against religion.[49]

Smollett maintained this unmodified and unsparing condemnation in the *Continuation,* where, surveying the events of the year 1760, he writes:

> The progress of reason, and free cultivation of the human mind, had not, however, entirely banished those ridiculous sects and schisms of which the kingdom had been formerly so productive. Imposture and fanaticism still hung upon the skirts of religion. Weak minds were seduced by the delusion of a superstition styled Methodism, raised upon the affectation of superior sanctity, and maintained by pretensions to divine illumination. Many thousands in the lower ranks of life were infected with this species of enthusiasm, by the unwearied endeavours of a few obscure preachers, such as Whitfield, and the two Wesleys, who propagated their doctrine to the most remote corners of the British dominions, and found means to lay the whole kingdom under contribution. [4:121–22]

Although himself very much of an enthusiast in political affairs, Smollett stated his abhorrence of enthusiasm in religion, and in the *Travels* found occasion to analyze the fanatic as type.

> The character of a *devotee,* which is hardly known in England, is very common [in France]. . . . For my part, I never knew a fanatic that was not a hypocrite at bottom. Their pretensions to superior sanctity, and an absolute conquest over all the passions, which human reason was never yet able to subdue, introduce a habit of dissimulation, which, like all other habits, is confirmed by use, till at length they become adepts in the art and science of hypocrisy. Enthusiasm and hypocrisy are by no means incompatible. The wildest fanatics I ever knew, were real sensualists in their way of living, and cunning cheats in their dealings with mankind. [Letter 5][50]

In the activities of the Methodists, Smollett certainly saw insubordination: the pretensions of the lower orders to some measure of religious authority and religious illumination, and the leveling of class distinctions in ecclesiastical practices. In the activities of the City, he saw a great but comparable example of insubordination. An indication that the two types remained linked in his thinking is the character of Humphry Clinker himself, who in the novel is brought to represent the antithesis of both luxury and fanaticism. In all the novelist's work from 1756 there is no direct reference to the positive, spiritual side of Christianity, certainly nothing approaching the Christian devotion of a Johnson, a Smart, a Cowper, or even a Boswell. It would seem that for him the valuable service of religion is to supply not a metaphysic, but an ethic. In the relationship between church and government, government is necessarily the dominant partner. And as ethics could be brought into the service of politics, so the eradication of luxury could be made as much a religious duty as a civic one.

THE POLITICS OF PEACE:
THE *BRITON* AND THE *ATOM*

Smollett's ventures into periodical journalism were probably undertaken as necessary jobs of work. He had a sizable stable of writers and translators as well as a family to support. Yet however pressed for time and money he was, his journalistic writing is not mere hackwork. Like Swift, he had both the habit and the ability to turn an occasion into an opportunity, a job into a crusade. Whenever he put pen to paper he resumed his lifelong debate with his own time, for he seemingly wished to do more than acknowledge the movement of history: he wished to alter it. His earlier periodical ventures permitted engagement in controversy. What was to be his last demanded it. By the spring of 1762 the conditions of 1710–14 appeared to have returned. Old lines of contention were being redrawn, old arguments rehearsed. And Smollett had taken Swift's place in the center of the storm.

It was to promote public peace and unanimity, as these were conceived by Bute, that Smollett undertook the *Briton*. Largely by chance, the founding of the *Critical Review* coincided with the initial stages of the Seven Years' War. By conscious design, the complete span of the

Briton coincided with the war's concluding stages. Capitulation of the French at Montreal in September 1760 was taken as a sign that eventual victory belonged to the English. Canada had been secured, and further military action, it was thought, would serve both to extend and to consolidate English conquests. With victory evidently assured, fierce controversy erupted over its terms. To the commercial interests and apparently to much of literate London, on one side, a favorable peace meant the end of the French trading empire—in Europe as well as in the western hemisphere. To this end City spokesmen were arguing at the accession of George III for a continuation of the continental campaign and the retention of all the rich conquests in the Americas (to include, by the end of 1762, Puerto Rico, Florida, Havana, Guadaloupe, Martinique, and the many smaller islands of the West Indies). Economic considerations were equally important to the other side, as George III suggested when he wrote to Bute that the waste of the war must end before "the reign of virtue" could commence. To the young monarch, his chief advisor, most of the court, and the country gentry, a favorable peace meant a rapid close to a very costly war. This position was founded on a willingness to end the German alliance, and hence the European war, and to barter away the newly acquired territory in favor of an early treaty. Thus from what may be called the Tory point of view the goal of the peace was a return to the European balance of power of the late 1740s. From that of the City Whigs, the only satisfactory goal was English hegemony over European and American trade.[1]

From 29 May 1762, four days after Bute assumed control of the Treasury, to 12 February 1763, two days after the signing of the Treaty of Paris, Smollett engaged in the defense of Bute's terms for peace and of Bute himself. His brief from the ministry had no doubt been more positive, yet the force of circumstance in mid-1762 placed him in a constrained position. If members of Parliament, upon whom acceptance of the terms of peace actually depended, would not be moved by the resources of a Treasury well-prepared to reward its friends, then they would not be persuaded by the lucubrations of a new political sheet of transparent origins. Nor could massive popular support be expected, given the general metropolitan view of the peace, its designer, and its defender. In the event, the mere existence of the *Briton* seemed indeed to spur new animosity toward the ministry and to raise political issues, like that of a government-controlled press, previously dormant—emotions and issues that persisted well beyond February 1763. Bute's lieutenants, moreover, did not give Smollett the practical support he needed to wage an even moderately successful campaign. For an important example, the novelist was evidently unaware of the details and even the timing of the preliminary articles of the peace before they were signed and made public in November 1762.[2]

But if in one sense Smollett was severely constrained, in another he was correspondingly free. He had four to six pages to fill every Saturday for eight months, a situation allowing for both the scope of the elaborate serial essay and the concentration of the single short essay. Such opportunity came seldom in the review framework of the *Critical* or in the time- and space-bound pages of the *Complete History* and *Continuation.* The nature of his task, furthermore, was such that he probably accepted it with alacrity and gusto. In order to represent Bute and the peace in the best possible light, he had two direct and plausible methods at hand: identification of Bute's position with the wisdom of the royal prerogative and ultimately with the king himself, and exposure of all those who challenged the chief minister and the negotiations. Since the novelist applauded what he took to be the young monarch's principles of government, and since the main detractors in the opposition were old enemies, Smollett was being asked simply to continue his political efforts of the past seven years, this time under governmental aegis. The outsider found himself inside at last. Thus, as the *Atom* is his version of *Gulliver's Travels,* the early numbers of the *Briton* have the flavor of nos. 14 and 15 of the *Examiner* of October 1710. In the first issues of the new periodical, Smollett displays a confidence and assertiveness approaching ebullience rare in his political and historical writings. Although this tone did not last beyond June 1762, the more fundamental moral earnestness it overlaid was never diminished. To put the situation another way, the assignment he accepted called for the talents of a nimble party writer of the more proficient class, of whom there were many readily available, as Arthur Murphy easily proved. Although he took on a job of hackwork, Smollett brought to it neither the methods nor the motives of a hack. His opponents in 1762 and 1763 charged that the *Briton* contained merely the standard partisan diatribe of the time. While granting the partial truth of that charge, one can point to the more important fact that the attitudes Smollett expressed in such language were definitely his own, however much they may have also been the ministry's, and had been expressed at least seven years earlier and were to be reaffirmed in publications at intervals over the succeeding eight years. In the *Critical* and the histories, Smollett played a large part in framing what by 1762 had become the language of political controversy. And indeed the *Briton* probably lost much of its propaganda value to the ministry precisely because Smollett was not taking dictation from the palace of St. James.

The *Briton* therefore represents Smollett's single most concentrated attack upon the manifestations of luxury: its agents and abettors and their specious self-justifications. It is to the *Critical* as the second layer of a palimpsest is to the first. Smollett's attacks upon the integrity of writers and politicians in the 1750s and 1760s are not only connected with, but similar in tone to, his condemnation of luxury. All were refrains in the *Critical,* major themes in the *Briton,* and figures of contempt in the *Continuation* and the *Atom.* Yet, just as he makes no attempt to define precisely what he means by luxury, neither does he disclose anywhere his criteria for a responsible politics or a responsible press. To take the latter issue, nowhere in his voluminous signed writings or in the periodicals he edited can one discover anything approaching a philosophical discussion of the nature of public commentary. Nowhere do he and his writers suggest rules to govern the publication of news and opinion; nowhere does he attempt to delimit the duties and responsibilities of the press. What one does discover are pejorative statements about the integrity of his opponents; on political questions the charges are specific, practical, and partisan. When the *Critical* or the *Briton* deplored an item in another periodical or, more severely, called for legal action to be taken against it, they were customarily referring to a particular journal whose point of view clashed with Smollett's. And in his journalistic work, this point of view was controlled by more immediate and practical concerns than the integrity of the press. His reviews were of course themselves known for their pugnacious and tendentious methods and language, and the novelist spent eleven weeks in King's Bench Prison convicted of public libel. Given then the sufficiency of the evidence, the conclusion is inescapable that in decrying the press in *Humphry Clinker* Smollett was recalling his own personal rivalries, particularly the months of inflamed dispute with the *Monitor* and the *North Briton* in 1762 and 1763.

Scholars as late as 1974 have tended to take the novelist's language at face value. Unlike Smollett's contemporaries, they tend to assume that his use of such terms as *reason, good order,* and *corruption* was absolute, objective, and self-evident.[3] Some hold that Smollett's opposition to the continental war was based on humanitarian grounds and therefore interpret Bramble's attacks upon the press as a condemnation of some of the obvious excesses of the time. In each case, scholarly eludidation has merely repeated Smollett's positions without analyzing them. Yet proponents of the continental campaign also stated their arguments in humanitarian language, saying that without England's assistance her European allies would be left to the ravages of Louis's armies. Again, the *North Briton* may well represent one aspect of the journalistic excesses of the 1760s, but so do the *Briton* and the *Auditor.*

In many places Smollett calls attention to the excesses of the City; nowhere does he undertake the same task against the Tories, the court, or the landed interest. In the *Briton* he seeks to expose putative inconsistencies in the arguments of the City papers; so many and so gross

are they, he asserts, that they prove the worthlessness of their proponents. Yet he is himself capable of several lapses in argument. For one
instance, he portrays Pitt as solely a creature of the main chance, then
has no explanation for the minister's forsaking the largest opportunity
of his later career. Pitt's retirement, by Smollett's own testimony, brings
rebuke from both friends and enemies. Again, Smollett calls the mob as
foolish in its rejection of Pitt as it had been in its earlier adulation. Yet
he claims that Pitt had come to treat "mere citizens" with patent contempt—a circumstance that if true would certainly justify rejection,
however belated. He charges that when in power Pitt did nothing but
fleece the people. What talents and what influence would Pitt then have
"to rescue a beleaguered constitution"? When Bramble and Lismahago
term canvassing for votes an "avowed system of venality," they are not
so much expressing a philosophical judgment as repeating a partisan
political slogan used against the popular methods of certain Whig politicians. In actuality, the only practical alternative to the solicitation of
votes—and one frequently used—was the purchase and distribution of
parliamentary seats by the Treasury. When Bramble likewise despises a
politician of birth who will "put himself on the level with the dregs of
the people," he is, first, almost certainly denouncing Pitt and, second,
giving a characteristically Smollettian meaning to the phrase, *the dregs
of the people.* The bottom 40 to 60 percent of the people, on an economic scale, were regarded as untouchable by all political groups, as
Smollett, Pitt, and Beckford alike knew well. To an unsympathetic
observer, it may have seemed that Pitt put himself on the level of the
middling sort of tradesmen, but these last could hardly be described in
any objective sense as "the dregs of the people." Similarly, it was not an
impartial observer who saw canvassing for votes as inherently more
selfish and illiberal than Bute's purchase of the loyalty of provincial
placemen.[4] Here as elsewhere Smollett is utilizing the partisan slogans
of the court and ministry. Indeed, he uses the terms *dregs* and *vulgar* in
precisely those contexts where Beckford uses *people.* In no. 31 of the
Briton, for instance, Smollett sought to refute the anonymous but decidedly Whiggish author of the pamphlet *An Address to the Cocoa-Tree*
(1762). He writes:

> I know our addresser and his friends, in all their speeches and
> writings, take it for granted, that the *people* of England, in their
> collective capacity, are disaffected towards the present minister.
> I deny the supposition; I am under no difficulty of admitting, that
> the *vulgar* of London are; but, I am certain, so far as any fact of
> that kind can be ascertained, that the majority of the *people* of
> England, at this very instant, is greatly in his favour. [Italics added]

It would, in short, be difficult to find, after Swift, a major eighteenth-century author who uses with more regularity not only the issues but also the actual language of contemporary politics.

The *Briton* is at once the most ample illustration of Smollett's habits in the use of political language and the best single gloss on that language. In individual numbers he is concerned not with definition but with persuasion; his normal mode is emotive assertion. Yet when taken together, the whole collection of the essays of the *Briton* serves to clarify each part. For eight months Smollett had one principal message: The Whig opposition is base. Stated in the first, it was reiterated in virtually every one of the thirty-eight numbers. In the course of those months he stated and restated his thesis in so many ways—extension, simplification, elaboration, deduction, and others—that his essential meaning is unmistakable.

Certain issues were intended to be unmistakable from the beginning. And to the City Whigs the most arresting aspect of the first number (29 May 1762) of Smollett's new journal must have been its masthead. Under the coat of arms of the king of England and in tones of a manifesto, Smollett declared that the function of the *Briton* was "to oppose and expose and depose *The Monitor*," an infamous sheet that had "undertaken the vilest work of the worst incendiary" and had had "recourse . . . to insinuation against the throne and abuse of the ministry."[5] Thus one half of his rhetorical formula: the opposition was unspeakably bad. The other followed directly: the government was ineffably good. The ministry was unquestionably able and had the complete confidence of the monarch. His emphatic identification of George III with Bute's policies was an open invitation to the City to challenge the king's judgment and was to appear often in his pages. In this opening number he wrote:

> Our Sovereign's character is in all respects so amiable as to engage the affection of every one not blasted with envy . . . his heart benevolently sympathizes with all the children of distress . . . his hand is liberally opened to every appearence of merit . . . his sole aim is to augment and secure the happiness of his people with the independence of his crown.

In no. 4 he said, "The Sovereign can have no interest independent of the happiness of his people." Later, in no. 17, he calls George III a "Patriot-king, whose chief aim is the happiness of his people." The direct identification is repeated in no. 18:

> Let us depend upon the paternal affection of a virtuous Sovereign, who can have no views distinct from the interest and happiness of

his people. Let us depend upon the care and fidelity of an honest minister, who is engaged by every tie of loyalty, of honour, and of interest, to promote the patriot designs of his Master, to consult the glory and welfare of the nation.

Friend and foe alike, contemporary observers found the *Briton* least persuasive when Smollett undertook such positive defense of Bute's policies. Henry Fox secured Murphy's services for a second ministerial weekly within days of the appearence of Smollett's, and Temple affirmed "that *The Briton* left to himself is left to his worst enemy."[6] It was soon pointed out, for example, that Smollett was representing the monarch as both extremely cordial to the ministry and also judiciously independent of it. The novelist responded with the assertion that the role of the ministry, like that of the whole Tory party, was to protect the king's independence and his royal prerogative. He compounded the paradox by noting further that, in any event, Bute's ministry could not be termed either Whig or Tory.[7] A comparable dispute arose over no. 3, in which he replied to a challenge from the *North Briton* to state the achievements of the current ministry by citing the conquest of Martinique and the neutral islands of the West Indies. The *Monitor* and the *North Briton* retorted quickly that he had previously extolled Bute's war policy precisely because it condemned further conquest, and that the capture of the islands merely fulfilled the plans and preparations made by Pitt.

Smollett's evident slowness in the ebb and flow of week-to-week practical politics has caused the *Briton* to be largely ignored, even by scholars. Yet it could be argued that his role of apologist was uncharacteristic and therefore of lesser significance for an understanding of the work. In his historical and journalistic writings, his most effective defenses—and there are many—are of himself and his personal associates, and even these are for the most part attacks upon their detractors. What he most enjoyed was jamming common sense down the throats of men he considered fools. He was the man of wit turned man of the nation's business. The *Complete History* is vivid in representing the events of 1688 as a devolution from some earlier, more wholesome condition of English society, but that earlier state is not defined or described. In the *Briton,* likewise, Smollett's writing is most vigorous in those essays from which the personalities and the policies of the ministry are absent. Vindication of Bute, I contend, was but a necessary distraction from what he took to be his major task: to destroy the political influence of the City and its allies. To this end he needed to make no efforts to link the City with Pitt in opposition to the peace, for Pitt had already done so publicly. On 9 October 1761, Pitt and Temple resigned from the cabinet. Shortly thereafter, in order to explain his reasons for resigning and accepting a pension, Pitt addressed an open letter to Beckford which was published by City periodicals. And as early as the *Briton* no. 2, Smollett opened the assault upon Pitt's integrity that was to continue to the end of the journal.[8]

From the beginning of June 1763, Smollett was compelled to include the new political review, the *North Briton,* in his indictment of the City press. In this early stage of rivalry with Wilkes and Churchill, he argued that the government and the laws were too lenient against the treasons of the opposition press, and, alternatively, that legal action against an opposition author was an almost certain means of creating popular sympathy for him. In no. 4 Smollett compares the author of the first *North Briton* with Orator Henley, who "was in hopes of attaining the pillory, or of being brought to the cart's-tail; events which would have given him consequence among the multitude on whom he depended." The novelist retained this divided view on the value of legal suppression to the writing of *Humphry Clinker.* In the final volume of the *Continuation,* probably written sometime in 1764, he voiced both opinions. Describing the origins of the *North Briton,* he said: "One Mr. Wilkes, member of parliament for Aylesbury, was at very little pains to conceal that he was the author of the paper, which, in point of wit, language, or argument, could never have attracted the attention of the public, had not the minds of the people, by the arts of faction, been inflamed to a degree of madness" (5:220).[9] Writing earlier about the rumors of an amorous connection between Bute and the Queen Mother, he had said that swift suppression would have resolved the affair.

> Had the promulgators of the first defamatory libels that appeared against the k——g and his family, been apprehended and punished according to the law, the faction would have found it a very difficult task, in the sequel, to engage either printer or publisher in their service . . . but they were emboldened by impunity to proceed in their career, to confirm their calumnies by unrefuted falshoods, and to give a loose to the most audacious scurrility; until the minds of the people were so deeply and so universally tainted, that it became hazardous to call the libellers to account. [5:120]

In its campaign against the City press, the *Briton* naturally received the support of the *Critical Review* and the *Auditor.* In September 1762 a reviewer for the *Critical* gave praise to a pamphlet that called for the suppression of "the torrent of abuse issued daily from that fountain of impurity against the most respectable characters." A later review stated: "We have often known it foreseen and lamented, that licentiousness may prove fatal to liberty; but of all licentiousness, that of the press is grown the rankest." At least one-third of Murphy's essays in the *Auditor* contained vilification of the opposition press, the remainder being taken up with glorification of the ministry. In a typical comment, Murphy called the authors of the *Monitor* and the *North Briton* "banditti of incendiary writers" and lamented "the unexampled lenity of the administration" in not punishing them.[10]

In no. 4 of the *Briton*, Smollett combines his attack upon the City press with one directed against the concept of popular government. This number expresses the conviction that the City is more irresponsible when it seeks popular support or, in his phrase, "appeals to the mob." Smollett asserts that the popular appeals of the *Monitor* can lead only to extravagance, disorder, and decline: "It is not to people who exercise their reason, that such appeals [those of the *Monitor*] are made. . . . No, they apply to the million; to the base illiberal herd, who have neither sense to attain conviction, nor sentiment to own the force of truth, who fatten upon the spoils of reputation and greedily snuff up the fumes of scandal, even to intoxication." Two issues later, in no. 6, he explains that, in contrast to City writers, when he addresses "the English people," he is *not* referring to "the base, unthinking rabble . . . without principle, sentiment or understanding." In no. 8 he equates those who want a quick end to the war with the "sensible and honest part" of the nation and calls the trading interests the "refuse of the vulgar." No. 11 contains the memorable fictional letter of Winifred Bullcalf, godmother and prototype of Win Jenkins, who protests in mangled English against the deceit of City politicians. Her husband had been promised huge reward for exhorting the mob around the Guildhall and Temple Bar, she writes, but for all his exertions got merely five shillings and a jug of rum. Most Londoners, Smollett would have his readers believe, knew Bullcalf under the name John Wilkes.

By August 1762, Smollett's accusations against the City had become harsh and blunt. Without circumlocution, he began calling the writers of the *Monitor* and *North Briton* scandalmongers and traitors, desperate men who would be appeased by the disgrace of their country and their natural superiors. "It would be doing too much honour to the talents of these revilers, to suspect they are employed by the French king as incendiaries, to raise a cumbustion in the bowels of their country," he wrote in no. 14, "but it cannot be unfair to charge them with having engaged as volunteers in this honourable service." The next number contained a yet greater amount of emotive abuse, as when Smollett asks,

> whence flow these tides of scurrility and treason, these deluges of filth and sedition that drown our daily papers, and stink in the nostrils of mankind?—From a fourth estate distinguished by the

name of *Rabble,* which I divide into three corporations, *viz.* Hedge coffee-house politicians, bankrupt machanics soured by their losses, and splenetic sots, who change their no-opinions oftener than their linens.

No. 14 continues this level of invective in a direct attack upon Wilkes. Smollett had been ridiculing the authors of the *North Briton* individually by giving them ridiculous names; Churchill appearing in the *Briton* as Bruin, Robert Lloyd as Paedagogus Latro, and Wilkes as Captain Iago Aniseen or Jacky-Dandy.[11] For the fourteenth number he concocted an Arabian Nights fable in which Wilkes is cast a Jahia Ben Israil Ginn, a goggle-eyed moral and physical monster. The great and liberal caliph of the time had established a paradise of freedom and prosperity for his people, but Jahia, an insignificant malcontent, wishes only to overturn the prosperity and to vilify his generous and forgiving ruler: "In this season of general felicity, there was a remnant of miserable wretches, who, from disappointed ambition, or inveterate envy, repined at the success of merit, and like so many demons, damned without all prospect of redemption, derived fresh torments from the happiness which their fellow-creatures seemed to enjoy."[12]

No. 16 of the *Briton,* published 11 September 1762, is at once a high point in Smollett's battle against the City, in which he gives vent to the quotidian resentments of many years, and, more significantly, one of the best summaries of the political views he had been expressing since 1756. Specifically, he seeks to make two points. First, the City and its allies are like the savage Goths who sacked Rome: "Uninspired by sentiment, unenlightened by science, and unrestrained by laws; instigated by sedition, and inflamed by intoxication." Second, the City advocates the leveling principle "that every individual has an equal right to intermeddle in the administration of public affairs"; at best this is "a principle subversive of all government, magistracy and subordination; a principle destructive of all industry and national quiet, as well as repugnant to every fundamental maxim of society." As a whole the number is the longest plain statement in all of Smollett's writings of his adherence to classical hierarchy and necessity and of his aversion to theories of social and political equality. Here is the wraith of the Country party under William and Mary and of Bolingbroke's Opposition under Walpole, still keening the world's ill fortunes, three-quarters of a century after the Glorious Revolution.

As so often in the *Critical Review,* he opens his attack upon luxury with an appeal to the lessons of ancient history. He proceeds by means of his customary method in controversy: having rendered a comprehensive assertion, he then argues within that assertion.

Every kingdom, and every age, for a series of centuries, has produced a set of speculative philosophers, who have endeavored to refine upon the constitution of their country; and almost all of these projectors have either affected, or actually felt, an enthusiastic attachment to the democracies of ancient Greece. Some have commenced advocates for the liberty of the people, merely from the pride of classical knowledge, and have extolled the laws of Solon, for no other reason but because they were written in Greek. Others have conceived republican principles from envy of their superiors in wealth and affluence. A third sort of reformers have espoused the plebeian interests, from an innate aversion to all order and restraint. And it is to be hoped, for the honour of human nature, that some few of those theoretical legislators have been actuated by motives of humanity and benevolence. This, however, I take to be a mistaken philanthropy, which, conceiving every individual to be equally free by nature, draws this erroneous inference, that every individual has an equal right to intermeddle in the administration of public affairs; a principle subversive of all government, magistracy and subordination; a principle destructive to all industry and national quiet, as well as repugnant to every fundamental maxim of society.

To give us a just idea of a mob-ruled commonwealth, we need only peruse the histories of Athens and of Rome, during those periods at which their government was purely republican. There we shall meet with nothing but faction, animosity, persecution, ingratitude and disquiet. We shall find the people of Athens led about by every turbulent orator in their turns, like an ill-tamed monster, from vanity to vice, from folly to caprice, from the lowest depth of despondence, to the most giddy height of elation. All was violence, tumult, injustice, and presumption.

Yet if the sensible, patriotic Greeks and Romans were susceptible to such extravagances, what, Smollett asks, is to be expected from the unrestrained and savage populace of a Gothic nation? Very simply, brutality, sedition, and intoxication: "Such were the mob-reformers which have appeared at different times, in almost every kingdom of Christendom." Lest his readers fail to apply this lesson to contemporary England, he moves rapidly to the present. He notes that, "the malcontents of our days have not yet proceeded to open insurrection . . . but . . . they have exactly followed the footsteps of their ancestors in those circumstances we have already mentioned, as well as in divers other particulars." They have boldly criticized the government and attempted to usurp the king's prerogative, keeping in constant view the example of Wat Tyler's rebels: "they have had the courage to scatter the seeds of sedition in public; to practice every species of defamation; to insult the government, and belie the ministry; to laugh at Bridewell and flagellation; and despise and brave the pillory, and even set the gallows at defiance." For his conclusion, Smollett drops all vestige of temperate language in favor of open diatribe, an attack upon the motives, character, and personalities of the opposition that seemed severe even to the strong tastes of the time.

As these Reformers have, upon all occasions, assumed the title of Free-born Englishmen, and denominated themselves *the good people of England;* it will not be amiss to enquire who the individuals are that compose this respectable community. Are they persons of wealth, property, or credit?—No.—Have they distinguished themselves as valuable members of the commonwealth?—No such matter.—Do they contribute to the necessities of the public, or of the poor, by paying scot or lot, King's tax, or parish-tax?—Not a farthing. They reverence no King: they submit to no law: they belong to no parish. Have they a right to give their voice in any sort of election, or their advice in any assembly of the people? They have no such right established by law; and therefore they deduce a right from nature, inconsistent with all law, incompatible with every form of government. They consist of that class which our neighbors distinguish by the name of *Canaille,* forlorn Grubs and Garetteers, desperate gamblers, tradesmen thrice bankrupt, prentices to journey-men, understrappers to porters, hungry pettifoggers, bailiff-followers, discarded draymen, hostlers out of place, and felons returned from transportation. These are the people who proclaim themselves free-born Englishmen, and transported by a laudable spirit of patriotism, insist upon having a spoke in the wheel of government.[13]

After its earliest numbers, the *Briton* received hardly any notice in the *North Briton.* Wilkes had been content to point out that Smollett was working for a Stuart—John, Earl of Bute—whose apparent goal was the restoration of the days of an earlier Stuart. When this point was driven home by repetition, Wilkes sought out larger targets than the author of the *Briton.* But no. 16 was extraordinary and called for rebuttal, and hence in no. 19 of the *North Briton* Wilkes printed a letter in response to Smollett from William Temple, the merchant from Trowbridge, which merits attention for several reasons. It reveals the heat surrounding Bute and his policies and represents the type of argument often used against Smollett. Besides replying in Lockean terms to no. 16 of the *Briton,* it paints a flattering picture of the City Whigs that shows beyond doubt that contemporaries were aware of Smollett's meaning and the actual objects of his opprobrium.

As the BRITON, of Saturday the 11th instant, is an impudent libel on all the good people of *England* in general, as well as on the city of LONDON in particular, representing all the *nobility, gentry, merchants, tradesmen, yeomen,* and all the commonalty, as a seditious rabble, which despises all government, because they express a dislike to some measures relative to a *peace;* and as our constitution is reproached with being an *ochlocracy,* or mob-common-wealth, because it permits our people to murmur with impunity at the conduct they cannot approve, which by-the-bye is inculcating the vilest tyranny ever practised by the worst monsters of all the *Roman* emperors, pray indulge me in communicating to the public a few remarks upon so extraordinary a performance. . . . He informs us *"that there are a set of speculative philosophical reformers.".* . . This extraordinary species of philosophers was reserved for the discovery of the *extraordinary genius,* the author of the BRITON. Well; . . . Could any poor creature write such stuff unless one lately eloped from *Bedlam?* But now for the root of this political evil, this philosophical aversion to order, arising from a regard to the interests of the people. This, our author tells us, proceeds from (remark him!) *the opinion that every individual is equally free by nature.* . . .

Government is a just execution of the laws, which were instituted by the people for their preservation: but if the people's implements, to whom they have trusted the execution of those laws, or any power for their preservation, should convert such execution to their destruction, have they not a right to intermeddle? nay, have they not a right to resume the power they have delegated, and to punish their servants who have abused it? If *our king can do no wrong,* his ministers may, and are accountable to the people for their conduct. This is the voice of *Locke,* the voice of our laws, the voice of reason; but we own not the voice of tyrants and their abetters, not the voice of the Briton. On the contrary, this wretch preaches up the doctrine, that some part of mankind, nay, the mass, are born slaves, who ought implicitly to be submissive to the caprices of a few, who by accident, knavery, or cunning, shall wriggle themselves into power. . . . Observe, *Britons,* what this despicable wretch, and tool of some in power, would reduce you to. Are these the sentiments of his paymasters? Is this the cue given him in his instructions, to boldly assert, that *Englishmen* are all born to be slaves. . . .

[The *Briton* holds that] the present citizens, merchants, traders, commonalty of LONDON, are just such another rabble as the mob under *Wat Tyler* and Jack *Straw* was formerly. He has given all manner of latitude and scope to his imagination, and indulged falsehood in all her wanton levities. . . . You neither want for capacity to discern his insults, nor for spirit to resent the abuse: no; for to do you justice, I must say, whatever the pride of presumption and the swell of vanity may induce some persons to think, the *merchants* of *London*, in their collective capacity, possess more honest, useful, political knowledge, and understand more of the true interest of their country, than all the ministers of state ever discovered, or were masters of.

Smollett meanwhile, sensing that the opposition was for the moment on the defensive, had no intention of meeting these arguments from Walpole's age, but attempted to pursue his advantage in no. 17 of the *Briton* by castigating the City and its press as "the vile retainers to a desperate faction" actuated by base and mercenary motives. He asks rhetorically which persons "so industriously blow the coals of discord" by opposing the peace treaty:

we must search for it [the answer] among the idle and profligate, who have neither diligence nor virtue to earn a subsistence in any calm, pacific course of life; among a set of selfish people who find their account in the war; an iniquitious band of money-brokers, usurers, contractors, and stock-jobbers, who prey upon the necessity of their country, and fatten on her spoils. These are joined by certain individuals in the public service, who sacrifice every patriotic sentiment to the desire of preferment: but those who raise their voices the highest in this discordant cry, are the vile hackneyed retainers to a desperate faction, actuated by implacable malice, rancorous envy, and guilty ambition.

Smollett's use of the pejorative term *faction* here and elsewhere in the *Briton* is to some extent uncharacteristic, inconsistent with the way he used it from 1756 until 1761. In defense of Bute, Smollett used the word to designate any political group or party in opposition to the existing administration. Previously he had usually used it—in the *Complete History* and the *Critical Review*—in a broader and looser sense to include all his political opponents, whether in government or without, as when he termed the Whig oligarchs under Walpole "an ambitious and greedy faction" unrepresentative of the English people. Once again the *North Briton* found occasion to gloss the novelist's habits in the use of political language and to turn the situation to its own advantage. In no.

30 the author says that most readers understand *faction* to be a careless term of abuse without meaning.

> But if by a *faction* we mean, according to a general acceptation, a set of men formed into a party on seditious and selfish principles, and determined, at all events, to oppose the friends and sacrifice the interests of the public to their own base and private views; in this sense of the word, it becomes us to be extremely cautious how we apply it.
>
> One sure and infallible *criterion*, by which every man may find out a *faction* with the most absolute certainty, is, the wicked art of sowing discord, and infusing the groundless jealousies among the people; whether directed against their old and firm friends, or their great and spirited allies. The first weekly political paper, which has appeared since the change of the ministry, and has been countenanced and paid by the government, was the BRITON, who has abused in the most indecent terms, his Majesty's royal grandfather, our protestant ally, the king of Prussia, the city of London, its first magistrate, and the *people of England*. This was the first wretch hired to ring the alarum bell of discord and sedition.
>
> Let facts speak. Are we not now become an uneasy, distrustful, and divided people? and, were we not a happy, confiding, and united nation, respected abroad, and blessed at home? Does not the present ministry occasion the greatest disunion and animosity ever remembered in this country? Are they not in the highest degree culpable of engendering the alienation of the best-intentioned subjects from the most gracious of sovereigns? Did not the late ministry preserve union and harmony in the nation; and had they not the confidence of the public in an unlimited manner? Whence has the change arisen? . . . a faction . . . seized the helm of government.

Having brought the *Briton* to a new and higher level of controversy, Smollett largely kept it there during the autumn of 1762. No. 20 reiterates some of his regular charges against the writers of the *Monitor* and the *North Briton,* calling them a "vile crew of incendiaries, the professed enemies of their Prince and his government, the prostitutes of a desperate faction, and, as far as in them lies, the parricides of their country." To these political charges he added, in no. 21, the explicit connection with luxury. Return of acquired territories is necessary, he declares, because conquest would merely aggravate further the syndrome of luxury: "The acquisition of Mexico and Peru would serve only to hasten the ruin of Old England. It would enervate our minds, debauch our morals, destroy our industry, and depopulate our country."[14] The following number, like the *Atom* and *Humphry Clinker,* declares indeed that such enervation is already apparent. The City could have supporters and its periodicals readers only if Londoners had gone insane.

> When we hear the present ministry reproached in every coffee-house, in every ale-house, and almost in every private house within the city of London: when we hear the plebeian politicians accuse them of want of capacity, of want of spirit and activity; and exclaim with an air of contempt . . . what can we think, but that heaven hath actually deprived the people of their senses; or that they are blinded by the most absurd prejudices, and transported by the most ungenerous and unjustifiable resentment.

> Is it possible, that rational beings should be so weak, so humble, as to resign all their own ideas and reflections, and listen with implicit faith, to the idle declamation of a few worthless incendiaries, who do not even take the trouble to amuse them with the faintest shadows of reason; but seem to overbear their intellects with a foul torrent of general abuse, totally devoid of truth, argument, and probability?

> To these abandoned wretches, who have devoted their talents, such as they are, to the propagation of slander and sedition, and perpetually ring the change upon *venal pens, ministerial hirelings, and mercenary writers, attempting to defend an infamous peace;* what should I oppose but an ineffable contempt, and silent disdain?

Smollett's disdain could not remain silent for more than a week, however. Opposition to Bute remained extraparliamentary and had no discernible effect upon the minister's plans for peace. On 1 November 1762 the king's emissaries signed the preliminary articles of the peace.[15] The opposition had failed in its primary objective, and circumstances called for a new ministerial offensive to complete the rout. The last three and one-half months of Smollett's writing for Bute accordingly reverted to his original positions of May and June, even though he altered their presentation and added a few novel thrusts. The first number after the signing of the preliminary treaty, no. 24, declared that: "The present, is the first aera in the annals of Great Britain, distinguished by a torrent of the foulest slander and abuse, poured upon the character of a Prince, who deserves to be the darling of his people; upon the reputation of a minister, whose conduct has defied the severest scrutiny of mallice." The next contains a strong attack, one of many to appear in the *Briton,* upon Beckford, now lord mayor of London. He is ridiculed for his want of character, his plantation holdings in Jamaica, and his sheeplike minions, "the common mob of that great metropolis."[16]

In no. 26, Smollett returned to the form of the fictional letter and produced one of the most effective issues of his paper and an anticipation of many of the letters of *Humphry Clinker,* especially those concerning the trials of Baynard and his luxurious wife. He recounts a political parable of one Mr. Fitz-George and his insolent servants, led by Will Pitot and Tom Give-place, or Buy-vote. While successfully ridiculing his opponents, he also provides a short history of the political events of the early 1760s. He seeks further to counter the City's main argumentative metaphor by using it himself: if the *Monitor* and the *North Briton* said the sovereign was the principal servant of the people, the *Briton* would reply that the people are nothing more than servants of the king. This unsigned letter served not only to stigmatize all Whig opposition as illegitimate, but also allowed Smollett to castigate specific personalities who had incurred his wrath: Pitt, Newcastle, Temple, Dashwood, Wilkes, Beckford, and Charles Say, most of whom were to reappear in *Humphry Clinker.* It is reproduced in full in an appendix to this book.

He was to resume his general castigation of the Whigs in January 1763 with a history of that party during the century, this time without the framework of fable. No. 35 repeats in exaggerated and summary form the attitudes he expressed in the final volume of the *Complete History* and looks toward the invective of the *Atom.* The premise of his argumentative essay is the singular nature of the royal prerogative: "British monarchy, however independent, must be limited by the constitution; if it is not, it is no longer British monarchy, but despotism. As to independency, unless it is independent within itself, if it is subject to the controul either of foreign power or domestic insolence, it equally ceases to be British monarchy." Throughout the century, he continues, the Whigs have been the constant source of domestic insolence, in part because they sought to reduce the strength of the monarchy: "The Whig ministers have always been known to plume themselves in the feathers they plucked from the prerogative; and have added to their own persons, that importance which they have filched from the crown." But this will never be tolerated again. The first two Georges were weak sovereigns overwhelmed by the machinations of the Whigs; their successor is of nobler fiber. Moreover, the Whigs were guilty of yet another type of treason against the crown, one now difficult to suppress. Some privileges that they usurped from the sovereign they distributed to the people at large, against their will. In some weak-minded persons the notion of popular government resulted, and it was these persons who created present-day scandals. But Whig attempts "to widen the bottom of government" had been defeated once and for all, and every reasonable man now agreed that "the popular principle of Whiggism" was naturally abhorrent to the great majority of Englishmen, who preferred a strong monarchy. Smollett concludes the essay with a repudiation of the Whigs as complete as that of no. 16.

The final issues of the *Briton* are dominated by recriminations against the City press. No. 31 distinguishes between "the People of England" for whom Smollett wrote, on the one hand, and "the vulgar of London" to whom the *Monitor, North Briton,* and *Patriot* appealed, on the other. No. 32 is replete with warnings that the government will not continue to endure the foul rantings of those "dregs of the populace," the writers for the opposition. In fierce tones, which find their reverberation in the words of Bramble (especially the letter of June 2) and Lismahago, Smollett asks what can stop this defamation: "What punishment does the malicious wretch deserve, who . . . lifts the murderous quill to stab the reputation of innocence, to sully the fair fame of the most shining merit, and unite the most treacherous disloyalty, with the most rancorous defamation." (Lismahago, in Bramble's letter of July 15, says liberty of the press "enabled the vilest reptile to soil the lustre of the most shining merit.")

> The shameless scribbler, like the village-idiot, when the clock was silent, still continues to strike sedition, from the force of habit, even though the springs that first moved him have ceased to operate. The weekly libel still appears, replete with nonsense, falshood and scurrility, and tho' banished with disgrace from every creditable society, finds readers among the vulgar herd of alehouse politicians. The most shocking exhibitions of infamous scandal and stupid obscenity, are publicly vended in the shops of this metropolis, to the reproach of government, and the disgrace of the nation, as if our people delighted in malice and indecency, and there was no law in the kingdom to punish the most brutal licentiousness.

He leaves no doubt that he demands the most severe punishment possible.

> We know it hath been adjudged, that an attempt, *forcibly to prescribe laws to the K——g, and to restrain him of his power, implies a design to deprive him of his crown and life; that words spoken to draw away the affection of the people from the K——g, and to stir them up against him, tend to his death and destruction, and are T——n;* and we know that *Scribere Est Agere.* [Original italics]

No. 33 calls the *North Briton* and the *Monitor* enemies of the nation whose address is "to the lower class of mortals," the rabble, to whom the City would give over the reins of government.

Smollett concludes the *Briton* on those themes with which he opened it. In the penultimate issue, no. 37, he avows that he was forced to come to the defense of the ministry. "The reader will remember, that I did not lift the pen in this dispute, until I saw my S——n, whom I am bound to honour, and his M——r whose virtue I had cause to respect, aspersed with such falshood, and reviled with such rancour, as must have roused the indignation of every honest man." The final number, no. 38, published on 12 February 1763, is another broadside against the Whigs generally and the City in particular.

The signing of the Treaty of Paris ended Bute's patronage and the life of the *Briton*. Smollett's letters and the *Travels* suggest that these eight months were among the most intense in his eventful life. In retrospect, they also seemed to him the most frustrating, even harrowing. A year after he had begun the journal he was broken in both body and spirit, and in June of 1763 he took his family away to France. Earlier he had written of his failing health to Moore: "My constitution will no longer allow me to toil as formerly. I am now so thin you would hardly know me. My face is shrivelled up by the asthma like an ill-dried pippin, and my legs are as thick at the ankle as at the calf."[17] In the opening letter of the *Travels,* written later, he spoke of the bitterness induced by his work on the *Briton;* he had been "traduced by malice, persecuted by faction" and "abandoned by false patrons" in a "scene of illiberal dispute, and incredible infatuation."

This period of his life was embittering not so much because the task he accepted was unfamiliar or difficult as because its results were so unsatisfactory. Personally Smollett went unrewarded; whatever he had been promised, he received no sizable remuneration. Politically the results were at best ambiguous. The ground swell of conservative, royalist support the *Critical* had been predicting since mid-1760 never materialized to embrace the *Briton* or its sponsors. The peace treaty had been drafted and ratified as Bute wanted, yet the minister remained in power only a few months beyond its ratification. Intended as a first step toward "the reign of virtue," the peace had exhausted its designer as well as its defender. The means had become an end and, for Bute, a dead end. Though Bute had won his campaign for the peace, moreover, the City had not altogether lost. In the course of his months of writing for the minister, Smollett had been compelled to reverse several of his positions on important political issues, such as the integrity of Pitt, the reliability of the French government, and the value of territorial conquests. Although he was regularly denounced for inconsistency, his consistency actually never faltered and was of the most basic sort: he sought by all arguments available to him to destroy the influence of the City Whigs. Yet he and Murphy had not succeeded in their smaller, preliminary task, that of destroying the credibility of the City press; if anything, ministerial attacks assisted in raising such credibility. The *Monitor, North Briton,* and *Patriot* had no hope of swaying members of parliament, and they did not. But with their selected audience, the middling group of the capital, their credit had grown prodigiously. The ministry in 1763 was weak in victory. The City, beginning twenty years of accelerated political agitation, was strengthened in defeat.[18]

In 1763 as in 1714, the Tories could gain the peace they desired, but not the stability and authority: they could manage a negotiating conference but not a country. Smollett's responses were much like Swift's. He soon abandoned England and later composed a political apologue, a summing up of his attitudes beyond the threshold of hope. *The History and Adventures of an Atom* retraced the historical ground Smollett had traveled before without presenting any new "facts." But it provided him with two opportunities he did not have in his periodical work: to express his disappointment over the chances lost by Bute and his administration, and to restate with the license of fiction his utter detestation of Whig politicians, especially Newcastle and Pitt, and their myrmidons, the Legion. The resulting work grows expressly from his earlier concerns. It outlines again the political history of luxury in the corruption of Whig power and describes the source of that power in what the novelist saw as its full obscenity. And it contains what amounts to his final statement of independence from partisan, practical politics—a partial explanation, at least, of the political detachment of *Humphry Clinker.*

Although the *Atom* is relatively short, it presents more of what Smollett took the actual stuff of politics to be than do the *Complete History* and *Continuation.* It represents a secret history of private maneuvers, behind closed doors and among milling crowds. The chronicle is narrated by an omniscient and indestructible atom, now lodged in the pineal gland of one Nathaniel Peacock, which is able once every millennium to impart the enormous knowledge it possesses: "For the benefit of you miserable mortals, I am determined to promulge the history of one period, during which I underwent some strange revolutions in the empire of Japan, and was conscious of some political anecdotes now to be divulged for the instruction of British ministers."[19] The one period the atom wishes to describe minutely lies between the death of Henry Pelham and the rise of Newcastle in 1754 to Bute's failure in 1763. The opening portion of the atom's story concerns the general condition of England from the revolution to 1754.

The major elements of this condition are by now familiar in Smollett. The English are a fickle, stupid, and docile people: "such inconsistent, capricious animals, that one would imagine they were created for the purpose of ridicule. Their minds are in constant agitation. . . . They seem to have no fixed principle of action, no certain plan of conduct. . . . One hour [an Englishman] doubts the best established truths; the next, he swallows the most improbable fiction. His praise and his censure are what a wise man would choose to avoid, as evils equally pernicious" (pp. 392–93). Moreover the English,

> value themselves much upon their constitution, and are very clamorous about the words liberty and property; yet, in fact, the only liberty they enjoy is to get drunk whenever they please, to revile the government, and quarrel with one another. With respect to their property, they are tamest animals in the world; and, if properly managed, undergo, without wincing, such impositions, as no other nation in the world would bear. In this particular, they may be compared to an ass, that will crouch under the most unconscionable burden, provided you scratch his long ears, and allow him to bray his bellyfull. They are so practicable, that they have suffered their pockets to be drained, their veins to be emptied, and their credit to be cracked, by the most bungling administrations, to gratify the avarice, pride, and ambition, of the most sordid and contemptible sovereigns, that ever sat upon the throne. [Pp. 393–94]

Monarchs who are contemptibly weak and foolish are perhaps apt but nonetheless incompetent rulers for such a people. George I is an ignoramus, but his successor is worse—expelled, not born, "*a posteriori* from a goose." "He was rapacious, shallow, hot-headed, and perverse; in point of understanding, just sufficient to appear in public without a slavering bib; imbued with no knowledge, illumed by no sentiment, and warmed with no affection. . . . His heart was meanly selfish, and his disposition altogether unprincely" (p. 397). His favorite amusement is "kicking the breech" of his ministers, an office assumed naturally by the Whigs, for they are the only group totally without honor or decency.

The Whigs are natural heirs of early Hanoverian policy because they are at once stupid and unscrupulous. For a time Newcastle is the most powerful political figure in the nation because he enjoys having his arse kicked: "He presented his posteriors to be kicked as regularly as the day revolved; and presented them not barely with submission, but with all the appearance of fond desire; and truly this diurnal exposure was attended with such delectation as he never enjoyed in any other attitude"

(p. 401). This admirable appetite is supported by a politic vacuity of mind, an actual "hollowness in the Brain"; "He had no understanding, no economy, no courage, no industry, no steadiness, no discernment, no vigour, no retention. He was . . . profuse, chicken-hearted, negligent, fickle, blundering, weak, and leaky" (p. 398). He is in fact the perfect specimen of the Whig oligarch: "A statesman without . . . the smallest tincture of human learning: a secretary who could not write; a financier who did not understand the multiplication table; and the treasurer of a vast empire who never could balance accounts with his own butler" (p. 400).[20] The inferior, metropolitan wing of the Whig party, led by fat aldermen who dine on turtle and venison, are more anarchic, disreputable, and unpredictable than the old duke and his friends. Yet they too are imbeciles willing to unite under the Hanoverian creed: "that two and two make seven; that the sun rules the night, the stars the day; and the moon is made of green cheese" (p. 416).

When Smollett reaches the period of the Seven Years' War, there is a sharp change in tone, one he himself notes: "I shall now proceed to a plain narration of historical incidents, without pretending to philosophize like H——e, or dogmatize like S——tt" (p. 416). The first two Georges, Newcastle, and their ilk Smollett can ridicule, for they are absurd and their activities make for farce. But from the mid-1750s the plain narration must also include Pitt and the mob, whom he can only loathe, for they are horrible. According to him, the old Whigs helped create the new sordid turn of affairs by initiating a policy of pandering to the mob: "'The multitude . . . is a many headed monster it is a Cerberus that must have a sop:—it is a wild-beast, so ravenous that nothing but blood will appease its appetite: it is a whale that must have a barrel for its amusement:—it is a demon to which we must offer up human sacrifice. Now, the question is, who is to be this sop, this barrel, this scape-goat?'" (p. 426). The victim chosen is of course Admiral Byng.

Pitt wanders into this opening as leader of the "self-constituted college of the mob." He possesses a loud braying voice, a fluency of abuse ("a species of music to the mob") which earns him the title, "first demogogue of the empire." His chief gift in diplomacy is to feign service to others while pleasing only himself. Performing the osculation a posteriori required of all public officials, he secretly disables his rivals. Filling his pockets with the treasure of the empire, he contrives a new food to beguile the starving, "a mess that should fill their bellies, and, at the same time, protract the intoxication of their brains, which it was so much his interest to maintain." Turning national policy to disgrace and apostasy, he holds the mob spellbound with his tricks, twists, and tumbles. Smollett sees Pitt as a virtuoso in the new English politics, mobocracy, having him declare, "I will ride the mighty beast whose name is Legion." He is the first power in the kingdom because he is a professional "mob-driver," a modern politician self-trained "to bridle and manage the blatant beast whose name was Legion." His natural constituency comprises the new order of public philosophers: "grocers, scavengers, halter-makers, carpenters, draymen, distillers, chimney-sweepers, oyster-women, ass-drivers, aldermen, and dealers in waste paper." Recognizing the stench of its own filth, the beast follows its master everywhere, and Pitt "milked the dugs of the monster till the blood came." Pitt's rivals are equally fascinated and horrified, convinced that the orator had sold his soul to the devil in exchange for power to move the mob. This is an interpretation the atom can credit: "I not only know there is a devil, but I likewise know that he has marked out nineteen-twentieths of the people of this metropolis for his prey" (pp. 461–62).

To the narrator-atom, Pitt and the Legion are practically inseparable and indistinguishable, and a full third of his tale is taken up with such passages as, "This furious beast not only suffered itself to be bridled and saddled, but frisked and fawned, and purred and yelped, and crouched before the orator, licking his feet, and presenting its back to the burdens which he was pleased to impose." And, "No fritter on Shrove Tuesday was ever more dextrously turned, than were the hydra's brains by this mountebank in patriotism, this juggler in politics" (both p. 437). Thus, as its Victorian critics charged, the *Atom* is indeed a scurrilous and virulent broadside against English politics during Smollett's lifetime. It does use such physical acts as eating, kissing, licking, vomiting, defecating, and many more to express a sense of disgust past despair. Most of the novelist's enemies pass in opprobrious review: Beckford as "an half-witted politician, self-conceited, headstrong, turbulent, and ambitious"; Churchill as a lewd priest able to rouse the blatant beast "by dint of quaint rhymes"; Wilkes as an artist in "making balls of filth which were famous for sticking and stinking." However, it was considerably more to Smollett's contemporaries, and should be so to anyone interested in the ideas of the age.

It expresses the novelist's final estimate of Bute, as a man of capacity and public spirit who is also checkered with "childish vanity, rash ambition, littleness of mind, and lack of understanding." The minister erred greatly when he prevailed upon the monarch to vest him with all the trappings of honor available in the kingdom; his fate was then sealed. It contains Smollett's disarmingly candid assessment of his own work on the *Briton*. He calls himself a dirt-thrower who played his part tolerably well. Although his missiles "were inferior in point of composition" to those of the City, they did at least bring a smarting to the eyes of Pitt and his minions (pp. 526–27). Finally, it shows Smollett near the end of his career reclaiming the role of objective statesman he had set for himself in 1756. Actual reference to the two political parties that divide England does not appear until near the close of the work (though the Whigs had been condemned all along), and then the purpose is to call for a plague upon both. One is composed mostly of fools, the other of knaves; both operate by "every art of corruption, calumny, insinuation, and priestcraft. . . . In short, both parties were equally abusive, rancorous, uncandid, and illiberal" (pp. 498–99). Very abrupt and appropriately bleak, his ending discloses Bute "hurried by evil counsellers into a train of false politics," facing with horror the prospect of yet another war, this time with the American colonists. The *Atom* reveals its author in an attitude of grave concern for, but personal detachment from, Britain's future. It is this uncommon sense of simultaneous involvement and disengagement that Smollett in his final work lent to Bramble and Lismahago.

Part Three

THE ATTACK UPON LUXURY AND
THE FORMS OF *HUMPHRY CLINKER*

*... if research requires a division of forces, a humane
education requires a synthesis, however provisional, of the results
of their labours, and to encourage us, by seeing these results,
not as isolated fragments, but as connected parts of a body of
living tissue, to acquire a more synoptic and realistic view of the
activities composing the life of society. The subject ...
is concerned not merely or mainly with the iridescent surface
of manners, fashions, social conventions and intercourse,
but with the unseen foundations, which, till they shift or crumble,
most men in most generations are wont to take for
granted.—R. H. Tawney, "Social History and Literature"*

Seven

THE POLITICS OF
HUMPHRY CLINKER

*We are not what we were; patriotism is not the growth
of these days; luxury has taken root too deeply for sudden
eradication.* —Critical Review, *1756*

*. . . the wise patriots of London have taken it into their heads, that all
regulation is inconsistent with liberty; and that every man ought to live in
his own way, without restraint—Nay, as there is not sense enough left
among them, to be discomposed . . . they may, for aught I care, wallow
in the mire of their own pollution.* —Matthew Bramble, *June 8*

Thus far it has been necessary to consider luxury in its material aspect
—its presence and influence in European history, in eighteenth-century
controversy, and in Smollett. It is now possible to make the inevitable
transition to its formal features. For three millennia the attack upon
luxury conveyed the dominant values and attitudes of Western society,
and moralists pursued their condemnations with certain impunity, for
no one would seriously defend immorality. Well before the birth of
Christ the attack had acquired a distinctive form. It had become so
common as to be conventional, so familiar as to take on a definite
shape. Individual writers would retain this general shape—as preachers
would keep the overarching form of the homily—while contributing
their own specific details. Theirs would be variations upon a traditional
theme, contemporary manifestations of a universal malaise.

215

The attack upon luxury may be regarded as a relatively distinct literary mode, with its own characteristic devices and methods of persuasion. It can more usefully be considered a mode rather than a genre, for it has been expressed in many genres. Because it seeks to reveal the (often hidden) dimension of causes, relations, and devolutions, it is primarily a heuristic, narrative mode, usually found in those forms which express developing awareness or expanding experience: quest, journey, psychomachia, imaginary voyage, retrospective elegy, nostalgic pastoral, panoramic survey, or moral history. It is the mode of Cato and Seneca, the *Republic* and the *City of God, Paradise Lost* and *Aureng-Zebe, Joseph Andrews* and the *Deserted Village;* of Swift and Bolingbroke, Davenant and John Brown. When that awareness is directed toward the historical past—as in Samuel and Kings, Sallust, Plutarch, and Gibbon—it nonetheless culminates in lessons drawn to redeem the present. And even in those rare instances where the attack has been shown to be successful—as in Prudentius and the Christian theologians— that victory over luxury must be guarded by constant vigilance and discipline.

From the Deuteronomic writers through Brown, Fawconer, and Goldsmith, the attack upon luxury normally represented an explanation and a warning, a portrait of a nation in rapid decline, perhaps in final devolution. The lesson is stated, then demonstrated in a series of marked contrasts: obedience – rebellion; old glory – new misery; political unity – competition and insubordination; social harmony – crime and ambition and confusion; the proud men of the ancient order – the debased representatives of the present; places of past greatness – sites of new debauchery; rural felicity – urban corruption; disciplined youth – depraved youth; a society guided by divinity and masculinity – one ruled by effeminate passion. So terrible and so persistent was the idea of luxury that it made an indelible imprint upon the European sensibility, and the list could be extended almost indefinitely. What had been a theological lesson became a theological pattern, forecasting God's punishment onto the present and future. It then yielded a logical pattern, a historical one, and a literary one. One sign of the vitality of the literary pattern is its early refinement. By the time of Herodotus the story is told by someone who is (or claims to be) relatively objective—a sage, historian, or foreign visitor. And within a generation, by the time of Aristophanes, the technique is developed further, with the superaddition for contrast of the views of various kinds of victims—the young, the naive, the gullible, and the unscrupulous.

Preceding chapters have sought to demonstrate that Smollett used this familiar mode in his major nonfiction after 1756. Is there reason to believe it is present also in his final work, the novel that is considered his masterpiece? On the prima facie level of direct textual evidence, the answer is clear. Twice in the first quarter of *Humphry Clinker,* Bramble delivers long and memorable tirades against the social customs of his time, first in Bath, then in London. He concludes his diatribe against Bath with the generalization: "All these absurdities arise from the general tide of luxury, which hath overspread the nation, and swept away all, even the very dregs of the people" (MB, April 23). In London he again sees a "tide of luxury" inundating the capital in social evils he has taken pains to specify: "they may be all resolved into the grand source of luxury and corruption" (MB, May 29). As Bramble turns his mind, briefly, to more pleasant matters during the journey northward, the theme—and the metaphor—is taken up by Lismahago: "Mean while the sudden affluence occasioned by trade, forced open all the sluices of luxury and overflowed the land with every species of profligacy and corruption; a total pravity of manners would ensue, and this must be attended with bankruptcy and ruin" (MB, July 15). Such open, direct denunciation is voiced by five different characters—Bramble, Jery, Lismahago, Dennison, and Baynard—and elaborated in eighteen different letters, letters that as a rule are the longest in the novel.

Such evidence establishes that the attack upon luxury is materially present, but it does not establish its necessity to a work of fiction. For this latter task only close analysis of forms will suffice. I shall argue in this and the following two chapters that *Humphry Clinker* does indeed deserve to be read in the light of the Western tradition, eighteenth-century controversy, and Smollett's own two decades of attack—in their light and as their epitome. While this contention is in no way iconoclastic, so far as I can discover no major work of English or Continental literature has been the subject of such a reading. The argument follows from the earlier portion of this study and from two truistic assumptions. First, the novel is inexhaustible and merits reading in as many ways as possible. The attack upon luxury is not the single golden key that will unlock its treasures. There is no such unique key, for Smollett is patently engaged in tasks (like the celebration of Scotland) other than the exposure of luxury. Yet it is the only approach not yet pursued by modern criticism, and it does provide access to much that can be gotten at in no other way: Smollett's method of combining general and particular satire, his cultivation of a mixed response for a bittersweet portrait of contemporary Britain, and the tradition in which it was written and read. The value of further access is clear if one accepts the argument of E. D. Hirsch that readers usually approach a new work through mode or type.[1] Retrospectively, we today tend to view eighteenth-century fiction under the all-absorbing rubric of *novel.* Contemporary readers, however, could not and did not. For what we know as the early novel was a fluid and hybrid form, the major writers incorporating much that was old into the "new species of writing." One has but to recall the influence of spiritual autobiography upon Defoe, model letters upon Richardson, the epic upon Fielding, and Rabelaisian satire upon Sterne to realize how comfortable Smollett would have been expressing his loathing of luxury in the new form.

Second, an idea like luxury can easily enter into the formal constituent part of a literary work. To admit that the attack upon luxury can be a literary mode is to acknowledge that ideas can be embedded in the narrative structure itself. An accomplished novelist like Smollett requires us to absorb the experience of his fictional characters, to assume it, to comprehend it, to regard it as natural. To present a luxurious world in action is by definition to make a series of metaphysical statements, for luxury is precisely that concept which for Smollett and others encloses all vital issues of human value. Novel-writing could be akin to cultural criticism. Moreover, the attack upon luxury may be metaphysical in still another sense. In an early essay Lionel Trilling writes of "the real basis of the novel" in England and on the Continent as "the tension between a middle class and an aristocracy which brings manners into observable relief as the living representation of ideals and the living comment on ideas."[2] Trilling's observation is not self-evidently valid for all great novels, but to the extent that it holds for many it elevates the importance of luxury. A traditionalist like Smollett would explain the tension Trilling finds in terms of the cultured few upholding a standard, a national way of life, a sanctified truth, "an England," against the subversive luxury of the barbarian horde. Extending Trilling, one could say that the attack upon luxury is "the real basis" of "the real basis of the novel."

To read *Humphry Clinker* as formally an attack upon luxury is to alter several modern critical emphases, including those that see Smollett as essentially simple (or if that is too harsh, then *transparent*), separate the man from his work, dismiss the social and political commentary, regard all main characters as coequal, reduce Bramble and Lismahago to decorative eccentrics, and see the organization of the novel as random and purposeless. To cite but one example, in a work cited earlier McKillop considers the milieu of the novel a region of endless absurdity but little indignation: "While the great world may rage without, the obliquities of these originals are harmless, and manifest themselves in a well-grounded order of things."[3] This is a plausible modern reading. But contemporary readers were aware that the great world indeed roars within the pages of the novel as the genesis of the endless absurdities McKillop notes; and if the obliquities of Bramble and Lismahago now strike us as harmless the reason is far different from the one he finds.

The well-grounded order of things Smollett cherished has in fact been much eroded, and the imprecations of his characters are delivered against a changing order they regard as disturbing and inferior. A Bramble and a Lismahago possess the confidence of buoyant assertation and do indeed embody values which are clear and self-confident, but they stand together as adversaries, not representatives, of the development of English society. So deeply and so carefully is the attack upon luxury embedded in the novel that the task of criticism is almost one of excavation. This and the following two chapters will seek to uncover the primary elements of Smollett's attack, in the political configurations, development of characters, and narrative structure of the novel. The remainder of this chapter attempts to demonstrate, in plain but ample fashion, that *Humphry Clinker* is a highly political novel, one of the most politically charged of the century.

To call *Humphry Clinker* a political novel might strike a modern reader (to put it charitably) as mildly paradoxical. Although many political figures are introduced, few are worthy, most contemptible; at best we meet men like the monarch who keep aloof from the routine duplicity of factions and parties. Political action, insofar as it is shown, is enveloped by chaos—sometimes hilarious, sometimes mortifying; political policy, we learn, is deceit practiced upon ignorance. Yet there is a familiar resonance to the scene. It had been predicted by Plato, Seneca, Bolingbroke, and Smollett—the time when the public graces have been swallowed up by the voracious maw of luxury. It is moreover the scene explained and described by Bramble in his first letter from London, May 29. Luxury has been as acid upon the nation he once revered, dissolving all into corruption, rebellion, and political frenzy. Moving from the general to the particular, Bramble personalizes the dissolution in several ways, most poignantly by reference to past friendships: "I have seen some old friends . . . but they are so changed in manners and disposition, that we hardly know or care for one another." The sentiment returns, he finds, throughout his tour of England, for merit and reward no longer travel together. Most of his old friends have changed for the worse: those who have retained their integrity have lost income and standing; those who have kept social position have squandered their morality. The traveler's sense of loss is indicative of the political tone of the novel, a withdrawal approaching despair. The madness luxury has released has driven out all hope for major, public reform; English politics is exhausted in vain self-interest. Only private hope, personal dreams remain. This fact marks a certain diminution in Smollett's ambitions, literary as well as political, and may explain part of the vitality and attraction of the novel. In contrast to his other projects, *Humphry Clinker* is a work of limits, restraint, proportion.

Relatively, it is a work of modest ambition, the kind appropriate to an age of rancor and excess. Certainly not mellow, it is simply measured—a political novel for a time when legitimate politics is dead.

On the one hand, Smollett sought to give the novel an appearance of political involvement but impartiality. This was the role he has assumed for himself as early as the *Complete History*, writing in it, the *Continuation,* the *Critical Review,* and the *Briton* that he was of no party. (In the last he also wrote that neither Bute nor any member of his ministry was politically partisan. Like contemporary opponents, however, later historians have tried in vain to discover a genuine Whig within the administration.) In the novel his chief male characters are close observers of contemporary politics, Bramble as a former Member of Parliament, Jery as an aspirant to its chambers, and Lismahago as a student of the law. Yet they are explicitly noted to be nonpartisan. Introducing Barton, a friend and fellow Oxonian, Jery remarks:

> He has not gall enough in his constitution to be enflamed with the rancour of party, so as to deal in scurrilous invectives; but, since he obtained a place, he is become a warm partizan of the ministry, and sees every thing through such an exaggerating medium, as *to me, who am happily of no party,* is altogether incomprehensible—Without all doubt, the fumes of faction not only disturb the faculty of reason, but also pervert the organs of sense; and I would lay a hundred guineas to ten, that if Barton on one side, and the most conscientious patriot in the opposition on the other, were to draw, upon honour, the picture of the k—— or m——, *you and I, who are still uninfected, and unbiassed,* would find both painters equally distant from the truth. [JM, June 2, italics added]

In the same letter Bramble mentions his own political independence: "Whilst I sat in parliament, I never voted with the ministry but three times, when my conscience told me they were in the right." In Namier's terms, Bramble was therefore of the independent country party during the ministries, presumably, of Newcastle and Pitt, and hence a proper commentator upon those two politicians. As a freeholder and country gentleman, he is placed in a relatively disinterested political position, untainted by the selfish motives of professional politicians, courtiers, merchants, and financiers.[4] The third major character, Lismahago, is represented as equally free from partisan spirit. Himself a victim of much political chicanery, he calls for a plague upon both parties. The specific political commentary, wide-ranging though it is, is largely confined to five of the more than eighty letters of the novel: JM, June 2; MB, June 2; JM, June 5; MB, July 15; and MB, September 20. Even in these, Smollett feels compelled to defend its inclusion. In Bramble's letter of September 20, for instance, Lismahago's political opinions—identical to Bramble's—are reported in detail, and the novelist has Bramble conclude: "So much for the dogmata of my friend Lismahago, whom I describe the more circumstantially, as I firmly believe he will set up his rest in Monmouth'shire." Bramble seeks to limit the influence of that "daemon of party" not only in his own life, but also in the life of literature and the arts; hence his alarm that "the daemon of party seems to have usurped every department of life. Even the world of literature and taste is divided into the most virulent factions, which revile, decry, and traduce the works of one another" (MB, June 2). For Smollett, who wrote or edited nearly seventy volumes of historical and political commentary between *Count Fathom* and *Humphry Clinker* and was increasingly associated with partisan causes, such isolation and restraint are quite striking. They may be interpreted as either the self-restraint demanded by the novel or the reduction to proper size of the role of partisan issues in everyday life; I would argue that they are both, the transcendence of false politics by the true. What is certain is that Smollett endured a series of bitter disappointments after 1763; vicious personal attack, the failure of the *Briton,* Bute's ingratitude and later fall from power, repeated acute illness joined to chronic ill-health, failure to receive a government post abroad, continued worry over money, and most important, the death of his only child, the fifteen-year-old Elizabeth. Political and paternal grief are intermingled in his summary of recent years for the opening letter of the *Travels* (1766):

> You knew, and pitied my situation, traduced by malice, perse-cuted by faction, abandoned by false patrons, and overwhelmed by the sense of a domestic calamity, which it was not in the power of fortune to repair.
> You knew with what eagerness I fled from my country as a scene of illiberal dispute, and incredible infatuation, where a few worthless incendiaries had, by dint of perfidious calumnies and atrocious abuse, kindled up a flame which threatened all the horrors of civil dissention.

On the other hand, he fashioned in *Humphry Clinker* a highly political design: the counterpointing of England and Scotland, city and country, change and tradition; the major characters' Welsh background; Bramble's flight from moral squalor to moral virtue, the equation in his person of physical sensitivity and moral sensibility; the journey of education of Jery and Lydia; the presence of a distressed veteran of the colonial wars; the alternation in the letters of frivolous and mature points of view. Each of these circumstances underlines Smollett's intention to provide serious comment upon familiar, public topics. Moreover, the novel is at its most vigorous as a tract against the times. Giving colorful illustration of what it condemns, *Humphry Clinker* proceeds with the logic of discourse. The irritations of Hot Well are succeeded by the provocations of Bath and the enormities of the capital. At Bath we are introduced to the nature and manifestations of luxury, at London to its agents and brutal consequences. Similarly, in discussing London Smollett first gives us the venal politicians who pander to false tastes (June 2, June 5), and then their handiwork in the near ruin of everyday living (June 8). Famous personages appear together in the three London letters, where they are introduced as if on permanent exhibit in a great hall of statuary. Thus Bramble asks, in the midst of the tour, "'Well, Mr. Barton, what figure do you call next?' The next person he pointed out, was the favorite *yearl;* who stood solitary by one of the windows" (JM, June 2). Barton makes his judgment, Bramble sustains or denies, and Jery finds for his uncle. Commenting upon issues, the London letters reinforce one another closely, with an opinion broached in the first letter repeated in the second and again in the third. To a lesser extent Smollett uses the same method with personalities, such as Newcastle, who is *said* to be an ass in the first and *shown* to be one in the third. The two later letters from Scotland, representing Lismahago's political disquisitions, serve to recall and further reinforce those of the English half. Smollett insured that his considered thoughts on luxury and politics would appear in each of the original three volumes of *Humphry Clinker.*

Certain opinions, such as that of the licentiousness of the press, are sustained throughout the five letters. Jery asserts the evil of the press in the first. In the second Bramble affirms the charge and Barton reaffirms, then illustrates it. In the third Bramble repeats himself; in the fourth and fifth Lismahago echoes and reechoes Bramble. On many occasions in the Scottish half of the novel, it will be remembered, Bramble is allowed to forget his earlier positions in order to stand as temporary adversary to Lismahago, thereby softening a little the lieutenant's didactic voice. Yet Lismahago does have his own particular function as political spokesman for Smollett, as he describes the methods of English exploitation of Scotland. And it is he, proud Scotsman and veteran soldier, who is called upon to defend the Treaty of Paris. Two-thirds of the way through the novel—hundreds of miles away, that is, from the king, Bute, Pitt, and the City—Smollett inserts a brief reference to the cause linked so intimately with his name: "One of the company chancing to mention lord B——'s inglorious peace, the lieutenant immediately took up the cudgels in his lordship's favour, and argued very strenuously to prove that it was the most honourable and advantageous peace that England had ever made since the foundation of the monarchy" (MB,

July 15). Bramble, acting here in the uncommon role of disinterested narrator, immediately closes the episode for Dr. Lewis by noting: "Nay, between friends, he offered such reasons on this subject, that I was really confounded, if not convinced."

Smollett's powers of dramatic presentation are at full stretch not with the glories of Edinburgh, but with the horrors of London. Even within the Scottish half, the pattern recurs. Whereas we are told of the hospitality of Commissary Smollett, we are shown the household of Lord Oxmington, and Jery's comments come not as summary but as introduction: "His lordship is much more remarkable for his pride and caprice, than for his hospitality and understanding; and indeed, it appeared, that he considered his guests merely as objects to shine upon, so as to reflect the lustre of his own magnificence.—There was much state, but no courtesy; and a great deal of compliment without any conversation" (JM, September 28). In addition, Smollett seems to be offering solutions to quasi-political problems. More often than not, the resolution of temporary grievance is not through persuasion and agreement, but through the direct use of force. To obtain quiet in his lodgings at Bath, Bramble must cudgel the offending musicians. He and Lismahago both recommended the severe beating of libelous printers. The travelers can gain Oxmington's respect only by a massive show of arms and strength, and Lismahago's kick is shown to be the proper response to the nobleman's lackey. Baynard cannot salvage his estate merely by following wise counsel: he and his affairs must be placed totally in the hands of Bramble and Dennison.

Seldom varied, the pattern of Smollett's political tour of England is renewed each time the party travels to a new place. Upon arrival, one of the males—usually Bramble and usually in the manner of the *Present State*—provides a synoptic view of the ills pervading the town. Against later letters from the same place, this introduction is taut and concise, vivid and impassioned: it is so relentless a portrait of human folly that we at first assume it must be eccentric to a novel of comic intentions, so extreme that it must be qualified, if not erased. As the party moves about the town, however, subsequent letters reveal the incarnation of those very ills in the men and women who dominate social affairs. The later letters, penned mostly by Jery, are more numerous, tentative, disinterested, and tolerant; yet their ultimate effect is to affirm the keenness and truth of the opening survey.[5]

Humphry Clinker includes many of Smollett's old crotchets, and the overarching issues are the most familiar, what we have come to know through his own work as the syndrome of luxury. In the wake of the vice flows an unholy emphasis upon trade and commerce. Hence Bramble follows his attack upon the luxury of Bath with a tirade against merchants and their morality of profit (MB, April 23), Lismahago asserts that "a glut of wealth . . . destroys all the distinctions of civil society; so that universal anarchy and uproar must ensue" (MB, September 20), and the Scotsman exposes, in the long passage already cited, the effects of English luxury in the depletion of the Scottish economy. Explaining why commerce must be tightly supervised, Lismahago also voices in a metaphor the novelist's rather feudal view of fluctuations in trade: "the nature of commerce was such, that it could not be fixed or perpetuated, but, having flowed to a certain height, would immediately begin to ebb, and so continue till the channels should be left almost dry; but there was no instance of the tide's rising a second time to any considerable influx in the same nation" (MB, July 15). He observes further:

> That commerce would, sooner or later, prove the ruin of every nation, where it flourishes to any extent. . . . He observed, that traffick was an enemy to all the liberal passions of the soul, founded on the thirst of lucre, a sordid disposition to take advantage of the necessities of our fellow-creatures. . . . Mean while the sudden affluence occasioned by trade, forced open all the sluices of luxury and overflowed the land with every species of profligacy and corruption; a total pravity of manners would ensue, and this must be attended with bankruptcy and ruin. [MB, July 15]

As Smollett had done in his histories, Lismahago in a later letter conjoins the effects of commerce and the behavior of the multitude.

> "Woe be to that nation, where the multitude is at liberty to follow their own inclinations! Commerce is undoubtedly a blessing, while restrained within its proper channels; but a glut of wealth brings along with it a glut of evils: it brings false taste, false appetite, false wants, profusion, venality, contempt of order, engendering a spirit of licentiousness, insolence, and faction, that keeps the community in continual ferment, and in time destroys all the distinctions of civil society; so that universal anarchy and uproar must ensue." [MB, September 20][6]

Bramble and Lismahago likewise express by implication what Smollett elsewhere states directly: commerce is the efficient cause of English degeneracy. It is associated in the novel with virtually all the horrors of London life and most of the ills of the rest of Britain—inflation, highway crime, depopulation of the country, ruin of the small landowner, eradication of frugality and simplicity, the decline of education and the arts.

Corruption of government is the most despicable of the many horrors of the capital, and among its many contemporary manifestations

Bramble continually remarks a nearly universal currying of favor. Instead of doing the work of the kingdom, English politicians are absorbed in endless rounds of otiose flattery and bribery, the ugliest of which is cultivation of the mob. In an oblique reference to Pitt, Bramble exclaims:

> Notwithstanding my contempt for those who flatter a minister, I think there is something still more despicable in flattering a mob. When I see a man of birth, education, and fortune, put himself on a level with the dregs of the people, mingle with low mechanics, feed with them at the same board, and drink with them in the same cup, flatter their prejudices, harangue in praise of their virtues, expose themselves to the belchings of their beer, the fumes of their tobacco, the grossness of their familiarity, and the impertinence of their conversation, I cannot help despising him, as a man guilty of the vilest prostitution, in order to effect a purpose equally selfish and illiberal. [MB, June 2]

A sure sign that Smollett's polemical flame was still lambent, this passage covers three-quarters of the population under the slurs "mob" and "dregs of the people." It recalls the criticism of Antony by a cold Octavius that Antony would "keep the turn of tippling with a slave" and then "stand the buffet / with knaves that smell of sweat." A figure like Pitt would certainly come into physical closeness with the middle-class voters of the City. But "dregs," "low mechanics," "prejudices," "belchings," "beer," "grossness," and "impertinence"–these terms identify the mass of workers and unemployed who, whatever their fearsome habits, had no voting rights and no direct political influence. Smollett would have his readers dismiss such distinctions.

With Lismahago the indictment becomes broader, as the old soldier argues that elections are themselves a species of bribery and that even the English form of limited representative democracy is evil. Calling Parliament "the rotten part of the British constitution," Lismahago traces present corruption to Walpole's putative habit of buying a legislature to suit him. Elections, at least those under George II, therefore amount to no more than "an avowed system of venality, already established on the ruins of principle, integrity, faith, and good order, in consequence of which the elected and the elector, and, in short, the whole body of the people, were equally and universally contaminated and corrupted." As if to anticipate all ripostes, Lismahago pursues his logic to a fatal stop:

> He affirmed, that of a parliament thus constituted, the crown would always have influence enough to secure a great majority in

its dependence, from the great number of posts, places, and pensions it had to bestow; that such a parliament would (as it had already done) lengthen the term of its sitting and authority, when-ever the prince should think it for his interest to continue the representatives. . . . With a parliament, therefore, dependent upon the crown, devoted to the prince, and supported by a standing army, garbled and modelled for the purpose, any king of England may, and probably some ambitious sovereign will, totally over-throw all the bulwarks of the constitution; for it is not to be sup-posed that a prince of a high spirit will tamely submit to be thwarted in all his measures, abused and insulted by a populace of unbridled ferocity, when he has it in his power to crush all opposi-tion under his feet with the concurrence of the legislature. [MB, July 15][7]

This passage reflects two aspects of Smollett's polemical writing. He strives to produce a bold and vivid assertion and then argues aggressively within the terms of the original assertion. More a habit than a conscious technique, this aspect of the novelist's style gives his argument an air of confidence while also avoiding the disquieting problems of definition, qualification, and evaluation. It also leads on occasion to a clash of con-flicting assertions. If, as Lismahago holds, the crown has the power to create a Parliament of its own design and thereafter to retain it, then that Parliament is the impotent, not the rotten, part of the British constitution. The passage further shows the novelist's penchant for repeating with small changes of phrase his cherished statements from earlier works. To his familiar warnings of a manipulated Parliament, he here adds a reference to the political controversies of the earlier 1760s— "a prince of high spirit . . . abused and insulted by a populace of un-bridled ferocity"—which would recall the alleged libels of the *North Briton*.

If Lismahago is anxious over the possibility of a tyranny imposed from above, Bramble is yet more exercised over signs of a revolution from below. Like thousands of moralists before him, the Welshman is convinced that insubordination represents the death fever, the final madness of a nation infected by luxury. In almost every English city he visits, he perceives its symptoms, particularly in social leveling, factions, freedom of the press, and the operation of the jury system. Since he believes that the various ranks of a society are immiscible, he finds frequent occasion to deplore such places as Vauxhall where classes and sexes mix more readily than elsewhere. On the one hand, the respectable persons found there are guilty of degrading themselves: "When I see a number of well-dressed people, of both sexes, sitting on the covered

benches, exposed to the eyes of the mob . . . I can't help compassionat-
ing their temerity; while I despise their want of taste and decorum"
(MB, May 29). On the other, the common people are guilty of criminal
failure to conform to class distinctions in dress: "Every clerk, apprentice, and even waiter of tavern or coffee-house . . . assumes the air and
apparel of a petit maitre—The gayest places of public entertainment are
filled with fashionable figures; which, upon inquiry, will be found to be
journeymen taylors, serving-men, and abigails, disguised like their betters." Even small examples of social mixing, like Win's comically ill-
fated visit to the theater, can be interpreted as political rebellion if one
assumes that every inch of new freedom granted to an apprentice removes that amount from the prerogatives of a lord. Hence Bramble's
conclusion follows from his premise: "In short, there is no distinction
or subordination left—The different departments of life are jumbled
together—The hod-carrier, the low mechanic, the tapster, the publican,
the shop-keeper, the pettifogger, the citizen, and the courtier, all tread
upon the kibes of one another: actuated by the demons of profligacy
and licentiousness . . . and crashing in one vile ferment of stupidity and
corruption" (MB, May 29). Repeating Smollett's earlier contentions
from the *Complete History*, moreover, he finds that the insubordination
of the poor inevitably leads not only to sedition but also to crime.

> The tide of luxury has swept all the inhabitants from the open
> country—The poorest 'squire, as well as the richest peer, must have
> his house in town, and make a figure with an extraordinary num-
> ber of domestics. The plough-boys, cow-herds, and lower hinds, are
> debauched and seduced by the appearance and discourse of those
> coxcombs in livery, when they make their summer excursions.
> They desert their dirt and drudgery, and swarm up to London, in
> hopes of getting into service, where they can live luxuriously and
> wear fine clothes, without being obliged to work; for idleness is
> natural to man—Great numbers of these, being disappointed in
> their expectation, become thieves and sharpers; and London being
> an immense wilderness, in which there is neither watch nor ward
> of any signification, nor any order or police, affords them lurking-
> places as well as prey. [MB, May 29]

In a nation beset by luxury, spurious political divisions are encouraged, while genuine authority and legitimate order go ignored.
Various groups are permitted to compete for the leadership that can
never rightfully be theirs. They rival one another with false claims, false
reports, false promises. As Bramble's above letter has raised the central
issues, Jery's next, of June 2, begins the process of illustrating the stinks
given off by the vice, noting, "Without all doubt, the fumes of faction

not only disturb the faculty of reason, but also pervert the organs of sense." In the same letter Bramble is quoted as saying that while in power Newcastle was rightly ridiculed, but when he lost power and "unfurled the banners of faction" he was hailed as "a wise, experienced statesman, chief pillar of the Protestant succession." Barton explains this contradiction by identifying faction with mob mentality: "I don't pretend to justify the extravagations of the multitude; who, I suppose, were as wild in their former censure, as in their present praise." In his letter of the same date, Bramble repeats and extends these themes. Explaining to Dr. Lewis why needed improvements of the British Museum "will never be reduced to practice," he says, "Considering the temper of the times, it is a wonder to see any institution whatsoever established, for the benefit of the public. The spirit of party is risen to a kind of phrenzy, unknown to former ages, or rather degenerated to a total extinction of honesty and candour" (MB, June 2). He then promptly moves to the most egregious public example of faction. "You know I have observed, for some time, that the public papers are become the infamous vehicles of the most cruel and perfidious defamation: every rancorous knave—every desperate incendiary, that can afford to spend half a crown or three shillings, may skulk behind the press of a news-monger, and have a stab at the first character in the kingdom, without running the least hazard of detection or punishment" (MB, June 2).

Barton is then introduced in order to confirm Bramble's opinion. Referring to his penchant for eulogizing the current ministry, Bramble notes that he had seen one of Barton's favorites so stigmatized in the press, "that if one half of what was said of him was true, he must be not only unfit to rule, but even unfit to live." He tells Barton that at first he could not credit the charges, but when the favorite failed to vindicate himself he began to entertain suspicions. Smollett's manipulation of his main character is obvious: in the space of two sentences Bramble is transformed from a cynic to an innocent. Barton's considered response is thus elicited, and echoing the conversation in *Macbeth* between Malcolm and Macduff, it turns upon the depraved tastes and perverted loyalties of the mob:

> "And pray, sir, (said Mr. Barton) what steps would you have him take?—Suppose he should prosecute the publisher, who screens the anonymous accuser, and bring him to the pillory for a libel; this is so far from being counted a punishment, *in terrorem,* that it will probably make his fortune. The multitude immediately take him into their protection, as a martyr to the cause of defamation, which they have always espoused—They pay his fine, they contribute to the increase of his stock, his shop is crowded with

customers, and the sale of his paper rises in proportion to the scandal it contains. All this time the prosecutor is inveighed against as a tyrant and oppressor, for having chosen to proceed by the way of information, which is deemed a grievance; but if he lays an action for damages, he must prove the damage, and I leave you to judge, whether a gentleman's character may not be brought into contempt, and all his views in life blasted by calumny, without his being able to specify the particulars of the damage he has sustained." [MB, June 2]

This belief in the delicacy of a gentleman's honor, something not to be entrusted to the judgment of such gross plebeians as usually make up a jury, is part of Smollett's contention that the freedom of the press and the composition of juries are parallel instances of rank insubordination, which if permitted to continue will produce not only scandal but sedition: "This spirit of defamation is a kind of heresy, that thrives under persecution. *The liberty of the press* is a term of great efficacy; and, like that of *the Protestant religion,* has often served the purposes of sedition." When Bramble interrupts Barton's harangue to comment further upon juries, neither the tone nor the substance of the passage is altered in the least: "Certain it is, a gentleman's honour is a very delicate subject to be handled by a jury, composed of men, who cannot be supposed remarkable either for sentiment or impartiality—In such a case, indeed, the defendant is tried, not only by his peers, but also by his party; and I really think, that of all patriots, he is the most resolute who exposes himself to such detraction, for the sake of his country" (MB, June 2). Lismahago's later attack upon the "illiterate plebeians" who generally make up a jury seeks to expose the injustice of the jury system.

> Juries are generally composed of illiterate plebeians, apt to be mistaken, easily misled, and open to sinister influence; for if either of the parties to be tried, can gain over one of the twelve jurors, he has secured the verdict in his favour; the juryman thus brought over will, in despite of all evidence and conviction, generally hold out till his fellows are fatigued, and harrassed, and starved into concurrence; in which case the verdict is unjust, and the jurors are all perjured. [MB, July 15]

Bramble, however, is aware of a likelier means of redress than "the ignorance and partiality of juries." To a gentleman traduced in the press, he recommends recourse to "the publishers bones" and "the ribs of an author." Should the gentleman himself be reluctant to try such measures he may employ "certain useful instruments, such as may be found in all countries, to give [an offender] the bastinado." Thus Smollett does find some occasional value in the violence of the mob. Although he has found an effective solution, Bramble is not able to relinquish the problem.

As for the liberty of the press, like every other privilege, it must be restrained within certain bounds; for if it is carried to a breach of law, religion, and charity, it becomes one of the greatest evils that every annoyed the community. If the lowest ruffian may stab your good-name with impunity in England, will you be so uncandid as to exclaim against Italy for the practice of common assassination? To what purpose is our property secured, if our moral character is left defenceless? People thus baited, grow desperate; and the despair of being able to preserve one's character, untainted by such vermin, produces a total neglect of fame; so that one of the chief incitements to the practice of virtue is effectually destroyed. [MB, June 2]

And in the second half of the novel Lismahago is once more called upon to return attention to the seriousness of the problem: "He said, he should always consider the liberty of the press as a national evil, while it enabled the vilest reptile to soil the lustre of the most shining merit, and furnished the most infamous incendiary with the means of disturbing the peace and destroying the good order of the community. He owned, however, that, under due restrictions, it would be a valuable privilege; but affirmed, that at present there was no law in England sufficient to restrain it within proper bounds" (MB, July 15).

The viciousness of the press was thus to Smollett another consequence of a climate of luxury and insubordination. It seemed to him that the masses wished to erase the distinctions that by nature existed between themselves and men of rank, to drag men of character down to their own level. (Bramble's letter of June 2, it should be noted, applies the epithet of *mob* to men able to pay the fines of popular publishers as well as to read their papers, and castigates as the *lowest* ruffian not only a man able to read and write but one who also can afford to buy the full apparatus of publishing.) The press became a vehicle of such infamous craving when it pandered to the tastes of the mob, a monster Bramble never could abide. The contemporary political condition of England was doubly perilous, moreover, because certain politicians as well as the press appeared to be pandering to the masses. Hence in his letter of June 2 Bramble moves quickly and effortlessly from a denunciation of the press to an attack on the complementary evil, the gentleman who flatters the mob. This theme is of course repeated by Bramble and Lismahago throughout the novel. In an earlier letter

Bramble had said: "Indeed, I know nothing so abject as the behavior of a man canvassing for a seat in parliament—This mean prostration, (to borough-electors, especially) has, I imagine, contributed in great measure to raise that spirit of insolence among the vulgar; which, like the devil, will be found very difficult to lay" (MB, May 19). The fundamental assumption is that the traditional exclusion of the great majority of Englishmen from the political process must be maintained; the primary condition of good order is stated plainly by Lismahago: "He said, he hoped he should never see the common people lifted out of that sphere for which they were intended by nature and the course of things" (MB, September 20).

Being the folly of the mindless and tasteless, insubordination is represented in *Humphry Clinker* by men and women who are largely faceless. Some are named, but most are merely neutered members of one or another organ of the mob—the City, the Methodists, the Legion. One could say that for Smollett they are not human personalities to be described, but problems to be solved, at best groups to be controlled. This is certainly not to say that the novelist could exclude his adversaries among the Old Whig Gang; about certain heads he could be as driven as any Mr. Dick. The founder of the gang, Walpole, is ushered in briefly by Bramble as "a first-mover, who was justly stiled and stigmatized as the father of corruption" (JM, June 2). Pitt, the present leader, appears as "the great political bully" and "that overbearing Hector" (JM, June 5), and directly in Jery's letter of June 2: "Ha, there's the other great phaenomenon, the grand pensionary, that weathercock of patriotism that veers about in every point of the political compass, and still feels the wind of popularity in his tail. He too, like a portentous comet, has risen again above the court-horizon; but how long he will continue to ascend, it is not easy to foretel, considering his great eccentricity." Newcastle is presented as the clown prince of the gang in two of the most comically acid scenes of the novel. In the one Bramble calls him "an ape in politics" for thirty years, and Jery describes him as hopelessly senile (JM, June 2). In the other he moves from one absurdity to another at his own levee, scandalizing visitors like the ambassador from Algiers: "he scarce ever opened his mouth without making some blunder, in relation to the person or business of the party with whom he conversed; so that he really looked like a comedian, hired to burlesque the character of a minister" (JM, June 5). The gang is rounded off with Townshend, who is in constant fear of Pitt (JM, June 5), and the pseudonymous factota, Pitt's "two satellites." The first is probably Wilkes: "without a drop of red blood in his veins . . . a cold intoxicating vapour in his head; and rancour enough in his heart to inoculate and affect a whole nation." The second, Temple:

"Without principle, talent, or intelligence, he is ungracious as a hog, greedy as a vulture, and thievish as a jackdaw" (JM, June 2).[8]

Relatively, these individualized sketches are few, enveloped by the collective presence of the mob. Seemingly omnipotent and omnipresent in England, the mob befouls everything it touches, from the spas to the churches, the courts to the papers, Ranelagh to Parliament. Put political-ly, the Whig oligarchs require no strength of numbers, for they possess such willing tools in the City, the Methodist chapels, and the gin shops. Smollett felt obliged to expose the folly and ignorance of the men of the City. That lesson is certainly part of the intention of *Humphry Clinker*. The original title page carried lines from the *Sermones* of Horace: *Quorsum haec tam putida tendunt, / Furcifer? ad te, inquam.* (To what object are these disagreeable facts directed, you rogue? To you, I said.) The most disagreeable collective portrait in the novel is of the men of the middle orders who come down from London and in their barbarity despoil the graces of Bath.

> Clerks and factors from the East Indies, loaded with the spoil of plundered provinces; planters, negro-drivers, and hucksters, from our American plantations, enriched they know not how; agents, commissaries, and contractors, who have fattened, in two succes-sive wars, on the blood of the nation; usurers, brokers, and jobbers of every kind; men of low birth, and no breeding, have found themselves suddenly translated into a state of affluence, unknown to former ages; and no wonder that their brains should be intoxi-cated with pride, vanity, and presumption. Knowing no other criterion of greatness, but the ostentation of wealth, they dis-charge their affluence without taste or conduct, through every channel of the most absurd extravagance; and all of them hurry to Bath, because here, without any further qualification, they can mingle with the princes and nobles of the land. Even the wives and daughters of low tradesmen, who, like shovel-nosed sharks, prey upon the blubber of those uncouth whales of fortune, are infected with the same rage of displaying their importance; and the slightest indisposition serves them for a pretext to insist upon being con-veyed to Bath, where they may hobble country-dances and cotil-lons among lordlings, 'squires, counsellors, and clergy. These deli-cate creatures from Bedfordbury, Butcher-row, Crutched-Friers, and Botolph-lane, cannot breathe in the gross air of the Lower Town, or conform to the vulgar rules of a common lodging-house; the husband, therefore, must provide an entire house, or elegant apartments in the new buildings. Such is the composition of what is called the fashionable company at Bath; where a very inconsid-

erable proportion of genteel people are lost in *a mob of impudent plebeians, who have neither understanding nor judgment, nor the least idea of propriety and decorum; and seem to enjoy nothing so much as an opportunity of insulting their betters.* [MB, April 23; italics added]

Once again the City Whigs represent the confluence of Smollett's national, political, and social antipathies, the intersection of large issues and small personalities. Bramble finds luxury and insubordination indigenous to London, whence they are carried outward, most notably to Bath, but also at times to the northern countryside (by persons like Mrs. Baynard and her aunt). The evils of the time encounter little resistance in England but much in Scotland, where they are fated to languish and die. Lismahago's two tirades (MB, July 15; and MB, September 20), though delivered on the road north, are directed against English influences. In Scotland neither commerce nor the men engaged in it are in any way subversive of the social and political order. On at least three occasions (MB, August 28; JM, September 12; and MB, September 20), Smollett gives praise to the effects of Scottish commerce and to the men who have brought it to such a productive state. In Scotland the pursuit of wealth is restrained by reason and virtue, as Lismahago asserts when he refutes the typical English notion of his country's deprivation:

"Those who reproach a nation for its poverty, when it is not owing to the profligacy or vice of the people, deserve no answer. . . . The most respectable heroes of ancient Rome, such as Fabricius, Cincinnatus, and Regulus, were poorer than the poorest freeholder in Scotland; and there are at this day individuals in North-Britain, one of whom can produce more gold and silver than the whole republic of Rome could raise at those times when her public virtue shone with unrivalled lustre; and poverty was so far from being a reproach, that it added fresh laurels to her fame, because it indicated a noble contempt of wealth, which was proof against all the arts of corruption—If poverty be a subject for reproach, it follows that wealth is the object of esteem and veneration. . . . An absurdity which no man in his senses will offer to maintain.—Riches are certainly no proof of merit: nay they are often (if not most commonly) acquired by persons of sordid minds and mean talents: nor do they give any intrinsic worth to the possessor; but, on the contrary, tend to pervert his understanding, and render his morals more depraved." [MB, September 20]

Scots merchants, it can be assumed, are thus to their English counterparts as Captain Brown is to Paunceford. (Just as Smollett nowhere attacks an individual or group of Scottish merchants, nowhere does he rebuke any contemporary Scottish political figure.) Furthermore, because of his inherent abilities, a Scotsman's true merit cannot be known from his outward appearance. Lismahago seems an impoverished veteran, but in fact he is a cultivated man of the world, trained in the law. In the same fashion, Bramble calls his apothecary "a proud Scotchman, very thin skinned, and, for aught I know, may have his degree in his pocket—A right Scotchman has always two strings to his bow, and is *in utrumque paratus*" (MB, June 8).

This dispensation applies with especial force to young Humphry Clinker. As Bramble's long-lost son, he shares in his father's strength of character and hence cannot be the "poor Wiltshire lad" he at first appears. On that initial appearance (JM, May 24), Tabby calls him "a beggarly rascal" and "a filthy tatterdemalion," and Jery finds his condition "equally queer and pathetic."

> He seemed to be about twenty years of age, of a middling size, with bandy legs, stooping shoulders, high forehead, sandy locks, pinking eyes, flat nose, and long chin—but his complexion was of a sickly yellow: his looks denoted famine; and the rags that he wore, could hardly conceal what decency requires to be covered—[JM, May 24]

Like native-born Scots, however, the sons of Welsh gentlemen cannot be known by their first appearance, as Jery reports.

> In the afternoon, as our aunt stept into the coach, she observed, with some marks of satisfaction, that the postilion, who rode next to her, was not a shabby wretch like the ragamuffin who had drove them into Marlborough. Indeed, the difference was very conspicious: this was a smart fellow, with a narrow-brimmed hat, with gold cording, a cut bob, a decent blue jacket, leather breeches, and a clean linen shirt, puffed above the waist-band. When we arrived at the castle on Spin-hill, where we lay, this new postilion was remarkably assiduous, in bringing in the loose parcels; and, at length, displayed the individual countenance of Humphry Clinker, who had metamorphosed himself in this manner, by receiving from pawn part of his own clothes, with the money he had received from Mr. Bramble. [JM, May 24]

The revelation is made complete when, under Bramble's questioning, Humphry discloses that he too is *in utrumque paratus*.

> "Suppose I was inclined to take you into my service, (said he) what are your qualifications? what are you good for?" "An please

your honour, (answered this original) I can read and write, and do the business of the stable indifferent well—I can dress a horse, and shoe him, and bleed and rowel him; and, as for the practice of sow-gelding, I won't turn my back on e'er a he in the county of Wilts—Then I can make hog's-puddings and hob-nails, mend kettles, and tin saucepans—" Here uncle burst out a-laughing; and enquired, what other accomplishments he was master of—"I know something of single-stick, and psalmody, (proceeded Clinker) I can play upon the Jew's-harp, sing Black-ey'd Susan, Arthur-o'Bradley, and divers other songs; I can dance a Welsh jig, and Nancy Dawson; wrestle a fall with any lad of my inches, when I'm in heart; and, under correction, I can find a hare when your honour wants a bit of game." "Foregad! thou art a complete fellow, (cried my uncle, still laughing) I have a good mind to take thee into my family—" [JM, May 24]

If the Scots and Welsh are invulnerable to luxury by reason of national virtue, the English upper orders are similarly protected by reason of superior birth. In his periodicals as in *Humphry Clinker,* Smollett attacks opponents among the higher classes not for their luxury, but for their politics, or more specifically, for their political characters. Unlike Bolingbroke thirty years before, he could not merely dismiss them as upstarts. Newcastle is a dolt, Pitt a despot, Townshend a knave. Lord Oxmington, likewise, is mean of spirit, but not luxurious (JM, September 28). Even Walpole is portrayed in the *Complete History* as not himself luxurious, but as the manipulator for his own corrupt ends of the luxury of others. Yet even this class-bound view of luxury is open to modification by politics. One English merchant, "G. H——," George Heathcote (1700–68), does receive Smollett's praise in *Humphry Clinker* as "really an enthusiast in patriotism." Although a lord mayor of London in 1742, Heathcote is not to be regarded as a Popular Whig. A nephew of one of the founders of the East India Company, he was usually allied with the oligarchic wing of Newcastle's coalition and considered the leader of the Jacobite party in London in the 1740s. In the 1750s he was denounced as "a great Jacobite" by members of the Common Council, and later Horace Walpole wrote of him as "a paltry, worthless Jacobite." A pamphlet Heathcote published in 1749 deplores the depravity of the times in tones reminiscent of Bolingbroke. While sharing many of Smollett's political attitudes, he is also an insider, and thus an effective critic of the "citizens of London," telling Bramble, "with the tears in his eyes, that he had lived above thirty years in the city of London, and dealt in the way of commerce with all the citizens of note in their turns; but that, as he should answer to God, he had

never, in the whole course of his life, found above three or four whom
he could call thoroughly honest" (MB, May 19).[9]

The narrator-atom of the *Adventures of an Atom* claimed that
nineteen-twentieths of the inhabitants of London were followers of the
devil, and Smollett had not reduced that proportion by *Humphry
Clinker*. While the City Whigs increase their sedition against authority,
the Methodists openly promote sedition against reason. Walking through
the city, Jery and his uncle discover Humphry haranguing a crowd in a
lane behind Longacre. When Bramble berates him for presumption,
Humphry pleads that he was moved by the new light of God's grace.
To which his employer responds: "What you imagine to be the new
light of grace . . . I take to be a deceitful vapour, glimmering through a
crack in your upper story—In a word, Mr. Clinker, I will have no light in
my family but what pays the king's taxes, unless it be the light of
reason, which you don't pretend to follow" (JM, June 10). Bramble
then continues:

> "Heark-ye, Clinker, you are either an hypocritical knave, or a
> wrong-headed enthusiast; and, in either case, unfit for my service—
> If you are a quack in sanctity and devotion, you will find it an
> easy matter to impose upon silly women, and others of crazed
> understanding, who will contribute lavishly to your support—if
> you are really seduced by the reveries of a disturbed imagination,
> the sooner you lose your sense entirely, the better for yourself
> and the community." [JM, June 10]

Bramble's suspicions are soon proved correct. What Humphry had felt
as "such strong impulsions, as made him believe he was certainly moved
by the spirit," Bramble discovers to have been the machinations of Lady
Griskin, who sought out the Methodist meeting as part of a scheme to
marry Tabby off to Barton and to that end prompted Clinker to
mount the rostrum, "to the true secret of which he was an utter
stranger" (JM, June 10). Humphry is shown to be free of fanaticism
(MB, June 14), and after London his Methodism is hardly perceptible.

Meanwhile, however, Tabby has attached herself with zeal to the sect;
she is of course both a silly woman and a person of crazed understanding, thus always vulnerable to the deceit and enthusiasm of the
Methodists. Bramble is unable to admonish his sister as he did Clinker,
but does guess that her religious devotion is no more than a convenient
cloak for a less spiritual quest. We are thus permitted a knowledgeable
smile upon learning that Tabby "has had the good fortune to come
acquainted with a pious Christian, called Mr. Moffat, who is very powerful in prayer, and often assists her in private exercises of devotion" (JM,
August 8). Later we appreciate the irony involved when Jery reports

that, "Mrs. Tabitha displayed her attractions as usual, and actually believed she had entangled one Mr. Maclellan, a rich inkle-manufacturer, in her snares; but when matters came to an explanation, it appeared that his attachment was altogether spiritual, founded upon an intercourse of devotion, at the meeting of Mr. John Wesley" (JM, September 3). Resolution of Tabby's search, in the shape of Lismahago, serves to confirm Bramble's early observation, when the passion of love does indeed abate the fervor of her devotion (MB, July 15). This view is tinged with brotherly tolerance, and we have reason to surmise that in this instance Smollett has transposed the usual roles of Bramble and Lydia. Usually mild and romantic, Liddy is frank and harsh in her appraisal of her aunt's behavior:

> My poor aunt, without any regard to her years and imperfections, has gone to market with her charms in every place where she thought she had the least chance to dispose of her person, which, however, hangs still heavy on her hands—I am afraid she has used even religion as a decoy, though it has not answered her expectation—She has been praying, preaching, and catechising among the methodists, with whom this country abounds; and pretends to have such manifestations and revelations, as even Clinker himself can hardly believe, though the poor fellow is half crazy with enthusiasm. . . . God forgive me if I think uncharitably, but all this seems to me to be downright hypocrisy and deceit—[LM, September 7]

In the activities of the Methodists, Smollett certainly saw insubordination: the pretensions of the lower orders to some measure of religious authority and illumination, and the leveling of class distinctions in ecclesiastical practices. In the activities of the City, he saw a complementary kind of political rebellion. He has Humphry Clinker assume the repudiation of both. Humphry easily proves himself a stranger to luxury, but remains suspect in Bramble's eyes until he can answer charges of fanaticism. After catechizing him over his preaching to the mob, Bramble affirms, "If there was anything like affectation or hypocrisy in this excess of religion, I would not keep him in my service; but, so far as I can observe, the fellow's character is downright simplicity, warmed with a kind of enthusiasm, which renders him very susceptible of gratitude and attachment to his benefactors" (MB, June 14). In keeping with his habits of association, Smollett here suggests that as simplicity with obedience is proof against luxury, so simplicity with humility is proof against fanaticism.[10]

Discovery of Humphry brings Bramble much personal comfort during the expedition, but it does nothing to allay his anxieties over the state of England. He finds a companion and later a son, but his search for honest politics and decent politicians is futile; there are no worthy men of influence to be found in England. Against the venality of the times stands only one public figure, George III, whom Bramble calls "A very honest kind-hearted gentleman . . . he's too good for the times" (JM, June 2).[11] Yet the monarch cannot administer the kingdom alone and must make do with the caliber of politician elected to Parliament. The contrast is stark between honest, kindhearted king and dishonest, heartless ministers and sycophants. No *public* response to the ills introduced by luxury appears possible. The process of degeneration has gone too far. The people, their representatives, and their institutions have all been corrupted. What is left is a humbler, smaller opportunity. Private men of good will can maintain their privacy against the infiltration of the times; they can renounce public haunts and public squalor. When national values have been twisted, personal choices alone remain, and these cannot represent the ideal but merely the inevitable. Hence *Humphry Clinker* ends, for Bramble and Lismahago, with retreat and self-exile in Monmouthshire.

$\mathcal{E}ight$

THE CHARACTERS OF
HUMPHRY CLINKER

For many twentieth-century readers the politics of Tobias Smollett is outrageous, repulsive, dead. But the politics of *Humphry Clinker* is cogent and alive. If this is paradox, it is the kind out of which literary history itself comes alive. The novel captures the essence of an attitude toward life, indeed toward an era, as only a work of nostalgia can do. Over two centuries it has enjoyed a large and diverse audience, and few have doubted the authenticity of that nostalgia. Like *The Way of All Flesh,* another work of nostalgia, Smollett's novel is a memoir and an indictment. While the one is a classic study of father-son enmity, the other examines the enmity dividing the social orders of a society. As Butler's use of the theory of acquired characteristics enhances rather than diminishes the accomplishments of his novel, so Smollett's use of the concept of luxury transcends the fading ideology of his time. Lamarckian theory provided a cogent frame for Butler's cautious optimism and his search for evolutionary purpose. Luxury provided an intellectual form for Smollett's cultural pessimism and sense of devolution: his preference for reason over enthusiasm, for logic over evidence, authority over empiricism, custom over innovation, and tradition over experiment. Ernest Pontifex enters a world freer and better than that known by his father; but Jery Melford will find the world far less hospitable than his uncle, in his youth, once did. As Butler repudiated Darwin's idea of purposelessness, so Smollett repudiated Hume's idea of limited progress.

Yet like irony, nostalgia does have its ambiguities. Source studies are often accused of diminishing the richness of a literary work, of reducing and flattening complexity into formula. The charge has its modicum of truth, for every compelling work of art encloses more activity than can be marked by a critic. But the accusation is ultimately unfair. Most twentieth-century critics have enjoyed *Humphry Clinker* as a work of ironic characterization, the partial and subjective views of its many comic figures qualifying one another; with contemporary reviewers of the novel I have argued that the acceptable views expressed in the novel radiate from Bramble. This latter interpretation does not, I think, deplete its fullness, but does the reverse. It grants Smollett yet more subtlety than do Jamesian critics: the achievement of a more effective unity under the surface of effective variety. If the novelist can perform his illusions upon the most adept of modern readers, then his reputation is indeed secure. Nor should awareness of his methods detract from their effects. The keenest followers of professional magicians, it is said, are the stagehands, from whom no sleight of hand can be concealed.[1]

By literary standards *Humphry Clinker* is, among many other things, the most successful conservative attack upon luxury written in any genre during the 1750s and 1760s, a pearl in a generation of sand. In it Smollett tapped one of the fountains of eighteenth-century emotion, taking the galvanic but nonetheless drab, gray stuff of old controversy and transforming it by the force of his powerful imagination. Like a Renaissance master, he captured the adventive moment and made all its colors fast. Among the reasons for this success, two are noteworthy. First, he could control the milieu of his novel, closing it to unanswered questions, unresolved ambiguities, and ambivalent conditions as he could not in his histories and journalism. Here there is no necessary division between the thing to be expressed and the medium of expression. Luxury need no longer be treated as an abstract entity to be denounced as a matter of course. It could be exposed where it actually existed—in the world of men. An acknowledged master of narrative design, Smollett could determine the terms and elements of both action and debate, thus fashioning a fictive world sufficient unto itself—and its readers. Vice, folly, and error appear of necessity in such a world, to arouse that response he declared he sought in *Roderick Random,* "that generous indignation which ought to animate the reader against the sordid and vicious disposition of the world." The Bramble party can be in that world but not of it. They are detached from their local roots and under no compulsion to defend their own estate against luxury. They are not beleaguered as Burdock and Baynard are, for they have each other and are welcome visitors in all remaining bastions. They are detached in precisely those ways Smollett himself was during the last eight years of his life.

Second, the attack upon luxury could in a natural way infuse the organization and characterization of *Humphry Clinker.* Smollett had not published a novel since the serialization of *Sir Lancelot Greaves* in 1760-61, and his last major novel, *Peregrine Pickle,* had appeared ten years before that, in 1751. As it had done in the *Travels* and the *Present State,* the attack upon luxury gave focus and coherence to his final work, whose travel form was not innately disciplinary. It was perhaps yet more useful to the novel than to the works of 1766 and 1768-69, for in *Humphry Clinker* it could be joined with ease to Smollett's inveterate habits of association and invention. In the final volume of the *Complete History,* to cite a long and early contrast, his use of luxury is not so clear and seems extrinsic—an appendage or superimposition. But in his last novel it is intrinsic, fully fleshed, and fully illustrated. It might indeed be argued that nineteenth- and twentieth-century students have been little concerned with Smollett's ideas precisely because of his successful integration of story with idea. *Humphry Clinker is* what Smollett thought about luxury in contemporary England, present, a Saintsbury might exclaim, in such a plenitude of substance that its essence need hardly be defined further.

Several of the foremost critics of luxury in the ancient world had fought the vice with deeds as well as words. Like Thucycides, Xenophon, Polybius, Josephus, Sallust, and Tacitus, they were active political partisans who, upon defeat of their practical hopes, turned to literary descriptions of the forums they had forsaken. Having done their best to reform their worlds directly and having failed, they withdrew a proper intellectual distance from practical affairs in order to transform fervent partisanship into reasoned analysis. Political loss would yield literary gain: history would be told by the men who made it, and it would acquire a distinctive blend of engagement and detachment.

Bramble's strategic retreat to Monmouthshire is a characteristic part of Smollett's attack upon luxury. He is an apt diagnostician of the distemper that is England, for he has been thoroughly inoculated, has known it intimately—as Augustine knew the city of men and Imlac the world beyond the Happy Valley. Having served long in Parliament and followed the antics of a generation of mercenary politicians, he has renounced direct involvement himself. He nevertheless declares practical experience in politics a necessity, seeking it for Jery and calling it superior to any amount of library reading. Engaged yet detached, he is intellectually involved yet physically distant. He has no hope that the disease of the age will be cured, but he does foster the humble aspiration that good men will do what they can to slow and isolate it. His valedictory journey has been shaped to that modest end, as a testimonial good-bye to all that, a form of contemporary history written by a patriot for the edification of other patriots.

In 1771 *Humphry Clinker* was a frankly topical book, but it also entered what George Steiner calls a field of prepared echo—resounding still to Seneca, Cicero, and Sallust, Augustine and Aquinas, Dennis and Law, John Brown and Samuel Fawconer, and to Smollett's own seventy much-read, much-discussed earlier volumes. Drawing upon a literary mode older than Europe itself, the novel could proceed by means of unfolding reiteration, allusion, and variation upon an established repertoire of motifs and characters. The gullibility of women and the mob had been preached—to cite but a few diverse examples—by Aristophanes, Cato, and Tertullian. The ruin visited upon men who were ruled by women was a refrain for Stoic and Christian alike. Commandments to cleanse the marketplace, to discipline the new rich, to distrust the claims of city-dwellers, to instruct carefully the young men who would guard the nation's future, to venerate the learning of age and experience—these are lessons carried from Plato's Athens to Smollett's London by way of all of the centers of learning in Europe. The repertoire would be eternally fresh and timely, for it was eternally fixed and timeless. Human nature was flawed: men are merely what they are, women more so.

In an attack upon luxury expressed through fiction, the central figure, as important as all others combined, is the moral guide. Although flawed himself, he must be acute and reliable. Although mortal, he must by his mere presence raise all the immortal issues—order, merit, justice, individual and social health. Although sharply individualized, his experience must embrace the range of social reality, from the minutiae of personal manners to the workings of national institutions. He is merely a man and that of a degraded age; yet he is a man of justice.

At first glance *Humphry Clinker* seems to possess two main narrators, for uncle and nephew share by far the greatest number of letters (and even greater number of pages) that make up the novel. Yet the division of focus is merely apparent, not substantial. By repetition the novel forces us to concentrate upon the scenes, characters, and issues it places before us. Jery provides the basic reportage, the journal of who traveled when, where, and by what route; Bramble examines the significance of the journey. While the nephew relates the event, the uncle gives us the feeling—often the taste and smell—of the event. Jery's letters after Bath seldom contain opinion; when they do, the opinion is normally Bramble's. Bramble's letters (certainly those in England) are virtually all opinion—first his own, later his and Lismahago's. It is through Bramble's offices that Smollett works his magic. Characterization becomes revelation and plot, confirming demonstration.[2]

The revelation of true character and motive first occurs with Bramble himself, for neither is clear at the start. In his opening two letters Bramble complains of his vexations—gout, constipation, melancholy—and soon thereafter refers to his bootless twenty-year search for happiness.[3] Jery's opening letter echoes the complaint: "My uncle is an odd kind of humorist, always on the fret, and so unpleasant in his manner, that rather than be obliged to keep him company, I'd resign all claim to the inheritance of his estate" (JM, April 2). Indeed Bramble seems as vulnerable to the luxury of the times as the other members of his household. Physically he has been indolent and splenetic, even his bowels, he laments, proving ungovernable. Psychologically he has been prey to discontent, a gnawing restlessness he feels is unsuited to his age and station. In his mid-fifties, with considerable wealth and influence, he is pestered by politicians who would find use for both possessions. His philosophical pursuit of true felicity has encompassed the life spans of Jery, Liddy, and Humphry (and perhaps has coincided with his period of direct involvement in politics), and he is determined to resolve it. The disquiet of Bramble's inner life converges at the opening with the outer disarray within his family. His sister has grown unmanageable, fantastically at odds with everyone in Monmouthshire, even the good Dr. Lewis. His nephew has seemingly gained nothing from Oxford save pertness and has embroiled himself in a low quarrel. The niece, his other ward, has formed a demeaning attachment with an indigent actor, the antagonist in Jery's quarrel. Even his servant grows more insolent by the day. The apparent situation is of an irascible, egoistic valetudinarian traveling for double relief, from the gout and from the demands of his dependents.

It is, however, no more than an opening gambit, a device to initiate interest and movement. Bramble is asking Lewis to prepare him something for the gout in his last letter (November 20) as well as in his first (April 2). The most perfect and salubrious place in all of Britain, Bramble makes clear, is Brambleton Hall, the place of departure, to which he would immediately return—he says eight times in the original opening volume of the novel—if he were not bound by other obligations. About his abrasiveness he comments more often and more forcefully than does any other character. Jery's one sentence of early criticism is mild in comparison, and even this is very soon dispelled by growing admiration:

> Mr. Bramble's character . . . opens and improves upon me every day.—His singularities afford a rich mine of entertainment: his understanding, so far as I can judge, is well cultivated: his observations on life are equally just, pertinent, and uncommon. He affects misanthropy, in order to conceal the sensibility of a heart, which is tender, even to a degree of weakness. This delicacy of feeling, or soreness of the mind, makes him timorous and fearful; but then he is afraid of nothing so much as of dishonour; and although he is exceedingly cautious of giving offence, he will fire at the least hint of insolence or ill-breeding. [JM, April 24]

Thus Smollett quickly opens and improves *our* first impression of Bramble: he is certainly a man of knowledge and responsibility. He quotes the Roman poets and historians, Shakespeare, and a variety of contemporary authors. Besides literature he has read law, art, politics, history, geography, and philosophy. He seems to know as much medicine as his physician-friend Lewis: "I forgot to tell you, that my right ancle pits, a symptom, as I take it, of its being *oedematous,* not *leucophlegmatic*" (MB, April 20). Although Jery has just come down from university, he cannot compete with his uncle in breadth of reading—or in depth of understanding. Jery's account of Bramble's misanthropy (April 2) is far more superficial than Bramble's own (April 17, 20, 23). The latter are both more harsh and more explanatory; Bramble knows and tells more about himself than any other character can or will. He explains his physical irritability by revealing his moral sensibility (something Jery later confirms). Where Jery in this instance merely recounts superficial effects, Bramble reveals profound causes. The contrast is of course yet greater with the remaining letter-writers, Lydia, Tabby, and Win. By the time the party reaches Bath, we realize that Bramble is not merely in selfish pursuit of comfort. For his family more than for himself, he is in search of the conditions of health—peace, honor, and contentment. In Bath he longs for "my solitude and mountains" as Ishmael in clotted Manhattan cries out for the sea. In London he acknowledges that the tour would be cut short were he the only traveler: "With respect to the characters of mankind, my curiosity is quite satisfied. . . . Every thing I see, and hear, and feel, in this great reservoir of folly, knavery, and sophistication, contributes to inhance the value of a country life" (MB, June 2). Personally appalled by this great reservoir, he endures its stench for the sake of his family, who as yet cannot tell incense from offal; he informs Lewis he will soon move northward: "But I must, in the mean time, for the benefit and amuse-ment of my pupils, explore the depths of this chaos; this mishapen and monstrous capital, without head or tail, members or proportion" (MB, May 29).

By the close of the novel Bramble's pupils have included, primarily, Jery, Liddy, and Humphry; secondarily, Lismahago, Tabby, Win, and such temporary attendants as Linden and Barton; by extension, nearly one hundred named characters; and by further extension all of Smol-lett's readers. To note his anxieties at the beginning is to esteem his achievement at the end. His powers of instruction have been taxed fully but happily; order and harmony have been restored and renewed at Brambleton Hall. Through good sense and good fortune, he has been able to redeem each member of his party, by the by performing the same office for meritorious acquaintances, like the mother of the con-sumptive child at Bristol, Martin the highwayman, Burdock, and Baynard. He has, moreover, learned as warmly as he has taught, the vigorous exercise of his faculties proving the precise regimen he has so long required. His venture—to "take a plunge amidst the waves of ex-cess, in order to case-harden the constitution" (MB, October 26)—has proved efficacious. His quest—like his nerves, estate, and future—has been settled. Never again, he remarks, will he allow his life to lose its balance (November 20).

Administrator and quixote, philosopher and modest citizen, Bramble possesses the varied nature needed to hold together a work seeking a mixed response. He is sometimes rash in his impressions, as about Jery's audacity, Humphry's fanaticism, and Lismahago's extravagance. Yet he is the first to speak against hasty judgments and does not remain per-manently deficient in any of his assessments. Though hardly flawless, within the bounds of the novel he is almost ideally just—to chance acquaintances as well as lifelong tenants, to women as well as men, to the base as well as the mighty. Though he appears initially a creature of blatant prejudice, he is shown to be extraordinarily free of blindness. He can with ease bring himself to applaud even urban and mercantile life—in Scotland, in Glasgow and Edinburgh—where luxury has not effec-tively penetrated. He has that quality which in shorthand form Smollett called intuition, a unique and active combination of learning, experi-ence, intelligence, and respect for natural law.

Because Bramble is a touchstone for justice, he suffers deeply and often. He is not a military hero like his friends Cockril, Balderick, and Lismahago, yet his code of honor is as demanding as theirs. He requires valor, dignity, and magnanimity of others, not merely because he requires them of himself, but because in a threatened civilization they are virtues of universal necessity. About the frailties of ordinary, individual human nature his tolerance is Roman. But about collective enterprises—war, politics, architecture, urban "improvement," public recreation, mercantile policy—he is adamant in his demands and scathing in his denunciations. In these he sees human folly magnified and deified. He will not allow the view that bleached bread and diluted beer represent minor abuses of taste, for under luxury no abuse is innocuous and all are connected. Perhaps in an earlier, more innocent age, an assembly at Bath provided trivial dissipation. But no longer. Now it provides "*a compound of villainous smells,* in which the most violent stinks, and the most powerful perfumes, contended for the mastery" (MB, May 8). With a phrase adapted from Falstaff and his own emphasis, Bramble discloses the assembly to be criminal as well as foul. His intuitive response given, he feels no need to describe further the shambles before him; it is more than enough that his senses cry out against a condition that would make a moral man sick: "arising from putrid gums, imposthumated lungs, sour flatulencies, rank arm-pits, sweating feet, running sores and issues, plasters, ointments, and embrocations, hungary-water, spirit of lavender, assafoetida drops, musk, hartshorn, and sal volatile; besides a thousand frowzy steams, which I could not analyze."

Bramble's exquisite senses also afford protection. In such a time of national disease, he says, every man must be his own physician. For this task most Englishmen are disabled, "their very organs of sense are perverted, and they become habitually lost to every relish of what is genuine and excellent in its own nature" (MB, June 8). For himself and his pupils, contemporary recipes for health and happiness are mostly degrading illusions. Hence he will distrust popular political and religious figures, refuse to believe the papers, avoid celebrated drinking waters, and take cold baths when conventional wisdom calls for warm (and the opposite). He realizes the journey may prove nuptial for some of his party, but he refuses to credit newer conceptions of marriage, for example, that sexual love can transform a man's character for the better. With Burdock, Baynard, Milksan, Sowerby, and others, he sees many men turned by women, and in each instance the man is worse for the transformation. For him sexual love must be judged by its social and political benefits, not seen as good in itself; he has himself been willing to pay for nine bastards, but no wife: "Thank heaven, Dick, that among all the follies and weaknesses of human nature, I have not yet fallen into that of matrimony" (MB, September 30). Physical attraction and marriage are merely fillips that should lead to masculine dominance in the family and social harmony in the nation. In luxurious England, however, goals have been eliminated and society has been turned topsy-turvy. Successful marriages for love are possible, he acknowledges in describing the Dennisons, but only when both partners are inoculated against the age; like Lewis and apparently Mr. S——, he prefers not to assume the risk.

In an age of tasteless insubordination, Bramble is a rare type, thorough individual *and* good citizen, a man who would abide by natural law even when the task calls for inordinate strength. "What temptation can a man of my turn and temperament have, to live in a place where every corner teems with fresh objects of detestation and disgust?" he asks in London (June 8). His answer is quick, for his duty to himself and his charges is self-imposed, although its fulfillment requires resistance to everything his age calls "fashion" and "society." He searches at large for honor, is disappointed, and therefore cherishes all the more those few friends in whom it remains alive. To the strong who can equal his demands, he gives his admiration. To the weak or unfortunate who cannot, he gives pity; if they are sensible enough to seek help, he supplies it readily. For the vain and frivolous who will not, he reserves his contempt. His quest for the good society must be ultimately disillusioning, since he seeks the conditions of national honor and finds only the possibility of personal ethics. Like Plato he believes that good politics best fashions good men. Like Cicero his conservatism is moral and aesthetic as well as political: he would have public life exemplary, glorious, and honorable. His is the dilemma of a search for the public good undertaken when legitimate politics is dead, the paradox of the man who while rejecting individual ethics as the primary touchstone discovers that only personal choices remain. And like Socrates he knows that the philosopher's dedication to his search appears ridiculous to the multitude.

The nature of that quest (as of Smollett's gifts) insures that Bramble will be a figure in comedy, if not a comic figure. Smollett follows Aristotle and Fielding in finding the ridiculous the spring of pure comedy. The most hilarious scenes are those that cause no lasting harm to anyone—such as ones precipitated by Win, Humphry, Lismahago, Bullford, Mackilligut, and Micklewhimmen. Like Parson Adams, Bramble is sometimes the object of laughter, as when Humphry "saves" him by the ear from still waters, or when he subjects himself to pills, purges, and pungent odors. More often he provokes laughter by seeking quixotically after decorum in situations inherently vile. In places like the Pump Room and Vauxhall, where all of polite society endures noise and stink, he demands peace and fragrance. In places ruled by sophisticators, he dares ask for pure food and drink. He is so at odds with English attitudes that he is continually caught up in contradictions, which to the fashionable world prove his boorishness. For Captain O'Donaghan, Lady Griskin, Lord Oxmington, and often Tabby, he is no more than a meddlesome oaf; yet we have reason to suspect that the derision he faces from "superior" personages in England is reflexive, without power to goad or alter him. Liddy nicely captures his reactions to the world of fashion assembled at Bath: "My uncle sometimes shrugs up his shoulders, and sometimes bursts out a-laughing" (LM, May 6).

If hearty laughter is one antidote to the distemper of the times, then simple avoidance is the other. After the refreshment of Scotland, Bramble is forced by the sorrows of Baynard back to an original question. "At what time of life may a man think himself exempted from the necessity of sacrificing his repose to the punctilios of a contemptible world?" (MB, September 30). The answer is found in his earliest letters, reiterated and demonstrated throughout the journey. In a contemptible world a man can create his own harmony, in retirement and vigilant cultivation of his own estate. "It must be something very extraordinary that will induce me to revisit either Bath or London," he tells Lewis in his last letter (November 20). Instead, the future will hold good exercise and good companionship: "I have got an excellent fowling-piece from Mr. Lismahago, who is a keen sportsman, and we shall take the heath in all weathers." Personal and political resolutions thereby coincide. When he determines that civic life in England has degenerated beyond recall, Bramble is prepared to accept the option of honor and retire. Like Cato and Lucius Piso, Cicero and Seneca, and like Smollett after mid-1763, he is self-exiled. He has fulfilled his moral obligation, that of passing on his knowledge of the fruits and frailties of the world to the young people of his family, as Cicero had done for his son in *De officiis*. Active, concerted resistance is now futile, and he will retreat to his small but comfortable lot in Monmouthshire, there to find remission from a wretched world for which he had become unfit. His just sense of history and his own worth dispels gloom. Other societies and other men have been under attack from luxury. He will not be intimidated; he will not despair.

Bramble is one of the outstanding creations in a great age of English fiction. Besides being a vital and interesting figure in his own right (independent in one's memory of the novel), he must bring about the communion of values that animates the novel. That is, he must win the assent and sympathy of his pupils and of Smollett's readers alike. He must convince them and us—fully and simultaneously. The task is not a simple one. Before the eighteenth century, literary attacks upon luxury could proceed under two presumptions: the clarity of the tradition and a direct, unmediated relationship between writer and reader. Yet by the time Smollett's last novel appeared, neither held with such tenacity. Although most readers might still regard luxury, traditionally conceived, as the great enemy, their relationship to authors had been radically altered by satire and the novel. Without the implicit authority of a Sallust or an Augustine directly addressing his readers, novelists resort to rhetorical devices of various kinds. Defoe and Richardson choose a first-person narrator of evident candor, Fielding an omnipresent narrator whose selection of language guides readers into his own unique angle of vision, Goldsmith a naive narrator whose strengths and limitations are for the most part transparent. Having used the direct approach in his histories and several devices of satire in his journalism and previous fiction, in *Humphry Clinker* Smollett tries something fresh.

As a literary mode, the attack upon luxury had for centuries depended upon an easy recognition of a series of contrasts elaborated into a typology: masculine – feminine, old – young, country philosopher – city sharper, and so on.[4] What distinguishes *Humphry Clinker* is not the mere inclusion of familiar patterns, but the lively variations Smollett plays upon them. With Bramble established as hub and touchstone, the novelist is free to roam like his travelers over character, circumstance, and geography, confident that his center will hold. (The reader's coming to terms with Bramble could be considered the earliest subplot of the book.) His contrasts are many and integral, but never simple and seldom static. As critic of the times Bramble stands opposed to Tabitha; as brother he stands watch over her. Seemingly, Quin is entrepreneur to the corruptions of Bath; actually, Bramble's claret-cousin, he is the city's secret scourge. Win Jenkins is always a jink; yet she is winsome, and by the end she is also a winner. Lismahago is one of the most poignant victims of the nation's moral squalor; he is likewise one of its keenest analysts. Paunceford is set against Serle, then Bramble and Jery, and finally Captain Brown. As Bramble's old companion, Baynard is a worthy man; as tool of a luxurious woman he is a pitiable wretch. As with other families in the novel, the Baynards provide an example and its opposite. Sons are to be compared with fathers, with mothers, and with other sons; wives with their husbands and with each other.

For the first third of the novel Smollett encourages the semblance of five discrete narrative versions of events: after Bramble come Jery the arch, Lydia the naive, Tabby the gullible, and Win the simple. Thereafter variations quicken. In her earliest letters, for instance, Lydia is an ingenue, less an observer than a girl acting out a fond role from remembered romances. These come hard upon her uncle's normative commentary and her own later letters, which represent the shrewd judgments of a penetrating young woman. As with Liddy and her uncle, much of the characterization and plotting moves by reversals: from official version to unbiased description, impression to certainty, appearance to reality, rind to heart. Wilson the nefarious actor turns effortlessly into George Dennison, paragon of young manhood. A cycle turns back upon itself when Matthew Bramble reveals a Matthew Loyd in his past in time to secure a Matthew Loyd for his future. Theatergoers and readers of fiction would be prepared for such revolutions of name and station; yet they might not expect the evolution of Jery the pup into Jery the prudent, or of Tabitha the terrible into Tabby the (relatively) tame. Thus while the characters of the novel must be considered in the light of the attack upon luxury, they are usually too full and too various to be stillborn types. And the groupings in which they appear pass unobtrusively through several levels of contrast into pairs, unions, reversals, balances, divisions, negations, equations, and juxtapositions.

Insofar as it is an attack upon luxury, *Humphry Clinker* is a novel about relationships: a social-political order that has been undermined, the many personal relationships that were destroyed in the collapse, and the few that have withstood the shock. Like the legislator in Genesis defining the threshold of luxury, Bramble defines for us the failures of merchants and politicians, citizens and families. From him radiate those relationships that impart movement and dimension, and through him we learn how well other figures cope with luxury and each other. For the most part the worth of a character in the English sections varies with the closeness of his relation to Bramble. Closest are his male friends and the young people of his blood, furthest the older men and women of inveterate luxury.[5]

The group that resembles Bramble most are the older, mature men who have been educated as he has and whose lives have been witness to the ravages of the age. It includes men who have small roles, like Serle, Balderick, Cockril, Bentley, Heathcote, and Mr. S——, as well as those with large roles like Lewis, Dennison, and Lismahago. It extends to the men who, although antagonists to luxury, are wedded to it by circumstance. Quin is bound by temperament to the stink of the Pump Room; Burdock, Baynard, Milksan, and Sowerby are bound by marriage. It is Bramble's respect that obtains our sympathy for such men, even as it is his own motive for assisting them. Half of his first letter, the first of the novel, it should be recalled, is devoted to specific, practical, and presumably effective advice on how to relieve various persons from temporary distress. His last is preoccupied with settling the affairs of his family and his household. As he has done for himself, he shall demonstrate to others that inner aspiration need not be crushed by external circumstance.

Humorous stranger to Bramble, then in stages gentle antagonist, friend, boon companion, and brother-in-law, Lismahago is of course the pivotal figure among the seasoned men carrying their experiences and misfortunes into the Bramble family. Our first view of him, like the first view of Bramble, is a ludicrous one. In two consecutive letters (July 10, 13) Jery details every comic feature of countenance, physique, dress, mount, accent, pride, and pugnacity. As he admits to Phillips, Jery at once grasps the amusement value in Lismahago's appearance: "In my last I treated you with a high flavoured dish, in the character of the Scotch lieutenant, and I must present him once more for your entertainment." In his initial report, however, Bramble plunges immediately into the Scotsman's opinions, with a few words of preface about the man's spirit of contradiction, indefatigable study, and desire "to refute established maxims" (MB, July 15). Though brief, this preface is adequate to Smollett's purpose. Lismahago has been legitimized, established as exactly the kind of man Bramble is himself, exactly the kind of character needed to introduce the Scottish portion of the book. Approaching Scotland, Bramble is required by Smollett's theme to relax, to enjoy fully a land free of England's disease. So that he may, Lismahago expounds the ramifications for his country of the luxury of the South, reiterating almost verbatim Bramble's earlier accusations against mob, press, juries, factions, inflation, commerce, merchants, effeminacy, and leveling politicians. The two men discover in Scotland that genuine friendship remains possible. That link forged, they discover in England that they can act in concert, in the affairs with Oxmington, Bullford, Baynard, and Tabby. By the close Bramble has succeeded in bringing good cheer to the lieutenant's austerity: Lismahago's joke in riposte to Bullford is so apt that it surprises and impresses all concerned (JM, October 3); and "His temper, which had been soured and shrivelled . . . is now swelled out, and smoothed like a raisin in plumporridge" (JM, November 8).[6]

Thematically it is Bramble's relationship with older males, allowing for a rotating criticism of luxury, that anchors the novel. Formatively it is his relationship with Jery and the rest of his family that allows it gradually to unfold. Jery, and to a lesser degree Humphry and Liddy, are being tried, tested for intellectual ripeness. From Homer through Fielding Western literature has recast the story of a young man in quest of knowledge and a family: in *Joseph Andrews* and *Tom Jones* the title character is a youth seeking wisdom and a lost father. In *Humphry Clinker* this single figure has been divided into two, doubling thereby the kind and amount of instruction that can be rendered. As it divides the attention directed to the pupils, this device concentrates our focus upon the teacher. Similarly, *Joseph Andrews* offers two older male figures for Joseph's emulation: Adams as moral guide for the journey, and Wilson as discovered father and future model. In Smollett the roles of tutor and father are united in Bramble. Jery requires an education whose progress and consequences will become the substance of his letters; these in turn represent a form of notebook the reader is per-mitted to inspect. Humphry needs a family and a place; his education is subordinated to his needs and his service. Already possessed of his father's moral fitness—Fielding's "Good Nature"—he is not solely a pupil; at times he can and does teach.

Like the other young men in eighteenth-century fiction, Jery Melford requires a structured expedition before he will be fit to assume the responsibilities of manhood. As Rasselas must put aside bootless yearn-ing before he is fit to rule, so Jery must discard the jejune arrogance he has put on at Oxford. Bramble notices Jery's immaturity, referring to him as "a pert jackanapes, full of college-petulance and self-conceit" (MB, April 17) and calling him down as an inexperienced pup, "a young fellow . . . when he first thrusts his snout into the world" (MB, May 6). But by the time the party reaches Bath uncle and nephew are commenc-ing to respect each other. For Jery the process begins with greater contact.

> The truth is, his disposition and mine, which, like oil and vinegar, repelled one another at first, have now begun to mix by dint of being beat up together. I was once apt to believe him a complete Cynic; and that nothing but the necessity of his occasions could compel him to get within the pale of society—I am now of another opinion. I think his peevishness arises partly from bodily pain, and partly from a natural excess of mental sensibility; for, I suppose, the mind as well as the body, is in some cases endued with a morbid excess of sensation. [JM, April 18]

Bramble discerns that Jery's brittle edges cover a young man of charac-ter, and Jery remarks approvingly of the older man's fineness of feeling, against which his own seems quite coarse: "Mr. Bramble is extravagantly delicate in all his sensations, both of soul and body. . . . His blood rises at every instance of insolence and cruelty, even where he himself is no way concerned; and ingratitude makes his teeth chatter. On the other hand, the recital of a generous, humane, or grateful action, never fails to draw from him tears of approbation, which he is often greatly distressed to conceal" (JM, May 10).

Such perception discloses that hereafter Jery is prepared actually to join his uncle in uncovering instances of insolence and cruelty, especially among the nouveaux riches. In neglect of Serle, his former benefactor, Paunceford receives the censure of uncle and nephew alike. While both agree that Paunceford has violated all rules of decency and friendship, it is Jery who delivers their verdict:

> This man, after having been long buffetted by adversity, went

abroad; and Fortune, resolved to make him amends for her former coyness, set him all at once up to the very ears in affluence. He has now emerged from obscurity, and blazes out in all the tinsel of the times. I don't find that he is charged with any practices that the law deems dishonest. . . . But they say, he is remarkable for shrinking from his former friendships, which are generally too plain and home-spun to appear amidst his present brilliant connexions; and that he seems uneasy at sight of some old benefactors, whom a man of honour would take pleasure to acknowledge—[JM, May 10]

The phrases "tinsel of the times" and "practices that the law deems dishonest" demonstrate that Bramble's lessons have taken hold. Jery has begun to penetrate current fashions in morality in just those ways that characterize Bramble. He is indeed so apt a pupil that in his next letter, May 17, he is able to observe for himself the vagaries of a luxurious society, noting that the Bath season has ended "and all our gay birds of passage have taken their flight." With Bramble's eye for physical detail, he perceives signs of enervation all about him: "There is always a great shew of the clergy at Bath: none of your thin, puny, yellow, hectic figures, exhausted with abstinence and hard study, labouring under the *morbi eruditorum;* but great overgrown dignitaries and rectors, with rubicund noses and gouty ancles, or broad bloated faces, dragging along great swag bellies; the emblems of sloth and indigestion." Earlier Bramble had found all of Bath swollen and congested by insolence; here Jery discovers concrete examples. Earlier Bramble had denounced the fools who flocked to Bath to be sucked dry by parasites; here Jery closes his letter with the tale of a would-be politician, George Prankley, betrayed by cowardice and vainglory into giving preferment to a mercenary parson, Tom Eastgate.

The effect of Jery's learning is such that at Bath Smollett is able to add a major voice, subordinate only to those of Bramble and Lismahago, to the indictment of luxury. Without sacrificing any of his rich resources of language, the novelist has bestowed distinctive voices upon uncle and nephew. Bramble's style is usually that of intuitive judgment forcefully rendered, Jery's a more neutrally descriptive tone effectively verifying and elaborating the older man's generalizations. To his Oxford chum Phillips, Jery announces his intention to describe everything of interest; that is, only he among the writers formally commits himself to observation of detail. While Bramble may transcribe his or Lismahago's lengthy monologues, only Jery has the habit of recording dialect and dialogue. When Bramble finds novelty in England, it is normally of the repulsive kind he has no patience to remark minutely. Jery, however, must walk three times around an object before forming an opinion. Hence it is to Jery that the great set-pieces of the novel are given: Bramble's deeds of valor and honor, as with the distressed widow (JM, April 20); Sunday dinner with Mr. S——, which opens with Bramble's casual remark that brilliant writers are usually quiet in company and proceeds to show us S—— reigning by dint of physical presence alone (JM, June 10); and those scenes of high comedy whose effect arises from simple placement of incongruity against incongruity (Tabby against Mackilligut, Lismahago against Bullford, Bramble against Linden, Lismahago and his horse, Humphry and the coach). The dialectical relation between Bramble and Jery goes so far that on occasion Smollett forgets his illusions. Bramble at the close of his letter of July 15, for example, tells Lewis of an open contest for Win's affections between Clinker and Dutton. As if forgetting that he alone corresponds with Lewis, he adds: "Jery has been obliged to interpose his authority to keep the peace; *and to him I have left the discussion of that important affair*" (italics added).

As Lismahago is a bridge between the English and Scottish parts of the novel, so Humphry Clinker is a bridge between the elder, intuitive men and the younger men in want of instruction. Somewhat less obtrusively, he also calls attention to the rural-urban poles of English luxury. He joins the expedition on the road between Bath and London –appropriately outside the centers of city temptation and dissipation, where like Joseph Andrews and Tom Jones he might have been drawn into the general whirlpool of degradation. In the rural virtues he abounds: he is simple, talented, obedient. But he is not yet proof against urban deceptions and cannot fully protect himself, being taken in turn by Justice Buzzard, the Methodists, and Lady Griskin. From Bramble Jery requires education by demonstration, Humphry education by admonition. To Bramble the ward-nephew can return respect and admiration, the servant-son loyalty and devotion. The young men become complementary pupils, each learning and being taught according to his presumptive station, and suggesting, by the by, that readers of all levels can benefit from Smollett's novel. Until the final revelations, their differing stations are underscored; when referred to by name the nephew is virtually always called by his Christian name; the servant "Clinker" and "Humphry Clinker" more often than "Humphry."

Humphry enters at the point when Bramble is beginning to doubt the sanity of his mission-quest. With his irritability rising and the stench of Bath in his nostrils, he chances upon "honest Humphry"–as Jery and Bramble each three times call him–an undoubted example of honest virtue unblemished by the fraud and sophistication around him.[7] Uncle immediately perceives and nephew at length confirms him as a model of positive simplicity. Bramble writes, "the fellow's character is downright simplicity" (MB, June 2), and he is "pleased with the gratitude of Clinker, as well as with the simplicity of his character" (MB, June 12). For Jery, "Humphry Clinker . . . is a surprising compound of genius and simplicity" (JM, June 10). He is sufficiently aware of "the poor fellow's simplicity" to see correctly Humphry's sole flaw, the "danger of falling sacrifice to his own simplicity" (JM, June 11). When Clinker does indeed fall victim, taken as a highwayman, Bramble is certain of his innocence, for he is "the very picture of simplicity" (MB, June 12). Although Bramble does occasionally become vexed with his new servant, the emotion is quickly assuaged by Humphry's "great simplicity of heart" (MB, July 4). Jery terms his own new valet, Dutton, "the very contrast of Humphry Clinker" and distinguishes between the genuine and the luxurious: "Humphry may be compared to an English pudding, composed of good wholesome flour and suet, and Dutton to a syllabub or iced froth, which, though agreeable to the taste, has nothing solid or substantial" (JM, July 18).

Bramble is willing to devote his care and energy to the tuition of Jery and Humphry because they will be future models themselves; Jery, in fact, represents Bramble at an earlier stage of his life. For the same reason, we learn, young George Dennison has been thoroughly tutored by his father. The virtue of such young men in turn stands in stark relief to the youths whose instruction has been neglected or left to their mothers, like young Burdock and Baynard. The story of Martin, the man of parts turned highwayman, parallels then converges with that of Humphry, indicating that unprotected young men are easy prey to the metropolis. Bramble has little time to assist him—initiates wager "he swings before Christmas"—but with men of merit short is sufficient. Although Martin's accomplishments are many, he has fallen victim to the snares indigenous to a luxurious city. His past misfortunes he owes to attaching himself to the merchant class: "he lived some time as a clerk to a timber-merchant, whose daughter Martin privately married, was discarded, and his wife turned out of doors" (JM, June 11). His present situation derives from the male folly especially common to the tribe of Macheath: "namely, an indiscreet devotion to the fair sex, and, in all probability, he will be attacked on this defenceless quarter." As Martin has intervened to save Humphry, so Bramble intervenes to save him. The letter recommending Martin to the East India Company (founded perhaps on Heathcote's former connection with the company) is the sole use Bramble finds in the novel for the world of English commerce.

A luxurious society offers too few opportunities to the goodly young men of the novel; their capacities are too circumscribed by frivolous pursuit of fashion and lucre. On the other hand, a debauched society offers too many freedoms to young women; their capacities are taxed beyond their limits. Smollett introduces relatively few young women into his tale—the ratio of older to younger characters generally must be about twenty to one—and places only Liddy and Win in the foreground. Their role is to be guided by the models of mature womanhood Bramble discovers, all except one of whom are proper wives to sensible men: Moore, Campbell, Colquhoun, Melville, Queensberry, Dennison. (Mrs. Pimpernel, who is virtuous despite her tyrannical husband, gets but one sentence.) Yet these ideal figures remain faint. They have no independent existence, are introduced only after their husbands, and are extensions into another personality of the qualities of their husbands. The best of them, the uncommon Mrs. Dennison, is praised by Bramble as an apposite consort to Dennison: her "disposition is suited to his own in all respects," and she is therefore "admirably qualified to be his companion, confidant, counsellor, and coadjutrix" (MB, October 8). It may also be that they are extensions in a different sense of Bramble and Jery, since each time the men reach a new place, they need someone to care for the women; for example, at Drumlanrig, "The dutchess was equally gracious, and took our ladies under her immediate protection" (MB, September 15). In any case Bramble exerts himself more in denouncing, say, Mrs. Burdock, than he does in praising all the virtuous wives combined.

It is protection, Bramble makes clear at the start, that Liddy needs more than any other service, for while intelligent she is "soft as butter, and as easily melted" and "as inflammable as touch-wood" (MB, April 17). What instruction she does receive on her journey seems to be by example, positive from her uncle and negative from her aunt. Her two letters from Bath and two from London reveal a heart of naive wholesomeness. Because she is immature and sentimental, she is occasionally unable to distinguish the luxurious and false from the simple and genuine and must be rescued continually (seventeen times by rough count) from the predators with which England abounds. At Bath she is gulled into believing that "a great many gentlemen and ladies of Ireland" frequent the Spring Garden (LM, April 26). The situation recurs in London when she mistakes notorious women of pleasure for famous ladies of fashion (LM, May 31). In contrast to her uncle, she finds that "Bath is . . . a new world—All is gayety, good humour, and diversion," where "The eye is continually entertained with the splendour of dress and equipage, and the ear with the sound of coaches, chaises, chairs, and other carriages" (LM, April 26). In London she says that her "imagination is quite confounded with splendour and variety," and compares the city to the world of romance, "all that you read of wealth and grandeur, in the Arabian Nights Entertainment, and the Persian Tales" (LM, May 31). Like her experiences with the reality of England, her romantic effusions are few and short and are set between the caustic letters of Bramble and the realistic ones of Jery. The moral—stated by uncle and brother alike—is that Liddy must be closely watched lest her innocence betray her. She will not be entirely safe until she is delivered into the arms of a man as well inoculated against the degeneracy of the times as Jery and Bramble. Such a man, we know, is not likely to be found in Bath, and certainly not in London.

Smollett does not allow Liddy to mature as deeply or as quickly as her brother. Yet her appreciation of Scotland signals a quickened perception. The first letter she has devoted to the members of the party, from Glasgow, September 7, is a précis of the revelations we have been witnessing. Jery is an affectionate, constant brother, having only her interest at heart. Win is "really a good body in the main," but "is weak in her nerves, as well as in her understanding." Clinker "is really a deserving young man," but Dutton is "a debauched fellow." She is as acute in self-assessment, aware that Scotland "being exceedingly romantic, suits my turn and inclinations." Her most arresting insights turn upon the deplorable women she has encountered and on Tabby's hunt for a husband among the Methodists. These are as bluntly caustic as anything written by Bramble, charging her aunt with ranting hypocrisy and women generally with cunning and deceit: "My dear Willis, I am truly ashamed of my own sex." For those who might have missed Liddy's transformation and permanent conversion to her uncle's views, Smollett has her exclaim to Bramble, "My dear uncle!—My best friend! My father!" and provides her with the following reflection:

> Nature never intended me for the busy world—I long for repose and solitude, where I can enjoy that disinterested friendship which is not to be found among crouds, and indulge those pleasing reveries that shun the hurry and tumult of fashionable society— Unexperienced as I am in the commerce of life, I have seen enough to give me a disgust to the generality of those who carry it on— There is such malice, treachery, and dissimulation, even among professed friends and intimate companions, as cannot fail to strike a virtuous mind with horror. [LM, October 4]

A prologue to Liddy's own future, this is of course a conscious echo of Bramble's hymns to Brambleton Hall, delivered in Bath and London.

When Liddy reports that Win is in the main "really a good body," we realize her mind is another thing entirely and that she is in need of extraordinary protection. From Tabby her mistress she receives tyrannical control, from Jery amused surveillance, and from Humphry tender devotion. There is a nice symmetry in the affection shared by the two servants: Humphry genuinely simple, Win a genuine simpleton, each falling in love at sight of the other's bare backside. In England she is naturally drawn to luxurious fashions, but her errors are ludicrous, domestic, and harmless. Win errs by imitation: "Nature intended Jenkins for something very different from the character of her mistress; yet custom and habit have effected a wonderful resemblance betwixt them in many particulars" (JM, July 18). She is overly fond of propriety and shares Tabby's concern with her prize possessions, "Three-quarters of blond lace, and a remnant of muslin, and my silver thimble" (WJ, May 15). And like all the ladies of the family, she is overawed by the attractions of London: "O Molly! what shall I say of London? All the towns that ever I beheld in my born-days are no more than Welsh barrows and crumlecks to this wonderful sitty! Even Bath itself is but a fillitch, in the naam of God—One would think there's no end of the streets, but the land's end" (WJ, June 3). She of course possesses the weaknesses of her class and delights in dressing above her station: "Last night, coming huom from the meeting, I was taken by a lamp-light for an iminent poulterer's daughter, a great beauty—" (WJ, June 3). In the end the true goodness everyone has testified to brings Win her reward: she has the novel's last word.

Tabby, however, is another story. Whereas Bramble, Jery, and Liddy suffer the waves of excess in order "to case-harden the constitution," Tabby simply likes to get wet. In her Smollett unites the extremes of two satiric types: the weak and empty vessel of the woman, open to the whole spectrum of vanities; and the person possessed of the normally opposed vices of luxury and avarice.[8] If with Liddy his powers of characterization are not pronounced, with Tabby his gifts of travesty are at their fullest. Bramble's solicitude tells us early that she is silly, not wicked—in Fielding's terms a representation of the Ridiculous. He tells Jery that she is "insensibly a part of my constitution—Damn her! She's a *noli me tangere* in my flesh, which I cannot bear to be touched or tampered with" (JM, May 6). She redeems his tolerance by caring for him when he is ill, and at the end—when her "vinegar . . . is remarkably dulcified" (JM, October 14)—by a proper choice of husband, the same he wished for her. Yet along the way she affords a sacrifying enough picture of luxury to scotch the need for a Mrs. Burdock.

Tabby's first letter of April 2 actually introduces the attack upon luxury, since it like all the rest is concerned solely with her possessions. In none of her letters does she remark journey, place, or emotion. Nothing beyond self touches her; she exists below the attractions of art, nature, reason, and experience. She is oblivious, Slipslop tutored by Mrs. Western. Rather than attend to the journey, she concentrates her formidable energies upon maintaining her store of goods in Brambleton Hall, while adding to it in the item of one husband. Throughout the expedition her perversity of judgment has two sides. On the one, she is never merely mistaken, but is always *completely* wrong, wrong 180 degrees. When she applauds the mirth of Bath or the honesty of the Methodists or the beauties of London, we have confirmed the antithetical views of brother and nephew. When she sees Humphry as a worthless beggar, Mr. Moffat as a fine gentleman, and Brambleton Hall as an early Cold Comfort Farm, we obtain important information, delivered in code. What is more, the other characters themselves delight in breaking the code. Bramble reports that Tabby is "inclined to give the whole Scotch nation to the devil, as a pack of insensible brutes," then adds the crucial phrase, "upon whom her accomplishments had been displayed in vain." Jery records her peevishness in Edinburgh and her desire to leave—until she chances upon a susceptible male. Even Win joins the game; as Tabby is railing against all things Scottish, Win tells us, "As for mistress, blessed be God, she ails nothing.—Her stomick is good, and she improves in grease and godliness" (WJ, September 7). Left to herself, she and her topsy-turvy world harm no one.

But when her vice turns social, embroiling others, she moves in the direction of Lady Griskin and Mrs. Baynard. Initially Jery sees her as "exceedingly starched, vain, and ridiculous" (April 2). But after traveling with her for a month, his view is sharper—and darker: "In her temper, she is proud, stiff, vain, imperious, prying, malicious, greedy, and uncharitable. . . . Her avarice seems to grow every day more and more rapacious" (May 6). During that month she has begun to issue the insatiable demands that characterize her luxury and that will not be quelled until she is ruled by Lismahago. Lydia remarks that the atmosphere of Bath is too feverish, but "Aunt says it is the effect of a vulgar constitution, reared among woods and mountains; and, that as I become accustomed to genteel company, it will wear off" (LM, April 26). She not only doubts, but revolts against her brother's generosity to the widow and her consumptive daughter at Bristol, even after Jery explains the situation: "Child, child, talk not to me of charity.—Who gives twenty pounds in charity?—But you are a stripling—You know nothing of the world—Besides, charity begins at home—Twenty pounds would buy me a complete suit of flowered silk, trimmings and all" (JM, April 20). Her letter of diatribe, May 19, charts the distance between her selfish attitude toward the servants and her brother's compassion.[9] She flirts with dozens of false gentlemen, foolishly sees Barton's favors directed toward herself, tries to entice a bereaved Baynard, and would have everyone (Squikinacoosta included) dressed in the latest Parisian fashions.

When Bramble exclaims, "I an't married to Tabby, thank Heaven!" he is drawing a pertinent distinction. Tabby is guarded round by a family of inordinate strength bent upon protecting her from herself—brother and nephew comment regularly on her "manageability"—and her *folies des luxes* are normally witless. She is probably related, by misadventure, to another fictional sister, Bridget Allworthy, both modeled upon the focal female figure in Hogarth's "Morning" (see Jery's description, May 6). What would the consequence be if she were brighter or uncontrolled or married to a man weaker than she? Put another way: what would the result be for England if most *men* were as frivolous as she? It is the very pettiness of Tabby's vices that serves to stress the danger of a climate of luxury, for frivolity can be translated swiftly into disaster. Tabby has power merely to irritate her brother, but the social rabble can overturn Bath, the political mob destroy London, and Mrs. Burdock and Mrs. Baynard bring heartbreak to their husbands.

Avatars of luxury dominate England. Indeed Tabby is a direct link, since she attracts mercenary "gentlemen"—about two dozen named and unnamed—as a rich coach draws highwaymen. (In Scotland it is *she* who does the pursuing.) She also establishes that luxury can threaten even the most virtuous of families, a lesson repeated with the entry of Bramble's cousins, Lady Griskin and Squire Burdock. That the Bramble party itself does not succumb is proof not of the enemy's weakness, but of its own strength. The forces of luxury are led by the political hacks and "uncouth whales" of commercial fortune noticed in the previous chapter. Their followers are mostly parasitic men and women whom Bramble with ample cause disdains to name: "If you pick up a diverting original by accident, it may be dangerous to amuse yourself with his oddities. He is generally a tartar at bottom; a sharper, a spy, or a lunatic" (MB, June 8). The remainder range from agents like Sir Ulic, Jack Holder, Squire Prankley, Colonel Tinsel, and Paunceford to their working-class imitators like John Thomas and Dutton.[10] In order to maintain an emotional equilibrium against such fashionable vermin, Bramble finds some means to keep them at a distance. He flees them, refuses to acknowledge them, or drives them from his vicinity. Like Oxmington and Tabby's ersatz suitors, most are cowards easily dissuaded. Yet occasionally words are not forceful enough. When two slaves owned by Colonel Rigworm, "a Creole gentleman" with neither taste nor breeding, play their French horns on the common staircase, Bramble's indignation is fierce. He promptly batters both horns and heads, promises the same to their master, and is disturbed no more.

Certain instances of luxury Bramble is obliged to confront without flinching. As a visitor to England cannot easily avoid Bath or London, so Bramble cannot in conscience skirt the home of a relative like

Burdock or a friend like Baynard. In such households he must acknowledge the power of effeminacy blindly to destroy the ways of Old England. They reveal the consequences of female rule and disclose how wives prey upon the weaknesses of worthy men, obtaining control even when their husbands know the better course: "I believe it will be found upon enquiry, that nineteen out of twenty, who are ruined by extravagance, fall a sacrifice to the ridiculous pride and vanity of silly women, whose parts are held in contempt by the very men whom they pillage and enslave" (MB, September 30). Burdock and Baynard should be as steeled against luxury as the other seasoned men of the novel, but, schooled by their wives, they merely demonstrate that dissipation has reached well into the North of England.

A flagrant example of the new rich, Mrs. Burdock is insensitive, illiberal, arrogant, brutal, and cold. The house she has turned into "a great inn," "neither elegant nor comfortable," a house without warmth. For the older virtue of generosity she has substituted mere splendor; her husband admits, "Country gentlemen now-a-days live after another fashion.—My table alone stands me in a cool thousand a quarter, though I raise my own stock, import my own liquors, and have every thing at the first hand" (MB, June 26). All normal bonds of duty and affection she has broken. Hence the son is a young fool just returned from Italy who "slips no opportunity of manifesting the most perfect contempt for his own father." The servants, without loyalty or subordination, are insolent, inattentive, and rapacious, "so greedy," Bramble reports, "that ... I can dine better, and for less expence, at the Star and Garter in Pall mall, than at our cousin's castle in Yorkshire." Her signal achievement is to be equally abusive to everyone, husband or chance visitor. At the moment Bramble arrives she and her son are expressing their love for Burdock by having him needlessly trepanned. The squire takes his near-death in stride, for he "hates her mortally; but . . . truckles to her dominion, and dreads, like a schoolboy, the lash of her tongue." Although he is a tough old dog, his dread is such that he cannot invite Bramble to stay the wet night.

When he visits the Baynards, Bramble meets with not an instance, but a whole colony of luxury, three men "driven by their wives at full speed, in the high road to bankruptcy and ruin" (MB, September 30). The women vie with each other and with wealthier women of the region for more and costlier clothes, plate, china, furniture, servants, horses, and carriages. Because their husbands are of differing temperaments, they must exercise "three different forms of female tyranny."

> Mr. Baynard was subjugated by practising upon the tenderness of his nature. Mr. Milksan, being of a timorous disposition, truckled

to the insolence of a termagant. Mr. Sowerby, who was of a temper neither to be moved by fits, nor driven by menaces, had the fortune to be fitted with a helpmate, who assailed him with the weapons of irony and satire.

Of all the fictional characters in *Humphry Clinker,* Mrs. Baynard most fully represents the vain triumphs of luxury; every detail Bramble provides in this, the longest inset story in the novel, reeks of social perversity. Her birth—"daughter of a citizen, who had failed in trade"—places her among those "shovel-nosed sharks," the English women of the middle orders, whom Bramble has deplored everywhere along the journey. As a tradesman, her father was certainly a rascal: "Your tradesmen are without conscience" (MB, June 8). But what is worse, he was also a failure: if "cits" are not good for trade, they are good for nothing. In her own education "for the usual purposes of the married state," she has repeated his failure.

> She excelled in nothing. Her conversation was flat, her stile mean, and her expression embarrassed—In a word, her character was totally insipid. Her person was not disagreeable; but there was nothing graceful in her address, nor engaging in her manners; and she was so ill qualified to do the honours of the house, that when she sat at the head of the table, one was always looking for the mistress of the family in some other place.

Only after marriage does she disclose her guiding passion, "vanity . . . of a bastard and idiot nature, excited by shew and ostentation." Only then does she pronounce her intention to rule all (and spend all) they have. Only then does she reveal her answer to all expostulation—prolonged faints and violent fits.

Her trickery, elaborately described in one of Bramble's rare transcriptions of dialogue, summarizes all the major acts of deceit recounted in the novel. Through it she gains an extravagant house in the city, an extravagant estate in the country, and an extravagant tour of the Continent. She tours Europe as Tabby does Britain, learning nothing, but gathering expensive parasites and bric-a-brac, disgusted with a country when her presence goes unnoticed. "Her travels," Bramble reports, "had no effect upon her, but that of making her more expensive and fantastic than ever." This is to be contrasted with the effect travel has had upon the Bramble family.

Upon returning to England, Mrs. Baynard assumes the rank of arbiter "in every article of taste and connoisseurship." She proves her genius by destroying the facade of the house and the perfection of the gardens and by duplicating the fashionable meals of London.

The pottage was little better than bread soaked in dishwashings, lukewarm. The ragouts looked as if they had been once eaten and half digested: the fricassees were involved in a nasty yellow poultice; and the rotis were scorched and stinking, for the honour of the fumet. The desert consisted of faded fruit and iced froth, a good emblem of our landlady's character.

The same as Jery proposed for Dutton, the lady's emblem is a syllabub, the emblem Bramble would choose for all of fashionable England. In her moments away from aesthetic projects, she superintends the tuition of her son, "a puny boy of twelve or thirteen," who according to Bramble "will be ruined in his education by the indulgence of his mother." She watches complacently as he steals a kiss from Liddy and thrusts his hand inside the bosom of her dress. With such guidance young Baynard will doubtless prove a fit companion in the Pump Room for young Burdock.

With exquisite care and expense, Mrs. Baynard has turned the estate into a gallery of contemporary English vices. Travelers with little time need not make the Bristol-Bath-London-Harrigate circuit, for here they may sample the same depraved food, morals, manners, architecture, and family relationships. Here they may meet individually those types that give the crowds of the spa and the capital their special stink: overbearing women, broken men, false friends, disloyal relations, insolent children, and thievish servants. A museum at once of English history and English destiny, it contains for Bramble "every thing . . . cold, comfortless, and disgusting." Chef d'oeuvre of the place is the lady herself, who, when not removed for fit or faint, may be viewed at length: form for the women who tread upon the kibes of their betters and the backs of their husbands; foil and warning to Liddy, Jery, Humphry, Baynard, Bramble, and the Dennisons.

Smollett's insistence upon this synecdochic epitome is so sharp that we hardly need, but cannot avoid, glosses by Dennison, Bramble, and Baynard. Dennison, Bramble tells us, is a beacon, a standard of reason in a disordered world—precisely the man into whose family Liddy should be entrusted. At every point where the Baynards fell victim to luxury, Dennison remained vigilant and carried his wife with him. He draws the contrast himself when he says he was resolute in avoiding "'pride, envy, and ambition. . . . Those, in times of luxury and dissipation, are the rocks upon which all small estates in the country are wrecked'" (MB, October 11). Bramble's commentary is more complex. At the Burdocks' he had been unsettled by a situation he could despise but not remedy. Baynard is a closer, worthier friend, willing to be advised, and moreover suffering the physical symptoms of mental distress that Bramble himself endured earlier. As he had cured himself, Bramble is determined to release his friend. Yet the exchange between the two men at first appears quite odd, with Bramble demanding, the other supplying, conversations of twenty years ago and humiliating confessions of weakness. Finally the gravamen become clear. When Bramble presses Baynard to resist his wife, the latter answers, "But there are certain lengths which my nature—The truth is, there are tender connexions, of which a bachelor has no idea—Shall I own my weakness? I cannot bear the thoughts of making that woman uneasy—" (MB, September 30). Bramble's response—"I was shocked at his infatuation, and changed the subject"—is thematic (he never willing changes the subject), since his companion's apology is of a piece with Adam's "the woman beguiled me and I did eat." Old Adam's plight remains pretty much the same into the eighteenth century. Whether the novelist seeks to recall the Fall is less important than his creation of a modern Eve. Whereas the archetype of feminine passion disobeyed the law and plucked the fruit, her descendant refuses to recognize any law beyond self and chops down the whole orchard.

If Bramble and Mrs. Baynard are polar opposites in the moral world of *Humphry Clinker,* they stand together in marking Smollett's gifts in the creation of character. The one stands above even the most famous tutor figures of the century: more vital, complex, and interesting than Grandison, Adams, Wilson, Allworthy, Imlac, or Primrose. The other is certainly more evocative of evil than the empty, dimensionless type of contemporary polemics. We glimpse her movements somewhat indirectly, through the magnifying projections of her curt dialogue, Bramble's bitter adjectives, and Baynard's lugubrious recollections. By careful preparation, the novelist can maintain the social definition of her type yet transcend its aesthetic limitations, allowing him to place her at the thematic climax of his narrative. To outline the form from the start, he offers us Tabby and Win, followed by dozens of anonymous female Yahoos in action at the Pump Room, Ranelagh, Vauxhall, and elsewhere. Thereafter he is ready to pause briefly over a figure like Lady Griskin, then to linger with a termagant like Mrs. Burdock. Coming immediately on the heels of such women on the trip north, Mrs. Baynard would not have been so surprising or effective. But Smollett withholds her until the visit to idyllic Scotland has passed, until Jery and Bramble have sung tributes to Scottish women, and until we have lapsed into the fond hope that the party has outdistanced the ravages of luxury. Then and perhaps only then will Baynard's wife provide a sufficient shock. Placed unexpectedly at the close of the book, she can be vapid in and of herself yet potent enough to evoke memories and resonances from everywhere in England. Her parts are entirely negative, yet she becomes greater than the sum of those parts.

The fact that Mrs. Baynard does draw together so many strands of the novel gives us a further instance of Smollett's achievement. He has dared to set his attack upon luxury in a land where luxury is the rule, the norm. On the most elementary level, five-sixths of the action (measured by the number of pages in the original edition) takes place in degenerate England, where the Bramble party and friends are outnumbered by villains in a ratio of hundreds to one. In power and influence good is easily overwhelmed by evil. Yet while England is dominated by villains, the novel is not. The party moves through pitch but is undefiled. It has many narrow escapes, but always extricates itself. The epistolary technique is essential in this regard. For we cannot look to the intervention of either Defoe's divine providence or Fielding's benevolent, omnipotent narrator. Instead, we watch while credible human beings help one another and at leisure write about their success. Smollett has projected a world in which the personal and the particular virtue of Bramble and his pupils is sufficient to withstand the general wickedness that envelops England.

At the opening of the novel Smollett pits a luxurious England at the peak of its material strength against a Bramble family at its psychological nadir. Faced with such omnivorous vice, Bramble is vexed, Jery callously amused, Liddy bewildered, Tabby and Win beguiled. In rapid succession at Bristol, Bath, and London we learn of other decent families who against their wills are pulled into the vortex or pushed into the hinterlands. Uniting around Bramble, this family will not be drawn or divided. At the close it is bound together as never before. It is moreover trebled in size and worth, having attracted Humphry, Lismahago, the three Dennisons, the Wilsons, Baynard, Miss Willis, and Archy M'Alpin. The family that had been Bramble's bane becomes his blessing, the source of his distress transformed into the spring of his joy—the first he has known in many years.

The political despair with which the novel concludes is thus balanced by the glow of personal renewal. Each positive character has completed a significant rite of passage, has achieved what he most needs, and has vanquished his own peculiar deadly sin. Perhaps to perpetuate his uncle's model pilgrimage, Jery himself appears ready to assume the role of moral guide; at the close of his last letter he offers to lead Phillips in a "scheme of peregrination." For his own part, Bramble covets the heath and hearth of Brambleton Hall, content to leave the fashionable English to "wallow in the mire of their own pollution."

THE STRUCTURE OF
HUMPHRY CLINKER

We have been at court, and 'change, and every where;
and every where we find food for spleen,
and subject for ridicule—Matthew Bramble, June 2

Of the eighty-two letters that make up *Humphry Clinker* Jery writes twenty-eight, Bramble twenty-seven, Liddy eleven, Win ten, and Tabby six. With two-thirds the total number of letters, the men also have seven-eighths the total number of pages; the only substantial letters by the women are three by Liddy. These surface facts suggest in a general way something about the nature of relationships in the novel. If pursued further they disclose part of the reading structure of the book. Jery has no "topics" that are uniquely his own, and his letters are in effect elaborations of Bramble's; Liddy's long letters provide either examples or extensions of her uncle's observations. The Bramble-Jery relationship of judgment and verification can then be traced with other male characters. Upon stopping in England, Bramble the traveler and outsider will characterize the new place, then converse at length with older men who are knowledgeable insiders—like Quin, Heathcote, Bentley, Balderick, Lismahago, Burdock, Baynard, and Dennison—and who confirm with incontestable detail his gravest suspicions. Smollett thus develops the incidents of *Humphry Clinker* in such a way that they constitute both the narrative itself and an attitude toward it, the structure he provides telling us not only what occurs but also how to interpret those occurrences.[1]

As it entered eighteenth-century England, the attack upon luxury possessed a closed, rationalist structure, expressing first principles from which no appeal—no new evidence or alternative interpretation—was possible. Yet over the century, as it grew more political and more closely allied to the genre and techniques of the novel, it also became increasingly empirical. Although some philosophers and theologians continued to pursue the attack by way of assertion and deduction, other writers proceeded by (or at least included a measure of) demonstration. In *Humphry Clinker* rationalist and empirical elements are in nice equilibrium. Political commentary is Smollett's way of describing the civic corruption of England as well as of accounting for its origins. Various characters are likewise led to gloss their own behavior and the workings of the plot. Jery is summarizing for us the effect of the journey upon all the young people of the party when he says, "Without all doubt, the greatest advantage acquired in travelling and perusing mankind in the original, is that of dispelling those shameful clouds that darken the faculties of the mind, preventing it from judging with candour and precision" (JM, October 14). Yet these rationalist devices are not sufficient for Smollett: they yield clarity but not force.

To say that *Humphry Clinker* is the story of an expedition told in letters is to call attention to its balanced elements. On the one hand, Bramble as head of the household sets the pace of the journey, its direction, route, and stopping points. It is at his insistence that the tour is panoramic, international, and comparative. Like Cato, Sallust, and Plutarch, and like Smollett in the *Travels, Present State,* and *Atom,* he demands that nation be judged against nation, people against people, city against country, vice against virtue, and present against past. His control is of itself sufficient to prevent stasis and to insure constant movement from place to place, time to time, and conversation to conversation. His control tells us, moreover, that threats to the family will be short-lived, that respite is always somewhere ahead. On the other hand, Smollett does not content himself with these traditional kinds of movement. By having five writers compose eighty-two letters over a period of about eight months, he multiplies many times the transitions of the novel. Each movement from day to day, style to style, or letter to letter carries the party forward but brings readers to a brief halt; we must pause to reorient ourselves, to recall who is writing, to fit together everything that has gone before. It is as though we were presented with a drama of eighty-two acts in which important action frequently takes place between the acts.

The two previous chapters have indicated some of the rationalist
patterns of the novel, the *what* and *to whom* of what happens. The
present chapter will concentrate primarily upon the empirical, the *how,
when,* and *where.* Every attack upon luxury seeks to reveal a plenary
truth: the horror of its nature and the virtual ubiquity of its influence.
Humphry Clinker accomplishes this end through all the means available
to a mature novelist with a consuming interest in the mechanics of
human activity. A documentary, encyclopedic quality is present in most
of Smollett's writing—as he seeks out how institutions are ordered, how
various activities are organized, how people live and move about, how
cities get planned and built, how machines are made and operate, what
particular jobs actually entail, how influence is generated and diffused,
how politicians are selected and corrupted. Converging with his symbolic sense, this inveterate interest in process generates much of the
vitality of the novel. As he is fascinated by specific details of how things
work, so his symbols are usually of the external or literal variety; that
is, he chooses for figurative use people and places that actually exist and
that take on a concentration of meaning by means of repetition and
accumulation. The one habit will convey how luxury manifests itself,
the other how it strikes and spreads its contagion: together they will
make the darkness visible. Structurally they also explain why the novel
seems obsessed with decadent England. Bramble is in search of peace
for himself and protection for his charges, he tells us. Yet for much of
the journey he leads them to and through the very heart of chaos and
danger. Of course he explains the contradiction in several ways: his
family must be case-hardened; no tour would be complete without the
great cities; he wishes to visit old friends; and so on. Yet the suspicion
persists that while Bramble is fleeing luxury, Smollett is actually pursuing it, searching out its tentacles, its spawn, and its foulings. Like the
historians tracing luxury to Eve or Cain or Nero, he seems bent upon
exposing the mainspring of evil, the universal villain, the omnipotent
conspiracy, the invisible network embracing insolent children, diluted
wines, and international commerce. Although there is no single criminal
genius presiding over this morass, Bramble is given the task of investigat-
ing it thoroughly. His is the hard duty to reveal that the type of generic
evil is no longer a fallen woman or a depraved tyrant, but a nondescript
mob.[2]

A structure of unfolding demonstration serves to emphasize that
luxury is a vice that destroys relationships among men as it destroys less
palpable social institutions. It is a matter of integrity with Smollett's
positive older males that fashion and misfortune do not change them.
They are most themselves when under duress, their steadfastness becoming self-sufficiency, the signal value in the chaos of England. Their

struggle—the struggle that brings them alive in the novel—is to keep themselves as they are. Their character is revealed not by inner process but by social and external conflict.

At the beginning of the novel all the letter-writers are testing themselves, each other, their correspondents, and the atmosphere of the spas. At Bristol, their first stopping place, Bramble perceives an air of neglect summarized in the widow and her sickly daughter. When he offers, privately, to relieve their distress, Tabby impugns his motive and deprecates his generosity. The clash between sister and brother reveals the nature of each and confirms Bramble's sense of the place. Jery, who recounts the episode, will not allow Bramble's judgment to be challenged so outrageously and responds on his behalf. By itself a diverting but minor scene, this is actually a small trial drawing together all that has gone before. Inadvertently losing his guise of amused observer, Jery is impelled to enter and judge the altercation, then to revise his estimates of uncle and aunt. The scene has accomplished much in a small compass and will be joined to subsequent scenes by another trial at the next spa.

Its temptations far greater, Bath receives far more attention than Bristol. As English luxury reveals itself more fully, the momentum of the novel gathers, larger challenge calling forth greater response. Here men of worth are sometimes merely ignored, but sometimes actively oppressed. Such distinguished friends of Bramble as Admiral Balderick and Colonel Cockril, "who have acted honourable and distinguished parts on the great theatre," are left to a life of indigence and frustration. They receive none of the distinction and reward their service to the nation merits, for Bath gives her attention only to the frippery and ostentation of new retainers of fortune. To Bramble's disgust and chagrin, men of true worth like Balderick and Cockril—who prepare us for the injustice that has befallen Lismahago—find the city not a haven, but "a stewpan of idleness and insignificance." "They have long left off using the waters, after having experienced their inefficacy. The diversions of the place they are not in a condition to enjoy. How do they make shift to pass their time? In the forenoon, they crawl out to the Rooms or the coffee-house, where they take a hand at whist, or descant upon the General Advertiser; and their evenings they murder in private parties, among peevish invalids, and insipid old women—This is the case with a good number of individuals, whom nature seems to have intended for better purposes" (MB, May 5).

Such scenes provoke Bramble but serve initially as a fillip to his nephew's entertainment. Jery's view of social intercourse at Bath will soon lead to another clash of personalities and judgments, and his pose of mediator will be thrust aside entirely.

> I was extremely diverted, last ball-night, to see the Master of the
> Ceremonies leading, with great solemnity, to the upper end of the
> room, an antiquated Abigail, dressed in her lady's cast-clothes;
> whom he (I suppose) mistook for some countess just arrived at the
> Bath. The ball was opened by a Scotch lord, with a mulatto
> heiress from St. Christopher's. . . . I cannot account for my being
> pleased with these incidents, any other way than by saying, they
> are truly ridiculous in their own nature, and serve to heighten the
> humour in the farce of life, which I am determined to enjoy as
> long as I can. [JM, April 30]

Similarly, he notes, "Another entertainment, peculiar to Bath, arises
from the general mixture of all degrees assembled in our public rooms,
without distinction of rank or fortune. This is what my uncle repro-
bates, as a monstrous jumble of heterogeneous principles; a vile mob of
noise and impertinence, without decency or subordination. But this
chaos is to me a source of infinite amusement." And again, "Those follies, that move my uncle's spleen, excite my laughter." From this
divergence a demonstration will issue, as it does every time Bramble and
Jery are coequal participants in a scene. It arises from a difference of
opinion obvious from the opening of the novel and establishes the
ground for all ensuing action. Smollett had begun contriving the situation in Jery's first letter and developed it carefully up to Bath. He gives
the young man an air of jejune callousness modified by a sense of fair-
ness: he has his opinion but is willing to have it tested. Already he calls
the crowd a chaos and reports his uncle's views at greater length than
his own.

> I took the liberty to differ in opinion from Mr. Bramble, when he
> observed, that the mixture of people in the entertainments of this
> place was destructive of all order and urbanity; that it rendered
> the plebeians insufferably arrogant and troublesome, and vul-
> garized the deportment and sentiments of those who moved in the
> upper spheres of life. He said, such a preposterous coalition would
> bring us into contempt with all our neighbors; and was worse, in
> fact, than debasing the gold coin of the nation. I argued, on the
> contrary, that those plebeians who discovered such eagerness to
> imitate the dress and equipage of their superiors, would likewise,
> in time, adopt their maxims and their manners, be polished by
> their conversation, and refined by their example. [JM, April 30]

Jery again gives himself the lesser argument, admitting he is "not
much conversant in high-life," but insists that the argument be resolved
by a "recourse to experience"—exactly the criterion Bramble has been
suggesting all along. He recommends the general tea-drinking as an ex-

periment, "no bad way of trying the company's breeding." Bramble and Quin agree to "abide by that experiment" provided they may watch from the safe distance of the gallery.

> The tea-drinking passed as usual; and the company having risen from the tables, were sauntring in groupes, in expectation of the signal for attack, when the bell beginning to ring, they flew with eagerness to the desert, and the whole place was instantly in commotion. There was nothing but justling, scrambling, pulling, snatching, struggling, scolding, and screaming. The nosegays were torn from one another's hands and bosoms; the glasses and china went to wreck; the tables and floor were strewed with comfits. Some cried; some swore; and the tropes and figures of Billingsgate were used without reserve in all their native zest and flavor; nor were those flowers of rhetoric unattended with significant gesticulation. Some snapped their fingers; some forked them out; some clapped their hands, and some their back-sides; at length, they fairly proceeded to pulling caps, and everything seemed to presage a general battle. [JM, April 30]

Smollett underscores the lesson by keeping Bramble's comments to a bare minimum; it will be Jery who will relate the "disgraceful situation" of the assembly, their "absurd deportment" and eventual "mortification." Quin is able to laugh at the result, for he had predicted that the different ranks of society would mix happily no more than "a plate of marmalade would improve a pan of sirreverence." But Bramble is hurt. "He hung his head in manifest chagrin, and seemed to repine at the triumph of his judgment . . . his victory was more complete than he imagined." Although Jery repudiates all of the combatants at the tea-drinking, the only persons he singles out for attention are women, "two amazons who singularized themselves most in the action." He reports: "One was a baroness, and the other, a wealthy knight's dowager." Bramble enforces the point by adding, "'I bless God . . . that Mrs. Tabitha Bramble did not take the field today.'" Jery concedes to avuncular wisdom and agrees that his proposed mixture leads to the disgrace and debasement of all. Never again in the novel will he challenge Bramble.[3]

The conversion of Jery at Bath recalls the events of Bristol and anticipates the lessons of the remainder of the expedition. The tea-drinking approximates the moment of recognition in drama, the point in dialectic when revolutionary change takes place, Jery abandoning his false conception of luxury with the realization that it had always been false. The process of discovery has involved change over time; yet the truth it discovers is changeless and timeless. Both characters are elevated: Jery is shown to have an authentic respect for truth, Bramble a genuine comprehension. The teacher-pupil distinction need no longer be so emphatic. One or more of such trial scenes will occur at every stage, testing the moral atmosphere of the new place, the integrity of new characters, and the triumphs of Bramble's judgment. In London, where virtue is openly attacked, Humphry will be the defendant at several—over his poverty, simplicity, religion, and innocence of robbery. All of these are actual tests except the last, when Clinker appears before an official magistrate, Justice Buzzard. Bramble will try a person only for just cause; English authorities prefer to seek out the patently innocent. Bramble's authority derives from his ability to discover reality. The influence of a Pitt, Newcastle, Wesley, or Buzzard, however, is due to his capacity for compounding error and misunderstanding. True justice survives in England only because private men recognize and dispense it for themselves; the representatives of law and religion are merely agents of luxury and deception. Humphry's experience in London will be repeated by Liddy, as she withdraws her trust from Tabby and Lady Griskin and places it more firmly with Bramble. No one in the novel bests Bramble; Lismahago is able to match him by reiterating his own arguments.

While they teach the young and reveal the honest, scenes of testing also expose the luxurious. From Bristol onward Bramble's senses are an outward monitor to the degeneracy of the age, to be flayed repeatedly until he crosses the Tweed. Compared with other English cities, Hot Well seems mild enough; still, Bramble finds it a place for fools: "the man deserves to be fitted with a cap and bells, who for such a paltry advantage as this spring affords, sacrifices his precious time, which might be employed in taking more effectual remedies, and exposes himself to the dirt, the stench, the chilling blasts, and perpetual rains, that render this place to me intolerable" (MB, April 20). And where fools reside, knaves will find them out. Here the reigning quack, playing hard upon the gullible, is the notorious Dr. Linden. For Smollett's purposes he is here to be exposed and purged. Bramble has little difficulty accomplishing the former task, telling Linden "with a view to punish this original . . . there was a wart upon his nose, that looked a little suspicious" (JM, April 18—Jery and Bramble again collaborating). Establishing that Linden cannot diagnose, Bramble allows him to show himself that he cannot prescribe. After a night of his own treatment Linden returns with "a considerable inflammation, attended with an enormous swelling; so that when he next appeared his whole face was overshadowed by this tremendous nozzle . . . ludicrous beyond all description." Bramble has thereby demonstrated to all present that the man is not to be trusted with anyone's health. That, however, is but part of Linden's function. He is present also to demonstrate in his own absurd person that charlatans are physically revolting. Hearing complaints of stench from the river, he enters "into a learned investigation of the nature of stink."

> He observed, that stink, or stench, meant no more than a strong impression on the olfactory nerves; and might be applied to substances of the most opposite qualities . . . that individuals differed *toto caelo* in their opinion of smells, which, indeed, was altogether as arbitrary as the opinion of beauty . . . that the Negroes on the coast of Senegal would not touch fish till it was rotten; strong presumptions in favour of what is generally called *stink* . . . that he had reason to believe the stercoraceous flavour, condemned by prejudice as a stink, was, in fact, most agreeable to the organs of smelling; for, that every person who pretended to nauseate the smell of another's excretions, snuffed up his own with particular complacency; for the truth of which he appealed to all the ladies and gentlemen then present: he said, the inhabitants of Madrid and Edinburgh found particular satisfaction in breathing their own atmosphere, which was always impregnated with stercoraceous effluvia . . . he affirmed, the last Grand Duke of Tuscany, of the *Medicis* family, who refined upon sensuality with the spirit of a philosopher, was so delighted with that odour, that he caused the essence of ordure to be extracted, and used it as the most delicious perfume: that he himself, (the doctor) when he happened to be low-spirited, or fatigued with business, found immediate relief and uncommon satisfaction from hanging over the stale contents of a close-stool, while his servant stirred it about under his nose.

With Linden's grotesquerie Smollett demonstrates that luxury is an affront to the senses as well as to the intellect; even the dullest should be repelled. At Bath the demonstration quickens and broadens, as Bramble is attacked through all his senses, and the atmosphere of luxury becomes evident, then oppressive, then horrid. The clamorous mob that crowds into the Pump Room will not be composed of the decent gentry Bramble had expected to find, but of broken-winded landladies, lame brandy-merchants, and paralytic attorneys who give off that "compound of villainous smells" that nauseates all but the degenerate; that is, no one but the Bramble family. The welter of sensory details Smollett provides is seldom gratuitous, for he gives them symbolic weight. Throughout England the simplest acts of everyday living are increasingly hard. Noise prevents conversation and rest, food is insipid or vile, foul odors beset one at every corner. Wines, ales, ciders, and

perries are undrinkable. In life as in art England has entered "a degenerate age, fast sinking into barbarism" (MB, April 28). At each major
stopping point on the journey Smollett will insert a catalog of the
effects of luxury, since for Jery and Bramble, history, nature, and sense
all cry out against it: as Bramble says at Bath, "All these absurdities
arise from the general tide of luxury, which hath overspread the nation,
and swept away all, even the very dregs of the people."

Bramble describes Bath as he will London: clotted, congested, sickly,
and sluggish. The streets are overcrowded with houses, set at odds,
"want beauty and proportion." They extend without planning or order,
as "growing excrescences" to create new confusion. He sees the city as
Rowlandson would later, as a place of permanent disorder, precisely the
spa to attract the very dregs of the people: "A national hospital it may
be; but one would imagine that none but lunatics are admitted."

> Thus the number of people, and the number of houses continue
> to increase; and this will ever be the case, till the streams that
> swell this irresistible torrent of folly and extravagance, shall either
> be exhausted, or turned into other channels. . . . This, I own, is a
> subject on which I cannot write with any degree of patience; for
> the mob is a monster I never could abide, either in its head, tail,
> midriff, or members: I detest the whole of it, as a mass of igno-
> rance, presumption, malice, and brutality; and, in this term of
> reprobation, I include, without respect of rank, station, or quality,
> all those of both sexes, who affect its manners, and court its so-
> ciety. [MB, April 23]

The upshot is that Bath too is sinking into barbarism, "the very center
of racket and dissipation" and a symbol of "a vile world of fraud and
sophistication." All substantial families are forced to flee, "the madness
of the times has made the place too hot for them, and they are now
obliged to think of other migrations—Some have already fled to the
mountains of Wales, and others have retired to Exeter. Thither, no
doubt, they will be followed by the flood of luxury and extravagance,
which will drive them from place to place to the very Land's End" (MB,
May 5). Like a charming actress turned tu'penny whore, the once
pleasant resort has been sophisticated by new and fast money. As
Bramble has said, England has turned topsy-turvy: the very places
people seek out for their health are sinks (and stinks) of disease, founts
of infection rather than cure. This combination of luxury and the mob
make the city intolerable for decent visitors. What is more, occasional
insubordination has now become general usurpation.

Even the wives and daughters of low tradesmen, who, like shovel-nosed sharks, prey upon the blubber of those uncouth whales of fortune, are infected with the same rage of displaying their importance; and the slightest indisposition serves them for a pretext to insist upon being conveyed to Bath, where they may hobble country-dances and cotillons among lordlings, 'squires, counsellors, and clergy. These delicate creatures from Bedfordbury, Butcher-row, Crutched-Friers, and Botolph-lane, cannot breathe in the gross air of the Lower Town, or conform to the vulgar rules of a common lodging-house; the husband, therefore, must provide an entire house, or elegant apartments in the new buildings. [MB, April 23]

Bath is become a mere sink of profligacy and extortion. Every article of house-keeping is raised to an enormous price; a circumstance no longer to be wondered at, when we know that every petty retainer of fortune piques himself upon keeping a table, and thinks 'tis for the honour of his character to wink at the knavery of his servants, who are in a confederacy with the market-people; and, of consequence, pay whatever they demand. . . . This portentous frenzy is become so contagious, that the very rabble and refuse of mankind are infected. [MB, May 5]

The point for Bramble is that there is nowhere to hide from the contagion. The momentum of portentous frenzy peaks in the capital with repeated scenes in which revulsion and discovery are inextricably mixed. He prepares for Lewis what he calls a "catalogue of London dainties," which he says could easily "swell into a treatise" were he to particularize every grievance he feels. With a full list of the most abominable foods in the civilized world, he includes the obstacles to a simple night of sleep:

I am pent up in frowzy lodgings, where there is not room enough to swing a cat; and I breathe the steams of endless putrefaction; and these would, undoubtedly, produce a pestilence, if they were not qualified by the gross acid of sea-coal, which is itself a pernicious nuisance to lungs of any delicacy of texture: but even this boasted corrector cannot prevent those languid, sallow looks, that distinguish the inhabitants of London from those ruddy swains that lead a country-life—I go to bed after mid-night, jaded and restless from the dissipations of the day—I start every hour from my sleep, at the horrid noise of the watchmen bawling the hour through every street, and thundering at every door; a set of useless fellows, who serve no other purpose but that of disturbing the repose of the inhabitants; and by five o'clock I start out of bed, in

> consequence of the still more dreadful alarm made by the country
> carts, the noisy rustics bellowing green pease under my window.
> [MB, June 8]

Actually the situation is far more grave, for in London he cannot summon up adequate personal analogues for the despair to which he is sub-
jected. Here alone on the expedition he finds life utterly contemptible.
Here his bodily pain is greatest and his family circle most vulnerable. At
every hand—in the arts, law, religion, politics, commerce, journalism—he
finds false schemes of "interest and ambition." Once the seat of wisdom and royalty, the jewel of Europe, London is now the *anus mundi*.

In two of the longest letters of the work, Bramble's of May 29 and
June 8, Smollett gives us three aspects of London: as an observed,
historical city; as symbol of a world in decline; and as theme, geographic
locus, source, and agent of that decline. As Rome was to the empire, so
London has become to Britain. In his writings of two decades, Smollett,
with these letters, comes closest to what his student Dickens achieved
in the Court of Chancery in *Bleak House* and Marshalsea prison in *Little
Dorrit:* the realization of a central, unifying emblem for what he
despised in society. On its surface, Bramble's attack is certainly conventional. Luxury had been regarded as the curse of cities from before the
time of Plato, and the association of the two was usual among Roman
writers. Among eighteenth-century English writers, moreover, satires
upon the capital were common, from Swift's two "Descriptions" to
Johnson's "London."[4] Yet, as previous chapters have shown, mid-
century London actually did contain all that the novelist stood against,
and his controversial writings are increasingly preoccupied with uncovering lines of influence within the city. The result in *Humphry Clinker* is
his use of two complementary images, invasion and degradation. London is certainly under attack from without by barbarian hordes, the
indigent poor of the provinces:

> the capital is become an overgrown monster; which, like a dropsical
> head, will in time leave the body and extremities without nourish-
> ment and support. The absurdity will appear in its full force, when
> we consider, that one sixth part of the natives of this whole ex-
> tensive kingdom is crowded within the bills of mortality. What
> wonder that our villages are depopulated, and our farms in want of
> day-labourers? . . . The tide of luxury has swept all the inhabitants
> from the open country—The poorest 'squire, as well as the richest
> peer, must have his house in town, and make a figure with an
> extraordinary number of domestics. The plough-boys, cow-herds,
> and lower hinds, are debauched and seduced by the appearance
> and discourse of those coxcombs in livery, when they make their
> summer excursions. [MB, May 29]

At the same time, it is being subverted by traitors from within, by base men intent upon fouling their own nest.

In these letters Bramble attempts to particularize for Dr. Lewis his charge that the metropolis is the fountainhead of luxury, the spring and channel of contemporary social vice. To a man of sense, it is uninhabitable. It is overcrowded and uncomfortable; all is hurry, noise, and confusion; prices are exorbitant, valuable goods scarce, and food adulterated; merchants are corrupt; the common people are depraved and intolerable; taste and friendship are impossible; necessary social divisions are eroded; women lose all decorum; fashions generally are silly, dress astonishing; crime and sickness spread unabated; servants are bold, greedy, and dishonest; the political situation is vicious and the government in constant danger; and much more. But the virulence of the contagion is such that it will not stop at the city's margins. London's demands for luxury are so voracious that it also despoils the remainder of the nation. The country is bereft of workers; population is falling; the land is stripped of resources; needed horses and cattle are plundered from the farms; small estates are wiped out and worthy men ruined; Scotland is exploited and Wales threatened; the primary virtues, especially subordination, economy, and simplicity, are banished. "There are many causes that contribute to the daily increase of this enormous mass," Bramble writes, "but they may be all resolved into the grand source of luxury and corruption" (MB, May 29). If Bath is a ruined actress, London is a queen grown blind, demented, and incontinent.

Smollett devotes more space to London than to the whole of Scotland. His party has looked into the abyss and his readers have been appalled. After this demonstration of England's decline he is able to resume the theme with allusion and variation. Jery reminds us that the rage of fashion respects no bounds, for "Harrigate treads upon the heels of Bath, in the articles of gaiety and dissipation" (JM, June 23); Bramble with his portrait of Mrs. Burdock testifies that shovel-nosed sharks also travel to northern waters. And Lismahago joins the group eager to discourse on the truth that "'a glut of wealth brings along with it a glut of evils; it brings false taste, false appetite, false wants, profusion, venality, contempt of order, engendering a spirit of licentiousness, insolence, and faction, that keeps the community in continual ferment, and in time destroys all the distinctions of civil society; so that universal anarchy and uproar must ensue'" (MB, September 20). Indeed the example of Mrs. Burdock and the warnings of Lismahago qualify the party's sojourn in idyllic Scotland. Enclosed on one side by Mrs. Burdock and on the other by Lord Oxmington and Mrs. Baynard, the visit to Smollett's homeland is like a holiday in a nostalgic past. Giving the Bramble party a much-needed respite, Smollett uses the Scots lieutenant to recall present economic and political realities. Lismahago holds that as London is plundering the rest of England, so England is plundering Scotland. Since the Union his country has relinquished vital portions of its trade, population, wealth, national resources, self-government, national spirit, and way of life. In return it has received merely a promise of military protection, dubious if not worthless.

Whatever the implications of this relationship, Bramble and his family are permitted to set them aside. To them Scotland is England turned right side up, a haven where relationships are radically altered. Gone are Bramble's pain, asperity, and craving for fellowship. Soon after arriving in Scotland, he finds, "I have met with more kindness, hospitality, and rational entertainment, in a few weeks, than ever I received in any other country during the whole course of my life" (MB, August 8). Where luxury has been withstood, felicity is still possible. North Britain is "the Scotch Arcadia," Edinburgh is "a hot-bed of genius," and the people greet one "not barely with hospitality, but with such marks of cordial affection, as one would wish to find among near relations, after an absence of many years." In answer to the proud Paunceford stands the good Scotsman Captain Brown, an "honest favorite of fortune" who also became wealthy in India. But unlike Paunceford, the captain gratefully returns to his devoted family, showering them with his generosity and moving Bramble (as Jery early said such acts would) to tears of joy (JM, September 12).

The nature of Smollett's demonstration has transformed the historical Scotland into a *paysage moralisé*. Most of the details seem chosen specifically to contrast with English habits. Scottish noblemen, politicians, merchants, professors, lawyers, doctors, farmers, and common people are all the subject of flights of eulogy. Every sign of English decay is here replaced with wholesome growth. Politicians are concerned only with national honor, merchants are restrained and honest, common people submissive, and juries properly constituted. And of course, "Scotch ladies . . . are the best and kindest creatures upon earth" (JM, August 8). Instead of the duplicity of a Justice Buzzard, Scotland offers a "college of justice" of unquestioned integrity. Instead of the churlish literati of London, Bramble finds Scots authors agreeable, instructive, and entertaining. Instead of the clerical drones and hypocrites of Bath and London, the Scottish kirk "abounds at present with ministers celebrated for their learning, and respectable for their moderation" (MB, August 8). A sense of the disparity—in Smollett's efforts as well as in national characteristics—is offered by two of Bramble's descriptions of food and drink, in London and in Cameron. In London, he says,

If I would drink water, I must quaff the maukish contents of an open aqueduct, exposed to all manner of defilement; or swallow that which comes from the river Thames, impregnated with all the filth of London and Westminster—Human excrement is the least offensive part of the concrete, which is composed of all the drugs, minerals, and poisons, used in mechanics and manufacture, enriched with the putrefying carcases of beasts and men; and mixed with the scourings of all the wash-tubs, kennels, and common sewers, within the bills of mortality.

This is the agreeable potation, extolled by the Londoners, as the finest water in the universe—As to the intoxicating potion, sold for wine, it is a vile, unpalatable, and pernicious sophistication, balderdashed with cyder, corn-spirit, and the juice of sloes. . . . The bread I eat in London, is a deleterious paste, mixed up with chalk, alum, and bone-ashes; insipid to the taste, and destructive to the constitution. The good people are not ignorant of this adulteration; but they prefer it to wholesome bread, because it is whiter than the meal of corn: thus they sacrifice their taste and their health, and the lives of their tender infants, to a most absurd gratification of a mis-judging eye; and the miller, or the baker, is obliged to poison them and their families, in order to live by his profession. The same monstrous depravity appears in their veal, which is bleached by repeated bleedings, and other villainous arts, till there is not a drop of juice left in the body, and the poor animal is paralytic before it dies; so void of all taste, nourishment, and savour, that a man might dine as comfortably on a white fricassee of kid-skin gloves, or chip hats from Leghorn. . . .

Of the fish, I need say nothing in this hot weather, but that it comes sixty, seventy, fourscore, and a hundred miles by land-carriage; a circumstance sufficient, without any comment, to turn a Dutchman's stomach, even if his nose was not saluted in every alley with the sweet flavour of *fresh* mackarel, selling by retail— This is not the season for oysters; nevertheless, it may not be amiss to mention, that the right Colchester are kept in slime-pits, occasionally overflowed by the sea; and that the green colour, so much admired by the voluptuaries of this metropolis, is occasioned by the vitriolic scum, which rises on the surface of the stagnant and stinking water—Our rabbits are bred and fed in the poulterer's cellar, where they have neither air nor exercise, consequently they must be firm in flesh, and delicious in flavour; and there is no game to be had for love or money. [MB, June 8]

To complete his catalog Bramble requires about ten pages of horrors; in Scotland he needs but one succinct paragraph to draw the contrast.

Do you know how we fare in this Scottish paradise? We make

free with our landlord's mutton, which is excellent, his poultry-
yard, his garden, his dairy, and his cellar, which are all well stored.
We have delicious salmon, pike, trout, perch, par, &c. at the door
for the taking. The Frith of Clyde, on the other side of the hill,
supplies us with mullet, red and grey, cod, mackarel, whiting, and
a variety of sea-fish, including the finest fresh herrings I ever tasted.
We have sweet, juicy beef, and tolerable veal, with delicate bread
from the little town of Dunbritton; and plenty of partridge,
growse, heath-cock, and other game in presents. [MB, September
6]

Bramble and Jery themselves draw one conclusion from such juxtapositions: Scotland represents a better because *older* way of living. Refus-
ing to bend to the blasts of fashion from the south, the people and their
institutions have kept fast the best of ancient traditions, remaining
hardy and virile. Jery applauds the refusal of the Scots to accept the
vices of the English, particularly their retention of "regulations of public and private oeconomy, of business and diversion" (JM, August 8).
Bramble admires the Highlands because the "country is amazingly wild.
. . . All is sublimity, silence, and solitude," and its men are admirably
rugged.

When disciplined, they cannot fail of being excellent soldiers. They
do not walk like the generality of mankind, but trot and bounce
like deer, as if they moved upon springs . . . they are incredibly
abstemious, and patient of hunger and fatigue; so steeled against
the weather, that in travelling, even when the ground is covered
with snow, they never look for a house, or any other shelter but
their plaid, in which they wrap themselves up, and go to sleep
under the cope of heaven. Such people, in quality of soldiers, must
be invincible. [MB, September 6]

While the unity of the clans is weakened, the strength of the country
endures, "founded on hereditary regard and affection, cherished through
a long succession of ages." In another scene of sensory demonstration,
Jery and Bramble visit the venerable Dougal Campbell in Argyleshire
and are delighted by a household that is "equally rough and hospitable,
and savours much of the simplicity of ancient times." They are gratified with the best of food, fellowship, music, and other entertainments.
With no meddling Mrs. Burdock about to say nay, they are graciously
invited to stay the night. They are shown to guest quarters while most
of the household retire to beds made of heath. Jery continues, "My
uncle and I were indulged with separate chambers and down beds,
which we begged to exchange for a layer of heath; and indeed I never

slept so much to my satisfaction. It was not only soft and elastic, but the plant, being in flower, diffused an agreeable fragrance, which is wonderfully refreshing and restorative" (JM, September 3).

With Scotland Smollett offers us the simple grandeur of Britain's past, embodied and embraced. (There is of course no room amid such greatness to note the poverty of ordinary Scotsmen.) That past has been in the background throughout, in Bramble's continual reflections upon Brambleton Hall. We need not be shown the estate in Monmouthshire, for we have seen its plenteous image. Scotland is a land of peace and refreshment; Brambleton Hall a retreat beyond retreat, a place of recreation beyond refreshment. Had the novelist sought to emphasize the practicability of an easy return to the past, he might have allowed the party to remain in Scotland or to pass immediately to Wales. Instead he makes Scotland a pivot, not a terminus. His art of contrasts has temporarily balanced Hades with Paradise, but the return journey through hell reminds us that Bramble and his family have not had an escape, merely a holiday. As Pope had it, he who would debase the sons, exalts the sires, and Smollett will balance Dougal Campbell with Oxmington and Mrs. Baynard.[5]

The epitome of Smollett's technical achievement in the novel is his ability successfully to transform matters of mere accidental taste into urgent moral issues. He is able to convince his readers that the bastard tastes of the English middle orders indeed signify falsehood and ignorance in morality, and further that the decline in morality portends the imminent dissolution of British civilization. When Bramble rails against the bleaching of bread, the scandalmongering of the papers, and the promiscuous mixture of classes at Vauxhall, he is particularizing a grievance greater than the sum of its manifestations, a national condition worse than anything he can say about it. And having once demonstrated his lesson, Smollett is able to give it resonance thereafter. After the spas and the capital we assume we have witnessed all possible variants of excess, have numbered all the abominations of desolation. Nevertheless, we are shaken and alarmed as Smollett unfolds the last long episode of the novel.

On September 30, Bramble writes to Lewis that his old friend Baynard is in the country and says, "I would not pass so near his habitation without paying him a visit, though our correspondence had been interrupted for a long course of years." The opportunity to renew his friendship gives Bramble a sense of delightful anticipation: "I felt myself very sensibly affected by the ideas of our past intimacy, as we approached the place where we had spent so many happy days together." Yet before he can set eyes upon his friend, his mood changes from eagerness to apprehension: "but when we arrived at the house, I could

not recognize any one of those objects, which had been so deeply im-
pressed upon my remembrance."

> The tall oaks that shaded the avenue, had been cut down, and the
> iron gates at the end of it removed, together with the high wall
> that surrounded the court yard. The house itself, which was for-
> merly a convent of Cistercian monks, had a venerable appearance;
> and along the front that looked into the garden, was a stone gal-
> lery, which afforded me many an agreeable walk, when I was dis-
> posed to be contemplative—Now the old front is covered with a
> screen of modern architecture; so that all without is Grecian, and
> all within Gothic—As for the garden, which was well stocked with
> the best fruit which England could produce, there is not now the
> least vestige remaining of trees, walls, or hedges—Nothing appears
> but a naked circus of loose sand, with a dry bason and a leaden
> triton in the middle. [MB, September 30]

In six sentences Smollett has unobtrusively recalled the lessons of four
hundred pages: the ubiquitous threat of luxury, the huge gulf between
Old England and the present age, the internal significance of external
signs. (He has also freely translated Horace's famous ode, "Of Luxury.")
Although we are alarmed that contemporary degeneracy has encroached
even within Bramble's circle, we are not surprised to find that Baynard,
though desperate, remains the good, gentle man Bramble knew him to
be. The intrusive agent of the changes in his estate—land, health,
finances—as well as of his present despondency, is his wife. She *has*
ruined her husband, but not in a spirit of gratuitous malice. Rather she
had simply indulged herself with the tastes of the times. In place of
the best fruit England could produce, middle-class taste has yielded
loose sand, a dry bason, and a leaden triton. As the reader's sympathies
are engaged in behalf of the unfortunate Baynard, his memory is recalled to Bramble's continuing verdict: "All these absurdities arise from
the general tide of luxury, which hath overspread the nation, and swept
away all, even the very dregs of the people."

Conclusion

LUXURY AND THE ACHIEVEMENT
OF *HUMPHRY CLINKER*

Examining what he calls the Norman yoke, Christopher Hill provides an apt analogue to the history of luxury. He recalls that the rulers of England had for centuries used the great myths of Western civilization to justify their superiority to an often resentful population. Vigilance was required, however, for the great myths had an unfortunate double-edged quality. They enabled medieval peasant rebels to ask,

> When Adam delved and Eve span
> Who was then the gentleman?

They nonetheless also obliged fourteenth-century bishops to recall the Fall of Man: Paradise could be gained only in heaven, and meanwhile sinfulness justified social inequality and subordination here on earth. When the Levellers asked for the creation of a New Jerusalem, Royalist and Puritan leaders alike spoke of the Tower of Babel—usually with the fall of Athens and Rome added for full measure. In the sixteenth and seventeenth centuries, when reformers insisted upon reclaiming the rights they had lost since the Golden Age, English rulers responded with the myth of primitive Arcadia.[1] For longer than the great myths, the attack upon luxury had served the interests of power and intellect, becoming the vital expression of their impulse to order. Any challenge to the social, political, or economic status quo could be dismissed as by definition a sign of wantonness. If a man wanted something he did not have, or if by chance he got something, he was perforce guilty of luxury. Certainly by the opening of the Christian era, the many different realms of human activity had been comprehended, laws laid down for the basic relationships—between man and woman and within the family, between man and God, and regarding wealth and authority—what the anthropologists term the primal trinity of sex, salvation, and sustenance.

This study has culminated in the attempt to reach and interpret the best-known of Smollett's works by way of some of the least-known. It has sought to understand the novelist's ideas as well as to explain them, to show the relationship that exists among the books of his last two decades, to reveal the personality that informed them, and to analyze that singular blend of genius, talent, and temperament that gives his writing its characteristic value and flavor. At the same time it has tried to be suggestive of an aspect of eighteenth-century thought older, larger, and more portentous than the social and political ideas of a single novelist. Once recognized and understood, Smollett's ideas can be seen to represent the tensions and ambiguities of an important portion of English society. With greater persistence and articulation, the novelist's work reveals the same concentration of attitudes to be found in generations of country gentlemen, politicians, clergymen, courtiers, and writers. What *Humphry Clinker* discloses is not merely a set of ideas, but also a mode or style of thought, a cluster of unspoken philosophic, social values.[2] Intellectually this mode of thought had been at bay from the early 1700s. But because its primary strength was not intellectual, the intellectual challenge was in the short run merely a minor irritation. When the formidable challenges did come—symbolically in 1745, economically in the 1750s, politically from 1763 onward—then the mode of thought clustered about the classical idea of luxury took on the aspect of a besieged garrison. English reformers, with the examples of the American, then French, radicals at hand, discovered that the old myths could be turned against the defenders of traditional privilege, and in 1783 Thomas Spence could claim with confidence that,

> The Golden Age, so fam'd by Men of Yore,
> Shall soon be counted fabulous no more.

Against this New Jerusalem Smollett and many others posed Old England.[3] To give the novelist his place in the currents of English life and thought, however, is in no way to deny the fullness of his achievement in either the nonfictional works or *Humphry Clinker*. Indeed his writings of the 1750s and 1760s in all likelihood represent the single most important body of conservative polemics of his generation. For nearly two decades he had used the classical concept of luxury to express a revulsion against certain aspects of historical change. This sense of the concept, infused into *Humphry Clinker*, was becoming increasingly ineffectual by the time the novel appeared in 1771. It was increasingly difficult, that is, for a ruling elite to demand effort and expansion while simultaneously urging restraint and retrenchment. Even as Smollett was writing in the mid-1760s the contradiction was apparent to many, and the attack upon luxury as a polemic weapon was being turned round by the insurgent middle orders, point blank against its previous aristocratic owners. He and Adam Smith were born but two years and sixty miles apart; yet on this issue they were separated by intellectual continents. In the age of Adam Smith, more nineteenth than eighteenth century, the Aristotelian view of luxury will not hold. When the classical conception was allowed to lapse into obsolescence, so too was the vast intellectual engine that supported it. Spence was premature, and it is too much to say with Burke that Smith had rediscovered God's law. But it is not too much to note that Richard Payne Knight had superseded Xenophon as interpreter of civilized values for Britain. Those values carried with them a tolerance for change and a sense of progress unacceptable to the age of Smollett. They allowed the growth of a different notion of human psychology, in which subjects need no longer be defined entirely by status and function but might be viewed as independent personalities. What had been regarded as devolution might now, under proper circumstances, be seen as evolution: in the lives of human beings, fictional characters, civilizations, and even nature itself. As Ronald Paulson has pointed out, narration now seemed to gain a new sense of purpose, in the pictorial as well as the literary arts.[4] Knight is far better known as the theoretician of the picturesque than as poet of the *Progress of Civil Society;* yet it may be that the two roles are not altogether different.

The attack upon luxury as Smollett used it was well fitted to his social and political pessimism, implicitly containing as it did the notion of a chronologically prior, ideal state. To private men like Bramble, Lismahago, Baynard, and Dennison—without, as the world turns, wealth or power—the struggle to preserve one's character and integrity inevitably led to a poignant sense of loss. To recall the past is not to renew it. Even the happiness of Smollett's ending—in which, to use Paulson's formulation, a missing father is found, lost lovers are united, a paternal estate is reclaimed, and everybody is rewarded—is essentially private and nonsocial. The triple wedding ceremony does not here have the over-tone of universal reconciliation that it has in Shakespeare. Rather, three specific women have subordinated their lives to three particular men; order and reconciliation have been sealed within one family alone. Integrity has not been vindicated in the arena of the great world; it has merely been protected unto another generation. The primary bene-ficiaries and youthful figures of hope—Jery, Liddy and George, Humphry and Win—are nevertheless much more pale and passive in their virtue than their tutors, the aging representatives of an older generation. Though their journey has been long, the young people have rarely earned a positive claim upon our attention. Fielding and Goldsmith use precisely this kind of resolution to express a world of new beginnings and new levels of vitality. Joseph and Fanny, Tom and Sophia, Sir William Thornhill and his Sophia, we must assume, will not permit the vigor of their lives to lapse into rural desuetude. To them the promises of a future England are at least as attractive as the achievements of Old England.

For Smollett the height of these achievements is implied in Bramble-Hall, the hub of the Bramble family's life and the terminus of the party's expedition. Yet in contrast to Paradise Hall or even Grandison Hall, Brambleton Hall is evanescent and abstract. Its characteristics are primarily negative, the negation of those of London. Its air is not pol-luted, its waters not stinking, its paths not clamorous, its veal not blanched, its bread not adulterated, its beer not sophisticated. Smol-lett's vision of genuine worth did not project an *alternative* society—as one in which charity should conquer selfishness. Rather he posited the values of an *earlier* society—one where life was simpler and where order, station, and identity were more firmly established and respected. (It is also, like Brambleton Hall, a world over which Matthew Bramble has undisputed sway.) In this retrospective search for a unified world, a better world we have squandered, *Humphry Clinker* anticipates such works as Carlyle's *Past and Present,* James's *The American Scene,* and Henry Adams's *Mont-Saint-Michel.*

The better world Smollett appealed to is at heart the world of in-herited rights: where the highest ranks of a society have exclusive responsibility for determining the nature of the good, where the laws of nature and the laws of tradition are regarded as synonymous, and where social position fixes one's activities and aspirations. In practice, the ethos of inherited rights was associated with that of inherited wealth, when land was the most important and lucrative real property. But as we have seen, land and the system of thought that supported it had lost their absolute supremacy by the time Smollett had reached his majority. The realities of wealth had changed substantially, and land was in many ways already less profitable than commerce. Mercantile economic theory exhausted itself when its categories of value became incapable of transformation, and the traditional condemnation of luxury degenerated into the scholastic, in the pejorative sense. That at least some educated laymen were aware of these changes in the 1750s is indicated by the essays of Hume and Johnson. Although politically conservative, each was aware that the past could not be preserved intact, that effective conservatism was also selective. Johnson's review of Soame Jenyns is a classic statement of the newer sensibility: the famous passage rejecting the utility of pain and misery indeed represents an almost revolutionary change in English sensibility.

The traditional concept of luxury accepted pain and misery as a permanent feature of the lives of the great majority of humankind. Smollett's attitude toward the English common people likewise carried an acceptance of their suffering and dispossession. His letters, especially those to Alexander Hume Campbell and Caleb Whitefoord, reveal an ardent claim to the rank of gentleman. In this respect he was like Dickens. But whereas Dickens upon attaining fame came increasingly to identify himself with the class below him, Smollett continued to aspire upward, identifying his interests with those of the men he considered the natural leaders of Britain. For most of his life Dickens was financially secure, but to his death Smollett was never so. To the gentlemen Smollett created, luxury is a many-sided threat. With its vulgarity and prostitution luxury undermines grace, hospitality, and fine manners. On a deeper level it directly threatens the material possessions upon which refinement is built. Deeper yet, it attacks the very ground upon which refinement and wealth are based: the ancient principles of necessity and hierarchy, summarized in the supposition that certain people have exclusive claim to the better things of life. It is perhaps one of the larger ironies of English and Scottish literary history that the Whig principles Smollett opposed so long and so vigorously should within the space of two generations stand as the foundation of the Tory Reaction. Smollett might not have noted the essential kinship between Bramble and the hero of the Waverley novels. The insolent Whigs of the City could never gain the breeding Smollett demanded, but they could very soon acquire the property.[5]

The terms of opposition in the novel are thus more varied and comprehensive than the city–country, Whig–Tory, England–Scotland contrasts in which they are usually conceived. Like his creations Bramble, Baynard, and Dennison, Smollett was educated by the city, and his journalistic career of a decade is testimony to the conviction that the future of Britain was to be determined, for good or ill, in the metropolis on the Thames. His tributes to Welsh country life are largely negative, to that of England stock, and to that of Scotland only slightly less perfunctory. What is more, he *does* praise urban life and urban commerce in Scotland, where social controls have not been relaxed. From one point of view the spirit of *Humphry Clinker* could be called Tory. Such a label would be adequate as far as it goes, but it would not go very far at all. For Smollett was interested in partisan politics only as a means, and the *Atom* makes clear that by the end of the 1760s no party or group approached his ideal of virtue. After 1763, it seems, he sought nothing so pedestrian as a new election, but a new and political reformation that would rid Britain root and branch of modernist influences. The spirit he wished to invoke through Bramble was of longer standing even than England. Among the Roman elements of the novel could be counted a reverence for Terminus, the god of bounds whom Ovid praised as the most admirable of Roman deities. It is a work into which he would pour everything of importance, but with every thing in proper place and proportion.

For the purposes of this study, the most significant contrast in *Humphry Clinker* is not between city and country, England and Scotland, or Mrs. Baynard and Mrs. Dennison. Instead it is the contrast between Smollett's own voices in the novel: Bramble and Mr. S——. On June 8 Bramble tells Lewis at great length why he will be pleased to quit London, asking "what is the society of London, that I should be tempted, for its sake, to mortify my senses, and compound with such uncleanness as my soul abhors?" And later, "Thank Heaven! I am not so far sucked into the vortex, but that I can disengage without any great effort of philosophy." Juxtaposed with Bramble's diatribe is Jery's long letter of June 10, in which he describes the obvious satisfaction Mr. S—— derives from life, especially literary life, in the capital. Encircled by entertaining and secretly admiring dependents (but no Mrs. S——), S—— rules benevolently and creates in his home in Chelsea one of the few places of positive value in England. For S—— London is the only possible cantonment, both a universe unto itself and a window from which to view the rest of creation. Smollett is the most urban of the five major novelists of the century—even more so than Defoe or Fielding in *Amelia*—and his final work is more engaged with the characteristics of urban life than any other major novel. If in his last years he should have been of two minds about the city and found means to project both onto the pages of *Humphry Clinker,* we have already seen some of the possible causes for ambivalence. Men of letters like Smollett and Mr. S—— could regard London as their proper habitat, the locus of wit, judgment, culture. Adamant traditionalists like Smollett and Bramble could regard it as barren ground, a once-proud haven ravaged by inferior men who befouled it and opened it to others more wretched than themselves. Charged with the social and intellectual history of its time, Smollett's *summa mundi, Humphry Clinker* summons up inventories of both aspects of the metropolis, perhaps more important to him at the end of his life, when he had abandoned it.

In Smollett the secondary world of imagination is always interpenetrated by the primary world of observation, and at many places in *Humphry Clinker* the two are almost indistinguishable. The commonplace about referential language in the novel takes on a further dimension in his last work. Whereas Fielding seeks to present fictions more complete and satisfying than disorderly reality could ever be, Smollett wishes to compel attention, which can be gained no other way, to the wretched condition of the phenomenal world. It is the difference, in our time, between Ralph Ellison and Richard Wright. Attempting ever to say complicated things straightforwardly, Smollett renders intensity of consciousness differently but no less fully than Sterne. The mediation of his many "originals" like Lismahago and Win works to heighten, not undermine, the seriousness of his moral—anticipating in practice an aesthetic theory that would absorb Dickens's generation. While a virulent attack upon luxury, the novel is framed by the letters of Dustwich and Davis, Tabby and Win. While providing all the refinements of moral judgment called for by Johnson in the *Rambler* no. 4, it also satisfies the demands of travel narrative, burlesque, domestic comedy, social satire, and comic romance. While written by a weakened, disappointed, dying man, it exudes vigor, vitality, and unquenchable spirit. While a portrait of social tragedy, it has for generations seemed one of the brightest of English comedies. While centered on the sensibility of a single character, it possesses the largest cast of memorable figures between Fielding and Dickens.

Smollett, it seems, was like his seasoned men, most himself when under duress, his gifts of fancy most engaged when most required. A mixture of the Rabelaisian and the rabbinical, he was prepared equally to laugh or to shame people free of what he considered absurd infatuations. In the course of the novel his gifts serve complementary functions: to expose injustice and to raise laughter. The scenes of England he gives us are disturbing and demoralizing; yet the retributive comedy he supplies is stabilizing, rejuvenating. It carries respite from the outrage of very real grievance. At Bath, for example, Bramble is mortified to find three of his old friends—Rear-Admiral Balderick, Colonel Cockril, and Sir Reginald Bentley—reduced to shells of men, overtopped by mere upstarts, and left to a cold day's dying. Yet our indignation at these injustices is controlled by a scene in immediate counterpoint. In the general tea-drinking at Bath, we are shown that upstarts and pretenders to fortune are shabby and disgraceful, sufficiently punished by their own absurdity. Instances of personal injustice abound in Smollett's narrative. Dr. Linden imposes his pretentious nonsense upon the gullible at Hot Well. Tabby mistrusts her brother's goodness to the mother at Bath and to the foundling, Humphry Clinker. Mrs. Burdock and her son attempt to have the squire needlessly trepanned. Mickle-whimmen, the Scots lawyer, delights in gross and dangerous practical jokes. Dutton seeks to entice Win from Humphry. Lord Oxmington and his lackeys seek gratuitously to humiliate Bramble and Lismahago. Although each of these incidents reflects the overarching callousness and deceit obtaining in Britain, each is resolved in a fresh gust of retributive laughter.

As the earlier *Briton* and *Travels* attest, Smollett's years of writing against the progress of national luxury provided him with abundant insight into the luxurious person as comic type. In *Humphry Clinker* observation and facility yielded a deftness of touch able to mark age, rank, and disposition in a few strokes of concentrated detail. He is able in one short scene to convince us that Newcastle is indeed a senile old fool and a political liability for any age—everything, that is, that Bramble has said he is. The reader is left more in wonder than resentment that the old duke should ever have held great power. Smollett's humor has therefore fulfilled its social function. The degeneration of his contemporaries has been rendered more visible by his skill and fancy. The fruits of luxury are shown to be absurd, and the absurd ought to be laughed at. Smollett's laughter is cathartic: it furnishes a release from the strains of living in a decadent society. Its audience is taught to distinguish the plate of marmalade from the pan of sirreverence, to honor the one and disdain the other. As tragedy and comedy are not actual opposites, so the deep disgust of the *Atom* is not antithetical to the hearty humor of *Humphry Clinker:* they are two sides of one coin.

Appendix

THE *BRITON* NO. 26

20 November 1762

The sauciness of servants is now become an epidemical evil. Go where you will, you hear nothing but complaints of them: but methinks, the case of one Mr. Fitz-George deserves particular notice and commiseration. This young gentleman, it seems, came to the possession of a plentiful estate, about two years ago, by the death of his grandfather. Being a humane, generous, good-natured man, he suffered most of the servants who were in the house in his grandfather's time to continue; and as for the few whom he found it prudent to part with, he gave them pensions for life. Mr. Fitz-George enjoyed his house and family with great peace and comfort for about a twelve-month, when one Will Pitot (for so I think they called him by way of nickname) gave his master warning in a great passion. People were very much surprised at this as they knew Will had had a very good place of it. But Will himself soon unfolded the mystery, by publishing a letter, in which he told us, that he had given his master warning, because he was not allowed to rule his master and the whole house. Many of the tenants of the manor were not sorry for

Will's leaving his place; for they say, that though he had been very zealous in maintaining the rights of the manor, yet he had such a number of over-seas acquaintances, to whom he sent presents out of the manor, that he some years laid out the whole rents upon them, which were about six millions. This the tenants murmured at very much; for in consequence of this, their Lord was obliged to raise their rents every year to maintain his house, and supply the exigencies of the manor, even to the amount, they say, of twelve millions a year some-times. This they reckoned very hard, as they had nothing to do with, nor received any advantage by, these acquaintances of Will's. And this they looked upon as the more unaccountable still, because Will, when he was an out-door servant, had exclaimed most bitterly against the servants before him, who had followed these practices, though they had never spent the half of the money upon their foreign acquaintances, that Will did upon his. But what provoked them most of all was, that they had helped Will to the place, merely with a view that he might break the neck of these things; and then they found, that instead of this, he increased them. But Will was a strange sort of fellow, and had got some peculiar notions of oeconomicks; for what was wrong when done by another, he thought right when done by himself. Nay, when he heard some whispers through the manor with respect to these things, after he left his place, he told the tenants in the letter already men-tioned, that indeed he should give himself no trouble to sollicit the return of their favour. This they considered as worse than all the rest, first to deceive them, and then to bid them defiance; but Will knew what he was saying, for, he had somehow or other, got an annuity for three lives.

Things continued in this posture about half a year, when another servant, who had lived long in the house, and been kindly used, I think his name was Tom Give-place, or Buy-vote, I don't know which, took it into his head to give his master warning also, unless he would double his wages. This was thought to be a very odd proposal, as Tom was now far advanced in years, and almost past his labour. The case, it seems, was this; money was wanted in the office to which Tom belonged; application was made to Mr. Fitz-George for it. He asked how much would do for such a time. Tom answered two millions. Mr. Fitz-George (as the money was to be raised upon his tenants) was willing to be as gentle to them as possible; he therefore asked some of his other servants, whether a less sum would not suffice; they replied, that, considering the burden the tenants had lain under for a great while, they thought one million was as much as they could in conscience demand of them, and that, with good management, would do very well; or if it would not hold out till the time proposed, their Lord might make a second demand when it was found necessary. Tom, taking this much amiss, left his place. Upon this, a great many of the out-door servants, raised a clamour, as they had done in Will's case before. The reason was, that Will had often cajoled some of them by saying, he liked their livery, *viz.* an alderman's-gown, better than his own, tho' he only played on them; so Tom had often employed others of them in jobbs about the house, for which he had every now and then given them a bit of a sop. This they were afraid they would now lose, and therefore mouth'd very undeservedly both against the master and the new servant he put in Tom's place. They objected that he was a stranger, though both he and his progenitors had belonged to the manor for several centuries; and long before some of themselves were so much as heard of in it. When this could not be denied, they then urged that he was however born on the northern part of the manor, and themselves in the southern or western; to this it was rationally enough answered, that the northern part belonged to the manor as well as the southern; and to prevent all objections of that kind for the future, proposed that the manor-house should be built exactly in the middle of the estate, and then the tenants would be all equally near it, according to their respective divisions. When they found therefore that these objections were treated only with ridicule by the opposite party, and people who had taken no side, they then trumped up a story, that he was not qualified for the place, because he did not know the way of the house. To this it was replied, If they meant the former way of it, they were undoubtedly right; for it was allowed, that formerly there had been a great deal of waste and profusion in it; but if they meant a way which would be most advantageous, both to the master and the tenants, they were mistaken, for he understood that as well as any man; and as a proof of it, they urged, that it was now plain from fact, that he had done the same service for one million, for which Tom (as mentioned above) had demand'd two. This new servant's name, I find, was Jack Scot, and related, they say, to Mr. Fitz-George's family. This fellow, it seems, had been much addicted to reading, which gave him something of the college, together with the court air. However, it made him master of a good deal of polite and useful literature, which afforded a handle to some to upbraid him with learned disquisitions upon cockle-shells, plants and flowers: and others, whose genius could not soar so high as this happy flight, came nevertheless very near it, by the curious invention of the name Jack-a-boot, which, it seems, they struck out by an uncommon effort of wit, from a titular name his family had long borne.

All these objections operated wonderfully upon many sensible people, both without and within the house; for one Harry Chamberman soon after gave his master warning likewise. Harry, we hear, had absented himself from his service for some time past; his master advertised him twice, but to no effect. However, whether of his own accord, or in consequence of a third advertisement, is not material, Harry did return; but it appears it was not to ask his master's pardon, or to apologize for what he had done, but to let him know he would serve him no longer. So Harry gave up his livery, and after dining with an old acquaintance, viz. Tom Give-place, went down to his friends in the country. In consequence of this, one Charley Check, whose business in the house was to see that the cooks, and other servants, put nothing to waste, gave Mr. Fitz-George warning also; the reason, they say, was not want of victuals, ill-paid wages, or being over-wrought, but that, being a relation of Harry Chamberman's, he would not stay in the house after he was gone. The same, we hear, was the case of one Peter Post-boy. His office was to carry his master's letters to and fro; but tho' his master paid him very liberally for it, kept him always in good livery, and never made him go in dark nights, yet he has given him warning too. Such is the way this young gentleman has been used by his servants; so that people of lower rank need not wonder if they are ill-used by theirs. Which of them have taken the example of the other, I cannot tell; but as to the designs of Mr. Fitz-George's servants in acting so, people seem to be universally agreed, that they want to force every body else out of the house, and to have the whole of it to themselves, and such as they shall put it. Whether Mr. Fitz-George will thus give up his house to them or no, no body as yet pretends to say. Many of the tenants heartily wish he would not; for they think it is a shame they should be so presumptuous: but however these things may be, there are two or three foolish curs, commonly called Monitor, North-Briton, Patriot, &c. but I understand their true name is Yelper, and all of one litter, who post themselves in dark corners, and snarl in an angry manner, both at Mr. Fitz-George, and his new servants, whenever they pass by; but when any of the old ones happen to come in their way they fawn, and lick their feet most wishfully, particularly Will Pitot's, tho' he has been longest out of the house. Whether Will had been kind to them while he was in it, by throwing them a little bone now and then, or whether they wanted to bespeak his favour beforehand, in case he should chance to come into it again, or whether they had something of an inbred antipathy against Scot, can't be certainly determined. Some are of opinion that there is a mixture of all three: be that as it will, Mr. Fitz-George and his servants, have hitherto gone out and in about their business, without taking any notice of them, because, I suppose, they don't think them worth their while.

This is the best and fullest account I can give you of this matter at present; but if you want further information about it, perhaps one

Charles Say, a news-man, or his eldest brother, may be able to satisfy you. These gentlemen have generally very early intelligence, with respect to what passes in Mr. Fitz-George's family, and one of them let us know the other day, that there is talk of seventeen more of that gentleman's servants going to give him warning. Whether this is true or false, time only can discover. But it is thought, if they should do so, Mr. Fitz-George will be in no difficulty to supply their places, as there are many in all parts of the manor who would be glad to serve him.

NOTES

INTRODUCTION

1. See, for example, the articles on luxury in the *Encyclopedia of Religion and Ethics,* ed. James Hastings (New York, 1916); *Encyclopedia of Social Sciences,* ed. E. R. A. Seligman (New York, 1954-59); *International Encyclopedia of the Social Sciences,* ed. David L. Sills (New York, 1968); *Dictionary of the History of Ideas,* ed. Philip P. Wiener (New York, 1973); and *Encyclopedia Britannica,* 15th ed. (Chicago, 1974).

2. In addition, he produced a seven-volume edition, *Compendium of Authentic and Entertaining Voyages,* in 1756, and a thirty-five-volume English edition of the works of Voltaire in 1765.

3. Roger Ascham, *The Whole Works of Roger Ascham,* ed. J. A. Giles (London, 1864), 3:153, 159. The discussion of luxury appears in 3:148-67.

4. Henry Fielding, *Enquiry into the Cause of the late Increase of Robbers* (London, 1751), p. 3.

5. Since 1800 approximately four hundred books and articles have appeared that discuss luxury in one connection or another. The usual context is of course the history of Rome. Three examples will suffice. Morris Bishop recounts the traditional causes assigned for the fall of Rome, among them "the moral answer: license, luxury, a decline in character and in discipline" (*The Middle Ages* [New York, 1970], p. 3). Crane Brinton provides a list of the ordinary daily luxuries of wealthy Romans: boasting, gambling, gluttony, drunkenness, sexual license, ostentatious display, and conspicuous consumption (*A History of Western Morals* [New York, 1959], pp. 114-17). W. E. H. Lecky, on the other hand, emphasizes the more extraordinary luxuries: the mutilation and crucifixation of house slaves to gratify the sadism of guests (*History of European Morals from Augustus to Charlemagne,* 3d ed. [1889; reprinted New York, 1955], 1:302-3). Even so profound a classical scholar—and one to whom I am in so great debt—as M. I. Finley conceives of luxury in modern terms. See his *Ancient Economy* (Berkeley and Los Angeles, 1973), e.g., p. 60. And to note that this conception is not limited to the world of

English-speaking scholars, see Paul Louis, *Ancient Rome at Work: An Economic History of Rome from the Origins to the Empire,* trans. E. B. F. Wareing (1929; reprinted London, 1965), pp. 126–30, 234–36. Some of the major works of scholarship on Rome argue with ample documentation that early views of Roman luxury are absurdly exaggerated. That is, they contest the conventional estimate but not the conventional definition of luxury. Among these are Ludwig Friedlander, *Roman Life and Manners under the Early Empire,* trans. J. H. Freese (1909; reprinted New York, 1968), 2:131–230; J. E. Sandys, *A History of Classical Scholarship,* 3rd ed. (Cambridge, 1920), esp. vols. 1 and 2; M. Rostovtzeff, *The Social and Economic History of the Hellenistic World,* 3 vols. (Oxford, 1941), passim; and Theodor Mommsen, *The History of Rome,* trans. William Purdie Dickson, 5 vols. (New York, 1900), passim.

Economic studies that use luxury to mean exorbitant spending are represented by E. J. Urwick, *Luxury and the Waste of Life* (London, 1908); R. I. MacBride, *Luxury as a Social Standard* (New York, 1915); Werner Sombart, *Luxury and Capitalism* (German ed., 1913), trans. W. R. Dittmar (Ann Arbor, 1967); and Emile De Laveleye, *Luxury* (London, 1891). Only two studies have attempted to view the concept historically—one directly, the other obliquely—and both assume the modern definition. H. Baudrillart, in his four-volume *Histoire du luxe privé et public, depuis l'antiquité jusqu'à nos jours,* 2d ed. (Paris, 1880–81), provides an informal but wide-ranging survey of ostentation in food, dress, building, and domestic arrangements. He finds the sources of luxury in the universal traits of vanity and sensuality. The controversy over it he discovers in the tension between two schools of ethical theory. One, typified by Rousseau, would prohibit all ostentation on moral grounds; the other, represented by Voltaire, would encourage it on economic grounds. By the final volume his historical goal is clear: he seeks to account for the French Revolution by contrasting the private opulence of eighteenth-century France with its public squalor. In *Primitivism and Related Ideas in Antiquity* (Baltimore, 1935), Arthur O. Lovejoy and George Boas note luxury several times as one of the ideas related to their central concern. Regarding primitivism they do proceed sensitively and historically. But they are committed to the search for but *one* unknown and therefore are impelled to treat luxury logically, as at all times and in all places the obverse of primitivism. They are unable with such an approach even to hint at the religious and political dimensions of luxury.

6. Even within the limited context of a single century, estimates of its significance vary widely. Leslie Stephen writes, "The cant of the day used the phrase 'luxury,' and luxury was admitted on all hands, to consist in a departure from the simplicity of nature" (*History of English Thought in the Eighteenth Century,* 3d ed., 2 vols. [London, 1902], chap. 10, 69). Duncan Forbes calls luxury one of the most familiar clichés of the time (introduction to Adam Ferguson, *An Essay on the History of Civil Society* [Edinburgh, 1966], p. xxxi). Hume's biographer, Ernest C. Mossner, takes it to mean simple consumption (*Life of David Hume* [Austin, Tex., 1954], p. 270). Maynard Mack, in *The Poet and the City* (Toronto, 1969), p. 199 n, uses it as nearly synonymous with greed. James William Johnson terms it "economic prosperity and cultural affluence" in *The Formation of English Neo-Classical Thought* (Princeton, 1967), p. 48. See also F. B. Kaye's introduction to *The Fable of the Bees* (Oxford, 1924), 1:xciv–xcvii; and Susie I. Tucker, *Protean Shape* (London, 1967), esp. pp. 82–83, 137–69.

Those studies that mention or discuss the concept with most respect tend to do so within narrow and specialized limits: as in studies of population, crime, European trade, mercantile theory, the decline of religion, the development of law, and the position of the laborer. Among the more prominent examples are: J. H. Plumb, *The Growth of Political Stability in England, 1675–1725* (London, 1967); Elizabeth Gilboy, *Wages in Eighteenth Century England* (Cambridge, Mass., 1934); André Morizé, *L'apologie du luxe au XVIIIᵉ siècle* (Paris, 1909); Edgar Furniss, *The Position of the Laborer in a System of Nationalism* (New York, 1920); Jacob Viner, *Studies in the Theory of International Trade* (London, 1937); Eli Heckscher, *Mercantilism,* trans. Mendel Shapiro, 2d ed. 2 vols. (London, 1955); E. A. J. Johnson, *Predecessors of Adam Smith* (New York, 1937); Philip Buck, *The Politics of Mercantilism* (New York, 1942); and A. W. Coats, "Changing Attitudes to Labour in the Mid-Eighteenth Century," *Economic History Review,* 2d ser., 11 (1958–59): 35–51. The one paragraph M. Dorothy George devotes to the idea in *London Life in the Eighteenth Century* (London, 1925), p. 14, is representative of the approach of such studies and also to the broadest generalization available:

Then, there was in the latter part of the eighteenth century, as in most times of social change, a general cry of national deterioration. This is based largely on two ideas, one, the terrible effects of increasing luxury, as seen for instance, in the nabob, or the lamp-lighter with silk stockings or the labourer's family consuming tea and sugar. The other is the decline of what Defoe called the Great Law of Subordination, a theory of course much stimulated by the fears of Jacobinism roused by the French Revolution. Though connected with opposite schools of thought, the two ideas merged; the well-dressed lamp-lighter for instance might be regarded as a symbol of either of the two great causes of degeneration.

A few studies of Smollett have noted his use of the concept, but usually in passing. Like most recent scholars, M. A. Goldberg follows Lovejoy and Boas in regarding luxury as the antithesis of primitivism. In *Smollett and the Scottish School* (Albuquerque, 1959), pp. 146-53, Goldberg associates the novelist with the moderate reformers Kames, Robertson, Ferguson, and others. Taking a different tack, David Bruce (*Radical Dr. Smollett* [New York, 1964], pp. 111-14) sees Smollett's opinions as those of a Radical Whig but offers no evidence. The most perceptive commentary appears in Byron Gassman, "The Background of Tobias Smollett's *The Expedition of Humphry Clinker*," diss., University of Chicago, 1960, p. 68. Gassman argues that Smollett's use of luxury is part of a pastoral tradition of opposition between city and country, a tradition that includes Pope, Fielding, and Goldsmith as well as Smollett. This approach reveals some notable similarities among literary figures but leaves the novel unrelated to Smollett's previous writings and to the social and political history of which they are a significant part. Finally, Lewis Knapp and André Parreaux follow Gassman in their respective introductions to the novel. Parreaux contrasts Bramble's "town grievances" with his "country comforts" (introduction to *The Expedition of Humphry Clinker* [Boston, 1968], pp. xxv-xxvi). And Knapp writes, "Another seemingly personal motif in *Humphry Clinker* is a strong love of the virtues of country life as opposed to the socially corrupting luxury and affluence of urban existence" (introduction to *The Expedition of Humphry Clinker* [New York, 1966], p. xiv).

7. Herbert Read, "Tobias Smollett," in his *Reason and Romanticism* (London, 1926), p. 192.

8. James L. Clifford, introduction to *The Adventures of Peregrine Pickle* (London, 1964), pp. xxviii-xxix.

9. Alan D. McKillop, *The Early Masters of English Fiction* (Lawrence, Kans., 1956), pp. 174-75.

10. W. H. Auden, *Forewords and Afterwords* (New York, 1973), p. 111.

11. This distinction has been made many times—to cite only works from this century—from Leslie Stephen's *English Literature and Society in the Eighteenth Century* (London, 1904) to Walter Jackson Bate's *From Classic to Romantic* (Cambridge, Mass., 1946) and Peter Gay's *The Enlightenment: An Interpretation*, 2 vols. (New York, 1966, 1969).

12. Also according to Johnson, the artist was "the interpreter of Nature and the legislator of mankind" who would preside "over the thoughts and manners of future generations" and "superintend the taste and Morals of Mankind." Johnson's emphasis upon the moral and the general is familiar to students of the century and is treated at length in René Wellek, *A History of Modern Criticism* (New Haven, 1955), 1:79-104; Bate, *The Achievement of Samuel Johnson* (New York, 1955); Jean H. Hagstrum, *Samuel Johnson's Literary Criticism* (Chicago, 1952); and Paul Fussell, *Samuel Johnson and the Life of Writing* (New York, 1971).

13. Jacob Viner, "Satire and Economics in the Augustan Age of Satire," in *The Augustan Milieu: Essays Presented to Louis A. Landa*, ed. Henry Knight Miller, Eric Rothstein, and G. S. Rousseau (Oxford, 1970), p. 86; see also pp. 87, 90-101.

14. Reviewing Viner's essay, Bernhard Fabian notes that at present eighteenth-century scholarship cannot explain the phenomena Viner discloses. He says further, "What is alarming about Viner's statements is that in the face of so much scholarship on satire he should find the satiric territory inadequately mapped by the literary historian and, moreover, many modern studies so esoteric as to be of limited value" (*ECS* 7 [1973-74]: 114).

15. Most literary studies of Smollett are silent on this period. The exacting ones are Gassman, "*The Briton* and *Humphry Clinker*," *SEL* 3 (1963): 397-414; and Robert Donald Spector, *English Literary Periodicals* (The Hague, 1966), pp. 95-99. For the remainder, Knapp, Fred W. Boege, and McKillop are representative. In his biography *Tobias Smollett, Doctor of Men and*

Manners (Princeton, 1949), p. 245, Knapp passes over the *Briton* as so much "vexation and drudgery" for which Smollett "was temperamentally unfitted." Boege writes: "Of Smollett's next literary undertakings, the editing of the *British Magazine* and the *Briton*, little needs to be said. The first seems to have gained him a firm friend in Goldsmith . . . the second cost him a good friend, John Wilkes, and his affiliation with Bute's administration was surely not designed to make him more popular. But his unhappy venture into political journalism had no direct effect on the fortunes of his novels" (*Smollett's Reputation as a Novelist* [Princeton, 1947], p. 23). McKillop states the conventional opinion in one sentence: "He was unfortunately involved in politics, and published the *Briton* (1762-63) in support of Bute's administration" (*Early Masters,* pp. 174-75).

It is true that at least twice in the late 1760s Smollett did complain of his earlier polemical efforts; yet his regret was, I believe, directed not toward the labor itself but toward its hostile reception. In any case, my argument is that, fortunate or not, he had been involved in politics long before 1762, and that social and political themes preoccupied his writings for most of the last two decades of his life. See his letter to William Hunter, 24 February 1767, in *Letters,* ed. Knapp (Oxford, 1970), pp. 132-33.

16. This is the view expressed in almost all histories of the novel; it can be traced from Thackeray through Saintsbury, Wilbur L. Cross, and Ernest A. Baker to Walter Allen, Lionel Stevenson, and others. It also informs the more specialized studies of Knapp, Parreaux, and McKillop. The most important demurrer is Paul-Gabriel Boucé, *Les romans de Smollett* (Paris, 1971), pp. 248-98.

17. Read, *Reason and Romanticism,* p. 192.

18. *Whitehall Evening-Post,* 15-18 June, 18-20 June, 22-25 June 1771; *Town and Country Magazine* 3 (1771): 317, 319, 327; the *Weekly Magazine; or, Edinburgh Amusement* 13 (1771): 76, 105, 272; *Edinburgh Advertiser,* 9-12 July, 16-19 July, 22-25 October 1771; *Hibernian Magazine* 1 (1771): 324.

19. *Universal Magazine of Knowledge and Pleasure* 49 (1771): 256; *Gentleman's Magazine* 40 (1771): 317.

20. Jonathan D. Culler, *Structuralist Poetics: Structuralism, Linguistics and the Study of Literature* (Ithaca, 1975), pp. 189-238, esp. pp. 192-93. The antiformalist position is stated more emphatically by David Caute throughout his *The Illusion: An Essay on Politics, Theatre and the Novel* (London, 1971), esp. pp. 23-25, 241-67. Caute holds that "the novel remains to this day an extremely fluid, open-ended literary form, sharing a lot and borrowing a lot from history, biography, philosophy, journalism, as well as other art forms like the drama and the cinema. This whore-like, open-legged personality is both a charm and a virtue of the novel; but the illusionists, the refiners and polishers, the magicians and conjurors, the mimetic realists and the salesmen of empathy, the hidden Gods—they would all have us believe that our coarse and rugged courtesan is in fact a porcelain princess without debts or duties" (pp. 264-65).

21. Ezra Pound, *How to Read* (1931; reprinted New York, 1971), p. 22.

22. This middle ground is coincident with Smollett's attitudes toward government and the desired organization of English society. Hence in chapters 4-6 I attempt a tentative outline of his political view during the final portion of his career. Such an outline, however incomplete, is needed because of a persistent confusion over his political ideas and because of the integral relationship between them and his concept of luxury.

As a sampling of comments on Smollett's political position, the following are notable and representative: (1) Smollett himself, writing of his labors on the *Complete History,* said, "I have kept myself independent of all Connexions which might have affected the Candour of my Intention . . . I have cultivated no Party." The statement appeared in a letter to William Huggins and is quoted in L. F. Powell, "William Huggins and Tobias Smollett," *MP* 34 (1936): 185. (2) The *Critical Review,* 6 (September 1758): 226-39, repeatedly asserts that the novelist is attached to neither party and is independent of both. (3) Scott, in his *Lives of Eminent Novelists and Dramatists* (London, n.d.), pp. 451-52, calls Smollett a moderate Tory and a monarchist. (4) Saintsbury, in his introduction to *Sir Launcelot Greaves* (London, 1895), calls him a Whig; but in the introduction to *Peregrine Pickle* in the same edition he says he has a Tory bent. (5) In his *Autobiography* (Edinburgh, 1860), p. 191, Alexander Carlyle says Smollett was unmistakably a Tory. (6) Thomas Seccombe, in his edition of the *Works* (Westminster,

1899–1901), 12:xiv, writes, "Smollett is clearly a political Ishmael, who has severed his ties with all parties." (7) Louis L. Martz, *Later Career of Tobias Smollett* (New Haven, 1942), p. 131, implies that he was politically ambivalent if not uncommitted. (8) In his biography, *Tobias Smollett,* pp. 303–4, Knapp holds that Smollett began the *Complete History* as a Whig but converted to the Tory point of view as he began to uncover the corruption of earlier Whig ministries. This contention is repeated in Laurence Brander, *Tobias Smollett* (London, 1951), p. 9; and Robert Gorham Davis's introduction to *Humphry Clinker* (New York, 1952), p. xv. (9) Goldberg opens his book, p. 3, with the assertion, "Smollett's political position is equally ambiguous and contradictory." (10) Bruce, throughout his book, finds the novelist's position to be that of a radical Whig. (11) Robert Donald Spector, in *Tobias Smollett* (New York, 1968), pp. 29, 33, finds him a conservative Tory. (12) Boucé (p. 50) notes the reception of his histories: "Ses critiques lui reprochaient une certaine partialité pour les "Tories," sa haine des "Whigs" et ses tendances jacobites."

23. Barbara Hardy, *The Exposure of Luxury: Radical Themes in Thackeray* (London, 1972). Significantly for my argument, Hardy does not attempt to define luxury but cites its usual associations in Thackeray: "rank, class, trade, commerce, money, insincerity and artifice, the corruptions of hospitality, fellowship and love . . . corrupt relations and values shown in object-worship and conspicuous consumption" (pp. 13–14). That is, while assuming a meaning quite different from Smollett's, Thackeray in the nineteenth century and Hardy in the twentieth use the same method of discussion—association—as Smollett used in the eighteenth.

24. William Makepeace Thackeray, *The Four Georges* (London, 1901), p. 63. Future references to this work will be to the same edition and will be given in the text.

25. Thackeray here tends to support one of Smollett's main contentions but contests another. While the latter may have agreed that the eighteenth century as a whole was probably the last period of patrician dominance, he would have said that his own lifetime—four-fifths of which coincided with the reign of George II—marked the time of visible vulgarization of English life.

CHAPTER ONE

1. Robert Graves and Raphael Patai, *Hebrew Myths: The Book of Genesis* (1963; reprinted New York, 1966), pp. 70–81; Louis Ginzberg, *The Legends of the Jews,* trans. Henrietta Szold (Philadelphia, 1909), 1:64–83; John Skinner, *A Critical and Exigetical Commentary on Genesis* (New York, 1900); Gerhard von Rad, *Genesis, A Commentary,* trans. John H. Marks (Philadelphia, 1961). A general treatment of women as tempter-victim is contained in H. R. Hays, *The Dangerous Sex: The Myth of Feminine Evil* (New York, 1964). More specialized are two works by Joseph Epstein: *Marriage Laws in the Bible and Talmud* (Cambridge, Mass., 1942), and *Sex Laws and Customs in Judaism* (New York, 1948); and J. J. Bachofen, *Myth, Religion and Mother Right,* trans. Ralph Manheim (Princeton, 1967). The belief in "Eve's curse" can be observed in a chronological and intellectual spectrum ranging from ancient Jewish law to the code of contemporary pimps. According to the latter, Adam was not the first man, but the first *trick* or fool; and women must continually be regulated by physical force. See Christina and Richard Milner, *Black Players: The Secret Life of Black Pimps* (Boston, 1972), chap. 6.

2. To understand the Hebrew conception of history I have drawn upon George W. Anderson, *The History and Religion of Israel* (London, 1966); C. F. North, *The Old Testament Interpretation of History* (London, 1946); and especially Johannes Pedersen, *Israel: Its Life and Culture,* 2 vols. (London, 1954). For Calvin and other later commentators, another basic text for the condemnation of luxury was Isaiah 2; see *Calvin: Commentaries,* trans. Joseph Haroutunian (Philadelphia, 1958), pp. 350–51.

The Deuteronomic sense of accursedness was often transposed to seventeenth- and eighteenth-century England and was caught well in Dryden's *Absalom and Achitophel* (1681):

The sober part of Israel, free from stain,
Well knew the value of a peaceful reign;
And, looking backward with a wise affright,
Saw seams of wounds, dishonest to the sight:

In Contemplation of whose ugly scars
They curs'd the memory of civil wars. [11.154-59]

3. 1 Sam. 12:21-25. This and all further quotations from the Bible are drawn from the King James Version; future citations will be given in the text. A comparable message is contained in Deut. 17:14-20.

4. The eighteenth-century English conception of luxury of course derives from later Roman and Christian commentary. There are nevertheless dozens of echoes of the Hebrew association of luxury, pride, and decadence. In a letter published in 1702, the traveler John Marshal describes the natives of the East Indies as "ignorant of all Parts of the World but their own; they wonder much at us, that will take so much Care and Pains, and run thro so many Dangers both by Sea and Land, only, as they say, to uphold and nourish Pride and Luxury. For, say they, every Country in the whole World is sufficiently endow'd by Nature with every thing that is necessary for the Life of Man, and that therefore it is Madness to seek for, or desire, that which is needless and unnecessary." John Marshal, "A letter from the East Indies . . ." (1702), quoted in Ray W. Frantz, *The English Traveller and the Movement of Ideas 1660–1732* (1934; reprinted Lincoln, Neb., 1967), p. 115.

It can be argued that the positive events of Jewish history also need to be associated with luxury. For it was only after Israel had been exhausted by luxury and crushed by the Babylonians that there arose the idea of a tragic fate and national identity for God's chosen people. In the midst of suffering and persecution, says the latter part of Isaiah, the task of the Jews is to bring about a reconciliation between God and all other peoples of the world.

5. Cf. Stanley Eugene Fish, *Surprised by Sin: The Reader in Paradise Lost* (New York, 1967), p. 332.

6. Walter W. Skeat, *An Etymological Dictionary of the English Language,* 4th ed. (1910; reprinted New York, 1956); A. Ernout and A. Meillet, *Dictionnaire etymologique de la langue latine,* 3d ed. (Paris, 1951); Eric Partridge, *Origins,* 2d ed. (New York, 1959); *Oxford English Dictionary.* The editors of the *OED* and Ernout and Meillet raise the possibility that the noun *luxus* derives from the adjective *luxus,* "dislocated, sprained"–a sense quite apt to the purposes of Greek and Roman historians.

7. Plato, *Republic* 2.372e-373e, 9.590b; *Timaeus* 4, 8; *Laws* 6.781a-b, 7.805d ff., 8.841a, 11.919b.

8. Cf. the fable of the unruly, luxurious steed in the palinode of the *Phaedrus* 253–54.

9. In Aristotle this position can be traced in the *Topics,* throughout the *Politics,* in the *Ethics* and *Athenian Constitution;* in the historians, Herodotus *History* 6–7; and Thucydides *Peloponnesian War* 3–6, 8.

10. Eduard Zeller, *The Stoics, Epicureans and Sceptics,* trans. Oswald J. Reichel (London, 1880), pp. 268-81, 301-4; E. Vernon Arnold, *Roman Stoicism* (Cambridge, 1911), pp. 332, 353-56; Ludwig Edelstein, *The Meaning of Stoicism* (Cambridge, Mass., 1966), pp. 22-44; A. A. Long, *Hellenistic Philosophy: Stoics, Epicureans, Sceptics* (London, 1974), pp. 205-9.

11. See *De benef.* 3.17-18; *Phaedra* 11.483-558; and the *Dialogi* 1.4, 4.21, 5.36. The elder Pliny's *Naturalis historia* and the *Discourses* of Epictetus elaborate further on the necessity for man to see rightly his place in nature. In the proemium to book 7, Pliny asserts the superiority of animals to men, for man alone of all living things courts grief in his endless pursuit of luxury, in every mode, for every member. Epictetus in book 4 of the *Discourses* used vividly for individuals the figures Socrates had applied to the state. He holds that most men can never attain virtue because they cannot comprehend it; their aspirations are entirely bound by luxury, which is to the soul what disease is to the body.

12. I follow the interpretation of Finley, *Ancient Economy,* pp. 40-44.

13. Diogenes had insisted that masters were more in bondage than their slaves; they *needed* slaves, but slaves did not need them. Cicero often illustrates this paradox when he shows that free men depend upon their dependents, those who are not free. Finley cites two further instances. About 400 B.C. an Athenian publicly pleaded poverty because he had no slaves to maintain him. Eight hundred years later Libanius the rhetorician argued before the council of Antioch the case of impoverished lecturers, so destitute they could afford no more than two or three slaves each (*Ancient Economy,* p. 79).

14. W. E. Heitland in *Agricola* (Cambridge, 1921) argues that such proponents of rural toil as

Cicero do indeed wish to keep most people on the land, but "the ever-repeated praises of country life are unreal. Even when sincere, they are the voice of town-bred men, weary of the fuss and follies of urban life, to which nevertheless they would presently come back refreshed but bored with their rural holiday" (pp. 200-201). For consideration of the influence of *De officiis* on the eighteenth century, see Henry Knight Miller's introduction to Henry Fielding, *Miscellanies* (Oxford, 1972), 1:xvii-xxvii. Other statements of Cicero's position may be found in *De finibus, Orationes Philippicae, Oration in Pisonem, Pro M. Caelio, Pro L. Murena,* and *De lege agraria.*

In *De oratore* (2.23) Cicero gives the concept of luxury aesthetic as well as moral value, declaring that an overripe style befits only a luxurious audience. Horace makes a similar point in the second of the *Epistolae,* and in *De sublimitate* (6.44, 95) Longinus warns that luxury destroys the spirit of a people and hence of their poets and writers.

15. Horace notes in the first of his epistles that though he belongs to no school he is indebted to the Stoics. Elsewhere he declares that wisdom teaches moderation and the rejection of luxury to poets as well as other men; the simple man is likely to be a *better* man than the spendthrift. See *Epistolae* 2.2. 122, 146-204; and *Ars Poetica* 71-72. In eighteenth-century thinking about luxury, Horace was probably best remembered for the fifteenth in his second book of odes. Usually given an English title like "Of Luxury" or "The Invasion of Luxury," this ode was doubtless well known to most literary men:

> Soon few for tilth the acres will remain,
> Such princely piles we raise. On every side
>   Fishponds, than Lucrine lake more wide,
>   We'll see. The Bachelor-plane
>
> Will oust vine-wedded elms; and violets blue,
> And myrtle's fragrance, and flower-scents untold,
>   Will scatter sweetness, where of old
>   The owner olives grew.
>
> Soon sultry sunshine by thick-planted bays
> Will be shut off. Not so taught Romulus' rule,
>   Or the unshaven Cato's school
>   And old folks' simpler ways.
>
> With them men's private wealth was scant indeed,
> But great the common good. No colonnade
>   With northern outlook yielded shade,
>   To please a private greed.
>
> None dared for house-building chance turf eschew;
> Cities and public temples, these at most
>   The laws bade deck at public cost
>   With pomp of stonework new. [Trans. John Marshall]

See also the *Satires* 1.1, 2.2; and Ovid *Remedia Amoris.* At least three—the first, sixth, and eleventh—of Juvenal's satires contain attacks upon luxury. The first calls the gross and luxurious fit targets for satire, citing men who "gorge whole patrimonies in a single course." The sixth calls luxury an evil of peace, more ruthless than war, which broods over Rome.

16. M. L. W. Laistner, *The Greater Roman Historians* (Berkeley and Los Angeles, 1947), p. 171; D. C. Earl, *The Political Thought of Sallust* (Cambridge, 1961), pp. 41-43. In these paragraphs I follow Earl's analysis of Sallust's thought.

17. *Catilinae* 10; *Jugurthinum* 41. Gibbon challenges this view in vol. 1, chap. 2, of the *Decline and Fall.* Cautionary tales of the subversive effects of luxury upon a victorious army can be traced at least to Alexander the Great. After defeating the armies of Darius about 330 B.C., Alexander and his generals reputedly adapted overwell to the indulgent life of the Persians. First rumors passed among the troops that Alexander had given himself utterly to the vice. Then, according to Plutarch, Alexander himself became alarmed at the ostentation and extravagance of his generals and cautioned them to "avoid the vices and follies of those we have conquered."

18. See esp. 41–42.

19. Cato, fragments 58–66, 154–75, in *Oratorum Romanorum fragmenta,* ed. H. Malcovati, 2d ed. (Turin, 1955); Livy *History of Rome* 1–2, 23, 35–43; *Periochae* 43, 47–48; Valerius Maximus *Factorum ac dictorum* 2, 6; Plutarch *Marcus Cato;* Polybius *Histories* 18, 35; Velleius Paterculus *Historiae Romanae* 1; Diodorus Siculus *Bibliotheca historica* 31; Aulus Gellius *Noctes Atticae* 2; Pliny *Naturalis historia* 10. Cf. Macrobius *Saturnalia* 3, 7.

Hellenistic writers may have been as influential as earlier Stoics upon the thinking of the historians. Philo Judaeus and Dio Chrysostom were among the philosophers attempting to discover the nature of luxury through the language used to describe it. They particularized the vices and passions of luxury in ways comparable to the jurists and do make clear where luxury was thought to be nurtured: in cities and the haunts of women, tradesmen, and the lowly. An environment of virtue is a place of men steeled by a simple rural existence devoid of possession.

20. In book 3 of the *Annals* Tacitus notes several speeches that blame women for the luxury to be seen in Rome. He also recounts that rare episode of political candor, Tiberius's famous letter to the Senate on luxury. When the Senate was pressed for stronger sumptuary codes, it equivocated and redirected petitions to the emperor. After some delay Tiberius responded with an open letter on the political exigencies surrounding the issue. He asks which of the manifold things called luxuries he is expected to limit. Each of his critics asks that a different item or freedom be banned, and those crying loudest for prohibitions are also those most busy seeking to exempt themselves. "The cure for other evils must be sought in our own hearts. Let us be led to amendment, the poor by constraint, the rich by satiety. Or if any of our officials give promise of such energy and strictness as can stem the corruption, I praise the man, and I confess that I am relieved of a portion of my burdens" (trans. Church and Brodribb).

21. Nero is described in books 13–16; Tacitus gives him and Agrippina the habits of both cruel rapacity and sadistic luxury. In his biography of Nero, Suetonius makes him the epitome of luxury: vain, wanton, greedy, lecherous, brutal, degraded. According to Suetonius he had two favorite sayings. Good for all occasions was, "True gentlemen always throw their money about." Reserved for the appointment of a magistrate was, "You know my needs, eh? You and I must see that nobody is left with anything" (trans. Robert Graves). He also particularizes what many others refer to, Nero's rage at the luxury of senators and knights and his enforcement and enactment of statutes to limit private expenditure. See also Annaeus Florus *Epitomae* 1–2.

22. The doctrine of self-denial and its sources are treated in K. E. Kirk, *The Vision of God* (London, 1931). In the story of Christ and the gift of the precious ointment (Luke 7:36–50, John 12:3–8) there is a striking parallel of the ancient injunction against human use of something intended for the divine. In John the scene is sharply dramatized: Mary's gift and her offer of her hair for drying Jesus' feet, the taunting of Judas and Jesus' response, "For the poor always ye have with you; but me ye have not always." Jesus' words were often used to justify the elaborate decoration of churches and cathedrals during periods of deprivation.

23. Lecky, *History of European Morals,* 2:66–68.

24. The best extended discussions are R. W. Carlyle and A. J. Carlyle, *A History of Medieval Political Theory in the West,* 6 vols. (Edinburgh and London, 1915), 2:56–75, 102–13, 3:92–114, 4:4–85; and David Brion Davis, *The Problem of Slavery in Western Culture* (Ithaca, 1966), pp. 87–121.

25. See e.g., *City of God* 4.3; and *Confessions* 6.15.

26. For Augustine's influence in the preservation of the Platonic tradition, see R. Klibansky, *The Continuity of the Platonic Tradition during the Middle Ages* (London, 1939).

27. See esp. *Confessions* 9, 12–13; *Tenth Homily* 4; *De vera religione* 38.69; *City of God* 9.17, 13.13; 14.15; and for useful background information, Herbert A. Deane, *The Political and Social Ideas of St. Augustine* (New York, 1963).

28. In the following paragraphs I draw upon Samuel C. Chew, *The Pilgrimage of Life* (1962; reprinted Port Washington, N.Y., 1973), pp. 1–34, 61–78, 144–73; and Morton W. Bloomfield, *The Seven Deadly Sins* (1952; reprinted East Lansing, Mich., 1967), pp. 59–66, 353.

29. In one of the few anticipations of my thesis, C. S. Lewis notes that Luxuria here also possesses the characteristics of Gula and Superbia: *The Allegory of Love* (New York, 1936), pp. 70–71. Sixteenth-century personifications of luxury are treated by Rosemond Tuve in *Allegorical Imagery* (Princeton, 1966), pp. 119, 182–83, 207–11, 442.

The alternative tradition of representation, in which luxury turns human beings into wild animals—usually asses, goats, hogs, and apes—is well illustrated by the engravings of Andrea Alciati in Geoffrey Whitney, *Choice of Emblemes* (1586).

30. Some sense of the pervasive, familiar quality of Renaissance depictions of luxury is contained in Frances A. Yates, *The Art of Memory* (Chicago, 1966). It is also striking that images of luxury were allowed to stand during the sixteenth-century Reformation in England; it was not one of the cluster of images destroyed by reformers and discussed by John Phillips in his *Reformation of Images: Destruction of Art in England, 1535–1660* (Berkeley and Los Angeles, 1974).

Typical representations are to be found in Chew, *Pilgrimage of Life,* figs. 75, 77, 79, 82, 89, 90, 103, 104, 141; Tuve, *Allegorical Imagery,* figs. 50, 51, 82–84; D. W. Robertson, Jr., *A Preface to Chaucer* (Princeton, 1962), figs. 2, 15, 16, 34, 68; Emile Mâle, *The Gothic Image,* trans. Dora Nussey (1913; reprinted New York, 1958), figs. 49, 50, 57, 59; and Erwin Panofsky, *The Life and Art of Albrecht Dürer,* 4th ed. (Princeton, 1955), fig. 216.

Jean Seznec discusses the transformation of Venus into Luxuria in *The Survival of the Pagan Gods,* trans. Barbara F. Sessions (New York, 1953), part 1, chap. 3. And in *Pandora's Box,* 2d ed. (New York, 1962), Dora and Erwin Panofsky describe the variety in Renaissance versions: Rosso Fiorentino's *Pandora Opening the Box,* René Boyvin's *L'ignorance chassée,* Bronzino's *Exposure of Luxury,* Andrea Mantegna's *Virtus combusta et virtus deserta,* and Jacques Callot's *Luxuria.*

31. Davis, *Problem of Slavery,* pp. 91–92.

32. Primary discussions of luxury and the passage where Augustine's influence is clearest is *Summa theologica,* first part of the second part, questions 6 through 89 (on Human Acts: Habits, Virtues and Vices), noted here as 1.2.6–89. Further discussion appears in 2.2.153–54. All are glossed by Etienne Gilson, *The Christian Philosophy of St. Thomas Acquinas,* trans. L. K. Shook (New York, 1956), part 3.

33. For Marlowe see verses signed "Ignoto"; for Webster, *The Duchess of Malfi,* 1.1.325–26. For Spenser see the following in the *Faerie Queene,* 1.4.1.5; 1.4.21.3; 1.12.14.9; 2.11.12.6; 4.10.23.1.

34. *Lover's Complaint,* 314; *Much Ado,* 4.1.41; *Henry V,* 4.4.19; *Hamlet,* 1.5.83. See also *Troilus,* 5.4.8; *Titus,* 5.1.88; *Richard III,* 3.5.80; *Macbeth,* 4.3.58; *Antony,* 3.13.120; *Merry Wives,* 5.5.94; and *Measure for Measure,* 5.1.501.

35. As usual Shakespeare looks as far forward as backward. *Lear* contains several speeches that use luxury in the sense of lust; it is also, throughout, very much about luxury in the modern sense. The famous "O, reason not the need!" speech of Lear (2.4) is but one of many places where Shakespeare's characters question the separation of necessities from superfluities in modern, psychological terms. Others are Lear to Edgar (3.2) and Gloucester to Edgar (4.1). Then, in the "What, art mad?" speech of 4.6, Lear in his mad lucidity penetrates to the core of the moral-social issue. When all distinction hangs upon office, "The usurer hangs the cozener. / Through tatter'd clothes small vices do appear; / Robes and furr'd gowns hide all. Plate sin with gold, / And the strong lance of justice hurtless breaks; / Arm it in rags, a pigmy's straw does pierce it."

36. See also *PL,* 11.711–13; *PR,* 3.297; 4.110–14.

37. In *The Savages of America: A Study of the Indian and the Idea of Civilization* (Baltimore, 1952), p. 5, Pearce notes that the Indian "became important for the English mind not for what he was in and of himself, but rather what he showed civilized men they were not and must not become." Jordan, in *White over Black: American Attitudes toward the Negro, 1550–1812* (Chapel Hill, N.C., 1968), comes to the same conclusion about the English perception of Africans. In this discussion I am indebted to Hayden White's illuminating essay, "The Forms of Wildness: Archeology of an Idea," in *The Wild Man Within,* ed. Edward Dudley and Maximillian Novak (Pittsburgh, 1972), pp. 3–38.

38. An obvious feature of the history of luxury has been its integral relationship with ideas concerning wealth. From the Attic kingdoms through the French Revolution, there was a parallel increase in the denunciation of wealth and its accumulation. The best-known statements of this point are to be found in Johan Huizinga, *The Waning of the Middle Ages,* trans. F. Hopman (London, 1924); Max Weber, *The Protestant Ethic and the Spirit of Capitalism,* trans. Talcott

Parsons (London, 1930); Ernst Troeltsch, *The Social Teaching of the Christian Churches,* trans. B. Wyon (London, 1931); Richard Schlatter, *Private Property: The History of an Idea* (London, 1951); and Crane Brinton, *A History of Western Morals* (New York, 1959). Since the censure of wealth was usually contained in an attack upon luxury, the intellectual situation of the eighteenth century becomes intelligible when it is understood that, historically, opposition to luxury was not an attempt to *prevent* the accumulation, but rather to *regulate* it. The year 1757 probably marked the peak of public condemnation of luxury in England, as represented by the reception of John Brown's *Estimate.* Yet in the same year Samuel Johnson could write with ample justification, "There was never from the earliest ages, a time in which trade so much engaged the attention of mankind, or commercial gain was sought with so general emulation."

39. A few comments on sources are required here:

1) There are several detailed studies of sumptuary laws in the ancient world and at least one for each modern European nation. For the most part these works acknowledge that the laws were intended to control behavior and spending; then they proceed to discuss only the latter kind of regulation. For example, a standard work on England is F. Elizabeth Baldwin, *Sumptuary Legislation and Personal Regulation in England* (Baltimore, 1926; also published with other works in vol. 44 of *Johns Hopkins University Studies in Historical and Political Science*). At the outset Baldwin describes such legislation as an effort to limit individual spending; next she establishes motives: "the desire to preserve class distinctions, so that any stranger could tell by merely looking at a man's dress to what rank in society he belonged; the desire to check practices which were regarded as deleterious in their effects, due to the feeling that luxury and extravagance were in themselves wicked and harmful to the morals of the people; economic motives; the endeavor to encourage home industries and to discourage the buying of foreign goods, and the attempt on the part of the sovereign to induce his people to save their money, so that they might be able to help him out financially in time of need. Sheer conservatism and dislike of new fashions or customs might be mentioned as a fourth factor which led to the passage of English sumptuary laws" (pp. 9-10). This is a fair statement as far as it goes, and it leads one to ask about those aspects of the legislation that went beyond spending to other forms of control upon class distinction and deleterious practices. And it leaves unasked the questions why some ranks were considered exempt from the laws and how the definition of luxurious practices was arrived at. The upshot is that, almost universally, modern studies of sumptuary codes use the modern sense of luxury as something known and deplorable and treat the laws as minor, moral, and paternalistic. They are to be distinguished from valuable contemporary works, such as Nicolas Baudeau, *Principes de la science morale et politique sur le luxe et les loix sumptuaires* (1798).

2) The most useful modern studies tend to be those that approach the law indirectly, by way of some larger concern: e.g., Peter Garnsey, P. A. Brunt, and M. I. Finley on social conflicts in Greece and Rome; W. W. Buckland and David Brion Davis on slavery; Sarah Pomeroy and Verena Zinserling on the position of women in antiquity; Doris M. Stenton on women in England; E. P. Thompson on the working class.

40. *Sumptuary* is the traditional adjective for a type of legislation that had several titles in antiquity and more in the Christian era; using a narrower range of laws from the seventeenth and eighteenth centuries, Maurice J. Quinlan in his fine study, *Victorian Prelude: A History of English Manners, 1700–1830* (New York, 1941), terms them vice laws. Often called "luxury statutes," or "laws against luxury," they have in common the philosophical purpose I have outlined and the announced purpose to combat the luxury rampant at the moment, usually opening with a preamble that declares that the present age is far more luxurious than any of the past and has evoked the following measure of restraint. (Annually, on the average, for three thousand years, with few long interludes, legislators pronounced their own age the most depraved the world had seen. This was entropy indeed.) Contemporary indexers for the *British Parliamentary Journals* tended to use the categories of "luxury," "poor law," and "civil disorder." Survivals in modern Britain and the United States would include the American Constitution (in its original distinctions of rank, race, and sex), the slave codes and later Jim Crow laws, and the temperance and "blue" laws of both nations. Parliamentary debates that led to the current English pub-closing statutes reveal that some legislators maintain a strong sense of the function of such

laws; they argued that regulating the hours pubs could be open would both restrict the profit a tradesman-owner could make and discourage laborers from avoiding work.

41. P. A. Brunt, *Italian Manpower, 225 B.C.–A.D. 14* (London, 1971), p. vii. See also Brunt's *Social Conflicts in the Roman Republic* (London, 1971).

42. Finley, *Ancient Economy*, pp. 67–68.

43. An obvious example, in force in most European countries from the establishment of the monarchy to the present day, is that royal marriages were exempt from the restrictions imposed upon the rest of the nation by nuptial laws. Louis XIV was involved in one of the most widely discussed examples of royal discretion exercised in the seventeenth century. In August 1661 the French minister of finance, Nicholas Fouquet, invited the young monarch (and six thousand others) to view his newly built estate, Vaux-le-Vicomte. Louis's response to the sumptuous establishment was a combination of jealousy and rage. He charged Fouquet with *luxe insolent et audacieux*, had him immediately imprisoned, and confiscated the treasures of Vaux for himself.

44. We have little direct information about how ordinary people were affected by a system of orders and status, but we do have such creative reconstructions as Eileen Power's *Medieval People* (London, 1924). The most important single mark of status was that of citizenship. Aristotle had held that politics was the business only of citizens, and in Greek and Roman law this threshold of favored status was legislatively defined and jealously guarded. In Athens citizens alone were entitled to hold land and to enter freely into marriage; their number, Finley estimates, was between one in six and one in three of all males. In 91 B.C. Augustus estimated about four million citizens of Rome in an empire of fifty to sixty million persons. See Finley, *Ancient Economy*, pp. 45–48; for the number and classification of Roman citizens, within Italy and without, see Brunt, *Italian Manpower*, pp. 61–83, 204–65; and, generally, see Peter Garnsey, *Social Status and Legal Privilege in the Roman Empire* (Oxford, 1970).

45. For this and other examples, see William L. Westermann, *The Slave Systems of Greek and Roman Antiquity* (Philadelphia, 1955), pp. 75–76, 91–93, 115.

46. The longevity of this view with all its contradictions is indelible in the Dred Scott case (1857), in deciding which the chief justice of the United States Supreme Court declared that black people "had no rights which the white man was bound to respect; and that the negro might justly and lawfully be reduced to slavery for his benefit." This judgment he noted was "an axiom in morals as well as in politics." The justice was of course historically quite correct, for the sumptuary laws defined not only legal culpability, but also moral-intellectual capacity. Four years later a judge in Alabama put the contradiction concisely: "Because they are rational *human beings*, they are capable of committing crimes; and, in reference to acts which are crimes, are regarded as *persons*. Because they are *slaves*, they are incapable . . . of performing civil acts; and in reference to all such they are *things*; not persons."

47. See [Andrew Horn], *The Mirror of Justices*, ed. William Joseph Whittaker (London, 1895), originally written or edited in the late thirteenth century; Brian Tierney, *Medieval Poor Law: A Sketch of Canonical Theory and Its Application in England* (Berkeley and Los Angeles, 1959); Paul Vinogradoff, *Villainage in England: Essays in English Medieval History* (Oxford, 1892); and Pierre Kramer, *Le luxe et les lois sumptuaires au moyen âge* (Paris, 1920).

48. Baldwin, *Sumptuary Legislation*, pp. 12, 101, 164–78; Lawrence Stone, *The Crisis of the Aristocracy, 1558–1641* (Oxford, 1965), pp. 27–30.

49. To observe the continuity of laws drawn to protect the land, one might compare, say, the Lex Agraria of 111 B.C. with the Statute of Artificers. The Lex Agraria and the legislation it superseded are discussed in E. G. Hardy, *Roman Laws and Charters* (1912; reprinted New York, 1975), pp. 35–92. The Statute of Artificers is the subject of Margaret Gay Davies, *The Enforcement of English Apprenticeship: A Study in Applied Mercantilism, 1563–1642* (Cambridge, Mass., 1956), esp. pp. 1–14; William Cunningham, *The Growth of English Industry and Commerce*, 6th ed., 2 vols. (Cambridge, 1919), 2:25 ff.; and Heckscher, *Mercantilism*, 1:224–32.

50. Leon Radzinowicz, *A History of English Criminal Law and Its Administration from 1750* (New York, 1948), p. 77. The most thorough account of the law is E. P. Thompson, *Whigs and Hunters: The Origin of the Black Act* (New York, 1975). On the use of mantraps and spring guns, see E. S. Turner, *Roads to Ruin: The Shocking History of Social Reform* (1950; reprinted

London, 1966), pp. 17–36. Douglas Hay provides an acute conspectus of how criminal law was used for social ends in his essay "Property, Authority and the Criminal Law," in Douglas Hay, Peter Linebaugh, John G. Rule, E. P. Thompson, and Cal Winslow, *Albion's Fatal Tree: Crime and Society in Eighteenth-Century England* (New York, 1975), pp. 17–63.

51. Baldwin, *Sumptuary Legislation,* pp. 186–91, 196–208, 229, and passim. Cf. John Martin Vincent, *Costume and Conduct in the Laws of Basel, Bern, and Zurich, 1370–1800* (Baltimore, 1935), pp. 42–95; and K. R. Greenfield, *Sumptuary Laws in Nürnberg* (Baltimore, 1918), passim.

52. Sarah B. Pomeroy, *Goddesses, Whores, Wives, and Slaves: Women in Classical Antiquity* (New York, 1975), pp. 46, 57, 178–82; Brunt, *Italian Manpower,* pp. 558–66.

53. Quoted in Chilton Latham Powell, *English Domestic Relations, 1487–1653* (New York, 1917), pp. 149–50, 147; see also Doris Mary Stenton, *The English Women in History* (London, 1957), pp. 29–74. For the rights of women in marriage, see George E. Howard, *A History of Matrimonial Institutions,* 3 vols. (Chicago, 1904); Gellert S. Alleman, *Matrimonial Law and the Materials of Restoration Comedy* (Wallingford, Pa., 1942); and Francis Lee Utley, *The Crooked Rib: An Analytical Index to the Argument about Women in English and Scots Literature to the End of the Year 1568* (Columbus, 1944).

54. I draw these instances from W. Warde Fowler, *The Religious Experience of the Roman People* (London, 1922); H. J. Rose, *Ancient Roman Religion* (London, 1949); and M. I. Finley, *Democracy Ancient and Modern* (New Brunswick, 1973).

55. The expedient equation of station with virtue was certain to catch Gibbon's sensitive eye. His fifteenth chapter (1776) explains:

> In their censures of luxury, the fathers are extremely minute and circumstantial; and among the various articles which excite their pious indignation, we may enumerate false hair, garments of any colour except white, instruments of music, vases of gold or silver, downy pillows (as Jacob reposed his head on a stone), white bread, foreign wines, public salutations, the use of warm baths, and the practice of shaving the beard. . . . When Christianity was introduced among the rich and the polite, the observation of these singular laws was left, as it would be at present, to the few who were ambitious of superior sanctity.

Horace Walpole, it will be recalled, said he went to church merely to set a good example to the servants.

56. In book 5 of the *City of God* Augustine holds that the cycle of fortune besets all nations, as luxury and pride lead to the downfall of even the most mighty. In Boethius, Boccaccio, Petrarch, and others the wheel of fortune usually rotates from peace to wealth to luxury to pride to war to poverty to humility to patience and back to peace. A literary gloss is Howard R. Patch, *The Goddess Fortuna in Medieval Literature* (Cambridge, Mass., 1927), pp. 170–71. A vivid illustration is the painting "The Dance of Life" by Nicolas Poussin.

57. Huizinga, Weber, Troeltsch, Schlatter, and Brinton all draw this conclusion in a general way. Stressing it specifically are Carlyle and Carlyle, *Medieval Political Thought,* 3:92–114; and Davis, *Problem of Slavery,* pp. 88–89.

58. Vincent, *Costume and Conduct,* pp. 3–11.

59. Quinlan, *Victorian Prelude,* pp. 9–22.

60. Contemporary accounts appear in London corporation records, Stow, and Cecil's memoirs: Corporation of the City of London, *Remembrancia,* 1:62; John Stow, *Annales of England* (1605); and Robert Cecil, first Earl of Salisbury, *Calendar of the MSS . . . Hatfield House, Hertfordshire,* ed. R. A. Roberts (London, 1883), 5:249–50.

CHAPTER TWO

1. *Gentleman's Magazine,* 27 (Supplement, 1757): 591. For further comments and reports during 1757–58, see the weekly columns headed "Colliers," "Mob," "Corn," "Wheat," and "Riots." For discussion of the riots see Robert B. Rose, "Eighteenth-Century Price Riots and Public Policy in England," *International Review of Social History* 6 (1961): 277–92; and James

E. T. Rogers, *A History of Agriculture and Prices in England*, 7 Vols. (Oxford, 1866-1902), vols. 6 and 7.

2. See the *Journals* of the House of Commons, especially for 1751-55 and 1757-60.

3. See also *London Magazine* 38 (April 1768): 683-84; 41 (November 1772): 539; 42 (February 1773): 68-70; 43 (October 1774): 481; 48 (December 1779): 537-39. Lois Whitney called attention to the controversy in the periodicals in *Primitivism and the Idea of Progress* (1934, reprinted New York, 1965), p. 46.

4. *Fable of the Bees*, Kaye ed., 1:108, 115.

5. J. G. A. Pocock, *The Machiavellian Moment: Florentine Political Thought and the Atlantic Republican Tradition* (Princeton, 1975), pp. 401-2. No one has treated the complex interrelations of history, language, and political theory during the period with more subtlety than Pocock. A beginning point for any serious study of the age is his "Machiavelli, Harrington and English Political Ideologies in the Eighteenth Century," in *Politics, Language and Time: Essays on Political Thought and History* (New York, 1971), pp. 104-47. He is concerned not with any particular idea or theory, but with the ways various theories collide and converge. In a general way he accounts not only for the presence of the attack upon luxury, but also for the decline of the attack later in the century:

> The language of politics is obviously not the language of a single disciplined mode of intellectual inquiry. It is rhetoric, the language in which men speak for all the purposes and in all the ways in which men may be found articulating and communicating as part of the activity and the culture of politics. Political speech can easily be shown to include statements, propositions and incantations of virtually every kind distinguished by logicians, grammarians, rhetoricians and other students of language, utterance and meaning; even disciplined modes of inquiry will be found there, but coexisting with utterances of very different kinds. It is of the nature of rhetoric and above all of political rhetoric— which is designed to reconcile men pursuing different activities and a diversity of goals and values—that the same utterance will simultaneously perform a diversity of linguistic functions. What is a statement of fact to some will symbolically evoke certain values to others; what evokes a certain cluster of factual assertions, and value judgments concerning them, to one set of hearers will simultaneously evoke another cluster and recommend another resolution of conduct in the ears of another set. Because factual and evaluative statements are inextricably combined in political speech, and because it is intended to reconcile and coordinate different groups pursuing different values, its inherent ambiguity and its cryptic content are invariably high. [*Politics, Language and Time*, p. 17]

6. Peter G. M. Dickson, *The Financial Revolution in England: A Study of the Development of Public Credit, 1688-1756* (London, 1967). For the context out of which this revolution grew, see L. A. Clarkson, *The Pre-Industrial Economy in England, 1500-1750* (London, 1971). The economic historian F. J. Fisher notes that the century was "the first period in which inventions played a significant part in the economic development of England." From the inventions came innovations in banking and agriculture and then a remodeled economic policy and new manufacturing practices. See *Augustans and Romantics, 1689-1830*, ed. H. V. D. Dyson and John Butt (London, 1961), p. 139. Fisher supposes that the new social structure that resulted from such changes was not visible as a whole until mid-century—the time of Smollett's historical and journalistic writing.

7. Isaac Kramnick, *Bolingbroke and His Circle: The Politics of Nostalgia in the Age of Walpole* (Cambridge, Mass., 1968), p. 4; see also pp. 30-55. William Pulteney expressed the situation more crassly and probably more accurately when he said that in an age of luxury the great families are at a disadvantage: they possess great wealth, but not ready cash. Cf. Peter Marris, *Loss and Change* (London, 1974), which studies in modern psychological terms the crisis of social change, entailing "the irretrievable loss of the familiar."

8. George Rudé, *Hanoverian London 1714-1808* (Berkeley and Los Angeles, 1971), pp. ix-x.

9. Carl J. Friedrich has said, "If Hobbes retained the verbiage of natural law while draining it of its substance, David Hume . . . is generally credited with its destruction" (*The Philosophy of Law in Historical Perspective*, 2d ed. [Chicago, 1963], p. 91). Both parts of Friedrich's statement are pertinent to the eighteenth-century situation.

10. The latter group is cited in Heckscher, *Mercantilism,* 2:290, the former in Johnson, *Predecessors of Adam Smith,* pp. 281-94; Buck, *Politics of Mercantilism,* pp. 14-20; Viner, *Studies,* pp. 6-51; and George, *London Life,* pp. 23-24. A partial list of the writers involved would include Petty, Grew, Davenant, Hale, Sheridan, Coke, Cary, Bellers, Yarranton, Firmin, Fortrey, Mun, Fauquier, and Gee. Those who attack luxury saw it as: (1) a pernicious example of bourgeois emulation of the nobility, (2) a temptation to the wealthy to squander their patrimonies, and (3) a waste of precious metals, through exports for payment and the manufacture of jewelry. Beneath and beyond these practical considerations lay the assumptions that the threat of bankruptcy was ever present and that an unequal distribution of wealth was necessary within Europe as well as within England. Since misfortune was a constant threat, economic activity became a desperate attempt to preserve the present. Accepting the axiom that one nation can prosper only at the expense of all others, these opponents interpreted luxury within their own country as a sign of national decadence and a spur to the economies of their competitors. They tended to see an economic structure at once predetermined and fraught with uncertainty. Calls for stronger control over trade and labor were a common attempt to resolve the paradox. Unregulated trade, they held, would permit consumption of useless, transient, or precious goods and thereby upset the balance of trade, squander gold and silver supplies, cause unemployment, and reduce the value of land. If the passion for French lace of women like Swift's female Yahoos and Smollett's Tabby was to be gratified, then England would be forced to increase imports. The transaction would require the loss of gold or needed raw materials to its traditional enemy. The next steps would involve natives left without work because of lost capital and the diversion of effort from agriculture to competing luxuries. Having been economically depleted, the nation would then be physically exhausted. Depopulation would follow from poverty, the abandonment of the land, the flight to the cities, and the neglect of subsistence farming. A proliferation of tariffs, prohibitions, and duties—many not removed until Gladstone's ministry—testify to the intensity of such fears.

11. Mandeville's own position will be discussed further in the following chapter. Here should be noted those studies that remark upon his significance as a bridge figure: Jacob Viner, *The Long View and the Short* (Glencoe, Ill., 1958), pp. 332-42; Kramnick, *Bolingbroke and His Circle,* pp. 201-4; and Hector Munro, *The Ambivalence of Bernard Mandeville* (Oxford, 1975).

12. [Nathaniel Forster], *An Inquiry into the Causes of the Present High Price of Provisions* (1767), pp. 47-48; Walpole's letters to Horace Mann, 1 July 1761 and 9 April 1772, in *Correspondence,* ed. W. S. Lewis (New Haven, 1937-), 22:49, 455; 23:400.

13. In *Consent and Consensus* (London, 1971), P. H. Partridge argues that consent of the governed is agreed to be the first characteristic of democratic government, but that modern use of the term "consent" is so vague that it can be employed to justify almost any regime. And while we are not disturbed, readers two centuries hence may wonder what is being requested when, say, Leon Radzinowicz and the London *Daily Mail,* Spiro Agnew and Jesse Jackson, all call for "law and order."

Of course many writers of historical or literary inclination continued through the nineteenth and even into the twentieth century to identify luxury with lechery. While economists like Veblen and Henry George were giving luxury a thoroughly modern cast, bookish and nostalgic critics like Saintsbury and Chesterton retained the older vocabulary. In his collection of *Miscellaneous Essays* (New York, 1892), Saintsbury writes disapprovingly of those who would introduce questions of morality into literature and observes that "you may write about murder all you like, and no one will accuse you of having committed that crime. You may depict an interesting brigand without being considered a thief. But so soon as you approach the other deadly sin of Luxury in any of its forms, instantly it appears self-evident that you not only take pleasure in those who do these things but also do them yourself" (p. 248).

14. Caroline A. Robbins, *The Eighteenth-Century Commonwealthman: Studies in the Transmission, Development and Circumstances of English Liberal Thought from the Restoration of Charles II until the War with the Thirteen Colonies* (Cambridge, Mass., 1959), esp. pp. 103-5; Lois F. Schwoerer, "The Literature of the Standing Army Controversy," *HLQ* 28 (1964-65): 187-212; Pocock, *Machiavellian Moment,* pp. 427-46; Kramnick, *Bolingbroke and His Circle,* pp. 236-60.

15. Charles Davenant, *The Political and Commerical Works of Dr. Charles D'Avenant,* ed.

Charles Whitworth, 6 vols. (London, 1771), 1:319. All other quotation from Davenant will be from this edition and cited in the text.

16. French theories of progress, some dating from the sixteenth century, are discussed in George Huppert, *The Idea of Perfect History* (Urbana, Ill., 1970). For English conceptions, see —in addition to the standard works on historiography and those by Pocock and Kramnick already cited—J. G. A. Pocock, *The Ancient Constitution and the Feudal Law: A Study of English Historical Thought in the Seventeenth Century* (Cambridge, 1957); G. H. Nadel, "Philosophy of History before Historicism," in *Studies in the Philosophy of History,* ed. G. H. Nadel (New York, 1965); and Isaac Kramnick, Introduction to Bolingbroke, *Historical Writings* (Chicago, 1972).

17. For the political quarrels of Anne's reign and documentation of the division of legislators, there are two excellent books of readings and two essential studies. The former are Geoffrey Holmes and W. A. Speck, eds., *The Divided Society: Party Conflict in England 1694–1716* (London, 1967); and J. A. W. Gunn, *Factions No More: Attitudes to Party and Opposition in Eighteenth-Century England* (London, 1972). The latter are Geoffrey Holmes, *British Politics in the Age of Anne* (London, 1967); and W. A. Speck, *Tory and Whig: The Struggle in the Constituencies 1701–1715* (London, 1970). For the influence of the Revolution of 1688 on the age of Anne, see Stuart Prall, *The Bloodless Revolution: England, 1688* (New York, 1972), pp. 21–39, 55–57, 245–93. Perhaps the best description of Anne's reign as an era of new peace, harmony, and prosperity appears in Pope's *Windsor Forest* (1713):

> Oh Fact accurst? What Tears has *Albion* shed,
> Heav'ns! what new Wounds, and how her old have bled?
> She saw her Sons with purple Deaths expire,
> Her sacred Domes involv'd in rolling Fire,
> A dreadful Series of Intestine Wars,
> Inglorious Triumphs, and dishonest Scars.
> At length great ANNA said—Let Discord cease!
> She said, the World obey'd, and all was *Peace*! [11.321–28]

18. *Works* (London, 1844), 1:115.

19. Addison notes the social distinctions within London in *Spectator* no. 403, for 12 June 1712:

> When I consider this great City in its several Quarters and Divisions, I look upon it as an Aggregate of various Nations distinguished from each other by their respective Customs, Manners and Interests. The Courts of two Countries do not so much differ from one another, as the Court and City in their peculiar ways of Life and Conversation. In short, the Inhabitants of St. James's, notwithstanding they live under the same Laws, and speak the same Language, are a distinct People from those of *Cheapside,* who are likewise removed from those of the *Temple* on the one side, and those of *Smithfield* on the other, by several Climates and Degrees in their ways of Thinking and Conversing together. [Bond ed., 3:506]

20. *Gulliver's Travels,* ed. Herbert Davis (rev. ed. Oxford, 1959), p. 201. The two following long quotations appear on pp. 199 and 201–2 respectively of the Davis edition.

21. Cf. part 4 generally and the remarks on the frugal diet of the Houyhnhnms and the luxury of the female Yahoos particularly.

22. Pocock, "Machiavelli, Harrington and English Political Ideologies," pp. 124–47; Kramnick, *Bolingbroke and His Circle,* pp. 76–83.

23. In at least four pamphlets Pulteney argues that the constitution is safe only when it is under the direct protection of "the Great and Rich Families in the several counties, Cities, and Boroughs." Such protection insures not only the safety of the constitution, but also the just administration of the crown. Pulteney's tracts are valuable as bills of particulars in the indictment of Walpole during the early 1730s. See especially *A Proper Reply to a late Scurrilous Libel* (1731); *The Politics on Both Sides* (1734); *An Humble Address to the Knights, Citizens, and Burgesses* (1734); and *An Enquiry into the Conduct of Our Domestick Affairs* (1734).

24. The *Craftsman* serialized Bolingbroke's "Remarks on the History of England" between September 1730 and June 1731, "A Dissertation upon Parties" from October 1733 through June 1734, and the briefer essays, "On Luxury" and "On the Policy of the Athenians." Most of his attacks upon luxury were reprinted in the *Collection of Political Tracts* of 1748. Pocock examines the shades of meaning within the term "corruption" in *Machiavellian Moment*, pp. 402, 477-86.

25. No. 59 (19 August 1727), 2:104. See also nos. 166, 178, 291, 312, 320. The argument dismissing party labels and attachments was a critical one for the Opposition and is the subject of Caroline Robbins, "Discordant Parties—A Study of the Acceptance of Party by Englishmen," *Political Science Quarterly* 73 (1958): 505-29; H. N. Fieldhouse, "Bolingbroke and the Idea of Non-Party Government," *History* 23 (1938): 41-56; and Norman Baker, "Changing Attitudes towards Government in Eighteenth-Century Britain," in *Statesmen, Scholars and Merchants: Essays in Eighteenth-Century History Presented to Dame Lucy Sutherland,* ed. Anne Whiteman, J. S. Bromley, and P. G. M. Dickson (Oxford, 1973), pp. 202-19.

26. Perhaps as many as half of the numbers of the *Craftsman* urge some version of this point. See for instance nos. 5, 9, 12, 19, 47, 56, 57, 71, 114, 127, 134, 151, 166, and 184. This model had much appeal to aggrieved landowners, the smaller squires anxious lest they be driven out entirely, the larger anxious that they would find as neighbors such of the new rich as lawyers, doctors, goldsmiths, and tradesmen. Their anxieties over taxes are reported in William Kennedy, *English Taxation 1640-1799* (London, 1913), pp. 64-100; over the movement of landholdings in H. J. Habakkuk, "English Landownership 1680-1740," *Economic History Review* 10 (1940): 2-17, and G. E. Mingay, *English Landed Society in the Eighteenth Century* (London, 1963), pp. 50-130. The more general changes in the quality of gentry life are considered in Edward Hughes, *North Country Life in the Eighteenth Century* (Oxford, 1952). Their hatred of stockjobbers is caught in the second of *Cato's Letters* (12 November 1720), occasioned by the Bubble: "The Resurrection of Honesty and Industry can never be hoped for, while this Sort of Vermin is suffered to crawl about, tainting our Air, and putting every thing out of Course; subsisting by Lies, and practicing vile tricks, low in their Nature, and mischievous in their Consequences" (3d ed., 1:8). What should be done about them? To Trenchard and Gordon, "The Answer is Short and at Hand, Hang Them!"

27. In "On Luxury" Bolingbroke writes, "They are puny politicians, who attack a people's liberty directly. The means are dangerous, and the success precarious. . . . But he is a statesman formed for ruin and destruction, whose wily head knows how to disguise the fatal hook with the baits of pleasure, which his artful ambition dispenses with a lavish hand, and makes himself popular in undoing."

28. *Works,* ed. David Mallet, 7 vols. (London, 1754-98), 3:299-300. See also 1:474 ff.; 2:65, 234, 333, 355-56, 373-74. One other essay of the 1730s merits brief attention because of a parallel with Smollett. In his letter from London of May 29, Bramble complains that "the capital is become an overgrown monster; which, like a dropsical head, will in time leave the body and extremities without nourishment and support." The metaphor of London as a dropsical head was used at least as early as the opening years of the seventeenth century, but its earliest occurrence within the controversy over luxury, so far as I have discovered, is in Erasmus Jones's *Luxury, Pride, and Vanity* (n.d. [BM catalog suggests 1735]), which went through at least five editions. Jones's concerns include the size and squalor of London and the consequent depopulation of the rest of the country: "It is not an ungrateful Spectacle . . . to behold the prodigious Growth and Encrease of this unwieldy *City.* . . . Who can reflect upon this, but must necessarily believe that the Head, in a very little time longer, will grow so much too big for the Body, that it must consequently tumble down at last and ruin the whole" (4th ed., p. 2).

29. William Wood, *A Survey of Trade* (1718), p. 158. See also Nicholas Barbon, *A Discourse on Trade* (1690); John Bellers, *An Essay for Imploying the Able Poor* (1714); and *Some Considerations on the National Debts* (1729). The most valuable account of the relation between economic hardship and political unrest in the 1760s is Walter James Shelton, *English Hunger and Industrial Disorders* (London, 1974).

30. See also Henry Knight Miller, *Essays on Fielding's Miscellanies* (Princeton, 1961), pp. 94-103; and Malvin R. Zirker, Jr., "Fielding and Reform in the 1750s," *SEL* 7 (1967): 453-56. A useful compilation of attacks upon the luxury of the poor from contemporary books, news-

papers, and documents is J. P. Malcolm, *Anecdotes of the Manners and Customs of London during the Eighteenth Century* (London, 1808).

31. John Fielding, *An Account of the Origins and Effects of a Police* . . . (1758), p. 8.

32. William Horsley, *The Universal Merchant* (1753), p. xv. For similar views, see John Campbell, *The Present State of Europe* (1750), esp. p. 22; Duncan Forbes, *Reflections on the Sources of Incredulity, with Regard to Religion* (Edinburgh, 1750); Matthew Decker, *An Essay on the Causes of the Decline of the Foreign Trade* (1744); and *Sixteen Discourses upon Doctrines and Duties* (1754).

33. See for example *Critical Review* 2 (August 1756): 2.

34. John Brown, *Estimates of the Manners and Principles of the Times* (1757), 1:35-38, 42-49, 58-59, 85-93, 201.

35. Brown's tirade contains several literary echoes, perhaps recalling for his readers the wit and learning of the natural leader. His description of England racked by luxury uses the language applied to an Antony ruined by luxury in speeches of Philo and Octavius in the opening act of *Antony and Cleopatra*. His account of the psychology of luxury recalls, from *Paradise Lost*, the dream Satan forces upon Eve: "distemper'd, discontented thoughts, / Vain hopes, vain aims, inordinate desires / Blown up with high conceits ingend'ring pride."

36. Why Bolingbroke should lead this group is not clear. Brown had attacked Mandeville and luxury earlier, in the second of his *Essays on the Characteristics of the Earl of Shaftesbury* (1751), where he calls the *Fable of the Bees* an "immense *Labyrinth* of Falsehood." Mandeville is termed "this coarse Writer" and "a dishonest Mind" whose appeal is to "our modish Coffeehouse philosophers" and to "a Set of Wrong-headed Enthusiasts." Nevertheless, Brown says little about the nature of luxury in the earlier work, except to note that it amounts to "unprofitable *Riot* and *Excess*." Volume 2 of the *Estimate* was published in 1758. For Brown's other comments on the consequences of luxury see 1:193-96; 2:26-27, 33, 49, 95-96, 105-7, 189-90, 194-95.

37. *London Magazine* 27 (May 1758): 223. For earlier comments in the periodical see 25 (January 1756): 15-17; 25 (October 1756): 473-76; and 26 (December 1756): 576. See also *World*, no. 157 (1 January 1756), pp. 116 ff.; no. 167 (11 March 1756), pp. 173; and no. 171 (8 April 1756), pp. 195; *Grand* 1 (February 1758): 68, 73; 1 (September 1758): 450; 1 (October 1758): 514; 2 (June 1759): 298-99. For the *Universal*, see 20 (supplement 1757): 308; 24 (January 1759): 4; 25 (August 1759): 70, 73-74. *The New Royal*'s views are contained in the issues for October (p. 152) and November (pp. 218-19) 1759. For the comparable opinions of the lesser periodicals, see the *Old Maid*, no. 31 (12 June 1756), p. 256; *Connoisseur*, no. 107 (12 February 1756), p. 71; no. 118 (29 April 1756), p. 128, and the *Prater*, no. 14 (12 June 1756), p. 79. The *Universal Visiter*'s comments appear in no. 6 (June 1756), pp. 264-65; and no. 8 (August 1756), pp. 353-54. For the background of this reception see Stephen, *History of English Thought*, chap. 10, pp. 67-70; and Robert Donald Spector, *English Literary Periodicals* (The Hague, 1966), pp. 63-66.

38. Quoted in *Critical Review* 6 (October 1758): 350. See also George M. Kahrl, *Tobias Smollett, Traveler-Novelist* (Chicago, 1945), p. 127, n. 21.

39. Quoted in *Monthly Review* 23 (July 1760): 26.

40. See also Henry Stebbing's *Sermons on Practical Christianity* (1759) and Dr. Bolton's *Letters and Tracts on the Choice of Company, and other Subjects* (1761).

41. Pocock, *Politics, Language and Time*, pp. 286-87.

42. Among other attacks set in the traditional vein after 1763 are Young's *Farmer's Letters to the People of England* (1767), letter 7; and the anonymous *Political Speculations* (1767), *An Infallible Remedy for the High Price of Provisions* (1768), and *The Present State of Great Britain and North America* (1767). The most influential of these latter attacks appears to have been William Paley's *Principles of Moral and Political Philosophy* (1785), which was used as a textbook well into the nineteenth century and saw fifteen editions by 1805. Paley, archdeacon of Carlisle from 1782, traces the degradation of the poor to their luxury and laziness; he notes that the rich, too, engage in luxury but defends them as elevated beings to whom common regulations do not apply.

43. *Collected Works*, ed. Arthur Friedman (London, 1966), 4:286. References to luxury appear in the poem in 11.295-314, 385-94. Goldsmith's other comments on luxury are to be

found in *The Roman History* (2 vols., 1769); the *Citizen of the World*, letter 25; and "The Revolution in Low Life" from *Lloyd's Evening Post*, 14–16 June 1762. Scholarly commentary includes Howard J. Bell, Jr., "The Deserted Village and Goldsmith's Social Doctrines," *PMLA* 59 (1944): 747–72; and Friedman's notes, 2:50 ff.

44. *Critical Review* 20 (October 1765): 315–16. But this is the only such "moderate" comment to appear during Smollett's lifetime.

45. *Monthly Review* 47 (Appendix 1773): 508.

46. Ronald L. Meek, *Social Science and the Ignoble Savage* (Cambridge, 1976), pp. 99–130, 150–76.

47. *Wealth of Nations,* ed. William R. Scott, 6th ed. (London, 1921), 1:79–80. The whole of this chapter is apposite; it is chap. 8 of book 1, "On the Wages of Labour." See also D. P. O'Brien, *The Classical Economists* (London, 1975).

48. Chapter 19 of *The Vicar of Wakefield,* in *Collected Works,* ed. Friedman. See also J. Trusler, *Luxury no political evil, but . . . proved to be necessary to the preservation and prosperity of States. Addressed to the British Senate* (c. 1780).

49. Stephen, *History of English Thought,* chap. 10, 68; Ian R. Christie, *Crisis of Empire* (New York, 1967), p. 113. Full accounts of commercial expansion after 1763 are contained in V. T. Harlow, *The Founding of the Second British Empire 1763–1793,* 2 vols. (London, 1952, 1964); and Judith Blow Williams, *British Commercial Policy and Trade Expansion 1750–1850* (Oxford, 1972). The growing awareness of new forces in the political economy is traced in M. Blaug, "Economic Theory and Economic History in Great Britain, 1650–1776," *Past & Present* 28 (1964): 111–16. Several times in his *Europe in the Eighteenth Century: Aristocracy and the Bourgeois Challenge* (New York, 1973), George Rudé comments upon a change in English attitudes visible after 1763.

50. M. Dorothy George, *Hogarth to Cruikshank: Social Change in Graphic Satire* (New York, 1967), p. 13 n.

51. From early in the century American abolitionists had argued that an unnatural desire for luxury was responsible for slavery. John Hepburn, in *The American Defence of the Christian Rule* (Philadelphia, 1715), charged that the inordinate thirst for wealth brought men, even once-pious Quakers, to enslave other men for profit and to ensnare themselves in idleness and sexual debauchery. Hepburn's position was approved and reiterated by Elihu Coleman in *A Testimony Against that Antichristian Practice of Making Slaves of Man* (1733), the first abolitionist tract to receive official acceptance by a Quaker meeting. The identification of luxury with slavery was to be a consistent part of Quaker polemics during the first half of the century and was elaborated by Ralph Sandiford in *A Brief Examination of the Practice of the Times* (1729) and by Benjamin Lay in *All Slave-keepers Apostates* (1735). Probably the most important statements of the Quaker position appear in the works of John Woolman, whose *Some Considerations on the Keeping of Negroes* (2 parts, 1754, 1762) and *Journal* (1774) argue that slave owners had passed on the corruption of luxury to their children and their children's children. Instead of the "inheritance incorruptible" of God's word, they had brought to the New World a succession of wars and calamities that was but a sign of the awful retribution of God's justice. In his *Letters from an American Farmer* (1782), Crèvecoeur pursues a theme from Woolman, the contrast between the potential vitality of America and a Europe "fatigued with luxury, riches, and pleasures" (letter 3). Benjamin Franklin later returns to the portrait of a luxurious, dissipated Old World.

52. Henry Mackenzie, chap. 21 of *The Man of Feeling,* ed. Brian Vickers (London, 1967)—the Oxford English Novels edition. Another sign of the declining force of traditional slogans against luxury is the humorous appearance of one of these in the mouth of the pompous Mr. Sneer in act 1 of Sheridan's *The Critic* (1779).

53. J. W. Archenholtz, *A Picture of London* (London, 1797), p. 122. See also Charles Morazé, *The Triumph of the Middle Classes,* trans. anon. (London, 1966), esp. chap. 1, "London-Berlin: A Contrast." For a fascinating account of economic change described through family history, see T. W. Beastall, *A North Country Estate: The Lumleys and Sandersons as Landowners, 1600–1900* (Chichester, 1975). Although Smollett might have been shocked at the idea of a citizen expressing contempt for his betters, he saw clearly that the "cits" would gain an even greater ascendency. He would have appreciated the irony of a nineteenth-century

descendant of Charles James Fox, and a fervent Whig, leaving in his journal this account of an annual dinner to honor Fox's birthday:

> Mr. Fox's birthday. I went with Lord Thanet to the Fox dinner. We sat for ever and I was bored. Lord Erskine, Mr. Lens, Mr. Scarlett, Mr. Dennison and many dirty, violent little black people, who talked about taxes, poverty, funds, war, peace, the wickedness of ministers generally, for they had no particular fact or person in view, and the usual prophecies of ruin, tyranny and revolution which wind up the sentences of speculative politicians. Good dinner at Grillon's Hotel.

The Journal of the Rt. Hon. Henry Edward Fox, ed. the Earl of Ilchester (London, 1923), p. 153; quoted by Archibald Foord, *His Majesty's Opposition 1714-1830* (Oxford, 1964), p. 460.

CHAPTER THREE

1. The new collection of 1760 was *Essays and Treatises on several Subjects,* published in London in four volumes. During the 1770s the word *refinement* served as a partial but convenient circumlocution for *luxury,* then the two were used in conjunction, and by the early nineteenth century *refinement* had completely supplanted *luxury* when progress was meant. See, for example, Adam Sibbit, *A Dissertation, Moral and Political, On the Influence of Luxury and Refinement on Nations* (1800).

2. In this and later chapters I associate Smollett with the views of anonymous reviewers for the *Critical* without identifying the two. Grounds for this association are given in chapter 5.

3. According to Joan Robinson, *Economic Philosophy* (London, 1962), chap. 1, Mandeville has never been successfully refuted. He was certainly not alone in his defense of luxury. A few other writers anticipated or repeated many of his ideas, among them: Dudley North, *Discourses upon Trade* (1691); *An Essay on Money and Bullion* (1718); *Some Considerations on the Nature and Importance of the East-India Trade* (1728); [Patrick Lindsay], *The Interest of Scotland considered* (1733); and Jacob Vanderlint, *Money answers all Things* (1734). See Viner, *Studies in the Theory of International Trade,* pp. 90-91. Although bound to Veblen's sense of luxury, Gordon Vichert has useful things to say about Mandeville's satire in "The Theory of Conspicuous Consumption in the Eighteenth Century," in *The Varied Pattern: Studies in the Eighteenth Century,* ed. Peter Hughes and David Williams (Toronto, 1971), pp. 253-67. See also Philip Harth's fine introduction to the Penguin edition of the *Fable* (1970).

4. Mandeville's conservatism is apparent in the full title of the 1714 edition, which holds that the work will "demonstrate, That Human Frailties, during the degeneracy of Mankind, may be turn'd to the Advantage of the Civil Society, and made to supply the Place of the Moral Virtues." That he wishes to benefit traditional, hierarchical English society is made explicit in his contempt for women and the "Essay on Charity and Charity Schools" included in the edition of 1723. See also Viner, "Satire and Economics," p. 95. Quotations from the *Fable* are taken from the edition by Kaye.

5. See, e.g., *The Miracles Performed by Money* (1695); *The Character of a Covetous Citizen* (1702); *The Cheating Age Found Out* (1705); *To that Celebrated Idol Mammon, Chief Governor of Men's Consciences and Both Spiritual and Temporal Lord of all Christendom* (1709); John Dennis, *An Essay upon Public Spirit* (1711); Swift's essays in the *Examiner* and his *History of the Last Four Years of the Queen;* and Kramnick, *Bolingbroke and His Circle,* pp. 201-4.

6. He also wrote, "What Men have learnt from their Infancy enslaves them, and the Force of Custom warps Nature, and at the same Time imitates her in such a Manner, that it is often difficult to know, which of them we are influenced by."

7. Pocock, *Machiavellian Moment,* p. 461.

8. See, e.g., the *Review,* no. 18 (14 April 1705); *Complete English Tradesman,* 2d ed. (1727), pp. 318-19; *The Great Law of Subordination Consider'd; or, The Insolence, and Unsufferable Behavior of Servants in England duly enquired into* (1724); *The Behavior of Servants* (1726); and *Street-Robberies, Consider'd* (1728).

9. Defoe, *A Plan of the English Commerce* (1727; reprinted Oxford, 1927), p. 5. Further

citations in the text are to this edition. Among his innumerable other statements on the subject, see esp. *The Consolidator* (1705); *Whigs turned Tories and Hanoverian Tories from their avowed Principles proved Whigs; or, Each side in the other Mistaken* (1713); *Torism and Trade can never Agree* (1713); and *A True State of Publick Credit* (1721).

10. *London Journal,* nos. 689 (9 September 1732), 706 (6 January 1733), and 605 (6 March 1731); Thomas Gordon, *Essay on Government* (1747); Robbins, *Eighteenth-Century Commonwealthman,* p. 5; and Kramnick, *Bolingbroke and His Circle,* pp. 117-19. In this and the following paragraph I draw heavily from Robbins's book, her article, "Discordant Parties," and from Kramnick, *Bolingbroke and His Circle,* pp. 117-36.

11. *London Journal,* nos. 575 (8 August 1730), 740 (1 September 1733), 768 (16 March 1734), and 769 (23 March 1734); John, Lord Hervey, *Ancient and Modern Liberty Stated and Compared* (1734).

12. *London Journal,* nos. 592 (5 December 1730) and 777 (18 May 1734); *Daily Courant,* 28 August 1731; *A Full and True Account of the Strange and Miraculous Conversion of the Tories in Great Britain by the Preaching of Caleb d'Anvers, Prophet and Apostle to these Nations* (1734). The subject is treated in depth in J. H. Plumb's *The Growth of Political Stability in England 1675-1725* (Boston, 1967).

13. *London Journal,* no. 571 (11 July 1730); *Daily Gazetteer,* nos. 72 (20 September 1735), and 120 (15 November 1735).

14. *London Journal,* nos. 558 (11 April 1730), 606 (13 March 1731), 770 (30 March 1734), 783 (29 June 1734), and 799 (19 October 1734); *Free Briton,* no. 128 (11 May 1731); *The Case of the Opposition Stated Between the Craftsman and the People* (1731).

15. *The Letters of Tobias Smollett,* ed. Knapp, p. 136.

16. I have been unable to locate a copy of the original edition of this pamphlet. Here I rely upon the nine pages of extracts printed by the *Monthly Review* 9 (March 1753): 191-99. Page numbers following quotations from the work refer to this issue of the *Monthly.*

17. Like the *Critical,* Smollett in his histories generally denies that the lower orders suffer demonstrably in periods of shortage. The contrary position is to be found in most of the studies of the period: David Davies, *The Case of the Labourers in Husbandry* (1795); Frederic Eden, *The State of the Poor* (3 vols., 1797); W. J. Ashley, *The Bread of Our Forefathers* (London, 1930); J. D. Chambers and G. E. Mingay, *The Agricultural Revolution, 1750-1880* (London, 1966); and John Burnett, *A History of the Cost of Living* (London, 1969).

18. W. Hazeland, *A View of the Manner in which Trade and Civil Liberty Support each Other* (1756); Malachy Postlethwayt, *Great Britain's True System* (1756), and *Britain's Commercial Interest Explained and Improved* (1757); William Mildmay, *The Laws and Policy of England, relating to Trade Examined . . .* (1765); *Observations on the Number and Misery of the Poor* (1765); [Nathaniel Forster], *An Enquiry into the Causes of the Present High Price of Provisions* (1767); James Steuart, *An Inquiry into the Principles of Political Economy* (2 vols., 1767); *Considerations on the Effects which the Bounties, Granted on Exported Corn, Malt and Flour, have on the Manufactures of the Kingdom* (1768); [Soame Jenyns], *Thoughts on the Causes and Consequences of the Present High Price of Provisions* (Dublin and London, 1767); *An Answer to a Pamphlet entitled Thoughts . . .* (1768); *Considerations on the Exportation of Corn . . .* (1770); *An Inquiry into the Connection between the present Price of Provisions and the Size of Farms . . .* (1773); *An Inquiry into the Late Mercantile Distresses in Scotland and England . . .* (1772); and Francis Moore, *Considerations on the Exorbitant Price of Provisions* (1773).

19. In 1795-96, when there was another great outcry against the cost of corn, wheat, and bread, at least seven pamphlets appeared that repeated or extended Forster's argument. See the British Museum catalog under "Price of Provisions" for a convenient listing.

20. Trade is discussed in chapters 19 and 20 of book 2; the status of laborers in chapters 11, 17, and 18 of the same book.

21. The *Critical's* bias becomes plainer when such reviews as the above are compared with those of the *Monthly Review.* See the *Monthly* 2:326; 6:22; 8:197; 11:137; 19:104; 23:25; 25:342; 30:168; 33:48; 36:279-84, 365-78, 469, 518; 37:470-73.

CHAPTER FOUR

1. A likely explanation of Smollett's interest in politics and social theory comes from J. H. Plumb. During the earlier portion of the century the powerholders, the dominant oligarchical wing of the Whigs, were for the most part interested only in technique; they became managers, technicians, and pragmatists. Theory was left largely to the political "outs." Plumb writes: "In a world of political stability, intellectual inquiry into the nature of politics and rational criticism of institutions is unlikely to be encouraged. After 1720 it was to be found only in important circles of opposition, amongst the dissenters and, above all, across the border in Edinburgh and Glasgow." Smollett, it will be recalled, was born the year after Walpole assumed control of the Treasury (Plumb, *In the Light of History* [Boston, 1973], p. 8). On what Smollett would have considered working-class insubordination, a useful study of the later part of the century but with application for the earlier is John Foster, *Class Struggle and the Industrial Revolution: Early Industrial Capitalism in Three Industrial Towns* (London, 1974).

2. For Pope, as for Smollett, the bubble could not be forgotten, for it marked the moment when:

At length corruption, like a general flood
(So long by watchful Ministers withstood)
Shall deluge all; and Avarice, creeping on,
Spread like a lowborn mist, and blot the sun;
Statesmen and Patriot ply alike the stocks,
Peer and butler share alike the Box,
And Judges job and Bishops bite the Town,
And mighty Dukes pack cards for half-a-crown
See Britain sunk in lucre's sordid charms.   [*Moral Essays*, epistle 3, 11.135–43]

3. In many places, though not in the narrative of events of 1720, Smollett seems to associate the Whigs and especially Walpole with the whole career of the Bubble, and not simply with its resolution. The *Critical* did this openly, and this transfer of blame had been practiced by Tory political figures throughout the 1720s. Smollett's acceptance of the maneuver thirty years later is perhaps a measure of his willingness to condemn Walpole. Modern accounts nevertheless establish that the stock operation was a Tory affair: W. R. Scott, *Joint Stock Companies to 1720* (London, 1955); Eric Wagstaff, "Political Aspects of the South Sea Bubble," diss., London 1934; and John Carswell, *The South Sea Bubble* (London, 1961). Carswell (p. 190) notes that whatever Blunt, Hungerford, and Aislabie were, they were certainly not Whigs; the early support of Harley and Bolingbroke, moreover, was of great value to the scheme.

4. After discussing Johnson's moderate attitudes toward the Puritans and the civil war, Donald J. Greene comments, "Yet those things never become to Johnson as they do to, say, Thomas Hearne and Thomas Carte, Shebbeare and Smollett (to whose writings one may turn for examples of genuine Tory prejudice) matters calling for direct personal resentment" (*The Politics of Samuel Johnson* [New Haven, 1960], p. 33). The *Monthly Review* often challenged the authority of Smollett's histories; see 18:293–302; 19:249; 34:421; and 12:535. With the *Craftsman*, the *Complete History* is probably the source of the stereotype of Walpole as archdemon of political events, the cynical corrupter of all that was good in English life. Cf. Savage's *Epistle to Walpole* (1732).

5. Smollett's views of the ravages of Whig rule under George II are contained in volume 3 of the *Continuation*, published in 1763.

6. The consistent villain and source of calamity in the *Atom*, it will be recalled, is not any single political figure or group, but the mob, the Legion.

7. A similar passage occurs a few pages later in the *Continuation*, in which Smollett drops all attempts to confine his remarks to the subject at hand—parliamentary discussion of the poor laws—in favor of open partisanship upon a contemporary issue. While he had been writing, Parliament had been debating the licensing and control of those chief resorts of working-class recreation, the public houses. The proper decision, he holds, would be total suppression of these

"receptacles of vice" and "infamous recesses of intemperance" which are "the bane of industry, as well as population." Such places sap the wealth of the country by creating "the diminution of hands, the neglect of labour." Paradoxically, however, he concludes by arguing for both abolition and control, calling for legislation,

> that would abolish those infamous places of entertainment, which swarm in every corner of the metropolis, seducing people of all ranks to extravagance, profligacy, and ruin; that would restrict within due bounds the number of public houses, which are augmented to an enormous degree, affording so many asylums for riot and debauchery, and corrupting the morals of the common people to such a pitch of licentious indecency as must be a reproach to every civilized nation. [3:63]

Throughout the *Continuation* Smollett takes note of the "riotous and turbulent spirit" of the common people. Describing a grain shortage in the northern counties in 1753, he writes:

> At Leeds, a detachment of the King's troops were obliged in their own defence to fire upon the rioters, eight or nine of whom were killed on the spot; and, indeed, so little care had been taken to restrain the licentious insolence of the vulgar by proper laws and regulations, duly executed under the eye of the civil magistracy, that a military power was found absolutely necessary to maintain the peace of the kingdom. [3:71]

8. In the Admiral Byng affair, Smollett saw a fierce, clamorous, licentious, and intractable mob roused by a greedy faction to condemn the unfortunate officer. See the *Continuation*, 1:322, 479.

9. The most important work on this major aspect of social history has been done by George Rudé: "'Mother Gin' and the London Riots of 1736," *Guildhall Miscellany*, no. 10 (September 1959); "The London 'Mob' of the Eighteenth Century," *Historical Journal* 2 (1959): 1-18; "The Gordon Riots: A Study of the Rioters and Their Victims," *Trans. Royal Hist. Soc.*, 5th ser., 6 (1956): 93-114; *Wilkes and Liberty* (London, 1962); and *Hanoverian London* (Berkeley and Los Angeles, 1971). A useful summary of Rudé's earlier research is contained in chapters 1 and 9 of *Wilkes and Liberty*. See also Jack Lindsay, *1764* (London, 1959).

10. Martz discusses Smollett's contribution to the *Present State* in *Later Career*, pp. 104-23.

11. See 1:406, 431, 451, 464-65, 474, 480, 490-92; 2:30, 148-49.

12. Smollett's other comments on the lower orders appear in 1:406, 431, 441, 464-65, 474, 480, 490-502; 2:11-13.

CHAPTER FIVE

1. I do not wish to suggest that Smollett's journalistic campaign was hackneyed, at least any more so than the earlier ones of, say, Addison and Fielding or the different ones of economists and clergymen. Rather, all attacks upon luxury tend to fall within familiar patterns, and journalistic attacks are usually more enlightening than others. With a minimum of philosophizing, they reveal specifically what is disturbing the writers or their patrons. A visual analogue to the novelist's work in the *Critical* and the *Briton* would be the *Election* series that Hogarth painted in 1753 and 1754.

2. For this comparison I have retraced ground already covered for different purposes in several studies, most recently and thoroughly in Robert Donald Spector's *English Literary Periodicals* (The Hague, 1966), a valuable guide to journalistic vagaries of the period. Of the twenty-five or so periodicals publishing in the 1750s, none was so consistently conservative as Smollett's. The *Critical* anticipated by months the pessimism that became widespread in reviews of Brown's *Estimate*. As early as April 1756 the review was arguing against luxury in the context of immediate political, economic, and social issues.

3. During two lengthy periods, however, he probably did little direct writing or editing for the review. He spent the winter of 1759-60 in prison. And in a letter to Garrick dated 5 April 1761 (*Letters*, p. 98), he states that during the past six months he had written only one article for the *Critical* and might not do more during the next six. In a later letter (p. 125) he wrote that he gave up all connection with the periodical before leaving England in June 1763.

4. For attacks directed at Smollett as "Mr. Critical," see Knapp, *Tobias Smollett*, pp. 176–81; Claude E. Jones, *Smollett Studies*, University of California Publications in English, vol. 9, no. 2 (Berkeley, 1942), pp. 107 ff; and six notes by Robert D. Spector: "Attacks on the *Critical Review*," *Periodical Post Boy* (June 1955), pp. 7–8; "Further Attacks on the *Critical Review*," *N & Q* 200 (1955): 535; "Additional Attacks on the *Critical Review*," *N & Q* 201 (1956): 425; "Attacks on the *Critical Review* in the *Court Magazine*," *N & Q* 202 (1958): 308; "Attacks on the *Critical Review* in the *Literary Magazine*," *N & Q* 205 (1960): 300–301; and "Attacks on the *Critical Review* (1764–1765)," *N & Q* (1957): 121.

5. See the *Letters*, pp. 40, 81, 152–53; and Edward S. Noyes, "Another Smollett Letter," *MLN* 42 (1927): 232, 234.

6. See Derek Roper, "Smollett's 'Four Gentlemen': The First Contributors to the *Critical Review*," *RES* 10 (1959): 38–44; and Knapp, *Tobias Smollett*, pp. 176–77.

7. Reflecting upon the war in the *Continuation*, Smollett was most critical of the continental campaign. See 1:423–24; 2:391–92, 426–27; 3:254–55, 293–95, 352; 4:15–16, 421–22; 5:160–65, 293–94. After remarking at one point upon the prudence of the king of Denmark for remaining apart from the European conflict, he wrote:

It was reserved for another nation [England] to adopt the pernicious absurdity of wasting its blood and treasure, exhausting its revenues, loading its own back with the most grievous impositions, incurring an enormous debt big with bankruptcy and ruin; in a word, of expending above an hundred and fifty millions sterling in fruitless efforts to defend a distant country, the intire property of which was never valued at one twentieth of that sum; a country with which it had no natural connection, but a common alliance arising from accident. [2:391–92]

Compare Bolingbroke's remark on the necessity to end "Marlborough's war": "Whenever we shall have got rid of our war, the landed interest will then rise, and the moneyed interest, which is the great support of Whiggism, must of course decline."

8. Such prosperity was of course literary, not financial. The review demanded attention and received it, as countless numbers of contemporary comments attest. In the most famous, Johnson suggested to George III in February 1767 that of the literary journals "the *Monthly Review* was done with the most care, the *Critical* upon the best principles."

9. All identifications of authorship are from the article by Roper, "Smollett's 'Four Gentlemen.'" While it has become a historical truism to note that the English were not prepared for either the prosecution or the consequences of the war, that fact has much bearing upon the *Critical*'s editorial positions. Smollett, Griffiths, and Beckford saw different events and saw events differently. The *Critical*, *Monthly*, and *Monitor* not only disagreed about the importance of various issues and goals of the war, they also disagreed about what those issues and goals were. Even distance from those events did not modify the discrepancies, as a comparison of Smollett's histories with, say, Walpole's memoirs reveals. It must suffice here to remark that, normally acting as partisans, Smollett and the other writers for the *Critical* had a highly selective view of what was happening during the course of the conflict.

Among secondary works, I draw upon: J. S. Corbett, *England in the Seven Years' War* (London, 1907); O. A. Sherrard, *Lord Chatham: Pitt and the Seven Years' War* (London, 1955); Bernard Schilling, *Conservative England and the Case against Voltaire* (New York, 1950); and Keith Feiling, *The Second Tory Party, 1714–1832* (London, 1938).

10. The reviews attributed to Smollett are 2 (August 1756): 35–44; 2 (October 1756): 251–52, 257, 278–79, 285–86. The others are 2 (October 1756): 281, 284; 3 (February 1757): 185; 3 (March 1757): 283. Over sixteen months, the *Critical* published at least twenty-three reviews on the subject of Byng. On the validity of the charges against the ministry, see James A. Henretta, *"Salutary Neglect": Colonial Administration under the Duke of Newcastle* (Princeton, 1972).

11. In the *Continuation*, Smollett implies that Byng was innocent of wrongdoing. Spector has examined the more important passages of that work in "Smollett and Admiral Byng," *N & Q* 200 (1955): 66–67.

12. *Critical* 4 (October 1757): 371. See also 4 (November 1757): 468; and 4 (December 1757): 550–52.

13. The extent to which Pitt's conduct was supported by Tory leaders is explored by Romney Sedgwick in "Letters from William Pitt to Lord Bute, 1755-1758," in *Essays Presented to Sir Lewis Namier*, ed. Richard Pares and A. J. P. Taylor (London, 1856), especially pp. 121-22.

14. *Critical* 15 (February 1763): 150. Knapp's "Smollett and the Elder Pitt," *MLN* 59 (1944): 250-57, brings together the novelist's major comments on Pitt, but without placing them in political context. Arnold Whitridge remarks briefly in passing upon the relationship between the two men in his *Tobias Smollett: A Study of His Miscellaneous Works* (Brooklyn, 1925), pp. 23-52.

15. There is perhaps one exception to this generalization during Smollett's tenure as editor. In the January 1759 issue (7:48-49), the reviewer of the work by Rousseau seems to repeat an argument from Hume, but his point is quite muddled and applied only to conditions in *France*.

16. For a few examples see the *Critical* 2 (August 1756): 95-96; 2 (December 1756): 460; 3 (May 1757): 451-52; 4 (September 1757): 219-20; 5 (April 1758): 290; 9 (April 1760): 263; 10 (July 1760): 42; and 14 (May 1765): 395.

17. *Critical* 3 (May 1757): 478.

18. For examples of such chiding see *Critical* 1 (April 1756): 257; and 2 (October 1756): 259-60. For its generosity see 2 (December 1756): 460; 11 (June 1761): 435-39; 13 (January 1762): 80; 15 (March 1753): 161; 16 (November 1763): 378-81; 17 (January 1764): 31-36; 17 (April 1764): 304-5; 20 (July 1765): 25-35.

19. See also 5 (1758): 72-75, 443-45.

20. See also 17 (January 1764): 55-58.

21. For Smollett's role in the enterprise see Martz, "Tobias Smollett and the *Universal History*," *MLN* 56 (1941): 1-14.

22. See, for example, *Critical* 8 (October 1759): 267; 9 (March 1761): 173-74; 12 (November 1761): 323-24; and 13 (February 1762): 109.

23. The exchange between Bramble and Lismahago, for comparison, is as follows.

I allowed the truth of this remark, adding, that by their industry, oeconomy, and circumspection, many of them in England, as well as in her colonies, amassed large fortunes, with which they returned to their own country, and this was so much lost to South Britain.—"Give me leave, sir, (said he) to assure you, that in your fact you are mistaken, and in your deduction, erroneous.—Not one in two hundred that leave Scotland ever returns to settle in his own country; and the few that do return, carry thither nothing that can possibly diminish the stock of South-Britain; for none of their treasure stagnates in Scotland—There is a continual circulation, like that of the blood in the human body, and England is the heart, to which all the streams which it distributes are refunded and returned: nay, in consequence of that luxury which our connection with England hath greatly encouraged, if not introduced, all the produce of our lands, and all the profits of our trade, are engrossed by the natives of South-Britain; for you will find that the exchange between the two kingdoms is always against Scotland; and that she retains neither gold nor silver sufficient for her own circulation.—The Scots, not content with their own manufactures and produce, which would very well answer all necessary occasions, seem to vie with each other in purchasing superfluities from England; such as broad-cloth, velvets, stuffs, silks, lace, furs, jewels, furniture of all sorts, sugar, rum, tea, chocolate, and coffee; in a word, not only every mode of the most extravagant luxury, but even many articles of convenience, which they might find as good, and much cheaper, in their own country. For all these particulars, I conceive, England may touch about one million sterling a-year.—I don't pretend to make an exact calculation; perhaps, it may be something less, and, perhaps, a great deal more.—The annual revenue arising from all the private estates of Scotland cannot fall short of a million sterling; and, I should imagine, their trade will amount to as much more.—I know, the linen manufacture alone returns near half a million, exclusive of the home-consumption of that article.—If, therefore, North-Britain pays a balance of a million annually to England, I insist upon it, that country is more valuable to her in the way of commerce, than any colony in her possession, over and above the other advantages which I have specified: therefore, they are no friends, either to England or to truth, who affect to depreciate the northern part of the united kingdom."

I must own, I was at first a little nettled to find myself schooled in so many particulars.—Though I did not receive all his assertions as gospel, I was not prepared to refute them; and I cannot help now acquiescing in his remarks so far as to think, that the contempt for Scotland, which prevails too much on this side the Tweed, is founded on prejudice and error. [MB, September 20]

Martz discusses a further pair of parallel passages, from the *Briton* and *Humphry Clinker*, in *Later Career*, pp. 171-73. A. J. Youngson provides a valuable historical gloss on the situation in his *After the Forty-Five: The Economic Impact on the Scottish Highlands* (Edinburgh, 1973).

24. See especially *Critical* 1 (March 1756): 97 (Smollett); 2 (August 1756): 48; 2 (September 1756): 121 (Smollett); 3 (March 1757): 238; 4 (July 1757): 46; 7 (April 1759): 375; 8 (October 1759): 271-72.

25. See, for example, *Critical* 5 (April 1758): 292, and the review's prefatory remarks to its extracts of the *Complete History* and *Continuation*.

26. See the previous section on luxury in the *Critical*, and 5 (April 1758): 285-319. In the preface to the opening volume (1758) of the *Grand Magazine of Magazines*, the editors criticized the bias of both the *Critical* and the *Monthly*: "The managers of the *Reviews* are not, perhaps, incompetent judges, but they are too slovenly or too remiss: too partial or too much interested in the characters they give; too much bigotted, or too free thinkers; too zealous Tories or too rigid Whigs, to judge with candour of the labours of their contemporaries; hence it is, that the characters they give, often stand in contrast to each other." Cited by Spector, *English Literary Periodicals*, pp. 190-91, n. 121.

27. Since the *Monitor* was a *political* and not a trade periodical, the call for reform amounted to its "platform," as it did with the allied periodicals the *Con-Test, Patriot,* and *North Briton.*

28. See *Critical* 2 (August 1756): 10-11, 44; 5 (January 1758): 1; and 7 (April 1759): 292.

29. *Critical* 9 (June 1760): 466-67.

30. Occupying the broad middle ground of Smollett's political vision was the companion of luxury, commerce itself, which the novelist came to distrust as later writers did industrialization and technology. Severely controlled, as it would be under the administration of a natural legislator, commerce would not disrupt the process of civil government and would surely not precipitate a costly war; rather, it would have a beneficent, consolidating effect upon the whole of English society. Under the Whigs, however, the meddling arrogance of mere merchants and tradesmen was tolerated, sometimes even encouraged, and commerce was permitted to assume unprecedented importance. Thus unrestrained, it upset the social order, threatened the constitution with sedition, and engendered "tumult, riot, and insurrection." During the last years of the reign of George II the *Critical* gave considerable, normally pejorative, attention to the effects of commerce, much of it in connection with the war and the price of food. Smollett was meanwhile also composing his acerbic remarks on the influence of commerce for the concluding volume of the *Complete History* and then resuming the theme in the initial volume of the *Continuation* (1760). Of the effects of the cessation of war in 1748, he writes in the *Continuation:*

Commerce and manufacture flourished again, to such a degree of encrease as had never been known in the island: but this advantage was attended with an irresistible tide of luxury and excess, which flowed through all degrees of the people, breaking down all the mounds of civil polity, and opening a way for licence and immorality. The highways were infested with rapine and assassination; the cities teemed with the brutal votaries of lewdness, intemperance, and profligacy. The whole land was overspread with a succession of tumult, riot, and insurrection. [1:56]

Four years later, unregulated commerce still threatened the kingdom.

The tide of luxury still flowed with an impetuous current, bearing down all the mounds of temperance and decorum; while fraud and profligacy struck out new channels, through which they eluded the restrictions of the law, and all the vigilance of civil polity. New arts of deception were invented, in order to ensnare and ruin the unwary; and some infamous practices, in the way of commerce, were countenanced by persons of rank and importance in the commonwealth. [1:128]

In the *Present State* (7:64), he equates "trade and commerce" with "cheating and over-reaching."

31. The greatest source of information about the City is contemporary periodicals themselves. Of secondary sources the most important are four studies by Lucy B. Sutherland: *A London Merchant* (London, 1933), *The East India Company in Eighteenth-Century Politics* (Oxford, 1952), *The City of London and the Opposition to Government, 1768–1774* (London, 1959), and the article "The City in Eighteenth-Century Politics," in *Essays Presented to Sir Lewis Namier*, ed. Richard Pares and A. J. P. Taylor (London, 1956), pp. 49–74. The strength of Whig sentiment in the City can be gauged by the entries in *The Diary of Sylas Neville*, ed. Basil Cozens-Hardy (London, 1950). Neville regarded himself as a staunch republican and was a friend of Wilkes. For another contemporary view, see *The Diary of the Late George Bubb Dodington . . . March 8, 1749 to February 6, 1761*, ed. Henry P. Wyndham (London, 1784); and *The Political Journal of George Bubb Dodington*, ed. John Carswell and Lewis A. Dralle (Oxford, 1965). Dodington may have been the man who recommended Smollett to Bute's attention as editor of the pro-administration paper that was to become the *Briton*.

Important specialized studies include A. H. John, "War and the English Economy, 1700–1763," *Economic History Review*, 2d ser., 7 (1954–55): 329–44; Walter E. Minchinton, "The Merchants in England in the Eighteenth Century," in *The Entrepreneur: Papers Presented at the Annual Conference of the Economic History Society at Cambridge, England April 1957* (Cambridge, Mass., 1957), pp. 22–31; and W. P. Treloar, *Wilkes and the City* (London, 1917).

An instance of City independence that Whigs of Smollett's age were proud to recall occurred in 1688, when in contravention of James II's "reforms" the lord mayor and aldermen continued to apply the Test Act, ordered that the Guy Fawkes Day celebration be maintained, declined to invite the new papal nuncio to dinner though ordered to do so at royal command, and did continue Anglican services in the Guildhall chapel.

32. On the political friction created by the City Whigs, within and without London, see the studies by Sutherland cited in note 31; Robbins, *Eighteenth-Century Commonwealthman*, pp. 9, 16, 228; Treloar, *Wilkes and the City*, pp. 126–36; Rudé, *Wilkes and Liberty*, chap. 9. An attempt to explain the friction in social terms appears in the second half of Anthony Giddens, *The Class Structure of Advanced Societies* (London, 1973).

33. *Memoirs of William Beckford of Fonthill* (London, 1859), 1:33. Beckford was apparently the principal financial backer of the *Monitor* when it was founded in 1755 and continued to be a major contributor. He was thus at the hub of reform politics, opposition journalism, and City commerce. The interrelationships among City figures were various. The main editor of the *Monitor*, Arthur Beardmore, was Temple's lawyer and a successful businessman. Richard Grenville, Lord Temple, was of course the brother of George Grenville and the brother-in-law of Pitt. The scholarly work of first resort, and the one I usually follow in this and the following chapter for information regarding important political figures and movements, is Lewis Namier and John Brooke, *The History of Parliament: The House of Commons, 1754–1790*, 3 vols. (London, 1964). Beckford's career is discussed in 1:329–30.

34. Cited by Sutherland, "The City in Eighteenth-Century Politics," p. 66. The City stressed electoral reform both because of its intrinsic merit as a political issue and because its success would lead, it was argued, to further acceptance of "the sense of the people." Until 1832 the City sent only four members to Parliament, with two additional supporters of metropolitan causes coming from Southwark and, on occasion, two more from Westminster. Meanwhile, as Defoe noted repeatedly in his *Tour* (1724–26), "barren villages" like Old Sarum and "miserable, dirty, decayed, poor, and pitiful towns" each sent half that number. Yet the disproportion was actually not as great as it at first appears, as was shown by Namier in his *England in the Age of the American Revolution*, 2d ed. (London, 1961), pp. 223–24. Forty-eight other members returned for the Parliament of 1761 provided latent support for City interests, since, whatever their nominal constituencies, they were London merchants. These forty-eight did not normally

share the political attitudes of the City Radicals, but they did to a large extent share their commerical views. In any case, City parliamentary strength taken at its highest numerical figure of fifty-six remained a paltry thing, for in 1761 Devon and Cornwall together returned seventy members. The theme was repeated widely outside of Parliament and the periodicals by scores of pamphlet-writers. For one example, the anonymous author of *Political Disquisions* (1763) contended that the present British constitution represented interests no longer predominant and that the merchant class must now obtain a greater share of governmental influence. The best recent account of the agitation is John Cannon, *Parliamentary Reform 1640-1832* (Cambridge, 1973).

35. Valuable contemporary accounts of this movement, from the point of view of a supporter, are contained in three works by John Almon: *A Review of Mr. Pitt's Administration* (1762), *A Review of Lord Bute's Administration* (1763), and *The History of the Late Minority* (1766). There is a copy of the last of these with marginal comments by Wilkes in the British Museum. Secondary discussions are Rudé, *Wilkes and Liberty;* Robert R. Rea, *The English Press in Politics, 1760-1774* (Lincoln, Neb., 1963); George Nobbe, *The North Briton* (New York, 1939); and James T. Boulton, *The Language of Politics in the Age of Wilkes and Burke* (London, 1963).

36. Spector makes this point briefly in his *"The Monthly* and Its Rival," *Bulletin of the New York Public Library* 71 (1960): 159-61. A thorough comparison would include discussion of the following comments from the *Monthly.* On political representation and commentary: 15 (July 1756): 1-2; 15 (September 1756): 233; 15 (October 1756): 408; 15 (November 1756): 518-21, 526-29; 17 (October 1757): 291; 17 (November 1757): 467; 18 (May 1758): 401. On progress in commerce and trade: 14 (January 1756): 37; 14 (February 1756): 81; 15 (September 1756): 217; 16 (February 1757): 163; 16 (April 1757): 302-3, 349-52; 18 (May 1758): 465.

37. See the attacks upon Smollett cited in note 4. Horace Walpole provided a sample in his *Memoirs of . . . the Reign of King George the Third:*

> Smollett was a worthless man, and only mentioned here because author of a History of England, of the errors in which posterity ought to be warned. Smollett was bred a sea-surgeon, and turned author. He wrote a tragedy, and sent it to Lord Lyttelton, with whom he was not acquainted. . . . Smollett's return was drawing an abusive portrait of Lord Lyttelton in Roderick Random, a novel; of which sort he published two or three. His next attempt was on the History of England; a work in which he engaged for book-sellers, and finished, though four volumes in quarto, in two years; yet an easy task, as being pilfered from other histories. Accordingly it was little noticed till it came down to the present times; then, though compiled from the libels of the age and the most paltry materials, yet being heightened by personal invectives, strong Jacobitism, and the worst representation of the Duke of Cumberland's conduct in Scotland, the sale was prodigious.
> [Ed. H. R. V. Fox (London, 1822), pp. 419-20]

Political and social divisions were also geographical divisions, there being great areas where no member of the London mob would be tolerated. Bramble, it will be remembered, wished to confine the vulgar who resorted to Bath to the lower town. Contemporary pamphleteers often referred, in a kind of shorthand, to the contests of "Soho vs. Wapping" or "St. Marylebone vs. St. George-in-the-East."

38. *The Adventures of an Atom,* in *Miscellaneous Works,* ed. Robert Anderson, 2d ed. (Edinburgh, 1800), 6:415. Further citations to the *Atom* are to this edition and will be given in the text.

39. For Murphy's political character and abilities, see Almon, *History of the Late Minority;* Spector, *English Literary Periodicals,* pp. 68-72: Nobbe, *North Briton,* p. 33; and *DNB.*

40. Those identified as Smollett's are: *Critical* 1 (January-February 1756): 88, 89; 1 (April 1756): 258-59, 259-60, 263-64; 2 (September 1756): 121 ff.; 2 (December 1756): 471-72. See also his related review, 2 (August 1756): 38-39. Those by other writers are: 2 (September 1756): 188; 3 (January 1757): 83; 3 (February 1757): 179-82; 4 (October 1757): 369-70; 5 (February 1758): 101; 6 (July 1758): 81-83; 6 (August 1758): 170-71; 6 (November 1758):

438. Related reviews are 5 (January 1758): 9-10; 5 (April 1758): 284; and 6 (September 1758), 228-39.

41. See for example *Critical* 11 (May 1761): 363-69, 389-90; 15 (January 1763): 68-69.

42. See for example *Critical* 2 (December 1756): 343-48; and 4 (November 1757): 379, 385.

43. Representative examples are *Critical* 9 (June 1760): 465-67; 12 (August 1761): 108-9, 13 (January 1762): 1-4; and 15 (June 1763): 449-67.

44. The *Critical* was far from being alone in raising this specter. See, for example, George Watson, *The Scripture Doctrine of Obedience to Government* . . . (1763); and John Brown, *Thoughts on Civil Liberty, on Licentiousness, and Faction* (1765). See also Rudé, "The London 'Mob' of the Eighteenth Century," *Historical Journal* 2 (1959): 1-18.

45. See *Critical* 10 (July 1760): 43. In the *Continuation* Smollett seems to suggest that crowds of common people gather for political meetings only when hired by sinister agents of faction. See, for example, 4:334.

46. See *Critical* 5 (April 1758): 312; and 9 (February 1760): 89-90. See also *Travels,* letter 9, for Smollett's comments on Joseph, his postilion.

47. See *Critical* 2 (November 1756): 348-50; 7 (May 1759): 427-28; 10 (October 1760): 290-91; and 18 (June 1764): 467. See also Schilling, *Conservative England and the Case against Voltaire,* pp. 23 ff., 69-83. In *English Literary Periodicals,* Spector draws this conclusion: "Yet in no periodical was the relationship of Church and state more emphatically argued than in the *Critical.* For its reviewers, religion and morality were interdependent, and the social order itself depended upon the perpetuation of traditional religious belief. Without religious morality to enforce civil duty, preservation of justice and mercy would rest upon 'the written laws of men; and . . . the unwritten laws of reason and conscience—both which [are] totally insufficient'" (p. 193). In *Humphry Clinker,* Bramble writes ironically (July 4) that a friend of his, George Hewitt, returns to Italy by way of Geneva "that he may have a conference with his friend Voltaire, about giving the last blow to the Christian superstition."

48. *Critical* 11 (January 1761): 40; and 8 (November 1759): 419.

49. *Critical* 16 (December 1763): 456.

50. The declaration that the enthusiast "is hardly known in England" is of course inconsistent with many of his other writings, but it is in keeping with his plan for the *Travels.* As noted in connection with his remarks on luxury, Smollett is here minimizing English vices while emphasizing those of the French and the Italians.

CHAPTER SIX

1. The diplomatic maneuvers of the period are discussed in Zenab Esmat Rashed, *The Peace of Paris 1763* (Liverpool, 1951). The terms of the alliance between Bute and George III are clarified in *Letters from George III to Lord Bute, 1756-1766,* ed. Romney Sedgwick (London, 1939), and in James Lee McKelvey, *George III and Lord Bute: The Leicester House Years* (Durham, N.C., 1973). One of the best running commentaries on the war of the weekly papers is volume 1 of *The Correspondence of the Late John Wilkes,* ed. John Almon (London, 1805). Almon includes three letters Smollett wrote to Wilkes before the paper war began, in one of which he addresses Wilkes as "my friend."

2. Besides the intervention and support of the *Auditor,* there are three items of evidence to indicate that the *Briton* fell short of the administration's purpose. (1) John Almon, whose *History of the Late Minority* is the only source for this kind of information, recorded at the time that "the number [of copies of the *Briton*] printed was but 250," implying further that not even this small number was completely distributed. The Whiggish *St. James's Chronicle* on 5 June 1762 noted the appearance of the new sheet with these remarks: "The late Revolution in the Ministry having again set the numerous Tribe of Pamphleteers, Politicians, periodical Paper-Writers, and others of the Machiavellian Class to work, the Public was presented last Saturday with a new Paper entitled the *Briton,* professedly written in Opposition to the *Monitor*: Of this Paper it was our Intention, agreeably to our accustomed Impartiality, to have laid an Abstract before our Readers; but on examining it, we found the Execution, besides

some very exceptionable Points in the *real* Intent of the Piece, to be infinitely beneath either our Notice or Criticism" (quoted in Nobbe, *North Briton*, p. 38). (2) After its first three issues, the *North Briton* largely ignored Smollett and the *Briton;* when it attacked the pro-administration press, it cited the *Auditor*. (3) If Smollett had succeeded in increasing the administration's popularity, Bute would probably have continued to finance the *Briton* beyond the peace treaty. As it happened, the treaty was signed 10 February 1763, and the *Briton* issued its last number 12 February.

3. Defending Smollett against numerous misconceptions, Knapp is eloquent in his biography on the novelist's behalf, citing as evidence, usually, his own answers to his detractors. This method—and the important research that permitted it—is an immeasurable improvement over nineteenth-century studies. When it involves issues of contemporary controversy, however, it is not always adequate. In addition to *Tobias Smollett,* see Knapp's "Rex versus Smollett: More Data on the Smollett-Knowles Libel Case," *MP* 41 (1944): 221-27; "Smollett's Early Years in London," *JEGP* 31 (1932): 220-27; "Ralph Griffiths, Author and Publisher, 1746-1750," *Library* 20 (1939): 197-213; "Smollett and the Elder Pitt," *MLN* 59 (1944): 250-57; and the introduction and notes to Knapp's edition of *Humphry Clinker*.

Gassman extended this method into areas of social and intellectual background in his "The Background of *Humphry Clinker,*" diss., University of Chicago 1960; "*The Briton* and *Humphry Clinker,*" *SEL* 31 (1963): 397-414; and "Religious Attitudes in the World of *Humphry Clinker,*" *Brigham Young University Studies* 6 (Winter 1965): 65-72. Other studies approaching the novelist in much the same way include Whitridge, *Tobias Smollett;* Goldberg, *Smollett and the Scottish School;* and Bruce, *Radical Dr. Smollett.* The most recent example is Robin Fabel, "The Patriotic Briton: Tobias Smollett and English Politics, 1756-1771," *ECS* 8 (1974): 100-114. Fabel regards Smollett as "the nonpolitical doctor" who transcended political disputes and who dismissed political groups of all types.

4. See Namier, *The Structure of Politics,* 2d ed. (London, 1957), pp. 99-100, 117, 210, 268-70, 280-82; and J. Steven Watson, *The Reign of George III* (Oxford, 1960), pp. 81-91.

5. In the third issue Smollett explained that the Briton was "Printed for J. Coote, at the King's Arms, in Paternoster Row."

6. *The Grenville Papers,* 1:457, cited by Nobbe, *North Briton,* p. 32.

7. As part of his political housecleaning, Bute upon becoming first lord began removing Whigs from office. Between October 1760 and February 1762, he expunged nearly all of the Whiggish country lords-lieutenant and justices of the peace, created seventeen new Tory peers and nine Tory lords, and in the largest category, many new Tory grooms of the bedchamber, part of which purge has been called "the massacre of the Pelhamite Innocents."

8. See the *Briton,* nos. 2 (5 June 1762), 7 (10 July 1762), 8 (18 July 1762), 11 (7 August 1762), 35 (22 January 1763). See also the *Continuation* 1:424; 2:4, 6, 18, 196, 261, 306, 381 ff., 426-27; 4:116, 327 ff.

9. See also *Continuation* 5:211-19.

10. See *Critical* 14 (September 1762): 238; 18 (August 1764): 150; and *Auditor,* no. 31 (18 December 1762).

11. In the *Auditor,* Murphy called Wilkes Colonel Squintum and Colonel Cataline. Temple was Lord Gawkee, and Beckford Alderman Sugarcane. See, for example, no. 16 (23 September 1762).

12. *Boswell's London Journal, 1762-1763,* ed. F. A. Pottle (New York, 1950), contains the two standard, but antithetical, views of this charge. On one side, Boswell—who was then reading regularly the *Briton, Auditor, Monitor,* and *North Briton*—found the *North Briton* a polished and witty journal of debate and discovered "a poignant acrimony in it that is very relishing." He records his admiration for Wilkes and even sends him an essay for publication (that was never used). On the other side, Pottle in his introduction calls Wilkes an "unscrupulous demogogue" who "roused the anger of the mob" and "played upon the fears of the mob." Nobbe's book *The North Briton* examines the traditional charges against Wilkes.

13. Smollett's argument here echoes the attacks of the *Critical* upon Rousseau's political teachings. While generally favorable to his style and imagination, the review objected strongly to his political theories. See 7 (January 1759): 48-59; 11 (January 1761): 65-66; 12 (September 1761): 203-11; 13 (February 1762): 101-7; 14 (October 1762): 250-70; 14

(November 1762): 336-46; 14 (December 1762), 426-40; 15 (January 1763): 21-34.

14. This argument provides further evidence of the political nature of his attacks upon luxury. For seven years, since 1756, Smollett had been arguing that such enervation, destruction, and depopulation *had already* ruined Old England, for in no other way could he explain the influence of such unworthy men as the City Whigs.

When reprinting the *Briton* for the *Political Controversy* collection, Wilkes appended the following note to Smollett's statement: "I never yet heard that wealth was the occasion of the ruin of any kingdom.—It must be allowed, indeed, that it introduces luxury, and enervates the disposition in impolitic governments, and so far may be reckoned a misfortune.—But in trading nations industry always keeps us active, tho affluence should render us extravagant . . . we have nothing to fear from our riches while we pay a proper attention to our laws. . . . Upon the whole, the Briton's arguments are calculated for the primitive ages of the world, when a king would feast upon a bit of bread and milk, and an Emperor was unacquainted with the luxury of a mutton chop or a decent pair of breeches" (2:28).

15. Upon hearing of the signing of the preliminary articles, Wilkes is alleged to have said that "it was certainly the peace of God which passeth all understanding."

16. In many ways the rival political sheets determined each other's contents. Whom the *Briton* would damn the *North Briton* must praise, and vice versa. Since Murphy and Smollett regularly denounced Beckford, Wilkes often lauded the lord mayor. In no. 39, for example, published on 26 February 1763, Wilkes reports Beckford's "*elegant* and *masterly* speech" in which he stated "*that the present Peace was in every respect more infamous than that of Utrecht.*" He continues:

> He did accordingly, from the duty he owed to his fellow-citizens, and from his steady, admirable uniformity of conduct, summon a common-council expressly on that great occasion, to explain and enforce with patriotic zeal the important cause of their meeting, and propose an address to the Legislature, to stop in time the progress of so alarming a negociation, founded on the strong evidence of the *preliminaries.* This was his clear duty, and this he nobly discharged. . . . He will therefore, never lend himself to *prop* the minister who made this *infamous peace* as he terms it; but will, I am persuaded, continue steady, indefatigable and animated in an opposition to him.

17. Edward S. Noyes, "Another Smollett Letter," *MLN* 42 (1927): 232.

18. In addition to the works previously cited on this point, see Carl B. Cone, *The English Jacobins* (New York, 1968).

19. *Miscellaneous Works,* ed. Anderson, 6:390. Further citations from the *Atom* will be to this edition and volume, and will be given in the text. The political analogies with Japan are discussed in James R. Foster, "Smollett and the *Atom,*" *PMLA* 68 (1953): 1032-46; and Knapp, "The Keys to Smollett's *Atom,*" *ELN* 2 (1964): 100-102. Hereafter I take the liberty to use the "translated" English names in the text.

20. The famous allegation that Newcastle did not know Britain to be an island is mentioned as fact twice in the *Atom,* pp. 398, 417.

CHAPTER SEVEN

1. E. D. Hirsch, *Validity in Interpretation* (New Haven, 1967), p. 74.

2. The essay is Trilling's "Art and Fortune" in *The Liberal Imagination* (1950; reprinted New York, 1953), pp. 247-71. The approach suggested here could be used with several early fictional narratives. In *Tom Jones,* for example, Fielding uses luxury as concept and as characteristic in the middle and latter portions of the novel. When Tom enters the inn at Hambrook or Upton, he is beholding a world of perfervid pretense as repellent as that Bramble found in the Pump Room at Bath, and the degeneracy he finds in London has the same roots as that Bramble found.

3. A comparable but more recent reading of the novel is John M. Warner's "Smollett's Development as a Novelist," *Novel* 5 (Winter 1972): 148-61. Warner's essay is a well-written and (in its own terms) closely argued exposition of what he considers to be Smollett's movement away

from satire and toward irony. It contains direct or tacit evaluations of all the important elements of *Humphry Clinker,* but without a single reference to the literary history of its own time. From his own perspective Warner can discover Smollett to be much closer as a novelist to Henry James and Lawrence Durrell than to Henry Fielding.

In what might become a similar situation, readers a century or so from now may wonder at the sudden and ambiguous appearance in the later 1960s of black characters in novels by white American authors who had previously left untouched all aspects of black life—for example, John Updike's *Rabbit Redux,* Bernard Malamud's *The Tenants,* Walker Percy's *Love in the Ruins,* and especially Saul Bellow's *Mr. Sammler's Planet.*

4. In his preface to the opening volume of the *Continuation* (1760), Smollett professes that,

> he will carefully avoid the imputation of enthusiasm. In the midst of his transports he hopes to remember his duty, and check the exuberance of zeal with the rigid severity of historical truth.
>
> This is the guiding star by which he hath hitherto steered his dangerous course; the star whose chearing radiance has conducted him safe through the rocks of prejudice and the tides of faction. Guiltless of all connexions that might be supposed to affect his candour, and endanger his integrity, he is determined to proceed with that fearless spirit of independence, by which he flatters himself the former part of the work hath been remarkably distinguished. [1:v]

5. I have not tried to demonstrate further the working of this pattern, for it will be taken up in following chapters. Nor have I attempted to encompass all the political issues touched upon in the novel, but have restricted myself here to the most prominent.

6. Compare the nobleman's lecture to Harrison on the effects of luxury upon a nation in book 11, chapter 2 ("Matters Political") of *Amelia.*

7. This passage has troubled several critics, who have wondered why on this issue alone Smollett should be challenging the government of George III. But as discussion of the *Complete History* has shown, Lismahago is here recalling the practices of Walpole under George II. The review of *An Additional Dialogue of the Dead* in the *Critical Review* for June 1760, cited in chapter 5, calls elections the chance politicians have for "soothing, cajoling, corrupting and destroying the morals of their constituents" (9:466). Its conclusion merits repeating: "Consult history, consult your own mind . . . there can [never] be a dependence on the integrity of the people, where luxury and interest contribute in rendering corrupt, those on whom they have devolved their rights, and constituted their representatives" (9:467).

8. These identifications are explained, and several others for pseudonymous characters attempted, in a forthcoming note in *Notes & Queries* (1977).

9. In the *Continuation,* Smollett interrupts his narrative to praise Heathcote and to apologize for an "injury done him in an earlier volume [*Complete History,* 4:575] in classing him with partisans of the ministry."

> We think it our duty to declare, upon better information, that alderman Heathcote, far from being a partisan of any ministry, always distinguished himself in parliament by a constant and uniform opposition to all ministerial measures, which tended to the prejudice or dishonour of the nation; and ever approved himself an honest, resolute, and zealous assertor of the rights and liberties of the people. [3:442]

Further information on Heathcote is contained in the *DNB;* Sutherland, *The East India Company in Eighteenth-Century Politics;* and Namier and Brooke, *History of Parliament.*

10. Byron Gassman takes a different approach to Methodism in the novel in his "Religious Values in the World of *Humphry Clinker,*" *Brigham Young University Studies* 6 (Winter 1965): 65-72. A valuable study of attacks on the sect is Albert M. Lyles, *Methodism Mocked* (London, 1961). In a letter to John Chute, 10 October 1766, Horace Walpole describes a Methodist chapel he visited at Bath and concludes that luxury can be found even here.

11. Repeatedly through the 1760s Smollett identified himself as a sturdy warrior on behalf of the king's causes. The recurring praise of the young monarch in the *Briton* had been preceded by the encomiums of the *Critical* and was followed by yet stronger advocacy in the *Continuation* and the *Atom.* In the *Continuation* he wrote:

[The people's] love was heightened to rapture and admiration . . . when they were made acquainted with the transcendent virtues of his heart, and the uncommon extent of his understanding; when they knew he was mild, affable, social, and sympathizing; susceptible of all the emotions which private friendship inspires; kind and generous to his dependents, liberal to merit . . . when they knew his heart was intirely British; warmed with the most cordial love of his native country, and animated with plans of the most genuine patriotism; when they learned . . . that he possessed almost every accomplishment that art could communicate, or application acquire. [4:151-52]

CHAPTER EIGHT

1. During the last thirty years or so, most of the critical commentary on Smollett's handling of character has emphasized the novelist's irony. Warner, in the article on Smollett's development cited above, says that no character is reliable of himself, since all are treated ironically; truth is found by splicing together the comments of all five letter-writers: "The scene of life . . . as the diversified points of view indicate . . . is approached from many angles and is seen to reflect truth not just from one of these but from all" (p. 159). A similar conclusion, making Smollett an early romantic in his vision of truth, is drawn by William A. West in "Matt Bramble's Journey to Health," *Texas Studies in Literature and Language* 11 (1969): 1207. More recent and elaborate examples of this approach (in studies otherwise quite different) are John Valdimir Price, *Tobias Smollett: The Expedition of Humphry Clinker*, Studies in English Literature, no. 51 (London, 1973); and Eric Rothstein, *Systems of Order and Inquiry in Later Eighteenth-Century Fiction* (Berkeley and Los Angeles, 1975), pp. 109-53, esp. pp. 100-21. Among the studies that relate Smollett's characters, especially Bramble, to contemporary fictional types, two of the best are Thomas R. Preston, "Smollett and the Benevolent Misanthrope Type," *PMLA* 79 (1964): 51-57; and John Sena, "Smollett's Persona and the Melancholic Traveler: An Hypothesis," *ECS* 1 (1968): 353-69.

2. In an instance of plebeian luxury, I take the liberty once more to separate that which is inseparable. Only for convenience of discussion can the characters of *Humphry Clinker* be divided from its politics or its structure.

3. According to long-standing Welsh and English beliefs, the bramble plant is curative as well as prickly. In one version, its leaves in solution were used to heal burns, infections, and diseases. In another, a plant that had rooted at both ends to form an arch was regarded as beneficent to all sickly persons and animals that passed under it. See E. M. Leather, *The Folk-Lore of Herefordshire* (London, 1912); and Edwin and Mona Radford, *Encyclopedia of Superstitions*, 2d ed., rev. Christina Hole (London, 1961).

4. In the preface to *Ferdinand Count Fathom*, Smollett speaks of the need for contrasting incidents and characters: "That the mind might not be fatigued, nor the imagination disgusted, by a succession of vicious objects, I have endeavoured to refresh the attention with occasional incidents of a different nature; and raised up a virtuous character, in opposition to the adventurer, with a view to amuse the fancy, engage the affection, and form a striking contrast which might heighten the expression, and give a *relief* to the moral of the whole."

5. This criterion seems to hold with even those figures who do not appear in his letters. Certain characters like Mr. S— and Squire Prankley we encounter only through Jery; yet it is a nephew who is exercising those methods of assessment he has recently learned from his uncle.

6. Martz in *The Later Career*, pp. 170-75, describes Lismahago's role in the novel as essentially didactic. For an account of the effect of English prejudice upon Scots, see George M. Kahrl, *Tobias Smollett: Traveler-Novelist* (Chicago, 1945), pp. 65-79.

7. Goldberg, *Smollett and the Scottish School*, pp. 169-75, builds his argument for the novelist's primitivism on the character of Clinker. Although he does not note that Clinker is not a hard primitivist (and Bramble is not a primitivist at all), he is perceptive on Clinker's moral function.

8. See for example *Spectator* no. 55, Pope's "Of the Characters of Women," William Whitehead's "Song for Ranelagh," and Chesterfield's famous "Women . . . are only children of a larger growth" letter, 5 September 1748. Patricia Meyer Spacks presents an interesting review

of the position of women, from the viewpoint of women writers, in "Ev'ry Woman Is at Heart a Rake," *ECS* 8 (1974): 27–46. One might say that for traditional critics of luxury, there lingered a Miltonic image, not of that "fair defect of nature" alone, but of Eve joined by Sin, half graceful woman and half loathsome serpent. In her *Marriage: Fielding's Mirror of Morality* (University, Ala., 1973), pp. 122–43, Murial Brittain Williams includes useful appendixes on marriage and divorce laws and popular attitudes toward women. Jean H. Hagstrum's forthcoming book on changing conceptions of love will trace the theme through eighteenth- and early nineteenth-century literature.

9. See also her letter of June 14, Jery's of May 29, Liddy's of April 26 and June 10, and Bramble's of June 12.

10. On many occasions from the *Critical Review* of 1756 to the *Atom* of 1769 Smollett was to remark what he considered criminal conspiracies among the working poor. Bramble's comments on the servants of Squire Burdock are anticipated in many places, particularly in the closing letter of the *Travels,* which is devoted to methods of extortion and advises weary travelers to oblige the "confederacy" lest their journeys be made intolerable. Apropos the delight Win and Dutton take in dressing like their betters, at least six times during Smollett's editorship the *Critical* attacked the dress of servants as indicative of the luxury of the laboring population. The strictures upon women's dress and habits in Smollett and the *Critical* should be compared with those found in *The Lady's Magazine; or, Polite Companion for the Fair Sex* (September 1759-).

CHAPTER NINE

1. My sense of the structure of *Humphry Clinker* is close to that Malcolm Bradbury finds in most fiction; see his "Towards a Poetics of Fiction: 1. An Approach through Structure," *Novel* 1 (1967): 51. There is a further parallel in Henry Knight Miller's excellent analysis "Some Functions of Rhetoric in *Tom Jones,*" *PQ* 45 (1966): 209–35. Miller demonstrates in Fielding's rhetoric an attempt to reach "every Reader in the world." Smollett's ambition was no less; he would have his work appeal to the reason, to the senses, and to all shadings of the two.

2. In stressing Smollett's attack upon luxury, let me repeat, I do not wish to be seen as neglecting or minimizing the novelist's relationship to his contemporaries. His indebtedness to earlier epistolary fiction, to Anstey's *New Bath Guide,* and to Fielding has been well treated before. Yet if one were to search out specific parallels, one would still be obliged to go to antiquity: to the attack on juries in the *Wasps* and on the comprehensive franchise in the *Knights,* for example, or to the dialectic of character and action in the Platonic dialogues, where a figure of known background and temperament enters with a question to be answered or a dilemma to be resolved and is guided to his own enlightenment. In any case, my argument here is concerned with uses, not sources.

3. Byron Gassman first noted the change in Jery's attitude in "The Background of . . . *Humphry Clinker,*" p. 61. Bramble's charge that the common people defile a spa has a historically familiar ring. For three centuries the authorities of Zurich ordained by law who was permitted to travel to the mineral springs at Baden, fourteen miles away.

4. See Louis A. Landa, "London Observed: The Progress of a Simile," *PQ* 54 (1975): 275–88.

5. Scotland, Dennison's small part of England, and Bramble's small part of Wales all offer a way of life that is providential as well as arcadian. To meet as many of the good people of North Britain as he wishes, Bramble must be vigorous in his pursuits. In London he was, it seems, content to spend the time writing long letters. (He also discovered there that the only decent food to be had was eggs "imported from France and Scotland.") In Scotland he is apparently too busy to write, and his letters are relatively few for the length of time he spends in the country. As he is vigorously exercised, he loses all signs of gout and constipation, incidently following Chowder's example of a healing regimen.

In Dennison's estate a few acres of Scotland seem to be transplanted, and in their descriptions of the two places Jery and Bramble provide what amount to Smollett's Discourses—offering the proper subjects, methods, and ideals for Imitation in Excellence. Like the typical Scotsman, Dennison is in features "hale, robust, and florid." Yet because he resides below the Tweed, he like Baynard requires a fortunate death in the family before he can be his own man. He inherited the estate when his elder brother "was happily carried off by a fever, the immediate consequence of a debauch" (MB, October 8).

CONCLUSION

1. Christopher Hill, "The Norman Yoke," *Puritanism and Revolution* (London, 1958), pp. 50-122.

2. In our day this mode of thought would be called an ideology, pertinently defined by Karl Mannheim as a pattern of thought characteristic of ruling groups who "in their thinking become so intensely interest-bound to a situation that they are simply no longer able to see certain facts which would undermine their sense of dominance" (*Ideology and Utopia,* trans. Louis Wirth and Edward Shils [New York, n.d.], p. 40). Yet perhaps the best gloss is also the most famous. When Alice questions his arbitrary use of words, Humpty Dumpty replies that only one issue is involved, "which is to be *master*—that's all."

3. To this myth Johnson is said to have replied: "Sir, it is not so much to be lamented that Old England is lost as that the Scotch have found it."

4. See his *Emblem and Expression: Meaning in English Art of the Eighteenth Century* (Cambridge, Mass., 1975), pp. 9-10 and passim.

5. When a new anti-Jacobin newspaper appeared in Edinburgh in 1819, Scott wrote to Lord Melville that the present discontent of the common people could "be easily extinguished if men of property will be true to themselves and use their power." He then identifies men of property. "It is the middle class which requires to be put on the guard—every man who has or cultivates a furrow of land or has a guinea in the funds or vested in stock, in trade or in mortgage or in any other way whatsoever" (*Letters,* ed. H. J. C. Grierson, 12 vols. [London, 1932-37], 6:31, punctuation supplied). Smollett was alarmed over the agitation of the City Whigs because, he said, they possessed no muniments—no titles, rights, or deeds. There is an important parallel in the rise of the City Whigs and the coming to power of the "country men" of the Roman Senate. For the latter see T. P. Wiseman, *New Men in the Roman Senate B.C. 139–A.D. 14* (Oxford, 1971). There is also a family resemblance among Smollett's vulgar plebeians, Cato's barbarians, and Hobbes's natural men.

INDEX

Periodicals and anonymous works are cited under titles; all other
works are included in entries under authors. Two abbreviations
have been used: S for Smollett, *HC* for *Humphry Clinker.*

Library of Congress Cataloging in Publication Data

Sekora, John.
  Luxury.

  Includes index.
  1. Smollett, Tobias George, 1721-1771 – Criticism and
interpretation. 2. Luxury. 3. Smollett, Tobias George,
1721-1771. The expedition of Humphry Clinker.
I. Title
PR3698.L88S4   823'.6   77-4545
ISBN 0-8018-1972-5

t